At Home in Postwar France

BERGHAHN MONOGRAPHS IN FRENCH STUDIES

Editor: **Michael Scott Christofferson,** Associate Professor and Chair of Department of History, Adelphi University

France has played a central role in the emergence of the modern world. The Great French Revolution of 1789 contributed decisively to political modernity, and the Paris of Baudelaire did the same for culture. Because of its rich intellectual and cultural traditions, republican democracy, imperial past and post-colonial present, twentieth-century experience of decline and renewal, and unique role in world affairs, France and its history remain important today. This series publishes monographs that offer significant methodological and empirical contributions to our understanding of the French experience and its broader role in the making of the modern world.

Volume 1
The Populist Challenge: Political Protest and Ethno-nationalist Mobilization in France
Jens Rydgren

Volume 2
French Intellectuals against the Left: The Antitotalitarian Moment of the 1970s
Michael Scott Christofferson

Volume 3
Sartre against Stalinism
Ian H. Birchall

Volume 4
Sartre, Self-Formation and Masculinities
Jean-Pierre Boulé

Volume 5
The Bourgeois Revolution in France 1789–1815
Henry Heller

Volume 6
God's Eugenicist: Alexis Carrel and the Sociobiology of Decline
Andrés Horacio Reggiani

Volume 7
France and the Construction of Europe, 1944–2007: The Geopolitical Imperative
Michael Sutton

Volume 8
Shades of Indignation: Political Scandals in France, Past and Present
Paul Jankowski

Volume 9
Mitterrand, the End of the Cold War, and German Unification
Frédéric Bozo

Volume 10
Collective Terms: Race, Culture, and Community in a State-Planned City in France
Beth S. Epstein

Volume 11
France in the Age of Organization: Factory, Home and Nation from the 1920s to Vichy
Jackie Clarke

Volume 12
Building a European Identity: France, the United States, and the Oil Shock, 1973–1974
Aurélie Élisa Gfeller

Volume 13
General de Gaulle's Cold War: Challenging American Hegemony, 1963–1968
Garret Joseph Martin

Volume 14
At Home in Postwar France: Modern Mass Housing and the Right to Comfort
Nicole C. Rudolph

AT HOME IN POSTWAR FRANCE
Modern Mass Housing and the Right to Comfort

Nicole C. Rudolph

First published in 2015 by
Berghahn Books
www.berghahnbooks.com

© 2015, 2020 Nicole C. Rudolph
First paperback edition published in 2020

All rights reserved.
Except for the quotation of short passages
for the purposes of criticism and review, no part of this book
may be reproduced in any form or by any means, electronic or
mechanical, including photocopying, recording, or any information
storage and retrieval system now known or to be invented,
without written permission of the publisher.

Library of Congress Cataloging-in-Publication Data

Rudolph, Nicole C.
　At home in postwar France : modern mass housing and the right to comfort / Nicole C. Rudolph.
　　pages cm. — (Berghahn monographs in French studies ; volume 14)
　Includes bibliographical references and index.
　ISBN 978-1-78238-587-5 (hardback) — ISBN 978-1-78238-588-2 (ebook)
　1. Housing—France—History—20th century. 2. Housing policy—France—History—20th century. 3. Architecture, Domestic—France—History—20th century. 4. Dwellings—France—History—20th century. 5. France—Social conditions—1945–1995. 6. France—Civilization—1945– I. Title.
　HD7338.A3R83 2015
　363.5'80944—dc 3

2014033559

British Library Cataloguing in Publication Data

A catalogue record for this book is available from the British Library.

Printed on acid-free paper.

ISBN: 978-1-78238-587-5 hardback
ISBN: 978-1-78920-804-7 paperback
ISBN: 978-1-78238-588-2 ebook

For my parents and for Michael,
for whom books are an integral part of a home,
and
for Vandana and Desmond,
who have had to share their home with this book

Contents

List of Illustrations ix
Acknowledgments xi
List of Abbreviations xiii

Introduction 1

Part I. Modern Homes for a Modern Nation

Chapter 1
Building Homes, Building a Nation: State Experiments in
Modern Living, 1945–1952 17

Chapter 2
Designing for the Classless Society: Modernist Architects and
the "Art of Living" 53

Chapter 3
The Salon des Arts Ménagers: Teaching Women How to Make
the Modern Home 87

Part II. Mass Homes for a Changing Society

Chapter 4
Housing for the Greatest Number: The Housing Crisis and
the *Cellule d'Habitation*, 1953–1958 117

Chapter 5
"Who Is the Author of a Dwelling?" From User to Inhabitant,
1959–1961 149

Chapter 6
Beyond the Functionalist Cell to the Urban Fabric, 1966–1973   186

Conclusion   223

Selected Bibliography   235

Index   247

Illustrations

Figures

Figure 1.1.	Six possible dispositions of kitchen and dining spaces proposed for an apartment	24
Figure 1.2.	Two apartments in Eugène Beaudouin's Cité Rotterdam	39
Figure 2.1.	The Henri Becque model apartment	60
Figure 2.2.	The "normal" HBM model apartment	61
Figure 2.3.	The "ameliorated" HBM model apartment	62
Figure 2.4.	The ILM model apartment	63
Figure 2.5.	Le Corbusier's 1928 "Maison Loucheur"	68
Figure 2.6.	André Lurçat's Maubeuge 4P, 1947	73
Figure 2.7.	Marcel Roux and Pierre Faucheux's Appartement idéal (Appartement Paris-Match), 1952	74
Figure 3.1.	Photo of living room from the CCAFRP's Logis 48 exhibit, 1948	105
Figure 3.2.	Photo of living room shown at SAM's Logis 49 exhibit, 1949	106
Figure 4.1.	Floor plan of Jean Prouvé's Maison des jours meilleurs, 1956	131
Figure 4.2.	Georges Candilis and Guy Brunache's Opération Million plan	133

Figure 4.3. Émile Aillaud's plan in a "bar" at the Cité de
          l'Abreuvoir, Bobigny   133

Figure 5.1. The *Appartement référendum*, 1959   154

Figure 5.2. The *Essai d'habitation évolutive*, 1960   157

Figure 6.1. Plan by Paul Chemetov and Jean Deroche   212

Figure 6.2. Two 4Ps and a 5P in Jean Renaudie's apartment
          complex in Ivry   216

Tables

Table 4.1. Evolution of Surface Area Allowances for Public
          Housing, 1947–1955   135

Table 5.1. Evolution of Surface Area Allowances for Public
          Housing, 1954–1963   165

Acknowledgments

As we teacher-scholars weave our way through ever-busier days and labor with ever-dwindling resources, I wish to thank the individuals and institutions that have generously offered so much of their time and capital to this project.

I am very grateful to Molly Nolan, Stéphane Gerson, and Rosemary Wakeman, whose comments on earlier presentations of this research have made the final product stronger, and I sincerely appreciate the helpful suggestions and feedback from the anonymous reviewers who read the book manuscript. *Mille mercis* to Karen Adler and Jackie Clarke, whose embrace of my research launched my career as a historian and whose insightful advice has been invaluable. I am indebted to Michael Christofferson and Steven Zdatny for having read the entire manuscript, having offered useful critiques for its revision, and having insisted that this book would make a significant contribution to the literature on postwar France. I appreciate the wonderful team at Berghahn Books who has made the production of the book such a pleasure; thanks especially to Molly Mosher, Elizabeth Berg, and Anna Skiba-Crafts for their meticulous work. Finally, I owe Herrick Chapman a debt that can never be repaid. His combination of gentle mentorship, rigorous erudition, and generous support is unparalleled in the academy.

Institutions have also been key to the production of this work, which has relied on research grants from the American Philosophical Society, the Franco-American Foundation of the Fulbright Commission, and New York University. My professional home, Adelphi University, has provided the release time and funds necessary to complete this project. Provost Gayle Insler, Deans Steven Rubin and Sam Grogg, and my department chair, Raysa Amador, have been especially supportive, and I thank them.

Two who championed this work are no longer with us, but I have tried to hold their wisdom in mind during the writing process: Phil Watts and Tony Judt, you are missed.

I am beholden to family and friends, most especially Carol Rudolph and John Bell, and also Kent and Arlene Menser, Mary Ellen Callahan and Tony Lynn, Joseph and Pauline Rudolph, Joseph and Barbara Rudolph, and Sebastian Monte and Kate Haas Monte, who have provided the emotional sustenance, financial support, and childcare necessary to this book's completion.

Finally, my greatest debt is to Michael, who has been an equal partner in parenting, who has done his half (and often more) of the housework, and who has still found time to work for the revolution: he is an inspiration, every day. Now, finally, it's his turn to write.

Some sections of this book feature revised and expanded discussions of research that has been disseminated in an earlier or different form in *Modern and Contemporary France* 12, 4 (2004), *Gender and History* 21, 3 (2009), and *Interiors: Design, Architecture, Culture* 5, 2 (2014).

Abbreviations

AFNOR	Association française de normalisation
AUA	Atelier d'urbanisme et d'architecture
CCAFRP	Caisse centrale d'allocations familiales de la région parisienne
CDC	Caisse des dépôts et consignations
CEDER	Centre d'études des équipements résidentiels
CEGS	Centre d'études de groupes sociaux
CIAM	Congrès international d'architecture moderne
CNRS	Centre national des recherches scientifiques
CPTFM	Cahier des prescriptions techniques et fonctionnelles minima
CPTFMU	Cahier des prescriptions techniques et fonctionnelles minimales unifiées
CRI	Commissariat à la reconstruction immobilière
CSTB	Centre scientifique et technique du bâtiment
DATAR	Délégation à l'aménagement du territoire et à l'action régionale
DGEN	Direction générale à l'équipement national
DGUHC	Direction générale de l'urbanisme, de l'habitation, et de la construction
ENA	École nationale d'administration
ENSBA	École nationale supérieure des beaux-arts
FNA	Front national des architectes
FNAH	Fonds National de l'Amélioration de l'Habitat
HBM	Habitation à bon marché
HLM	Habitation à loyer modéré
ILM	Immeuble à loyer moyen
INED	Institut national d'études démographiques
ISAI	Immeuble sans affectation individuelle (or, sometimes, immédiate)

JOCF	Jeunesse ouvrière chrétienne féminine
LEN	Logement économique de première nécessité
LOGECO	Logement économique et familial
LOPOFA	Logement populaire et familial
MC	Ministère de la Construction
MEL	Ministère de l'Équipement et du Logement
MLAC	Mouvement pour la liberté de l'avortement et la contraception
MLF	Mouvement de libération des femmes
MRL	Ministère de la Reconstruction et du Logement
MRP	Mouvement Républicain Populaire
MRU	Ministère de la Reconstruction et de l'Urbanisme
ONRI	Office national des recherches scientifiques et industrielles et des inventions
OPHVP	Office public d'habitations de la Ville de Paris
PADOG	Plan d'Aménagement et d'organisation générale
PAN	Programme Architecture Nouvelle
PMF	Pierre Mendès-France
PSR	Programmes sociaux de relogement
SAD	Société des Artistes Décorateurs
SADG	Société française des architectes diplômés par le gouvernement
SAM	Salon des Arts Ménagers
SAS	Syndicat des Architectes de la Seine
SCIC	Société Centrale Immobilière de la Caisse des dépôts et consignations
SEC	Services des Études de la Construction
SEMIDEP	Société d'économie mixte immobilière interdépartementale de la région parisienne
SERPEC	Société d'études et de réalisation de procédés économiques de construction
SNCF	Société nationale des chemins de fer français
SNEC	Syndicat national de l'équipement de cuisine
SONACOTRAL	Société nationale de construction de logements pour les travailleurs algériens
UAM	Union des Artistes Modernes
UDSR	Union Démocrate et Socialiste de la Résistance
UNCAF	Union nationale des caisses d'allocations familiales
ZUP	Zones à urbaniser par priorité

Introduction

> [H]ow recent the idea is that life should be "comfortable," that those who live it should be "happy."
> —Joan Didion, 1967[1]

How can a revolution be invisible? A revolution, by definition, entails the replacement of one social or political order with another. Surely, such an event would not escape our attention. Yet, Jean Fourastié, writing his classic work on the years 1946 to 1975 in France, chose to entitle it *Les Trente glorieuses, ou la révolution invisible de 1946 à 1975* (*The Thirty Glorious Years, or The Invisible Revolution from 1946 to 1975*). The first part of the title has become a widely used term in French, a shorthand reference to the period of economic growth and prosperity that France enjoyed during the three decades following World War II. The "invisible revolution," never similarly invoked, is usually described instead by the use of another word: modernization. When speaking of postwar France, modernization is understood to signify a number of (often interrelated) large-scale political and social transformations, including rural exodus and urbanization, development of mass consumerism, industrialization, Americanization, and decolonization.

It may be that the "invisible revolution" seemed so because much of it took place not in the streets, public space of the *citoyen*, but at home, within the putatively private space of the domicile. *At Home in Postwar France* argues that domestic space was a key site for a number of the social changes mentioned above and aims to tell the story of the modern French home from 1945 to 1975.

Housing was of critical political and economic importance during this period. For French architect Marcel Lods, World War II represented a "monstrous opportunity."[2] He meant by this that wartime destruction had its silver lining: a chance to rebuild French cities according to modern principles that would create a more just social order. The extent of the destruction—one out of every twenty buildings was destroyed, one out of every five damaged and a total loss of 1.2 million homes[3]—was such that reconstruction came to the fore as a national priority. Nor did the nation's attention to housing wane in the years following the first decade of reconstruction; demographic factors, including the baby boom, repatriation of French citizens from Algeria, immigration, and rural exodus, contributed to an enduring housing crisis. By 1975, over 8 million new housing units had been built, bearing out Lods's perception of a tabula rasa.[4] Lodging this many people meant literally incorporating them into a collective project to build modern France.

Home, that purportedly private sphere, and indeed celebrated as such by its inhabitants during the postwar period,[5] was thus also a means by which nations literally rebuilt themselves at the end of World War II. In a specific historical context governed by massive wartime destruction, shortages of shelter, manpower, and materials, and an evangelical belief that technocratic planning could create a better world, the planners and policymakers of the postwar period included domestic space in their modernizing projects. France was not alone in this regard; many nations sought to effect economic and social change through the design and construction of modern homes. At the 1951 Festival of Britain, a London neighborhood comprised a "Live Architecture" exhibition of modern flats that demonstrated the Labour government's commitment to bringing comfort to the masses. In 1959's famous "Kitchen Debate" between Soviet Premier Nikita Khrushchev and American Vice President Richard Nixon, the home eclipsed the missile as proof of each nation's superiority.

Moreover, many nations turned to a Modernist vernacular during reconstruction, adopting its streamlined forms and use of concrete, glass, and steel. The postwar housing production of the United Kingdom, the Netherlands, Sweden, Central and Eastern Europe, and the USSR manifests an enthusiastic embrace of International Style.[6] Yet the ubiquitous forms of Modernism obscure a diversity of meanings and pathways. In the USSR, for example, modern high-density housing was meant to parry the consumerist thrusts of the United States; its ability to be erected quickly combined with its emphasis on a collective way of life would demonstrate Soviet superiority.[7] In England, municipalities drove the erection of the "council flats," and they tended to favor lower-rise configurations of duplexes, row houses, and clusters of four- or five-story apartment complexes. Though housing policy was also state-led in Sweden and in the Netherlands, scholars have shown how interest groups mediated and intervened more substantively in state plans in those countries.[8] In France, on the other hand, the extent to which the state apparatus drove not only the construction but also the design of housing was exceptional.[9] Top-down programs and institutions like housing ministry design competitions, bonuses for using state-approved model plans, and the creation of a state-funded large-scale public housing developer worked to homogenize French housing design for the first two decades after the war.

Among the nations building modern homes and employing International Style, only France needed to overcome the shame of defeat and collaboration and a fear of decline. Even in the face of continuities of staff, agencies, and policy ideas that reached back into the 1930s and the Vichy regime, the leaders and planners of the mid to late 1940s subscribed to an ideology of rebirth and progress, hoping to rectify past errors, permanently solve recurrent problems, and regain a powerful role for France on the world stage.[10] Their ambitions included accelerating industrialization, promoting population growth, spurring scientific and technological innovations, putting the economy at the service of the nation instead of entrenched interests, and reducing the effects of social inequalities. Housing was well suited to the renewal paradigm because the scale of destruction precluded a return to business as usual; one could not simply pick up from 1939 because whole neighborhoods were damaged, and manpower and materials were in scarce supply. The situation was unprecedented and called for revolutionary approaches.

Beyond the physical act of reconstruction-as-rebirth, the French looked to the design and construction of modern homes to herald their renaissance because of Modernism's connotations of newness and democracy. Unlike Rastignac and Père Goriot's nineteenth-century boarding house, where, although members of different classes inhabited the same building, the furnishings, layout, and equipment of the apartments on each floor varied with one's station in life, and unlike American urban areas where modern apartment complexes were designated for either the middle or the working classes,[11] French mass homes were, at least in the first generation, imagined and built to be one-size-fits-most-classes apartments. In the context of a transnational adoption of Modernism for housing reconstruction, the French experience retains a distinct shape because of its particular vectors of production and dissemination and because of the historically specific meanings—of renaissance, renewal, and redemption—that the French assigned to Modernist forms.[12]

*****

As architectural historian Gwendolyn Wright has observed, "Embedded within the spaces, between the objects, of all homes are implicit roles for men and women, for individual and community, for majority and minority groups within any society."[13] In other words, the production of space is never neutral but reflects instead normative beliefs about social life. In France, the centralized and technocratic state set out to reconfigure domestic space to correspond to revised conceptions of gender roles, family life, and social organization. *At Home in Postwar France* aims to recover the acts of embedding, to unearth the debates around and reactions to choices made about how the French should dwell, and hence, who they should be. What can these debates and choices tell us about what was felt to be at stake in a changing France? Did the home itself actually change? And how did members of different classes, genders, and generations experience "modern" domestic life as it could be lived in these new constructions? Did living in these homes change them?

To answer these questions, *At Home in Postwar France* focuses primarily on interiors. Both the form of interiors and their importance have been largely neglected until now. They have most often served as a minor detail in larger narratives of reconstruction, urbanization, urban policy, or housing policy. These macro-level stories take a quantitative approach to housing, discussing the housing crisis and the state's efforts to resolve it through the large-scale production of the rent-controlled apartments known as *habitations à loyer modéré* (HLMs), or they focus on the qualitative insufficiencies of the ultra-high-density housing complexes. The latter, known as *grands ensembles,* quickly earned the nickname of "dormitory cities," due to their lack of collective services. From the beginning, they were—and continue to be—associated with juvenile delinquency, crime, and marginalization. As for architectural histories, these tend to highlight exceptional projects rather than the banal apartments into which hundreds of thousands of families moved between 1945 and 1975. Histories of women's lives have looked at the effects of the growth in household technology and mass consumerism as these pertain to women's relationship to domestic space over the course of the 1940s, 1950s, and 1960s, but, touching on many subjects including employment, family policy, and representations, they fail to provide a deep understanding of how the home interior evolved in response to—or prompted—such changes.[14]

When we put interiors at the center of the narrative, however, we better understand the goals of the policymaking for and the lived experience of ordinary citizens, for these spaces were at once the private "hearth" of the family and also the basic unit of a *grand ensemble*'s site plan. That is, just as the family was viewed as the building block, the biological "cell"—to invoke the contemporary term—of the organism that was French society, so the apartment was the keystone of the urban. Looking at apartment blueprints permits us to see quite clearly the relationships and roles imagined by planners for inhabitants of different genders and social classes specifically and for citizens in general. Homes were the object of a domestic civilizing mission, an attempt to acculturate rural and working-class dwellers into a modern art of living, a quotidian modernity that would reflect well on the nation. Planners also focused their efforts on women, who were not excluded from state modernization efforts, but at their center. State-sponsored endeavors to remake the home allow us a fuller view of French modernizing policies that encompasses more than economic growth, industrial and technological development, and a burgeoning consumer society.

Studying domestic space also helps us to understand attempts to shape, control, negotiate, and adapt to modernizing projects. Looking at postwar modernizing projects via the home, we can grasp the significance of the question splashed across the page of a 1946 issue of an architectural journal: "Do the French Want a Separate Kitchen?"[15] The article described the results of a survey performed by the Institut français de l'opinion publique (IFOP), which asked respondents to weigh in on the ideal kitchen. Should it open into the living area or be closed off? Should it be large enough to dine in, or should the dining area be elsewhere? The following year, the Institut national d'études démographiques (INED) published a lengthy examination of the preferences (also gleaned by survey) of the French in the "matter of urban habitation." The INED project asked the French to share their opinions on burning questions like terraces versus balconies, and whether they preferred to hang pots and pans on the wall or hide them from view.[16]

For a nation confronted at that moment with the preparation of a comprehensive social security program, bombings in Indochina, a referendum on the Constitution, and the adoption of the Monnet Plan, such questions might appear of little consequence. What possible difference could it make whether the kitchen was open or closed? Put another way, what was at stake in the various suggestions for urban housing? The IFOP and INED surveys suggest there was a shared sense that the home should be remade. That is, as France embarked upon an explicit project of economic modernization, it is clear that reconstruction planners also meant to extend the modernizing project to the domestic sphere in the interest of rebuilding the nation.

What were the dominant "traditional" models of housing that modernizing agents found insufficient or inappropriate for dwelling in the new, modern France? Before World War II, a handful of archetypes dominated French domestic architecture. The middle class and upper class lived in country villas or urban apartments, both of whose interiors comprised public, private, and service areas. Service regions were the spaces where domestic help worked, such as the kitchen, pantry, washroom, and nursery. The public quarters, like the parlor, foyer, and dining room, were devoted to receiving and entertaining visitors. Bedrooms and, for this lucky few, bathrooms composed the most private spaces in the house. The higher one ranked on the social ladder, the more the number of rooms proliferated to include highly specialized rooms like smoking rooms, libraries, offices, sitting rooms, boudoirs, or children's playrooms.[17]

For the working class, one- to three-room dwellings were the norm. Rural families' farmhouses blended the indoors and outdoors but were often much larger than the apartments and furnished hotel rooms into which working-class urban families squeezed. Some of the latter opted instead to live on a city's outskirts, building or renting homes on a small piece of land, in order to have access to jobs in the city and independence (and a vegetable garden) at home. Depending on their size and condition, these houses were either called *pavillons* (modest bungalows) or *taudis* (run-down shacks). Most of the rural and suburban homes that housed the French were poorly equipped, served by little in terms of infrastructure and even less in the way of household technology. In the first decades of the twentieth century, another type of housing for the urban poor had emerged. The *habitations à bon marché* (HBM), inexpensive housing also known as "social" housing, aspired to provide hygienic and wholesome living environments for large, primarily working-class, families, but, due to limited capital investment, such options remained restricted to only a small number of families.

The postwar French home diverged from these predecessors. The functionalist "4P"—four *pièces,* or rooms—introduced a new way of dwelling for all families, regardless of social class. The upper middle class lost their specialized rooms for receiving, as the parlor, the dining room, and the sitting room were all fused into the *séjour,* a living room–dining room area designed to be the sole public space and locus of family interaction. The rural and working-class families who gained access to indoor plumbing and central heating for the first time also lost their common rooms, where they were accustomed to preparing meals, dining, and gathering together as a family. Instead, the meal-taking "function" moved to the *séjour,* while meal preparation transpired in a miniscule space known as the laboratory kitchen, where built-in cabinets and counters offered storage and work space for the scientist-housewife, the archetype around whom the room was literally constructed.

Who was responsible for these changes, that is, for the construction, design, and popularization of the French modern home? Two groups of actors were particularly dominant; the first included officials at the Ministry of Reconstruction and Urbanism (MRU) who had the mandate to rebuild France. A new ministry created by Charles de Gaulle in 1944, the MRU oversaw construction and shaped the modern home by establishing the parameters and guidelines governing home designs. The second influential group was architects, of course, and specifically, Modernist architects.

During the interwar years a group of avant-garde architects interested in reinventing domestic architecture as a basis for remaking society had gathered together at the meetings of the Congrès international d'architecture moderne (CIAM). This pan-European association sought to mobilize new techniques, materials, and designs to re-create the home and its relationship to the urban. One of their leaders, Le Corbusier, had thrown down the gauntlet in 1923, declaring in his manifesto, *Toward a New Architecture*: "Architecture or revolution." While World War II staved off that revolution, the postwar period offered these architects a golden opportunity; because they had pioneered the use of inexpensive building materials like reinforced concrete and the first techniques of mass construction, planners eagerly sought their expertise for a rapid reconstruction.

The interactions between state planners at the MRU and Modernist architects form only one part of the story, especially since the modern mass home ultimately emerged from a process of negotiation among planners, architects, tastemakers, and dwellers. The book thus also examines the diffusion, mediation, and reception of ideas about modern dwelling. One of the most important vectors for this process was the Salon des Arts Ménagers (Domestic Arts Exhibition, or SAM), a yearly exposition showcasing all the novelties having to do with modern domestic space, including appliances, paint, siding, and furniture. While other nations had similar exhibitions (like the *Daily Mail*'s Ideal Home Exhibition in Britain), the scope of the Salon des Arts Ménagers, which ran from 1923 to 1983, was unique to France, since it was not only a commercial exposition but also the publisher of a monthly women's magazine. Moreover, the SAM organizers worked with home economists to promote good housekeeping, even sponsoring an annual contest to choose the *Fée du logis*, the best homemaker in France. The SAM was not only a point of contact between housing professionals and potential inhabitants of the modern home, but also an actor, actively engaged in teaching the French how to make and inhabit the modern home.

Most important, of course, is the reception of these homes. By embracing or rejecting certain features of the standard HLM apartment, residents helped to shape its form. Inhabitant surveys, sociologists' studies, memoirs, interviews, the minutes of the associations formed by new HLM residents, and the homes that residents themselves designed reveal what becoming modern meant to ordinary people. The modern home as a product of the postwar period was thus a composite result of all of the debates, conflicts, discussions, and compromises among state officials, architects, tastemakers, sociologists, and residents.

My analytical approach situates the story of postwar French housing at the nexus of social history, cultural history, policy history, and architectural history: the book parses change and continuity in the material aspect of homes, in the demographic and professional groups building and inhabiting them, and in the representations of domestic space in the mass press, the professional press, and popular cultural events like the Salon des Arts Ménagers. Two kinds of sources form the basis for my analysis: traditional discursive sources, taken from archives, the mass and professional presses, and resident surveys, but also material evidence, like floor plans of projects that were actually built, as well as the blueprints submitted to architectural competitions and the idealized depictions and models of the "average" home shown in women's magazines and at the SAM.

The book is divided into two sections. The first, which includes three chapters, covers the period from 1945 to 1953 and examines the genealogy of the modern French home and what the different sets of actors had at stake in its development. Chapter 1 considers the creation of the MRU and its efforts to pursue experiments with new housing, ranging from prefabricated bungalows to neoclassical apartment building interpreted in reinforced concrete. Seeking to use housing as a means of finally resolving the social question, state planners looked to the implementation of technical "comfort"—indoor plumbing and central heating—to raise the standard of living for French families. Chapter 2 describes the architects involved in MRU experiments with mass homes and locates the origins of the postwar functionalist modern home in the Modernist designs of the 1920s and 1930s *and* in interwar models of social housing. Through a close reading of blueprints, we learn that the one-size-fits-all-social-classes apartments designed by these avant-garde architects owed more to middle-class dwelling practices than to revolutionary interwar projects. Chapter 3 analyzes the SAM as a proponent of a domestic ideal that celebrated the modern home as ground zero for individual happiness and family unity; while promising to liberate housewives from their domestic slavery, however, the SAM also firmly reinscribed modern homemaking as the primary responsibility of French women. Acculturating the French to the new housing forms being designed by architects, the SAM identified a key role for women in modernizing France by modernizing their homes.

Part II takes the reader from the 1950s through the beginning of the 1970s, tracing the evolution of the modern home and focusing on important moments of change. These chapters present the interactions between and decisions made by groups of actors that had real consequences for home design. Chapter 4 depicts the turning point in housing policy that resulted from the effects of a worsening housing crisis in 1953–1954 and the state's decision to accelerate the mass production of housing. The embrace of the *grand ensemble* resulted in an ever-smaller and highly standardized—but still relatively well-equipped—apartment known as the *cellule,* or cell. Chapter 5 pauses to analyze events in 1959. As French residents moved into *grands ensembles* and reactions and evaluations of the new modern homes began to generate national study, publicity, and response, including feedback and counterproposals from the women whose housewifery made these homes function. A new figure in the debate—the urban sociologist—appeared on the scene, and, working in conjunction with residents, managed to successfully challenge the Modernist and technocratic orthodoxy of functionalism in dwelling. Finally, chapter 6 assesses the years from 1965 to 1970, during which the functionalist 4P fell out of favor with state planners, and a new period of experimentation with housing commenced. The political and social upheavals of the 1960s were accompanied by attempts to rethink the relationship of the domestic to the urban by considering the development of single-family detached homes as well as inventive juxtaposed apartments in large complexes. Just as these new efforts took off, however, they were brought to an end by the oil crisis of the 1970s, which prompted the state to stop financing new construction directly and to give loans instead to private initiatives, effectively terminating the state's job as a developer. Subsequently, attempts to shape social life through domestic space would devolve to non-state actors, such as activist architectural firms or private builders and developers like Maisons Phénix.

A note about terms: referents for the words "modernity," "modernization," and "modernism," as well as for their common adjective, "modern," are unstable. "Modernization," as employed by contemporary housing professionals, generally operated as a shorthand reference to the changes— social, economic, and cultural—taking place in postwar France; modernization could describe industrialization, urbanization, democratization, a decline of formality in social life, or the use of technology in the home. The term should not be understood as an endorsement of "modernization theory," the ideological framework of 1950s and 60s American social scientists who posited a teleological theory of the desirable transformation of the nation-state. Scholars have challenged the explanatory power of "modernization theory" on the grounds that tradition and modernity are not mutually exclusive, that the social does not necessarily have the same boundaries as the national, and that modernity does not have a single definition that includes specific and fixed political, economic, and social characteristics.[18] To analyze contemporaries' actions, I prefer the expression "modernizing project" to the word "modernization." *Projets de modernisation* and *plans de modernisation* figure prominently in contemporaries' discourse, and hence my use of "modernizing project" recoups actors' intentions rather than placing emphasis on a measurable or teleological result.

As the story of a modernizing project, this history of the French modern home also figures in the history of the "French model" of state power, which has been described as "part 'concerted economy,' part 'parental welfare state,' part 'technocracy'."[19] A number of shared assumptions guided the postwar policymaking that contributed to the genesis of the French model, particularly in the realms of economic, family, and housing policy: that planning would bring progress through prosperity, that specialists making decisions on the basis of extensive research were preferable to politicians guided by warring ideologies, and that the state should protect its citizens equally (we will return to this idea in a moment). Above all, leaders believed the errors and weaknesses of the Third Republic could be avoided by using studies and experts to solve problems and by mobilizing state power to implement their solutions.

Shared assumptions contributed to shared goals. Like family policy, housing policy was concerned with supporting the nuclear family and encouraging natalism. On the other hand, housing policy lacked the political infighting that marked family policy. Though there were tussles with other offices and agencies—turf wars with the Ministry of the Interior, or struggles to get Jean Monnet's General Planning Commission to include housing in its priority sectors—housing policy was relatively devoid of political wrangling during the Thirty Glorious Years. Day-to-day housing policy was often guided by technocrats like André Prothin, a civil engineer who became active in planning agencies in the 1930s and traversed Vichy urban planning and housing ministry posts, surviving ministerial shifts right through to the regime change of 1958. Like the Monnet Plan, housing policy sponsored research, used indicative planning, and suggested target goals for production, but it diverged from economic planning since it focused on only one sector of production. More generally, the history of housing encapsulates both the reach of and the limits to a *dirigiste* and technocratic approach to policymaking, and we will see how policy initiatives were shaped, reshaped, or rebuffed by constraints or critiques.

* * * * *

The once-experimental tall towers and long bars of Modernist architecture are now a permanent feature of the European landscape, and the critiques have never stopped coming. Maligned for their standardized concrete unsightliness, their location on the outskirts of city centers, and their paltry proportions, HLM neighborhoods in France have continually been associated with juvenile delinquency, poverty, racism, and urban unrest, most recently during the October 2005 riots. Critics include sociologists and historians, who see these housing projects as acts of hubris by Modernists who refused to give the people what they wanted, or as acts of authoritarian control over low-income populations. Supporters argue that recalcitrant traditionalists clinging to individualism foiled the realization of the Modernists' utopia. This interpretation of the *grands ensembles*, popular with architectural historians, sees them as affirmations of collective identity and community, whose full promise was negated by petit-bourgeois concerns with backyards and privacy. In the French historiography, discussions of postwar modern housing tend to invoke this failure-of-modernism argument in reference either to hypotheses about the causal relationship of *grands ensembles* to social unrest and class oppression or to consideration of whether such projects merit preservation and rehabilitation, as patrimony or as salvageable housing.[20]

Apart from being a thoroughly inadequate causal explanation of juvenile delinquency and institutionalized racism, either in the postwar period or in the twenty-first century, the "failure-of-modernism" discussion distracts us from other lessons we might take from the *grands ensembles*. As this book recounts, the historical specificity of the reconstruction—a massive need for homes combined with a privileging of the ideas of Modernist architects—facilitated two of the state's social engineering efforts: reduction of class conflict and the promotion of a nuclear family characterized by traditional gender roles. When one steps away from the "failure-of-modernism" debate and looks at the assumptions and goals of housing policy, one can see that the right to comfort guaranteed by the state in the form of an equipped home—along with other welfare state benefits like retirement pensions, unemployment insurance, and family allocations—was part of a belief that the French citizenry, regardless of class position, was entitled to state protection from insecurity, physical discomfort, and inequality.

Various commentators have identified this principle as the basis of a "new social contract" or a "new deal" established at Liberation in the form of the modern welfare state, even as its creation had roots in institutions and policies stemming from the 1920s, 1930s, and even during the Vichy regime.[21] While it built on principles of morality and solidarity affirmed by bourgeois social reformers, social Catholic activists, and Socialists in each decade since the 1890s, the new welfare state anchored its compact in a notion of social debt, affirming a break with the past. Contemporaries remarked how war had deemphasized social differences, calling equally upon all citizens for their sacrifice to the nation, and it was time for the nascent Fourth Republic to repay that debt by reinforcing in peacetime the social solidarity produced during wartime. Consensus around the notion of expanding and adding to preexisting redistributive schemes of health insurance and family allocations led to the creation of the welfare state, even as political groups on both left and right struggled to shape and control the forms the apparatuses would take.[22]

The modern mass homes designed and built in the postwar period were part and parcel of this mission, and we see this even more clearly if we follow historian Philip Nord's definition of the postwar compact as a "pledge" that "the state would undertake to make a better France for every citizen and that it would do so not just by reducing the risks and anxieties of day-to-day existence but by enriching the lives of all through the dissemination of a culture of quality."[23] This democratizing aspiration to enrich the average French person's cultural life reverberated in projects of home modernization, too. Planners, architects, and tastemakers all expected that construction of housing equipped with indoor plumbing and central heating would protect health and offer security; further, the rational and functional layout of these homes' interiors would not only offer men and women tranquility, but through their ease of upkeep, the leisure time to develop residents' minds and passions.

In the postwar period, one-size-fits-all domestic architecture *was* the revolution: modern homes became a synecdoche for a modern nation. If clean, comfortable modern homes failed to become the birthright of every citizen, it is no less true that the campaign for modern homes resonated with the postwar generations, raising the standard of living—and expectations—for millions. Since Henri IV, the benchmark had been a chicken in every pot. The planners of the Thirty Glorious Years audaciously raised the bar to having the equipped kitchen to cook it in. As the epigraph suggests, the idea "that life should be 'comfortable,' that those who live it should be 'happy'," was new. In France, it was a political and cultural invention of Fourth and Fifth Republic planners, Modernist architects, tastemakers, and mass marketers; that these beliefs became commonplace, that mentalities were changed, is due, at least in part, to the invisible revolution that took place at home in postwar France.

Notes

1. Joan Didion, "The Seacoast of Despair," in *Slouching Towards Bethlehem* (New York: Washington Square Press, 1981 [1968]), 209.
2. Joseph Abram, *L'architecture moderne en France*, vol. 2, *Du chaos à la croissance: 1940-1966* (Paris: Picard, 1999), 47.
3. François Clanché and Anne-Marie Fribourg, "Grandes évolutions du parc et des ménages depuis 1950," in *Logement et habitat: l'état de savoirs*, ed. Marion Ségaud, Catherine Bonvalet, and Jacques Brun (Paris: La Découverte, 1998), 77; Frédérique Boucher, "Abriter vaille que vaille, se loger coûte que coûte," in "Images, discours et enjeux de la reconstruction des villes françaises après 1945," ed. Danièle Voldman, a special issue of *Cahiers de l'Institut d'histoire du temps présent* 5 (June 1987): 157.

4. Figures derived from yearly production figures listed in Marcel Roncayolo, ed., *La Ville d'aujourd'hui*, vol. 5 of *Histoire de la France urbaine*, ed. Georges Duby (Paris: Seuil, 1985), 646.
5. On residents relishing the privacy of home, see Nicole Haumont, "Habitat et modèles culturels," *Revue française de sociologie* 9 (1968): 180–90; Claire Langhamer, "The Meanings of Home in Postwar Britain," *Journal of Contemporary History* 40, 2 (April 2005): 341–62; and Susan E. Reid, "The Meaning of Home: 'The Only Bit of Life You Can Have to Yourself'," in *Borders of Socialism: Private Spheres of Soviet Russia*, ed. Lewis H. Siegelbaum (New York and Basingstoke: Palgrave, 2006), 145–70.
6. For an examination of European postwar housing that traces the differing national contexts, see the special issue of *Home Cultures* 7, 2 (July 2010) on "European Housing in the American Century."
7. On Khrushchev's move to building single-family occupancy homes, see Steven E. Harris, "Moving to the Separate Apartment: Building, Distributing, Furnishing, and Living in Urban Housing in Soviet Russia, 1950s-1960s," Ph.D. diss., University of Chicago, 2003 and Greg Castillo, *Cold War on the Home Front: The Soft Power of Midcentury Modern Design* (Minneapolis, MN: University of Minnesota Press, 2010), esp. 161–70.
8. Mikael Hård, "*The Good Apartment:* The Social (Democratic) Construction of Swedish Homes," *Home Cultures* 7, 2 (July 2010): 117–33; Liesbeth Bervoets, "Defeating Public Enemy Number One: Mediating Housing in the Netherlands," *Home Cultures* 7, 2 (July 2010): 179–95.
9. Patrick Dunleavy, *The Politics of Mass Housing in Britain, 1945-1975* (Oxford: Clarendon Press, 1981).
10. On the tragic flaw of Third Republic self-interest and stagnation, see Marc Bloch, *Étrange Défaite* (Paris: Gallimard, 1990 [1946]); on renewal, see Richard Kuisel, *Capitalism and the State in Modern France* (Cambridge: Cambridge University Press, 1981), esp. chap. 7 on "the spirit of 1944," and Philip Nord, *France's New Deal: From the Thirties to the Postwar Era* (Princeton, NJ: Princeton University Press, 2010).
11. See for example, Samuel Zipp's chapters on New York City's Stuyvesant Town (for the white middle class) and the George Washington Houses housing projects in East Harlem for working-class blacks, whites, and Hispanics in *Manhattan Projects: The Rise and Fall of Urban Renewal in Cold War New York* (Oxford and New York: Oxford University Press, 2010).
12. The edited volume by Frédéric Dufaux and Annie Fourcaut, *Le Monde des grands ensembles* (Paris: Editions Créaphis, 2004) offers an overview of international examples of high-density housing complexes. As an edited volume, the collection lacks a sustained comparison but includes reflections on case studies in South Korea, Iran, South Africa, and Algeria.
13. Gwendolyn Wright, "Prescribing the Model Home," in *Home: A Place in the World*, ed. Arien Mack (New York: New York University Press, 1993), 214.
14. Anecdotally, I have noticed that French bookstores with a subsection on *grands ensembles* feature primarily sociological works on "difficult" or "sensitive" neighborhoods, suburban renewal, and the "paradoxical patrimony" of this housing. Book-length studies on urbanization, social housing, and housing policy include Jean-Paul Flamand, *Loger le peuple. Essai sur l'histoire du logement social* (Paris: La Découverte, 1989); Marcel Roncayolo, ed., *La Ville d'aujourd'hui*, vol. 5 of *Histoire de la France urbaine*, ed. Georges Duby (Paris: Seuil, 1985); Thibault Tellier, *Le temps des HLM, 1945-1975: La saga urbaine des Trente Glorieuses* (Paris: Autrement, 2007); and W. Brian Newsome, *French Urban Planning 1940-1968* (New York: Peter Lang, 2009). Architectural histories that cover the period of the Thirty Glorious Years include Bruno Vayssière, *Reconstruction-décon-*

struction: le hard French ou l'architecture française des trente glorieuses (Paris: Picard, 1988); Abram, *L'architecture moderne en France*, vol. 2; and Gérard Monnier, *L'architecture moderne en France*, vol. 3, *De la croissance à la compétition: 1967-1999* (Paris: Picard, 2000). For histories of women's lives in France consult Claire Duchen, *Women's Rights and Women's Lives in France, 1944-1968* (London and New York: Routledge, 1994) and the essays on France in Françoise Thébaud, ed., *Histoire des femmes: Le XXe siècle*, vol. 5 of *Histoire des femmes en Occident*, ed. Georges Duby and Michelle Perrot (Paris: Plon, 1992).
15. "Les Français veulent-ils une cuisine séparée?" *La Maison française* 1, 2 (November 1946): 35.
16. Institut National d'Études Démographiques [INED], *Désirs des Français en matière d'habitation urbaine* (Paris: PUF, 1947).
17. See Monique Éleb and Anne Debarre, *L'Invention de l'habitation moderne. Paris 1880-1914. Architectures de la vie privée* (Paris: AAM/Hazan, 1995).
18. For a description of modernization theory and a summary of challenges thereto, see Dean C. Tipps, "Modernization and the Comparative Study of Societies," *Comparative Studies in Society and History* 15 (1973): 199–226.
19. Nord, *France's New Deal*, 20.
20. See, for example, Vayssière, *Reconstruction-déconstruction*, and Frédéric Mitterrand, "Mettre en valeur l'architecture du XXe siècle," in Île-de-France, Direction régionale des affaires culturelles, ed., *1945-1975, une histoire de l'habitat: 40 ensembles de logements, patrimoine du XXe siècle* (Paris: "Beaux-arts" editions/TTM editions, 2010).
21. See Nord, *France's New Deal*. Pierre Rosanvallon (*The New Social Question: Rethinking the Welfare State*, trans. Barbara Harshav [Princeton, NJ: Princeton University Press, 2000], esp. 27–28) and Douglas E. Ashford (*Policy and Politics in France: Living with Uncertainty* [Philadelphia: Temple University Press, 1982], esp. 228–29) emphasize the development of the new social contract as rooted in the notion of national debt to the citizenry. Bruno Vayssière sees the "new social contract" offering a commitment to equality that drilled down to quotidian concerns, such as the guarantee that the newly created nationalized electric utility, Électricité de France, would offer, for the first time, identical connection fees for all clients ("Des premiers objets de l'après-guerre aux années molles…" in *Les bons génies de la vie domestique* [Paris: Éditions du Centre Pompidou, 2000], 132).
22. Herrick Chapman, "France's Liberation Era, 1944-47: A Social and Economic Settlement?" in *The Uncertain Foundation: France at the Liberation, 1944-47*, ed. Andrew Knapp (New York: Palgrave MacMillan, 2007), 103–20.
23. Nord, *France's New Deal*, 382–83.

Part I

Modern Homes for a Modern Nation

Chapter 1

BUILDING HOMES, BUILDING A NATION
State Experiments in Modern Living, 1945–1952

> Surely we are not going to, as we did in 1918, rebuild the same little houses along the same little streets? We are not going to sacrifice to the spirit of the old décor the possibilities of man's liberation that a new décor can bring us?
> —Eugène Claudius-Petit, future minister of the MRU, 1945[1]

In 1946, the preamble to the recently ratified Constitution of the French Fourth Republic established the terms of a new social contract: "The Nation shall provide the individual and the family with the conditions necessary to their development. It shall guarantee to all, notably to children, mothers and elderly workers, protection of their health, material security, rest and leisure." This explicit promise of a better life, even for those seen as the weakest members of society, arose from the consensus among Western European nations that, as Tony Judt put it in his masterful account *Postwar*, the "physical and moral condition of the citizenry was part of the state's responsibility."[2] State-sponsored and state-administered health insurance, family allowances, and pensions would henceforth buffet many Europeans from the scourge of disease and potential excesses of market capitalism.

Comprehensive social security was not the only insurance against the physical and moral deterioration of the populace. Housing also had a role to play, identified, as we shall see, by postwar actors as the primary site for the rest and leisure guaranteed by the Constitution. Yet war had taken a brutal toll on dwellings all across the Hexagon; over 1,800 communes (similar to American counties) had been classified as disaster areas. The largest included France's second city, Marseille, as well as major metropolitan areas such as Lyon, Toulouse, Nantes, Nice, Bordeaux, Strasbourg, Lille, Le Havre, and Clermont-Ferrand.[3] Moreover, the homes still standing lacked amenities. In 1946, there were nearly 14 million housing units available for a population of 40.5 million people; of these existing units, 48 percent had no running water, 80 percent did not have a toilet on the premises, and a full 95 percent did not include an indoor shower or bathtub.[4] Yves Salaün, a housing ministry official, observed in 1949 that not only had very little new housing been built since World War I, but very few efforts had been made to modernize existing homes. Particularly in comparison with other nations, he lamented, the French were living in antiquated housing conditions that failed to meet their needs.[5] Glimpsing in the enormous burden of reconstruction the possibility of improving everyday life for the French, the Ministry of Reconstruction and Urban Planning (Ministère de la Reconstruction et de l'Urbanisme, or MRU) embarked upon a program of experimentation designed to discover the most efficient means of producing modern homes.

The very existence of the MRU signaled an acknowledgement that the country needed to be rebuilt—literally. Charles de Gaulle, head of the Provisional Government of the French Republic, created the ministry by decree in November 1944 and charged it with rebuilding France. The responsibility was enormous; during the war, one building out of every twenty in France had been destroyed, and one of every five damaged. The new ministry[6] coordinated a monumental number of tasks, which involved clearing the country of land mines, assembling scarce but needed building materials, acquiring land for reconstruction, erecting wooden, barracks-like provisional homes for the homeless and for construction workers, and evaluating and distributing reparations for damaged or destroyed property. Though the immediate tasks of reconstruction were crushing, the MRU also wanted to plan for the future, and one of its projects was the mass production of functional and comfortable modern homes put within the reach of the average French family.

Most of the ministry's endeavors and resources in the realm of housing went to damage claim payments to property owners, to the erection of provisional housing for the homeless and for workers in high-priority industries, and to financing the repair of partially damaged buildings. The MRU was overwhelmed with projects and chronically short of funds. Thus previous accounts of the reconstruction have marginalized the ministry's attempts to imagine—and build—modern homes.[7] Yet ministry planners did not fail to propose new forms of housing. Indeed, like the architects of the Monnet Plan, MRU officials aimed to rebuild the nation through planning; instead of a planned economy, they would offer to the nation planned municipalities comprised of functional homes created from state-of-the-art construction techniques. This chapter takes a closer look at the MRU's experimental housing in order to study the state's vision of modernity as it related to everyday citizens and to nation-building.

The first part of the chapter briefly examines the initial years of the MRU and details its early research, which encompassed not only prefabricated homes and apartment buildings but also a survey to ascertain popular preferences in housing issues. The survey revealed class differences in dwelling practices, which the MRU had to decide how to address. Then, by looking more closely at the MRU's "experimental city" of prefabricated houses in the Parisian suburb of Noisy-le-Sec and at the three major architectural competitions it sponsored between 1947 and 1951, it is possible to extract some of the MRU's normative proposals for modern homes. For the MRU, modern living meant zoned living areas within comfortable homes furnished with central heating and hot water. In the last section of the chapter, I argue that underlying the MRU's expectations of domestic architecture is a belief that rational and comfortable interiors could play an important role in rebuilding France, complementing the political, economic, and social projects of the Fourth Republic by organizing relationships of class and gender.

The Early Years of the Ministry of Reconstruction and Urbanism

At Charles de Gaulle's request, Raoul Dautry served as the MRU's first minister, and, in return, at Dautry's request, "urban planning" was added to the name of the ministry of "property reconstruction" (*reconstruction immobilière*) that he had been asked to lead.[8] Dautry's insistence on town planning reflected the scale of his ambition; as he saw it, the ministry existed not simply to repair war's damage, but to reorganize the French territory on the basis of zoning and planned development. Dautry, like many of the planners who would come to dominate the postwar period, was both a reformer and a technocrat. Trained as an engineer at the prestigious École Polytechnique and subsequently an executive for the Northern Railroad and the state railroad (Chemins de Fer de l'État), Dautry had helped to organize the national railroad, the SNCF, in 1938. He had developed an interest in workers' or "social" housing during the Belle Époque, and like other reformers of his time, he believed homes to be an instrument of social peace. After the end of World War I, in a climate of labor tension, Dautry spearheaded a project to build homes for railroad workers; in three years, over ten thousand bungalow-style homes, to house sixty thousand people, sprung up in planned garden cities. Dautry also served as the head of the Ligue nationale contre le taudis (National Anti-Slum League). Based on his experiences with this organization, he drafted a report on housing that served as the basis for the 1928 Loucheur law, which authorized direct state financing for the Habitations à bon marché (HBM), low-cost housing for the working and lower middle classes. Dautry, who had been minister of Armaments for the Reynaud government in 1940, had chosen not to work for the Vichy regime. In addition to his reputation as an able administrator, an advocate of dirigisme, and a fervent technocrat, then, Dautry also had the advantage of an uncompromised reputation. Although he had not been a member of the Resistance, it was more important that he had not been a collaborator.[9]

Dautry's MRU was highly centralized and supervised decision making on an astonishing number of matters, from approving each city's reconstruction plan to assigning housing attributions to the displaced. Attempting to implement their agenda, the MRU personnel charged with rebuilding France met with several formidable challenges, most importantly a dearth of funds, manpower, and building materials. Ministry officials dealt primarily with the needs of the moment in the first years after Liberation. New construction between 1944 and 1948 devolved largely to private initiative, which financed nearly three-quarters of all new homes. But this contribution was minimal because new homes were still quite rare: privately funded housing totaled only 7 percent of the total housing units made available to the French during this period. The MRU funded over 90 percent of the remainder, in the form of repairs to 650,000 damaged homes and the erection of more than 100,000 provisional constructions.[10]

In addition to being hampered by shortages, new construction met with some popular and political resistance. People objected to the privileging of new construction over repair and to the rejection of faithful reconstruction. Dautry's intent to remake France through better urban planning led him to approve the razing of partially damaged buildings in order to rezone a neighborhood or create new thoroughfares, as in the case of Brest.[11] Such decisions were not popular with either homeowners or renters accustomed to paying low rents for modest dwellings. When, after de Gaulle's departure from the government in January 1946, Dautry left the ministry (and moved on to the directorship of the new French Atomic Energy Commission), the incoming MRU minister, François Billoux, a Communist, promised to prioritize instead the repair of partially damaged buildings. The Communists preferred solutions to the housing shortage that maintained the rent control of the prewar period; they interpreted Dautry's decision to raze salvageable buildings as profiting only construction companies. At the same time, however, the Communist federation of labor unions, the Confédération Générale du Travail, had condemned faithful reconstruction as "reconstruction of the same shops along the same streets, maintaining the same division of property."[12] In a 1978 interview, the secretary general of Billoux's cabinet, Jacques de Seguy, explained that their decision to privilege reconstruction over new construction lay in their concern for doing well at election time, as well as their lack of technical expertise. De Seguy contrasted the Billoux cabinet—"more proletarian"—with Dautry's, which drew upon alumni of the École Polytechnique and the École Centrale Paris (another elite engineering academy).[13]

Differences of politics, class, and education characterized successive administrations, and in the months between January 1946 and September 1948, the parliamentary instability for which the Fourth Republic has become known resulted in six different ministers at the MRU, each of whom had a tenure of only a few months. At the MRU's core during this period were non-political appointees; these included the technicians, engineers, and civil servants who had, by and large, been retained from the Vichy organizations tackling planning and reconstruction: the Direction générale à l'équipement national (Directorate-General of Equipment and Infrastructure, or DGEN) and the Commissariat à la reconstruction immobilière (Property Reconstruction Commission, or CRI). Many of Dautry's initiatives in the realm of modern homes outlasted his tenure due to the efforts of people like Jean Kérisel and Dautry's friend André Prothin. Kérisel hailed from Ponts et Chaussées ("Bridges and Roads," a selective institute training civil engineers) and had studied at the École Polytechnique before Ponts et Chaussées; he also held a doctorate from the Sorbonne. Kérisel had led the CRI's reconstruction effort and served the MRU as head of the Direction générale des Travaux (Directorate-General of Public Works). André Prothin, a civil engineer and urban planner, had been director of public works for the prefecture of the Seine in the early 1930s and acted as DGEN's director of urban planning during Vichy. Dautry asked Prothin to lead the Direction générale de l'urbanisme, de l'habitation, et de la construction (DGUHC) at the MRU. Both engineers shared Dautry's scientific bent and faith in planning.

One experimental program benefiting from their stewardship was the Immeubles Sans Affectation Individuelle (Apartment Buildings without Individual Assignment, also sometimes rendered as Immediate Assignment), the ISAIs. Launched in 1945, ISAIs took the form of apartment buildings that would incorporate standardized building components and various construction processes; Dautry had created the ISAI program as a means of ascertaining the most efficient methods of home construction. Hundreds of ISAIs were built across France, including two of the most famous French experiments in postwar housing: Auguste Perret's apartments in reconstructed Le Havre, now a UNESCO World Heritage site, and Le Corbusier's Unité d'habitation at Marseille. The MRU offered apartments in ISAIs to property owners in exchange for damage claims, but willingness to accept the state's offer depended upon how much the form of the building varied from more traditional styles of architecture and how expensive it was to maintain an apartment therein. Because chapter 2 examines in more detail the architectural treatment of ISAIs, here we will simply point to the ISAI program as evidence of the MRU's early commitment to reconceptualizing and building new homes.

While laying the groundwork for mass production of housing by financing research into prefabrication and standardization, Dautry also supported the investigation into and analysis of French public opinion about homes. In early 1944, the Fondation Française pour l'Étude des Problèmes Humains (French Foundation for the Study of Human Problems), working with the DGEN, undertook to canvass urban dwellers on their "desires in the matter of habitation." At the war's end, Dautry commissioned the newly created Institut national d'études démographiques (National Institute of Demographic Studies, or INED) to resume work on the study. Surveys took place throughout September 1945, and INED published the results in 1947. Widely publicized in professional and mass media, the results merit in-depth description here for two related reasons. From the moment they were published through the early part of the 1960s, they constituted much of the received knowledge about how the French wanted to live; they offer, therefore, the context for a deeper understanding of housing professionals' design choices over the course of the 1940s, 50s, and 60s.

Interrogated about everything from how they wanted to store pots and pans to the preferred fuel for heating stoves, the French public revealed itself to be unified on several questions. First and foremost, the majority (72 percent) of the nearly 2,500 people interviewed for the survey expressed their desire to live in a single-family detached house; even 56 percent of Parisians, long accustomed to apartment-dwelling, aspired to this situation. Nearly 60 percent would agree to live in a mass-produced home if it were equipped with heating and sanitary installations. Two-thirds preferred to own their own home, with half of renters seeking to own property eventually; consensus also reigned that rent should take up no more than 10 percent of the household budget.[14]

The authors remarked that when differences of opinion arose, these tended to be correlated with age or socioprofessional category. In general, they observed, neither geography nor gender appeared to skew results. The authors noted that younger generations were more open to innovations in heating, construction forms, or floor plans. They enthused, "It seems that a transformation in housing standards is taking place. Is this not a singularly propitious time to take advantage of this momentum?"[15] This remark implied that the older generations' preferences, represented as force of habit, did not need to be taken into account in the planning of new homes. The demographers added their voices to the chorus of those hoping to usher France into a new era of modernity.

Though unanimity still existed on questions regarding whether the toilet should be in the bathroom (no), whether built-in shelves were preferable to armoires (they were), or whether it was worth a rent increase to have both a basement and an attic (it was), the survey revealed class differences in the use of space. The most marked variations arose when respondents gave opinions about room size, room specialization, and dining areas. For example, participants were asked to choose between large bedrooms and a smaller communal living area, or small bedrooms and a larger communal space. There was a 10 percent difference between the upper middle class, who opted for larger living rooms, since they entertained more at home, and workers and salaried employees, who preferred to sacrifice the size of the living room for larger bedrooms, where parents could share their space with a crib.[16]

A greater cleavage emerged when interviewees weighed in on what was known in architectural terms as the "separation of functions." The separation of functions was a design principle that had been gaining ground in architectural theory since its origins in the interwar period; when applied to domestic space, functionalism called for homes to be conceived according to the needs that they had to fulfill, instead of either to abstract principles of harmony and balance or to the status of those who dwelled within. Room specialization—the devotion of a single space to as few needs as possible, separating the functions performed in each area—seemed to most efficiently accomplish this goal. Thus, bedrooms were for sleeping, the living room was for family interaction, and the kitchen was for meal preparation. Moreover, functionalism called for "night functions," like sleeping, to be spatially delineated from "day functions," such as laundering, dining, and children's play.[17] In the "Hygiene" section of the INED survey, the first question was, "In your opinion, can the kitchen be used for bathing?" Though the majority of respondents (67 percent) answered in the negative, once again responses varied by class. Forty-one percent of workers thought that, in fact, it was perfectly fine to bathe in the kitchen, whereas only 21 percent of members of the liberal professions and 18 percent of business owners agreed.[18]

Finally, the knottiest problem of differences in dwelling practices, one related to the principle of room specialization, arose when interviewers asked respondents to identify the best grouping of kitchen and dining arrangements.[19] The survey devoted eleven pages, one of the largest subsections of the study, to this question. The origin of the problem lay in a nearly even split between where families habitually took their meals. Half always ate in the kitchen, and another 45 percent dined regularly in the dining room. The survey did not ask whether all respondents in fact possessed both a kitchen and a dining room. Workers were the largest group

(72 percent) to dine in the kitchen, compared with 52 percent of salaried employees. Less than a quarter of the members of the liberal professions ate in the kitchen.[20]

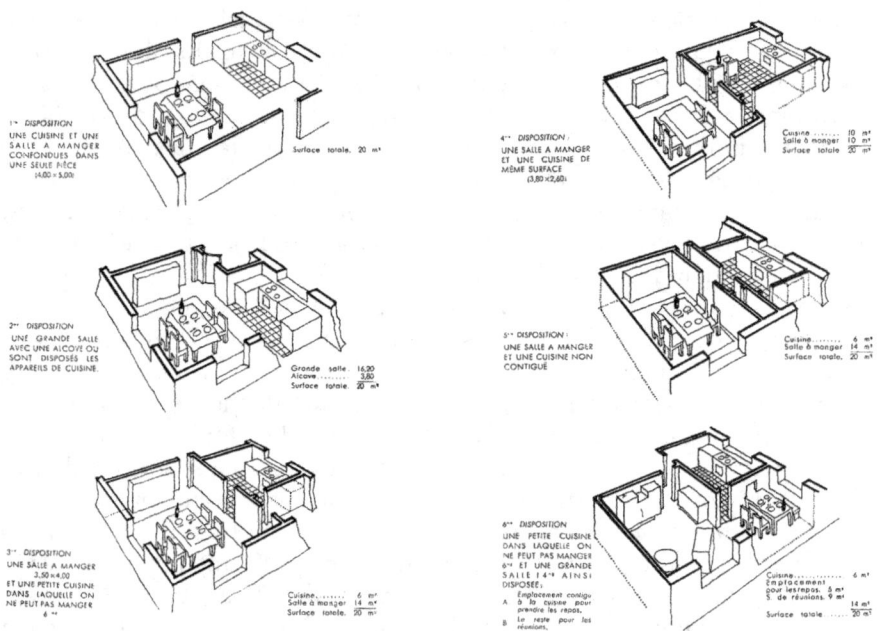

Figure 1.1. Six possible dispositions of kitchen and dining spaces proposed for an apartment. © Presses Universitaires de France.

Individuals were asked to evaluate six different layouts (Figure 1.1). The various dispositions essentially posed three questions: Should the kitchen be separated from the dining room? If so, should the two rooms be contiguous or separated by a hallway? Finally, should the kitchen be small or large (big enough to accommodate a dining table)? What was not made explicit, which may have led to some ambiguity for respondents, was whether the dining room was to be the exclusive site for family interaction or whether the kitchen and dining room choices were in addition to an unseen living room area. In this light, the sixth option was somewhat confusing. It provided an additional space, that of a parlor-type area. Some respondents may have chosen the sixth choice on the basis that they did not want their dining room to be the only place to gather; others may have believed that the kitchen and dining room choices shown were in addition to a living room.

On the whole, the French rejected the non-separation of the kitchen and dining area and preferred either a dining corner in an alcove of the living area or a kitchen and dining room of equal proportions, providing the option of dining in either room. There were regional variations (only 16 percent of those in northwest France liked the sixth choice, whereas 27 percent of those in the northeast did) and age variations (again, for the sixth choice, only 17 percent of those over 65 preferred it compared to 29 percent of those between 20 and 34). Twenty-nine percent of those who habitually ate in the dining room favored the sixth disposition, as opposed to 19 percent of those dining in the kitchen; the latter endorsed (by a majority of 36 percent) the fourth choice, which was ranked first by only 19 percent of those who customarily ate in the dining room. The fourth choice was the favorite for salaried employees, civil servants, and workers, while members of the liberal professions opted for the sixth choice.[21]

Though opinions varied about the form of the ideal kitchen, the responses to this question exemplify the survey's two key findings: (1) people inhabited domestic space in different ways, and (2) at least some of these people were open to new kinds of floor plans and new ways of using space. Because of INED's study, postwar planners knew from the outset that dwelling practices and preferences varied by generation, gender, class, and region, yet, as we shall see in the chapters that follow, they embraced standardization. At the time, it was not clear, given the survey's hypothetical approach, how residents would actually react when confronted with unfamiliar layouts and equipment. In fact, the MRU was in the process of measuring such reactions while the INED survey was being prepared for publication. In the next section, we look at the Experimental City, one of the MRU's special projects in the years following Liberation.

The Cité de Merlan at Noisy-le-Sec: Experiments in Living Rationally

Ordered by Dautry and supervised by the Service des Études de la Construction (Office of Construction Research, or SEC), a bureau of the DGUHC, the Cité expérimentale de Merlan at Noisy-le-Sec, in the outer suburbs of eastern Paris, was a housing development composed of over sixty prefabricated houses originating from seven nations. Rehousing only approximately two hundred people, the Cité expérimentale operated primarily as a laboratory for the MRU, so that housing professionals would be able to compare state-of-the-art prefabrication techniques and to examine how French families might fare in modern mass homes. Detailed surveys and evaluations of the Noisy-le-Sec experiment survive in the housing ministry's archives and provide meaningful traces of the MRU's expectations for modern domestic architecture. In this section, therefore, we turn to an in-depth examination of the Cité expérimentale.

The Experimental City included eleven American houses, seven from Britain, three from Switzerland, two from Finland, and one each from Canada and Sweden; the rest of the homes were French. The foreign homes were a product of MRU missions abroad, which were designed not only to publicize and raise funds for French reconstruction, but to determine what worked for other nations also suffering from housing shortages.[22] Jean Kérisel and the architect-urban planner Urbain Cassan had arranged to purchase several American homes while on mission to the United States in June 1945.[23] Selection criteria for the development included both type of prefabrication technique and availability of materials. Four of the American homes had already been shown in Paris at the Exposition des techniques américaines d'habitation et d'urbanisme in 1946. Ground was broken on the Noisy-le-Sec site in June 1946, and homes continued to be erected through October 1948.

The Cité expérimentale was essentially a residential tract development. This might seem surprising, given the disfavor that garden cities and single-family detached homes had recently fallen into among urban planners who championed instead residential zones composed of apartment complexes. Town planners had begun to argue that detached homes could lead to anarchic sprawl and, in any case, were too costly in terms of the infrastructure of roads, sidewalks, sewers and utilities that must necessarily serve each house. However, the MRU's official policy, under Dautry, was one of eclecticism. Following scientific method, many different strategies and innovations had to be tested in order to determine the most efficient model home. For the MRU, Noisy-le-Sec was less a test case for a new urbanism and more of a technical essay of materials and building processes.

If urbanism counted for little in the Noisy-le-Sec experiment, the SEC scrutinized interiors as carefully as it did new construction techniques. Homes had to be modern inside as well as out. Ministry personnel evaluated the different processes of lighting, heating, cooling, and ventilation employed in the homes. They also put the materials used in home design under the microscope. For instance, SEC personnel inspected over seven different flooring materials, such the new "English pitchmastic," to see how well they withstood grease, dirt, and wear. Finally, officials examined the equipment, furnishing, and layout of each home. A unique aspect of the Cité expérimentale was that the MRU's Housing Commission was in charge of furnishing homes as well as distributing them, since scientific method required modern homes to be furnished with modern furniture.

Applicants for the spaces were asked whether they would be willing to give up their old furniture in order to live in the Noisy-le-Sec prefabricated homes; desperate for homes, no one refused.

Who made up the community? There was no lack of volunteers for the Experimental City. Letters poured into the MRU from near and far, requesting one of the Noisy-le-Sec homes; however, only those families previously domiciled in Noisy-le-Sec were eligible. The housing office chose the majority of residents from families whose homes had been completely destroyed during an Allied air raid in April 1944, though some received an allocation of an Experimental City home after having been expropriated from their property to make way for new construction. Assignment began in July 1946 and continued through March 1949, meaning that some families waited nearly five years for a permanent home, making do in temporary barracks until then.

Allocations were officially based on family size, with large families taking priority. Unofficially, other factors came into play. Once the MRU's Housing Commission received a request from a qualifying family, the commission dispatched a social worker to evaluate the family. The questionnaire employed reveals not only that the commission was interested in the family's size and father's place of work, but that the social worker was also asked to give a general opinion of the family, as well as an estimation of the mother's "tidiness, cleanliness and orderliness."[24] In one family's case, the Housing Commission cancelled plans for an allotment because of reports that the parents had left their children unattended for four days.[25] Approximately 85 percent of the women were not employed outside of the home, and an evaluation of subpar housekeeping boded poorly for attribution. Presumably, slovenly homemakers would make bad "testers".

Only French families could move into the Experimental City. An Algerian family of seven who had lost their home in the air raid failed to receive a visit from a social worker because Algerians "had to be rehoused by the mayor's office," falling outside the official purview of the Housing Commission.[26] Yet, if the community was rather homogeneous when it came to ethnicity, the population was somewhat more diverse when broken down by the head of household's occupation: 43 percent workers, 18 percent salaried employees, 15 percent artisans, 12 percent liberal professionals, 7 percent civil servants, and 5 percent managers.[27] The local SNCF train station employed the majority of the workers, office employees, and managers in various capacities.

Once families began to move into the prefabricated homes, they received visits from the SEC officials sent to evaluate the success or failure of the interiors. An internal report assessing the kitchens in various homes makes clear some of the ministry's expectations: "The kitchen must no longer serve for bathing; bathrooms should be clearly separate from the kitchen. Kitchens should be directly linked to the living room–dining room area, so that mothers can easily supervise children. As a general rule, kitchens, being reserved solely for meal preparation, will measure seven square meters. Appliances should be arranged in order to reduce the homemaker's fatigue and facilitate her work. The kitchen should be well-ventilated and well-lit."[28]

These propositions evolved from three schools of thought with roots ranging from the end of the nineteenth century to the 1920s. As we saw in the previous section, the disconnection of the bathrooms from the kitchen obeyed the design principle mandating the separation of functions, as did the directive that the kitchen serve only for food preparation. Yet both also reprised elements of the fin-de-siècle hygienist agenda for workers' housing. The hygienists' definition of cleanliness—one aimed at the reducing the risk of epidemics—called for the division of corporeal care and waste from food preparation and consumption. Their belief in the medicinal effects of air and sunlight also contributed to the dictate that the kitchen be bright and well ventilated. In other words, modern homes should promote good health.

The ministry's commitment to room specialization appears in its review of a prototype submitted for inclusion at Noisy-le-Sec by Jean Prouvé, an engineer from Nancy who had spent much of the interwar period developing techniques for the mass production of both housing and furniture. Prouvé, a Modernist who had worked with Eugène Beaudouin and Marcel Lods on the most famous prewar example of Modern French housing, the Cité de la Muette at Drancy, had opted for an open plan, following Le Corbusier's design principles (see chapter 2). Prouvé's open plan provoked objections on several levels. The SEC's examination of the prototype noted that the failure to erect any barrier between the kitchen and the living room–dining room area was problematic, since "odors and vapors" produced by the "style of French cooking" would penetrate the living space.[29] Further, in a letter to Prouvé, the SEC informed him that he would have to make changes to the plan, explaining that "it is desirable to separate, in a home of this quality, the diverse functions: food, laundry, hygiene."[30] Prouvé made the modifications.

Though the separation of the kitchen and the living area was imperative for the MRU, the ministry's kitchen report did maintain that the kitchen should nevertheless be as close as possible to the dining area. This proposition, as well as the one that kitchen equipment should be arranged to reduce the homemaker's fatigue, stemmed from a third trend in domestic architecture, linked to the others and born in the 1920s: scientific management of the home. Much of the received knowledge about rationalized domestic space came from the prewar time and motion studies of housework conducted by German, Swedish, and American advocates of Taylorism for the home, research that was disseminated in France primarily by Paulette Bernège, a home economist.[31] Bernège consulted frequently with designers and architects, for whom the rationalization of space went hand in hand with functionalism. The chief goal of rationalist home design was to improve a household's productivity by reducing its expenditure of time, effort, and resources. SEC personnel demonstrated an ardent interest in rationalist design, particularly with regard to the ways in which it could improve women's everyday lives. Jean Magendie, head of the SEC's Bureau de l'Habitation, shared this concern, writing in a 1946 memo about ranges: "As a general rule, all work surfaces should be at an appropriate height for the housewife. She should not have to bend over, since this is the principal cause of fatigue. An inverse situation is that water should not run down her forearms when her elbows are at her sides. Surface heights thus depend principally on the housewife's size. Ninety centimeters is good for a woman measuring 1m65, so the most logical thing is to have bases of 5, 10 or 15 centimeters high on which we could place standard 80 centimeter cookers."[32] That the SEC staff devoted itself to this fine level of analysis indicates its conviction that modern houses should be energy-saving and comfortable, and, more broadly, its aim to build homes that would improve citizens' lives. At the same time, Magendie's memo illustrates an intention to build homes, literally, around the figure of the stay-at-home mother, a point to which we will return later in the chapter.

Feedback from other sources, such as social workers and residents of these new homes, serves to highlight other MRU aspirations, particularly when opinions diverged. Social workers were frequent visitors to the site, and the MRU, conscious that social workers had firsthand knowledge of families' everyday needs, eagerly sought their contributions. After one guided tour, sixteen female representatives from the Home Economics division of the Caisse centrale d'allocations familiales (the family allowances bureau) returned a questionnaire distributed by the MRU, which asked, among other items, if the 90-centimeter height for cookers was rational and whether it would be admissible to include laundry facilities in the kitchen.[33] For social workers, used to working with poor and often large families, the most salient aspect of modern home design was its labor-saving potential. Less concerned by the separation of functions, the women readily allowed that laundry could be done in the kitchen, though they were evenly divided on whether 90 centimeters was in fact the most rational height for a stove. (Several believed it should be five to ten centimeters shorter.)

Nonetheless, their interest in rationalizing domestic space did not mean that the social workers had no aesthetic preferences or biases. Because the MRU officially espoused eclecticism, it was open to the new forms, like flat roofs, that might accompany inventive prefabrication techniques; social workers were more conservative. In a 1950 letter to the MRU, the director of the Union nationale des caisses d'allocations familiales (UN-CAF, the new national agency responsible for the distribution of family allowances) reported the reactions of twenty-three departmental heads of social services during their tour of Noisy-le-Sec. These department heads offered their opinions of several of the homes. Remarking upon Jean Prouvé's home, the director reported, "The Prouvé house is, without a doubt, a formula more interesting for a collective, such as a day care facility, than a family home."[34] Though Prouvé had fulfilled the MRU's request to separate functions, he employed moving partitions to separate many of the rooms; as a result, the living area was a large open space and did not resemble a traditional apartment in which rooms opened up off of a distributing hallway. The visitors were more receptive to technological advances in gadgetry and furniture, praising a water heater operated by foot pedal in a French home and fold-down children's bunk beds in a Swiss house.

And what of the residents? How did they react to their new homes? Generally pleased with the high quality of the furniture and equipment in their new homes, inhabitants reserved the near totality of their complaints for foreign layouts that deviated from French ways of inhabiting space. This result indicated that another factor shaping dwelling practices, in addition to class and age, was national culture. One of the objections to American homes, for instance, was the absence of an entryway or foyer. Entering directly into the living room struck many Noisy-le-Sec residents as disruptive of familial privacy; they preferred that the view of the living area remain closed off until a visitor was invited in. Residents didn't like American kitchens separated only from the living room by a waist-high partition or bar and protested the placement of toilets in the bathrooms. They critiqued Swiss and Scandinavian homes where the bathroom facilities were too far from bedrooms (either in an opposite corner or on the first floor). The MRU staff also registered complaints about the lack of laundering spaces in all of the foreign homes except the Swiss ones.[35]

The SEC's kitchen report, however, reveals that it was not only layouts and equipment being evaluated by the MRU, but also the residents' behavior. The subsection on "usage" opened with the comment, "One might regret that, in practice, use of the kitchen does not correspond to the conception of the design and to the previsions which have been made for this conception." In other words, people were dining in the kitchen. The report's author lamented, "The kitchen, which was supposed to have been reserved solely for meal preparation, is used at mealtime by more than 70 percent of households, regardless of family size or the size of the room, which averages 7 1/2 square meters." How did the evaluator account for this? "This stems, on the one hand, from social milieu (55 percent [are] working class) and, on the other hand, from deep-rooted habits accumulated by living too long in tiny and badly-designed apartments. However, the reason offered by the mother has to do with the question of upkeep of the floors."[36] In spite of the fact that residents offered a rationale for their behavior that accepted the rationalizing aspect of the MRU's agenda for modern homes—eating in the kitchen helped to reduce labor because it was easier to clean the kitchen floor and because it helped to keep the living room tidy—the official attributed their behavior to class and bad habits.

In his memo on counter surfaces, Magendie downplayed women's concerns about the lack of laundering spaces in their homes; with a technocrat's eye for statistics, he explained that, unlike cooking, which occupied "all day," laundry "only" took place once or twice every two weeks. Although laundry was one of the most physically demanding aspects of housework, it merited less priority because it was done less frequently. Magendie dismissed some of the female residents' feedback as "housewives used to their routines."[37] Though MRU officials professed interest in easing the burden of housework, these comments demonstrate that they also believed that there were "correct" and "incorrect" ways of doing that work, as well as "proper" and "improper" places to dine. In other words, the MRU did not consider a housewife to be the ultimate authority on the most efficient way to run a home, and the ministry would have the final word on which elements of domestic life the modern home would rationalize.

The resident survey represents in microcosm the struggle between a technocratic state that self-identified as the agent of modernization and a populace characterized by the state as recalcitrant traditionalists. According to the resident survey, 77 percent of all families interviewed dined daily in the kitchen; only one family always took their meals in the living room–dining room area. The author of the kitchen report remarked that in addition to using the kitchen for family meals, women also ironed there, even when space had been allocated elsewhere for ironing. He observed, "In sum, the whole of family life takes place there during the week as well as on Sundays in numerous cases."[38] Confronted with this reality, the author concluded, "What this experiment suggests is that it would be desirable that living rooms, which are 20 square meters on average, be designed with a well-demarcated space called 'dining room,' which would open directly off of the kitchen and which could be separated from the reception area by a moving partition."[39]

Why not simply recommend larger kitchens? Why insist on maintaining the dining area in the living room? Why privilege the separation of functions over the rationalization of housework? The answers to these questions may lie in the author's class bias, in a belief in the hygienic importance of separation of functions, in some combination thereof, or somewhere else entirely. More important is the fact that the MRU representative's recommendation contains the germ of normative home design. Rather than trying to plan for diverse ways of inhabiting space, the MRU was moving toward the conception of a one-size-fits-all home. The Noisy-le-Sec experiment reveals that, rather than the modern home having to accommodate how real people lived, occupants were going to be expected to adapt to the modern home. For the MRU, the modern home was one where a functional layout combined with state-of-the-art technology to create a hygienic and rational environment; these qualities made it, a priori, the ideal home.

MRU Architectural Competitions: Committing to Comfort

The year 1947 was a turning point for the Fourth Republic, during which the Communists were expelled from the government, ending *tripartisme*, the coalition government of Communists, Socialists, and the Christian Democrats of the Mouvement Républicain Populaire (MRP). Massive strike waves in the railroad, bank, and automobile industries, among others, pointed to popular frustration with the Fourth Republic's failure to fulfill the promise of Liberation to end injustices. To a populace facing high inflation and weary of sustained shortages of food, housing, and coal, a return to the prewar status quo loomed large. Accelerating the French recovery became imperative, and to this end, the Monnet and Marshall Plans advocated a planned economy privileging the resuscitation of heavy industry.

The First (Monnet) Plan privileged six sectors of the economy: coal, steel, electricity, cement, agricultural machinery, and transport. It failed, therefore, to offer any financial priority to new construction, and the ministry lost the word "urbanism" from its name for the first half of 1947. The name change indicated that the ministry's vocation had been scaled back to the sole task of reconstruction. For the years 1947 to 1950, new construction received allocations of only 10 billion francs, whereas reconstruction received 610 billion.[40] Yet the expansion of the ministry's responsibilities in two arenas telegraphed the ministry's mission to build new homes for the French. First was the creation of the Scientific and Technical Center for Building (Centre Scientifique et Technique du Bâtiment, or CSTB), an organization attached to the MRU, whose purpose was to research, advise upon, and evaluate new materials, equipment, and building processes, and then to disseminate its findings. André Marini, the former head of the SEC, took the helm of the CSTB. In the years to come, by issuing a set of technical directives and recommendations for builders, architects, and engineers and by approving model plans and construction processes for use in MRU-financed housing projects, the CSTB would play a significant role in the normalization of interiors.

Second, the Habitations à bon marché program migrated from the ministry of public health to the MRU at the end of 1947. Influenced by studies showing overcrowding in the one- and two-room apartments then ubiquitous in the urban housing stock, the MRU established new and more generous norms for HBM surface areas when it took over the social housing program. Apartment size increased anywhere from 25 to 40 percent, depending on the number of rooms in the apartment. A four-bedroom apartment grew by 36.5 percent, and each bedroom received two more square meters than had been granted in 1922.[41] In 1951, HBMs became Habitations à loyer modéré (HLM), literally "reasonable or moderated rent" — rent-controlled — residences. The new appellation reflected the fact that rents for the apartments were not exactly "bon marché" (cheap), as well as an understanding that these were not only homes for the working classes, with whom the HBMs had been associated for half a century, but for a mixed-class constituency. The shift from HBM to HLM should be interpreted as an intentional redefinition of "social housing." That is, by affirming that HLM housing was meant for teachers, engineers, and salaried employees as much as workers' families, the MRU signaled its desire to put an end to spatial segregation and to help to resolve the social question by democratizing housing and communities. (See chapter 2 on the ways in which HBM housing had materialized dwelling preferences into designs for residents of different socioeconomic groups.)

To do this, it was imperative, according to the MRU, to determine the most rapid and least expensive building processes, and hence, by March 1947, the MRU had established a competition for new home construction. The contest had three modalities: two-story, three-bedroom detached homes; two-story, three-bedroom row houses (in sets of five); and four-story apartment buildings consisting of equal numbers of two- and three-bedroom apartments. Ten first prizes, twenty second prizes, twenty third prizes, and fifty fourth prizes were to be awarded, with the first- and second-place winners receiving, in addition to cash awards, contracts to build groups of approximately fifty units.

The contest directives specified that all plans should include an entryway, a large living area, and a bedroom for every two inhabitants. Architects could choose whether to attach the dining area to the kitchen or to the living area. On the other hand, proposals had to specify the location of a sofa, two armchairs, a desk, a dining table and chairs, and the beds, bedside tables, chairs, and dressers in the bedrooms.[42] Architects were also instructed to designate the location of the crib in the parents' bedroom, which indicates that the imagined occupants of these new homes were a young couple with at least one child and more on the way; the new modern home, then, was to encourage the attainment of the state's pronatalist objectives.

The competition's "Equipment Norms" specified the "minimum" equipment "indispensable" to a residence: running water, electricity (though provision was only made for one outlet), heat, cooking equipment, ventilation, and waste disposal. The instructions further stipulated that the running water had to be both hot and cold so that the bathroom (separate from the room with the toilet) could be used for bathing and laundering.[43] Given, as mentioned above, that 95 percent of contemporary homes did not have even a shower, and 80 percent of households lacked toilet facilities inside their residences, this "minimum" represented a great leap forward. The request that place for a refrigerator be incorporated into the layout of the kitchen also hinted at the MRU's optimistic expectations with regard to the mass adoption of household appliances; at the time only approximately 5 percent of households possessed a refrigerator.[44]

In addition to the word "equipment," the term "comfort" was beginning to signify these installations of heating, plumbing, and utilities. In 1948 Larousse defined "modern comfort" as "the ensemble of provisions destined to make an apartment building more comfortable, such as central heating, a bathroom, an elevator, electricity, etc." The 1946 census was the first to ask questions about "the elements of comfort" present in homes; these included electricity and gas hookups, running water in the apartment, a toilet, and a bathtub or shower. Central heating did not factor into the "elements of comfort" until the 1954 census, a fact that underscores the high ambitions of the MRU, which demanded the inclusion of central heating in its 1947 competition.[45]

Tellingly, when MRU officials employed the term "comfort," then, they were generally referring to heating, plumbing, and utilities. Their global conception of comfort, at least in 1947, went beyond its technical connotations, however. According to André Prothin's housing guidelines, space was as important a factor to the success of a house as its technical accouterments.[46] One could not reduce a home's surface area to a bare minimum and expect that improvements in comfort would compensate for tiny spaces. In a section of the 1947 competition instructions subtitled, "Usage Norms," the MRU specified that hallways and passageways should be minimized, "but large enough however to permit the rational usage of rooms and to ensure the independence of each room, which is one of the essential conditions of intimacy."[47] Even the building's orientation played a role in making a home livable. For example, it had long been assumed that the kitchens must face either north or east, in order to help prevent food from spoiling. New recommendations, anticipating the refrigerator's imminent entry into kitchens, advocated instead an orientation toward the south or west, so that the housewife who spent much of her time in the kitchen could enjoy a room filled with light for longer stretches of the day. Both the Noisy-le-Sec kitchen evaluation and the INED survey articulated this preference.[48] Thus, technology alone did not make a home modern, but planners believed that technological innovations were making it possible, for the first time in history, to design interiors for the sole purpose of the inhabitants' physiological and psychological well-being. That was the promise of the rational and comfortable modern home.

Aiming to fulfill this promise, over five hundred teams submitted entries for the MRU's contest. Though departmental juries submitted their recommendations for prizes, a national jury, led by Modernist architect Auguste Perret, reevaluated the plans, because the local evaluations were deemed too "erratic"; so, in keeping with the long French tradition of centralization, Paris had the last word, and in the spring of 1948, final winners were announced.[49] Out of 280 submissions for single-family detached homes, the jury awarded no first or second prizes, and only two third prizes and five fourth prizes. The results were not better for the 140 entries for row houses: again, no first or second prizes were awarded, and the jury conferred only two third prizes and four fourth prizes. The 144 proposals for apartment buildings found slightly more favor: the jury handed out one first prize, two second prizes, three third prizes, and six fourth prizes. The generally poor showing reflected the MRU's opinion that submissions tended to rely on traditional artisanal techniques and materials and failed to promote or suggest more rational and industrial construction methods and formulas.

The first-place design belonged to Arthur Héaume and Alexandre Persitz, the latter of whom was, at the time, editor-in-chief of the Modernist architectural journal *L'Architecture d'aujourd'hui* (Today's Architecture). Héaume and Persitz's winning plan, which appeared in the June 1948 issue of the journal, called for a rectangular-shaped apartment, and the architects had neatly divided the apartment according to the day-night principle. A small kitchen limited to meal preparation led directly—either by a door or by an opening through which dishes could be passed—into the dining area. Each bedroom had a closet, and the hallway contained both a linen closet and storage for cleaning supplies. The bathroom came with either a shower or a full bathtub. The master bedroom lay off of the living room area, placed as far as possible from the children's bedrooms. The architects noted that only a folding wall separated the master bedroom from the living area, so that during the day the living space could be enlarged if desired.

Though the MRU built 120 of these apartments in Calais, the ministry was disappointed by the contest's overall poor showing in terms of industrializing construction and economizing costs and decided to try again with a new competition in April 1949. By this point, the MRU was under the aegis of Eugène Claudius-Petit, a former member of the Resistance noted for his social Catholicism and passions for urbanism and Modernism. Claudius-Petit would spend over four years leading the MRU, and his influence was to be long-lasting. Claudius-Petit had cofounded the Union Démocrate et Socialiste de la Résistance (UDSR) political party in 1945 as a means of offering a political platform in support of workers' rights to non-Communist Resistance fighters. Claudius-Petit himself entered political life as an UDSR deputy from the Loire in 1946. Though he had hoped to be named the first MRU minister in 1944 and was disappointed when de Gaulle turned instead to Dautry, Claudius-Petit had remained active in the realms of urbanism, land-use development, and housing, intervening frequently on reconstruction debates in the National Assembly, serving on the editorial team of *L'Architecture d'aujourd'hui,* and participating in a number of committees and commissions related to reconstruction and urbanism. When the president of the Conseil des ministres, Radical-Socialist Henri Queuille, sought stability for his government by incorporating ministers from the UDSR, he turned to Claudius-Petit, who finally became MRU minister in September 1948.[50]

Like Raoul Dautry, Claudius-Petit believed in the need for a strong policy of new construction, yet, unlike the first MRU minister, Claudius-Petit privileged Modernism over eclecticism. Trained as a woodworker, Claudius-Petit became a high school drawing teacher in the 1930s; he was passionately interested in questions of art, architecture, and town planning and had become an ardent supporter of the radical proposals of Modernist architects like Le Corbusier. Claudius-Petit had also been influenced by Jean-François Gravier's 1947 best seller *Paris et le désert français* (Paris and the French Desert). Persuaded by Gravier's argument that decentralization and regional planning were the best means of managing urbanization and promoting economic modernization, Claudius-Petit submitted to the government the first national plan for *aménagement du territoire* (land-use management) in 1950. The plan proclaimed the absolute necessity of producing 240,000 housing units annually if the housing shortage was to be ameliorated.[51] With this proposal, Claudius-Petit defended the MRU's commitment to building new homes in addition to reconstructing those destroyed during the war and, in fact, passionately demanded expansion of its activities in that domain.

Since the goal of 240,000 units per year dramatically exceeded the rate at which new homes were being built (only 51,436 units had become available in 1949, a figure that included both reconstruction and new construction)[52] it was clear that improvements to the construction industry's productive capacity would still need to be sought. By 1949, the Noisy-le-Sec experiment was complete, the ISAI program had been terminated, and the 1947 competition had come to its sorry conclusion. Meanwhile, as the MRU conducted its experiments in modern living, some of the French attempted to take matters into their own hands, literally. Nicknamed the "Castors" (Beavers), these individuals sought to combine HBM funding with sweat equity to build their own homes in suburban communities. Rosemary Wakeman has shown how the Castors, who were active in groups ranging from 20 to 150 members, favored communities of individual homes arranged in such a way to facilitate mutual aid, communal exchange, participation, and solidarity.[53] Supported by progressive Catholic organizations like the Jeunesse Ouvrière Chrétienne (Young Christian Workers) and the Conféderation française des travailleurs chrétiens (French Confederation of Christian Workers) labor union, the Castors sought and received aid from the MRU in the form of loans and planning expertise. Yet this assistance stemmed largely from Claudius-Petit's sympathies with the Christian Democrats coordinating these efforts and the MRU's realization that it needed all of the help it could get in the domain of new construction, for the Castors' preference for individual homes conflicted, by 1950, with the ministry's shift in policy toward collective housing.

No initiative—state, private, or employer-based—had, as of yet, provided a cost-effective formula for quickly building mass housing, so Claudius-Petit began to orient the housing policy toward the high-rise apartment buildings advocated by Modernists. His 1949 MRU competition, while still encouraging developments in the domain of individual housing, called for taller apartment buildings. The 1949 competition, like its predecessor, had three modalities, but this time, architects could submit plans for one- or two-story detached homes to be built in Chartres, small apartment buildings of two to four stories for Creil-Compiègne, north of Paris, or tall apartment buildings of nine to twelve stories each for Villeneuve-Saint-Georges, south of Paris. First-place winners would receive contracts for two hundred units apiece. Under Claudius-Petit, then, the numbers of families to be housed in one grouping were getting larger, and the buildings were getting taller. What had been the tallest apartment size in the 1947 contest was now the mid-size option, and the tall buildings had more than doubled in size, becoming towers of apartments.

Marc and Léo Solotareff's proposal for tall apartment buildings won first place. The interiors lacked the elegance of Héaume and Persitz's apartments. The Solotareffs' plan neither maintained a crisp day-night separation nor provided the fully rational direct liaison between the kitchen and the dining room area. It did, however, facilitate privacy via a foyer and a long hallway and offered a small dining nook in the kitchen, where the space for a refrigerator had been eliminated. The system of construction in all of these competitions weighed more heavily in the judges' minds than did the sophistication of the interiors. Yet what makes the interiors important is that they illustrated the definition of a minimum standard of "modern comfort." In 1949, while the MRU may have relaxed its expectations somewhat regarding rational layouts and room specialization, each apartment still had to offer hot and cold water, kitchen and bathroom sinks, shower, toilet, and central heating.

In December 1950, the MRU initiated a new competition, one that made history by calling for a single contract of eight hundred units to be built in suburban Strasbourg. The competition instructions asked that each unit have enough space for "rest, family work, meal preparation, meals, bathing, WC [toilet], and storage space."[54] It is significant that "meals" was distinguished from the meal preparation space; clearly, this time, the urgings of the Noisy-le-Sec evaluator were going to be followed. Each apartment had to provide hot and cold water, a kitchen sink, a bathroom sink, a shower or tub, a flush toilet, at least five electrical outlets, central heat, and a gas line in the kitchen. This dedication to modern comfort is striking in the face of the MRU's continual and earnest efforts to bring down construction costs, a point to which we will return in the next section.

A highly publicized competition, the Cité Rotterdam contest attracted a number of noted architects, including Le Corbusier and Marcel Lods; the MRU ultimately approved only twenty-four teams of architects, engineers, and builders to submit final projects. The 22-man jury included MRU officials Jean Kérisel and André Prothin, as well as André Marini, former head of the SEC and now director of the new CSTB, and Adrien Spinetta, head engineer at the prestigious corps of engineers, Ponts et Chaussées. It also incorporated a number of Modernists, including Communist architect and Resistance member André Lurçat, Auguste Perret, and the engineer Jean Prouvé.

During the jury's deliberation, Lurçat expressed his regret that the jury did not include any women, who would be more qualified to express an opinion on how well the layout of the interiors would work. No one responded.[55] After a few rounds of voting, they selected a winner: Eugène Beaudouin, the architect responsible, with Marcel Lods, for the celebrated prefabrication experiments of the 1930s, the HBMs of the Cité des Oiseaux in Bagneux and Cité de la Muette in Drancy. The architectural journals praised Beaudouin's winning proposal for its site plan, which arranged a number of tall apartment towers, as well as some shorter buildings, around a long mall. The interiors garnered little comment, although the trade magazine *L'Architecture française* did note that the apartments allowed for light and ventilation, air through a balcony or terrace, and a kitchen that could be closed off or left open.[56]

Beaudouin's plan (Figure 1.2) was much more open, markedly so, than the previous winning designs. There was an entryway, but the absence of a door or partition meant that visitors could see directly into the living area. The boundaries between day and night functions were blurred by the inclusion of sleeping space directly into the living room–dining room area, as well as the lack of doors or other separators between that space and two of the bedrooms, including the master bedroom. Beaudouin had ignored the principle of day-night separation in order to facilitate maximum communal use of the entire apartment during the daytime. He did, however, provide a rational kitchen. The dining corner lay directly off of the kitchen for easy service; like Héaume and Persitz, but unlike the Solotareffs, Beaudouin did not include an additional dining nook in the kitchen. Beaudouin, consciously or not, was following the competition requirements as well as the advice of the Noisy-le-Sec kitchen evaluator and making it clear to residents where they should be taking their meals.

If the Cité Rotterdam had some of the elements requested by the French surveyed by INED—ample equipment, a spacious living area—

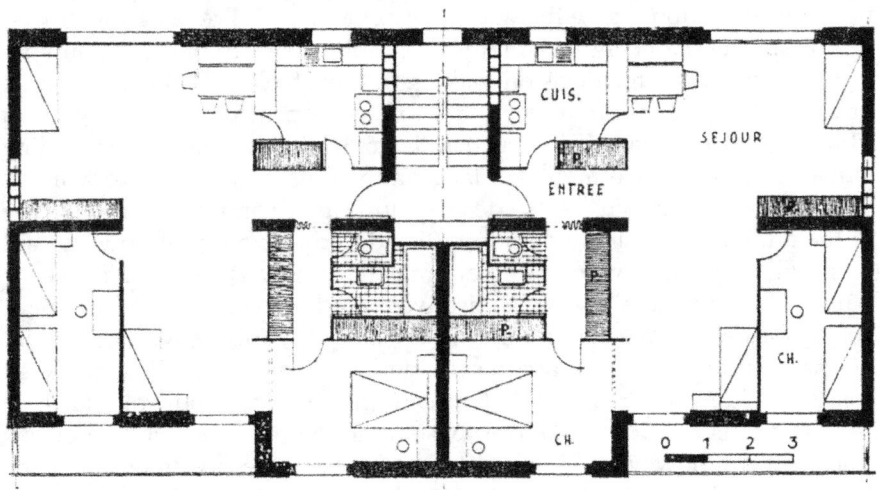

Type VI : 83 m², 30

Figure 1.2. Two apartments in Eugène Beaudouin's Cité Rotterdam. © 2014 Artists Rights Society (ARS), New York / ADAGP, Paris.

it also went against popular opinion by privileging tall collective buildings over individual homes and opting exclusively for kitchens too small to permit dining. Claudius-Petit believed that government officials had "to know how to resist public opinion," offering in its stead an enlightened strategy for construction that would be good for both France and the French.[57] What this description of the MRU competitions and winning designs demonstrates is the planners' attempts to create a modern interior, and what remained unchanged in these experiments was the provision of comfort. In all of its experimental projects from 1947 to 1951, the ministry called for the "indispensable minimum" which was, at the time, a real luxury for most of the population.

"Our Common and Ardent Desire to Make a New France"[58]

If the Ministry was interested in getting people to live rationally, and above all, comfortably, what was at stake in that decision? Its efforts to measure, test, and build comfortable and functional interiors attest to the ministry's belief that domestic space was important, but why did they think so? This section unearths the connections that the ministry made between building homes and rebuilding the nation; it argues that the MRU saw domestic space as having a role to play in France's renewal. Offering modern homes to its citizens would facilitate demographic growth, end social segregation, and in so doing give the world new evidence of French grandeur.

The specter of decline—economic, technological, demographic, and political—permeated the decision making of French elites.[59] Those in charge of urban reconstruction also pointed to the specific, poisonous legacy of Third Republic urban and suburban "anarchy." Land speculators selling *lotissements* (small allotments) of land on the outskirts of cities to workers with little money down created de facto dormitory communities with none of the amenities of planned sectors. The decentralization of housing and planning questions, which put planning and public works under municipalities' or communal purview, disadvantaged the small towns and poor communes where *lotissements* spring up, since the local governments did not have enough of a tax base to provide access to utilities, sewers, paved roads, or sidewalks.[60] As Annie Fourcaut points out, some workers, such as Italian masons, built wonderfully solid, ingeniously designed homes.[61] Many others, however, whose paltry savings had been exhausted by the purchase of the lot, built shacks from scavenged materials; consequently 2.8 million homes were classified as unsanitary in 1939, as compared to 150,000 in 1911. Moreover, by 1945, France had the highest incidence of overcrowding in Europe, and 640,000 of its people, including whole families, weren't living in homes at all, but in furnished single room occupancy dwellings known as *hôtels garnis*.[62]

The sentiment of French decline was reinforced by the housing statistics for Britain and Germany. The MRU's report of 1948 observed that 1.6 million new homes had been built in the years from 1919 to 1939. This put France behind Britain and Germany at 4.2 and 4.6 million new units respectively. In France only 20 percent of new units had been financed with public funds, compared to 38 percent in Britain and 42 percent in Germany.[63] Moreover, in the largest cities Britain and Germany had done more to mitigate housing costs for ordinary families. Between 1919 and 1939, Parisians had benefited from the erection of 70,000 homes for low- and middle-income inhabitants, whereas Berliners enjoyed new construction of 120,000 units, and London gained 250,000 council homes.[64]

In Germany and Britain, the pressure to use state or municipal funds to build low-income housing had been applied by political parties, but in France, political parties on the left pressed instead for preservation of a policy of rent controls that had been in effect since 1914, first due to World War I, then maintained in the face of inflation and economic depression. No government wanted to risk political suicide by legislating the rent increases that would bring rent to market levels comparable to other nations. These rent controls dissuaded private developers from building new housing, and landlords shunned renovations and repairs, since a higher tax burden meant that renting provided proportionally less return on investment. A second consequence of rent control was that renters devoted increasingly smaller proportions of their household budgets to rent. If, before World War I, renters had been accustomed to paying approximately 10 to 20 percent of their income on rent, the net effect of rent controls and freezes from 1914 to 1945 meant that families were now accustomed to paying somewhere between 2 and 6 percent. This phenomenon offered another French exception, for the figures in other nations remained higher: rent accounted for 19 to 20 percent of the household expenditures in Great Britain, the United States, and Germany. By 1948 the part of rent in total household expenditures in France was estimated to be 1 to 2 percent, a statistic that Eugène Claudius-Petit sensationalized in an article for *Le Monde*, whose headline read, "In 1948 the French spent 30 billion on their rent, 204 billion on their tobacco."[65]

French families had lived so long without comfort and with inflation that they would rather endure hardships or inconveniences than risk compromising the stability of the household budget. With the condescension typical of commentary on the working class, contemporary observers tended to ascribe the large amount of household funds dedicated to food to gourmandise. A good example of this is found in a 1948 report on

French housing. The article's author observed that "it seems to be more important that the family eats and drinks well than that it lives in really comfortable quarters. A higher rent must be paid each month, but the cost of a fine dinner has to be paid but once!"[66] If, indeed, the family was only dining finely periodically, then food would not have taken up so much of the budget, but the truth was that food scarcity led to inflationary pricing, which meant that food was taking up larger portions of the familial budget. As Tony Judt relates, "In French opinion polls taken in the course of 1946 'food', 'bread', 'meat' consistently outpaced everything else as the public's number one preoccupation."[67] Thus, as we saw earlier, the INED opinion poll on habitation reported popular consensus that an ideal rent was a mere 10 percent of the household budget, and this figure varied little from one social milieu to another. Moreover, remarked one contemporary scholar, INED's question focused on ideal rents: the sum that individuals were actually willing to or could pay was probably even lower.[68] INED interviewers in Rouen, Paris, and Dijon observed that people were interested in better homes, but not willing to pay for them. A canvasser in Dijon discerned that people made a distinction between what they would install if they were building their own home versus what they were willing to pay to a landlord. This investigator reported that the mothers "[a]ll wanted a little bathroom (they didn't dare say [wish for] a bathroom with a tub), but all told they prefer to endure the inconveniences they suffer from rather than have a more comfortable—but necessarily more expensive—abode."[69] Thus, in the immediate postwar period, there was no evidence that the French clamored for indoor plumbing, central heating, refrigerators, or more rationally organized layouts. The charge to modernize the home came from above and would entail a massive campaign to convince the French that a modern home would improve their daily lives and was worth the investment of a larger share of the household budget. But this message fell on deaf ears in the mid 1940s, in the face of postwar scarcity. Indeed, opting for low rent over comfort, some families remained in the MRU's provisional wooden barracks for nearly a decade.[70]

By 1948, MRU officials had reason for pessimism. The public was not going to be able or willing to shoulder the costs of modern housing any time soon, and the First Plan's failure to see housing as part of the nation's productive capacity meant that new construction continued to receive little priority in the ministry's budget. Nevertheless, ministry officials struggled to make both the government and the public understand the relationship between housing and productivity. Yves Salaün, of the DGUHC, pleaded the ministry's case:

> From even a simply economic point of view, without mentioning its social repercussions, the improvement of current living conditions imposes itself:

it concerns all households, and no demographic and health policy can be effectively pursued while it remains unresolved; production is affected by the deficiencies of the population which are essentially due, now that the supply of food has improved, to its poor housing conditions; the nation's general costs will rise, or at the very least will stay the same, if the diseases and vices (tuberculosis, alcoholism, juvenile delinquency) which have their origin, in large part, in a defective habitat, do not diminish their hold. ....[71]

The comfort delivered by heating and plumbing thus had a role to play in reproducing the labor necessary to modernizing France. A report on the health of Noisy-le-Sec inhabitants reinforced this line of thought. The report's author raved that when the man of the house "returns, tired from his work, whether it is in the evening or in the morning, like certain railway workers who work the night shift, he finds at home possibilities for bodily relaxation, thanks to the sanitary installations, and an atmosphere of calm and spaciousness."[72] It was hoped that these amenities would also encourage the man of the house to spend more time at home and less at the café, thereby contributing to family unity. Moreover, rational layouts would improve productivity within the home; the majority of Noisy-le-Sec's female residents surveyed confirmed this hypothesis, responding, when asked, that they spent less time in meal preparation than they did before they moved to the experimental city.

Inextricably linked to economic productivity, whether at home or at work, as Salaün suggested, was demographic renewal. De Gaulle's exhortation in a speech to the Consultative Assembly in March 1945 that France needed to produce 12 million "beautiful babies" forecast the Fourth Republic's decision to continue the natalist policies developed during the Third Republic and Vichy. There was broad consensus across the political spectrum in 1945 that French greatness was tied to population growth, as Andrew Shennan has shown.[73] Though less causally related to pronatalism than the extensions of family allocations instituted in 1945, rationally designed homes could nevertheless reinforce a family's decision to have more children by economizing household expenses as well as a stay-at-home mother's time and energy. As the Noisy-le-Sec health report stated, and as the resident survey confirmed, "A mother of a large family can have moments of leisure, which is unknown to her in a traditional layout."[74] Some, like Jean Magendie, believed that rational homes could possibly even convince women who worked for wages to become housewives, simultaneously facilitating economic and demographic recovery. Magendie received a visit one day from a certain Madame Fillon. Fillon had come to advise the ministry about the installation of day care centers for children (aged six months to seven years old) whose mothers worked outside of the home. Magendie noted in a memo that the best solution to the problem was not day care centers, but the return of working mothers to the home.

This, Magendie opined, would not only solve the problem of day care, but also the unemployment problem.⁷⁵

Though the link between social problems like unemployment and modern homes was rather implicit, and though Salaün had left the "social repercussions" of housing aside, Eugène Claudius-Petit articulated quite clearly the importance of housing to rebuilding French society in the postwar era. In addition to facilitating demographic growth, building hygienic and rational homes for all citizens would end social segregation and demonstrate a commitment to economic justice and human dignity. Observing that human constructions mirrored a civilization's society, he argued that the reflection worked both ways:

> [T]he home forms its inhabitants, the city or the town establishes the relations of a society ... No one can doubt the influence of the home, the neighborhood, the village or the city on the child, the family, the path of individual existence, the behavior of human groups brought together by life, the relationships between men and between groups, and, to say it all, on the character, [be it] of struggle, of indifference or of dignity, of human relations. ... Beyond our interests and habits, there is our civilization to save. Those who believe that it is only defended from time to time on the battlefields are insane. It is by daily action that we perpetuate it. We all say—it is easier to say than to do—that we want a classless society. Let us thus build the city without division.⁷⁶

Son of a railroad employee and a shopkeeper, Claudius-Petit had grown up in straitened circumstances in a neighborhood populated by artisans and workers and had developed a revolutionary's zeal for ending social segregation. Though his discourse sounded communistic, Claudius-Petit's political sympathies actually inclined more toward the center. Indeed, Claudius-Petit's two assertions—that homes influenced those who dwelled within and that housing could ease social conflict—reprised the paternalist principles underlying the foundation of the Société française des habitations à bon marché in 1889, a group created by prominent bourgeois professionals to sponsor and encourage the construction of low-income housing in the interest of public health, moral improvement, and social peace.⁷⁷

Claudius-Petit expressed frustration with what he saw as the unenlightened political agendas of the Communists and the Communist-led trade unions. In 1946, writing to Maurice Thorez, the head of the French Communist Party, Claudius-Petit urged him to reshape popular conceptions of the good life: "It would be too tragic to see workers defend 'petit-bourgeois' interests, 'petit-bourgeois' sensibilities, and to have the goal of getting everyone to become a home-owner."⁷⁸ Such a policy, Claudius-Petit believed, would lead only to a disorderly proliferation of suburban developments similar to the *lotissements*. By 1950, planners looked to technological installations of comfort, not to home ownership, to ensure social peace. Once accustomed to living well, MRU officials believed, families would want to work hard to maintain that standard of living. André Chastel, the art and architecture critic, reported as much for Le Monde after a visit to Noisy-le-Sec: "'Comfort costs a lot,' a railway worker told me, 'but we have a bathroom inside, and a refrigerator, and a hot water heater. And if we had to leave, we wouldn't find all that elsewhere, and we'd be mighty unhappy.'" Thus, Chastel concluded, "After several months of living in a modern home, this renter, in his wisdom, learned that, no matter who owns the property, the charm, the convenience and the healthiness of a residence justify a higher rent and fees." Chastel also noted that each interior he viewed was impeccably tidy and that residents accepted without complaint MRU rules about the upkeep of the yards and homes.[79] The Le Monde reporter's observation marked an ideological change with regard to reforming the working class. The civilizing influence that nineteenth-century reformers had prescribed for workers' housing appeared to be alive and well in these modern homes, but with an important difference. In the late nineteenth and early twentieth centuries, philanthropists and reformers promoted home ownership as a guarantor of social peace. The advances in technology that led to the introduction of comfort into modern homes meant—postwar reformers hoped—that such peace could be achieved without ownership.

Yet, as Claudius-Petit's words made clear, the ministry was not merely interested in the moralizing qualities of modern homes. It also believed the democratization of comfort to have political implications. The new social contract by which economic planning would guarantee to all what had been the privileges of a few, including not only social security but comfortable homes, spoke to the Fourth Republic's larger political project of reviving the grandeur of France after the inglorious precedent of Vichy and the perceived "Malthusian" stagnation of the Third Republic. Dautry had pledged to devote his efforts as minister to restoring France to the rank in the world that she had once enjoyed; developing low-cost, labor-saving, comfortable homes destined for the average French family would symbolize this French renewal by pointing to the new regime's commitment to equality.[80] Jean Fourastié, the economist, sociologist, and advisor to Jean Monnet's new General Planning Commission, also made the connection between housing and national renewal; he criticized the overcrowding and poor equipment of existing homes, saying that they corresponded to the "economic, social and technical stagnation that has characterized French history since 1914."[81] It would not be by rebuilding those homes as they had once been, but by offering modern homes whose comfort did not depend upon the status of their inhabitants that the new republic could distance itself from the old governments. Claudius-Petit agreed:

> After the night of oppression, the daylight casts an even harsher glare over the wounds of our used-up society, over the ugliness and rot of our suburbs and company towns, over the tomb-like darkness of our slums, over the filth of our factories and their anachronism. We understand very well now why France does not have enough children, and why the few that she has include far too many suffering from tuberculosis and rickets. ... What would the world think of a France that would preserve its slums in order to preserve its picturesque qualities, that would "recommence its past"? ... France owes it to herself, in order to regain her true grandeur, to give the world the style of our society.[82]

For Claudius-Petit, a hygienic and labor-saving modern home, built as part of a planned urban center, would rescue the French from the errors of the nation's past and would restore France to its rightful place among the world's great cultures.

It was not simply by providing central heat to working-class families that modern homes spoke to the project of rebuilding France. After a war in which the destruction and debasement of human life had reached horrifying nadirs, some saw modern homes as a tool that would aid individuals in their quest to reach their full potential. Jean Kérisel expressed this point of view on behalf of the ministry in an article about reconstruction and construction for the popular magazine *Science et vie*: "Man must shape his surroundings in harmony with his time and his activities in such a way that he can fully develop there [*qu'il s'y épanouisse pleinement*]."[83] *Épanouissement*, which means flowering, blossoming, or opening out, came to be the favorite term of those describing the ultimate purpose of the modern home. Jean Fourastié reprised Le Corbusier's famous assertion, explaining to his general readership that houses had evolved from passive shelters into "machines for living". Organized rationally and filled with equipment that would guarantee a family's health, protect inhabitants from the extremes of cold and heat, and liberate women from the hard physical work of housekeeping, the modern home would give, for the first time in history, the average person the opportunity for personal growth, whether it be intellectual, cultural, or moral.[84] Though comparatively few of these homes made it off of the drawing board from 1945 to 1952, the ministry had thrown down the gauntlet, establishing planned communities of comfortable homes for the masses as its priority, a utopian dream rejected by decision makers in other sectors of the government and shrugged at by ordinary French people, but one for which the MRU continued nevertheless to prepare.

Conclusion

The experimental projects undertaken by the MRU in the first years of its existence should be placed in the context of the manifold initiatives comprising the young Fourth Republic's attempt to build a new France. To this end, de Gaulle spearheaded the creation of several institutions designed to establish a renaissance based on the twin pillars of merit and scientific data. The new École nationale d'administration (ENA), for example, sought to evacuate class privilege from government service by establishing a meritocratic basis for this school for civil servants. As the ordinance establishing ENA observed, "Neither last century's industrial revolution and its economic and social consequences, nor the democratization of the State, which should have implied that of its components, have been sufficiently taken into account."[85] Two weeks after ENA's founding in October 1945, the Institut national d'études démographiques arose to provide the necessary demographic information upon which experts might base their plans for France's future. De Gaulle also established the Atomic Energy Commission in October 1945, which would marshal the resources necessary to bring nuclear capacity (for both electricity and national defense) to France. A few months later, in January 1946, the General Planning Commission emerged to coordinate the nation's production. By April 1946, the gas and electricity utilities had joined the automaker Renault and the largest banks as nationalized entities.

This renovation of physical infrastructure and political, economic, and scientific institutions signaled that nothing was to be left to chance. New approaches needed to be tried, measured, quantified, and evaluated, and this consciousness of preparing France's future can be seen in the experimental projects undertaken by the MRU. In these projects were the seeds of the housing that would dominate the French urban landscape over the next three decades. Nevertheless, we must not read this moment retroactively, as a period during which the groundwork was carefully laid for the course that new construction would take. The period from 1944 to 1952 offered few hints that the state would cast its lot wholly with the *grand ensemble* formula later in the 1950s. From the ISAIs to the architectural competitions, from Noisy-le-Sec to the Cité Rotterdam, the MRU experimented with collective housing and detached homes, avant-garde forms and more classical styles. Even the ministry's commitment to new construction itself fluctuated somewhat depending on the minister at its helm and on its budget. Nevertheless, when it came to prescribing interiors for new homes, the MRU evinced a preference for rational, comfortable spaces that were meant to fulfill all of an inhabitant's needs, and, ultimately, it was the ministry who had the last word on what those needs were and how they were best satisfied.

Functionalism in design mirrored the fever for planning. The separation of functions would promote personal and familial development and evolution in the same way that the planned economy would promote national growth. Rational, comfortable interiors would resolve the "social question" of class conflict in the context of a planned urbanism, since comfort and happiness need no longer, according to state planners like Claudius-Petit, be found only in bourgeois homes. Renewing the energy and protecting the health of working people, preserving the nuclear family, encouraging pronatalism, easing unemployment and class conflict, facilitating self-improvement, and symbolizing the Fourth Republic's commitment to equality: this was a weighty agenda for the modern home, even in its ideal form. The thousands of French desperate for housing were not expecting the state to deliver state-of-the-art modern homes and certainly didn't want to pay for them. When a 1948 law on rent control unregulated new construction, a system of housing allowances for qualifying families was simultaneously put into place to encourage families to move into new, more expensive, dwellings. Yet families' applications for these allowances could be—and were—rejected if the proposed move was to a home that still lacked running water, an indoor toilet, windows, or proper ventilation.[86] Officials at the MRU were firm: France would not be able to regain its grandeur if it left its inhabitants living in old-fashioned, outmoded, overcrowded dwellings. Using the opening provided by the need for reconstruction after the war, the planners and housing reformers employed at the Ministry of Reconstruction and Urbanism asserted that, one way or another, modern homes would become the only choice for French families.

Notes

1. Pierre Claudius (Eugène Petit), "Renaissance," *L'Architecture d'aujourd'hui* 1 (May–June 1945), 5; unless otherwise noted, all translations are my own. Pierre Claudius was the alias that the man born Eugène Petit had assumed during his time in the Resistance; after the war he became officially known as Eugène Claudius-Petit.
2. Tony Judt, *Postwar: A History of Europe Since 1945* (New York: Penguin Press, 2005), 72.
3. Danièle Voldman, *La reconstruction des villes françaises de 1940 à 1954: Histoire d'une politique* (Paris: L'Harmattan, 1997), 34–35.
4. Clanché and Fribourg, "Grandes évolutions du parc et des ménages depuis 1950," 85.
5. Ministère de la reconstruction et de l'urbanisme, Centre d'études de la Direction générale de l'urbanisme et de l'habitation [Yves Salaün], *Se loger* (Paris: MRU, 1949), 13.

6. The MRU, while a new ministry, was largely comprised of the staff of the Vichy offices charged with planning and preparing reconstruction during the war: the Commissariat à la reconstruction immobilière, the Délégation Générale à l'Équipement National, the Comité national de la reconstruction, and the Comité national d'urbanisme. Danièle Voldman's discussion of these organizations in *La reconstruction des villes françaises* is without peer.
7. The literature on reconstruction includes Danièle Voldman's canonical text, *La reconstruction des villes françaises*, as well as two strong collections: "Images, Discours et Enjeux de la Reconstruction des villes françaises après 1945," a special issue of the *Cahiers de l'IHTP* 5 (June 1987) edited by Danièle Voldman, and Bruno Vayssière, Manuel Candré, and Danièle Voldman, eds., *Ministère de la Reconstruction et de l'Urbanisme, 1944-1954: une politique du logement* (Paris: IFA-PCA, 1994). See also Hélène Sanyas, "La politique architecturale et urbaine de la reconstruction. France: 1945-1955" (Thèse de 3e cycle, Université de Paris VIII, 1982). For an overview of the architecture, consult Anatole Kopp, Frédérique Boucher, and Danièle Pauly, *L'Architecture de la reconstruction en France, 1945-1953* (Paris: Éditions du Moniteur, 1982) and Bruno Vayssière, *Reconstruction-deconstruction: le hard French ou l'architecture française des trente glorieuses* (Paris: Picard, 1988). Most of these works emphasize the ministry's incapacity to implement a real policy of new construction while coping with the imperatives, struggles, and constraints that accompanied reconstruction in the strict sense of the word.
8. Rémi Baudouï, "De Gaulle et la reconstruction," *Espoir* 103 (July 1995): 66–70.
9. For more biographical information on Raoul Dautry, consult Rémi Baudouï, *Raoul Dautry (1880-1951), le technocrate de la République* (Paris: Éditions Balland, 1992) and Michel Avril, *Raoul Dautry, 1880-1951: la passion de servir* (Paris: Éd. France-Empire, 1993).
10. Boucher, "Abriter vaille que vaille," 125, 158.
11. W. Brian Newsome, *French Urban Planning 1940-1968* (New York: Peter Lang, 2009), 65.
12. Kopp, Boucher, and Pauly, *L'Architecture de la reconstruction*, 84.
13. Cited in Kopp, Boucher, and Pauly, *L'Architecture de la reconstruction*, 85.
14. Institut National d'Études Démographiques [INED], *Désirs des Français en matière d'habitation urbaine* (Paris: PUF, 1947), 11, 13, 21, 33. It must be noted that the INED survey had a tendency to ask leading questions. For example, querying individuals about their preference for detached homes, the survey asked, "If you prefer living in an individual house, is this essentially in order to have a yard?" (23).
15. [INED], *Désirs des Français*, 13-14.
16. [INED], *Désirs des Français*, 40.
17. Christian Moley, in his article "La genèse du jour/nuit: scission de l'espace du logement en deux parties" (*In Extenso*, 9 [1986]: 259–81), argues that the day-night division becomes dominant in architectural circles in the mid 1950s; however, the many references to this division in both the architectural and popular presses well before this period suggest that it was advocated much earlier than that. Indeed, the INED survey proclaims that it is common "to distinguish between two distinct parts [of a home]: one constituted by the rooms where each person retires for sleeping, the other by the elements common to all and utilized during the daytime" (39).
18. [INED], *Désirs des Français*, 66.
19. The dilemma of the eat-in kitchen versus a dining room or living room–dining room area was a problem for nineteenth-century reformers and continues to stimulate debate among architects and design professionals today. See Nicole Rudolph, "La cuisine, cellule de base de la modernisation française. L'architecture, la modernisation et le genre dans la France des Trente Glorieuses" (Mémoire principal de Master 2, École Normale Supérieure / École des Hautes Études en Sciences Sociales, 1999).

20. [INED], *Désirs des Français*, 46–47.
21. [INED], *Désirs des Français*, 50–56.
22. For more on the MRU missions abroad, consult Danièle Voldman's article, "À la recherche de modèles, les missions du MRU à l'étranger," in *Images, Discours et Enjeux de la Reconstruction*, 103–18.
23. "Maisons préfabriquées prototypes pour l'exposition: Situation au 11 janvier 1946," 14 January 1946, located at the Archives Nationales' Centre des Archives Contemporaines at Fontainebleau (hereafter AN, CAC) 19771078/22.
24. The evaluation form filled out by social workers working for the Housing Commission can be found in AN, CAC 19771078/4.
25. Ibid.
26. See the Commission du logement's request files in AN, CAC 19771078/4.
27. Information on residents' socioprofessional backgrounds culled by author from attributions files in AN, CAC 19771078/4.
28. Anonymous handwritten report, "Cité d'expériences de Noisy-le-Sec: Études sur les Cuisines," AN, CAC 19771078/1.
29. The review of Prouvé's prototype, undated, was performed by the U.E.C. 2, Service des Études de la Construction, and can be found in AN, CAC 19771078/15. From other contemporary discussions of odors inherent in French cooking, it seems that the problem was chiefly related to the cooking of cabbage, a staple of the French diet at the time.
30. Letter from M. Demarre to Jean Prouvé, 4 July 1946, AN, CAC 19771078/15.
31. Bernège was involved with architects and home planners from the 1930s through the 1950s. Her books include *Si les femmes faisaient les maisons* (1928) and *De la méthode ménagère*, first published in 1928 and reissued until the late 1960s. For more on Bernège, see Jackie Clarke, "L'organisation ménagère comme pédagogie: Paulette Bernège et la formation d'une nouvelle classe moyenne dans les années 1930 et 1940," *Travail, genre et sociétés* 13 (April 2005): 139–57.
32. [Jean] Magendie, "Note pour Monsieur Demarre," 16 February 1946, AN, CAC 19771139/1.
33. The completed questionnaires, submitted 18 November 1949 by a Mademoiselle Lemonnier of the Enseignement Ménager du Service Social du CCAF, can be found in AN, CAC 19771078/1.
34. Letter from Jean Iliovici, Union Nationale des Caisses d'Allocations Familiales, to M. le Directeur de la Construction, 7 November 1950, AN, CAC 19771078/1.
35. Resident reactions are summarized in a report entitled "Familles de la Cité," sent to "M. Magendie," 24 November 1948, AN, CAC 19771078/1.
36. "Études sur les Cuisines."
37. Magendie, "Note pour Monsieur Demarre."
38. "Famille de la Cité"; "Études sur les Cuisines."
39. "Études sur les Cuisines."
40. Boucher, "Arbiter vaille que vaille," 91.
41. Susanna Magri, *Logement et reproduction de l'exploitation: Les politiques étatiques du logement en France (1947-1972)* (Paris: Centre de sociologie urbaine, 1977), 198.
42. Ministère de la reconstruction et de l'urbanisme [MRU], *Concours pour l'édification de maisons nouvelles*, March 1947, n.p., AN, CAC 19771078/1.
43. Ibid.
44. Figure derived from France's 1946 population of 40,503,000 and a statistical table describing the evolution of the appliance market in France. See "Evolution du marché français pour les principaux appareils ménagers," *L'Officiel hebdomadaire de l'équipement ménager* 500 (September 1977), special issue: *Livre d'or de l'électroménager européen*, 55.

Building Homes, Building a Nation   51

45. Olivier Le Goff notes that the Larousse definition of modern comfort dates to 1929. In a fascinating and detailed analysis of the Institut national de la statistique et des études économiques (INSEE) censuses during the Trente Glorieuses, Le Goff also advances the hypothesis that INSEE itself contributed to a normalization of comfort via the evolution of its categorizations. See Olivier Le Goff, *L'Invention du confort: naissance d'une forme sociale* (Lyon: Presses universitaires de Lyon, 1994), 52, 80–90. Jacques Dreyfus confirms comfort's technical denotation for contemporaries, noting that comfort was "principally defined by the available equipment and fluids" (*La Société du confort* [Paris: L'Harmattan, 1990]), 10.
46. W. Brian Newsome, "The Struggle for a Voice in the City: The Development of Participatory Architectural and Urban Planning in France, 1940-1968" (Ph.D. diss., University of South Carolina, 2002), 134.
47. [MRU], *Concours pour l'édification de maisons nouvelles.*
48. "Études sur les Cuisines"; [INED], *Désirs des Français*, 57.
49. Newsome, "Struggle for a Voice in the City," 138.
50. Benoît Pouvreau, *Un politique en architecture: Eugène Claudius-Petit (1907-1989)* (Paris: Le Moniteur, 2004), 110. Pouvreau's well-researched biography, using numerous sources including private archives and personal letters, is a wonderful source for the minister's motivations and aims, as well as his accomplishments and failures.
51. Voldman, *La reconstruction des villes françaises*, 401.
52. Boucher, "Abriter vaille que vaille," 155.
53. Rosemary Wakeman, "Reconstruction and the Self-Help Housing Movement: The French Experience," *Housing Studies* 14, 3 (1999): 355–66.
54. Ministère de la Reconstruction et de l'Urbanisme, *Programme du Concours pour l'exécution de 800 Logements à Strasbourg*, AN, CAC 19771081/1.
55. Minutes of jury meeting, 30 June 1951, AN, CAC, 19771081/02.
56. "Premier prix et exécution," *L'Architecture française* 117–18 (1951), 8.
57. Newsome, "Struggle for a Voice," 84–85.
58. Raoul Dautry, cited by Voldman, *La reconstruction des villes françaises*, 124.
59. On the proposals for renewal debated by political groups, see Andrew Shennan, *Rethinking France: Plans for Renewal, 1940-1946* (Oxford: Oxford University Press, 1989). On economic renewal, see Kuisel, *Capitalism and the State in Modern France*. On technological renewal, see Gabrielle Hecht, *The Radiance of France: Nuclear Power and National Identity After World War II* (Cambridge, MA: MIT Press, 1998).
60. Newsome, *French Urban Planning*, 29.
61. Annie Fourcaut, "Banlieue rouge, au-delà du mythe politique," in *Banlieue rouge 1920-1960. Années Thorez, années Gabin: archétype du populaire, banc d'essai des modernités*, ed. Annie Fourcaut (Paris: Éditions Autrement, 1992), 21.
62. Voldman, *La reconstruction des villes françaises*, 324.
63. *Se loger*, 57. Brian Newsome, citing figures from an article on reconstruction in the 1947 journal of the Centre national d'informations économiques, *Documents économiques*, gives these figures at 1.5 million for France, 3.66 million for Britain, and 4 million for Germany (*French Urban Planning*, 27). The MRU's higher figures may indicate different sources but also a desire to dramatize French deficiencies in order to increase budget allocations.
64. Marie-Jeanne Dumont, *Le logement social à Paris, 1850-1930: les habitations à bon marché* (Liège: Mardaga, 1991), 143.
65. On rent as percent of household budget, see Eugène Claudius-Petit, "En 1948 les Français ont dépensé 30 milliards pour leurs loyers, 204 milliards pour leur tabac," *Le Monde*, 8 March 1949, 4; Cicely Watson, "Housing Policy and Population Problems in

France," *Population Studies* 7, 1 (July 1953): 27–28; Anne Power, *Hovels to High Rise: State Housing in Europe Since 1850* (New York: Routledge, 1993), 40; and Newsome, *French Urban Planning*, 86 and 202 n.6.
66. C. Sidney Bertheim, "Housing in France," *Land Economics* 24, 1 (Feb. 1948): 52.
67. Judt, *Postwar*, 86.
68. Watson, "Housing Policy," 44 n.3.
69. [INED], *Désirs des Français*, 15–16.
70. Boucher, "Abriter vaille que vaille," 125; Jean-Pierre Rioux, *The Fourth Republic 1944-1958* (Cambridge: Cambridge University Press, 1989), 471 n.7.
71. [Salaün], *Se loger*, 209.
72. "Rapport de la santé," [sent to M. Magendie], 24 November 1948, AN, CAC 19771078/1.
73. Shennan, *Rethinking France*, 208–9.
74. "Rapport de la santé," and "Études sur les Cuisines."
75. J. Magendie, "Rapport sur la Visite au bureau de l'habitation le 27 juin 1945 de Mme FILLON, de 'Tourisme et Travail'," AN, CAC 19771078/1.
76. Eugène Claudius-Petit, introduction to *L'Architecture d'aujourd'hui* 32 (Oct.–Nov. 1950), special issue on "Reconstruction France 1950," 7.
77. For more on the Société Française des habitations à bon marché (SFHBM) and Belle Époque workers' housing, see Dumont, *Le logement social à Paris* and the many works of Roger-Henri Guerrand.
78. Cited in Pouvreau, *Un politique en architecture*, 101.
79. "La Maison du XXe siècle s'élabore à Noisy-le-Sec," *Le Monde*, 27 July 1949.
80. Avril, *Raoul Dautry*, 239.
81. Jean and Françoise Fourastié, *Les Arts ménagers* (Paris: PUF, 1950), 104, 114. Their emphasis.
82. Claudius, "Renaissance," 5.
83. Jean Kérisel, "Reconstruction et construction en France," *Science et vie* (1951), special issue on "L'Habitation," 13.
84. Fourastié and Fourastié, *Les Arts ménagers*, esp. 6–7, 48, 127.
85. Ordonnance no. 45-2283 du 9 octobre 1945 relative à la formation, au recrutement et au statut de certaines catégories de fonctionnaires et constituant une direction de la fonction publique et un conseil permanent de l'administration civile, *Journal officiel*, 10 October 1945.
86. Watson, "Housing Policy," 39 n.2.

Chapter 2

DESIGNING FOR THE CLASSLESS SOCIETY
Modernist Architects and the "Art of Living"

> *In fact, we must create a dwelling that responds to the requirements of family life, the activities and rhythm of which no longer differ so much from one social class to another.*
> —Alexandre Persitz, Editor-in-chief of *L'Architecture d'aujourd'hui*, 1948[1]

In its experiments with housing, the Ministry of Reconstruction and Urbanism turned to architects for help in determining the form that modern homes would take. In fact, the MRU explicitly incorporated architects in its efforts to rebuild France, for each reconstruction project had to include a number of architects. In his architectural history of the reconstruction, Anatole Kopp notes that this obligatory recourse to architects was something new.[2] Architects thus found themselves in a novel situation—and confronted with a new problem. Traditionally, the starting point of domestic architecture had been the client. Now the client was, in the words of Roger Gilbert, head of the Front National des Architectes (FNA), "France itself."[3] By this he meant not only that the state would pay the architects' fees, but also that architects were designing for the future of the nation, a prospect complicated by the fact that the nation comprised an infinitely varied number of inhabitants. Because the MRU had made it clear that the ministry would be pursuing a policy favoring prefabrication and mass production, architects knew that they would have to create something original: standardized, one-size-fits-all, housing.

What did architects propose? How did they define France's dwelling needs? What effects did changes in the profession and in the conditions of production have on the architects charged with building the nation's future? This chapter situates postwar Modernists' designs for the modern home in transformations in the architectural profession and identifies two sources of inspiration for inexpensive, egalitarian housing: state-sponsored HBM architecture of the 1930s and the more radical interwar projects of the Modern Movement. A close examination of some of the earliest materializations of postwar proposals, the ISAI apartments, reveals that architects essentially combined prewar HBM architecture with the formal and literal language of 1920s and 30s Modernism to produce an apartment designed for a middle-class occupant but imagined to be universally habitable. This apartment came to be known by its MRU designation: 4P, for four *pièces* (rooms). The 4P contained three bedrooms, a living room–dining room area, a small kitchen, and a bathroom. Analysis of the reception and discussion of the 4P in the Modernist architectural press then uncovers a tension between anxiety about this condensed, composite home and a desire to celebrate it as the perfect expression of a new art of living. This tension was a microcosm of a larger uncertainty, particularly prevalent among French elites, about how to respond to the advent of mass production, to changes in gender roles, and, especially, to the phenomenon of *moyennisation,* or, the expansion of the middle class to encompass larger segments of the population.

The Architectural Profession in the Immediate Postwar Period

In their professional publications, architects wrote enthusiastically and optimistically about the brave new world that they would help to create. Many of their articles concentrated on questions of urbanism and construction techniques, but home interiors also received ample attention and discussion in the late 1940s and early 1950s. *L'Architecture d'aujourd'hui* and *L'Architecture française* dedicated entire issues to the design and decoration of residences: enumerating the principles of the functional apartment, publishing minutely detailed measurements of furnishings and equipment, reporting on the new materials available for wall coverings, floors, and fixtures, and explaining how the latest models of refrigerators, ranges, and rubbish chutes worked. Modernists were excited about the prospect of bringing technological innovation into the home.

Yet architects, particularly in the first five years after Liberation, were also preoccupied with their professional future; they worried about the status of the profession and tried to determine the precise role that architects would play in French reconstruction. The old guard of architecture, represented by the powerful members of the Société française des architectes diplômés par le gouvernement (SADG),[4] continued to focus on and to teach the glories of monumental architecture, the magnificence of a beautiful façade, respect for artisanal construction methods, and the importance of regionalism to French grandeur.[5] But the Vichy Regime's celebration of regional styles and its privileging of rural arts and crafts had tainted regionalism as a design principle. Moreover, the need to ease the housing shortage as rapidly and as cheaply as possible imposed standardization at the expense of traditional building methods. Before the war Modernists had been fighting for legitimacy in architectural circles. But it was their very research into and experiments with prefabrication and mass production during the 1930s that gave proponents of the Modern Movement a certain amount of authority in the postwar context, because the MRU wanted desperately to cultivate such expertise.

The question of standardization interpellated each and every architect, calling into question the parameters and the goal of his work. Mass production not only seemed to impinge upon the free exercise of the architect's "liberal" profession, but also had the potential to dehumanize those who dwelled within by minimizing their individuality. Modernists tried to allay these fears. Future MRU minister and champion of Modernism Eugène Claudius-Petit argued the case for standardization on aesthetic grounds, claiming that Paris's Place Vendôme, in its uniformity, was far more beautiful than the "chaos" of neighborhoods where all of the houses looked different.[6] Paul Nelson, a prominent American Modernist architect working in France, introduced an issue of *L'Architecture d'aujourd'hui* featuring the Exposition des techniques américaines de l'habitation et de l'urbanisme by explaining the relationship of mass production to the architect's social mission. He proposed that the exhibition demonstrated how the "so-called peril" that standardization posed for the architect was actually "in his hands a factor of diversity and constant improvement in the standard of living."[7] Alexandre Persitz took a more matter-of-fact tack, dismissing the objections of those opposed to mass production as inappropriate, indeed unethical, given the enormity of reconstruction tasks:

> Whatever the reasons they invoke, these can be summed up, in fact, by the fear of seeing the "métier" limited. ... We believe that the role of the architect is undergoing a profound transformation. The field of his activity should be enlarged and combine more and more those of the urban planner and the sociologist. ... The architect who sees himself as doing battle with the problem of re-housing thousands of families, can he, humanely, materially, create for one neighborhood or district dozens of individual models, and is this even necessary? For such work on this scale, a certain standardization imposes itself whether one likes it or not.[8]

Persitz's pragmatism was prescient. The standardization of domestic architecture would indeed become the order of the day, and from Modernists' point of view, uniform, normalized housing units, imposed by economy, nevertheless had aesthetic, social, and even moral qualities to recommend them.

Persitz's observation that the architectural profession was changing was also astute. In December 1940, after a series of bills aiming to protect and restrict access to the profession had failed to become law throughout the 1930s, the Hautecœur law created the Ordre des architectes. Although membership in the Ordre did not guarantee that architects alone would receive contracts to design monuments, buildings, or other edifices, only those in the Ordre could claim the title of architect. To be eligible, one had to have received a diploma from a select number of (mostly Parisian) architecture schools. By 1944 the number of official architects had dropped from approximately 12,000 to 6,400.[9] At the end of the war, architects argued over the fate of the Ordre. As a product of the Vichy regime, should it continue to exist? In the end, the professional protection that the Ordre seemed to offer outweighed its Pétainist origins, and purging collaborationist members was deemed preferable to eliminating the Ordre entirely.

At the same time, Liberation brought a large number of new adherents to the FNA, founded at the request of the Parti Communiste Français by André Lurçat, a Modernist, resistance fighter, and Communist.[10] Anatole Kopp claims that this surge in membership stemmed from the belief that, as affiliates of the political party in power, FNA members would receive the lion's share of reconstruction contracts. For Kopp, the influx of opportunistic architects explains the stylistic "neutrality" of the FNA, by which he means the attenuation of the original Modernists' design tenets and social agenda (about which more will be said in the next section).[11] At the very least, a surge in the number of self-identified Modernists produced a wider variety of interpretations of Modernism. The term Modernist now encompassed a range of visions, from Le Corbusier's celebration of free plans to the more classical compositions of Michel Roux-Spitz, who, in 1942, had founded *L'Architecture française*, a competitor of the more avant-garde Modernist publication, *L'Architecture d'aujourd'hui*. Roux-Spitz's Paris School of Modernism was enthusiastic about non-traditional building materials like reinforced concrete but aimed to put these at the service of Beaux-Arts laws of elegance and proportion.[12]

In any case, the FNA did not prove to be a privileged source of contracts; instead, the MRU decided to regulate competition for contracts by establishing a ranking system for architects. In order to be considered for a government contract, a candidate first had to be a member of the Ordre, which reinforced the professional protection for which architects had long been clamoring. An eight-member MRU committee then assigned a ranking to each architect, which, for all intents and purposes, depended on his own reputation as well as the size and prestige of the firm for which he worked. The highest classification gave an architect eligibility to compete for contracts throughout France, but the majority of the rankings limited him to projects within his own *département*. Since most large firms were located in Paris, and because most of the architectural schools whose graduates were eligible for the Ordre were also Parisian, the ranking system reinforced the influence of Parisian architects.[13]

Not only did the state limit the field of operation for architects, but competition from urbanists and engineers seemed to further constrict the boundaries of the architect's expertise. Urban planners' stock had been rising steadily since the 1919 Cornudet law demanded that all cities of at least ten thousand inhabitants establish a detailed town plan, known as the *plan d'aménagement, d'extension et d'embellissement* (land use, extension, and beautification plan). Yet, as Danièle Voldman points out, despite the establishment of a professional course of study for urban planning at the Institut d'urbanisme, no one was "just" a planner. Most urban planners were already architects, or even architects and engineers, like the renowned Urbain Cassan. But the state established a professional hierarchy with its 1945 Architect's Charter, which placed urban planners above architects. In charge of each urban reconstruction project was a head urbanist. Working for him was the head architect, who supervised the "sector architects," who were responsible for particular neighborhoods, areas, or groups of buildings. They in turn guided the architects in charge of designing individual buildings, including apartment complexes, schools, municipal buildings, etc. By subsuming the head architect to the head urbanist, the MRU affirmed the primacy of urban planners in reconstruction efforts and more generally illustrated the contemporary preference for master planning. The ministry was aware of the possible offense that architects might take and employed a potent military analogy in the charter: "Although war demands hierarchies and disciplines harsher than those found elsewhere, the soldier does not feel diminished; he knows these are necessary and beneficial for his own protection, as well as for victory."[14]

Engineers were gaining in influence and prestige during this time, too; a 1934 law regulated the title of engineer, and engineers assumed a significant role in urban planning. In 1935, elective courses in urbanism appeared in the curriculum at the École nationale des Ponts et Chaussées, and in 1941, the school created a chair in planning. Outside of the classroom, engineers became increasingly involved with the elaboration and implementation of plans, and many found their way into the central and departmental administrations of the Vichy-era CRI (see chapter 1) and the

MRU. Unlike architects, engineers could work autonomously, outside of the purview of the head urbanist designated for any single reconstruction plan. Furthermore, as Danièle Voldman indicates, the industrialization of construction pointed more clearly than ever to the need for technical advisors, thus assuring a position for engineers in reconstruction.[15] Hence, Alexandre Persitz's recommendation to expand the architect's area of expertise ran counter to the professional specialization that was taking place.

Despite potential threats to the profession posed by standardization, government regulations, and the "jurisdictional claims"[16] of engineers and town planners, Modernist architects remained optimistic about their capacity to provide a substantive contribution to French reconstruction. The housing shortage, in particular, offered domestic space as a privileged sphere of activity and an opportunity to fulfill the architect's social mission by improving, as Paul Nelson had suggested, the average French family's standard of living. The head of the FNA, Roger Gilbert, wrote, "We can be the principal artisans of France's recovery. Our role is not limited, in fact, to translating current needs and tailoring our projects to the manner in which the French used to live and live today. We could and we should anticipate and orient social evolution."[17] What Gilbert was referring to here was the prewar Modernists' belief (about which more will be said later) that architects could hasten the democratization of French society by designing egalitarian housing.

In addition to imposing technical changes and occupational competition, reconstruction brought two other modifications to an architect's traditional ways of doing business. First was the fact that architects were no longer going to work exclusively for an individual patron. In the past, the starting point of any design was the needs and wishes as expressed by the customer. Now the state was asking architects to create standardized housing for an extremely diverse group, which diverged by class, by family size, by geographic location, and by age and other differences. How could architects design for this eclectic group?

The second immediate change in working conditions, related to the first, was the constant presence of financial and material constraints. In the past, the client had provided the necessary resources for financing a project. Now architects faced a situation in which, at least for the foreseeable future, the state would be asking them to trim budgets to a bare minimum and would be limiting the amount of space with which they had to work. The Modernist decorator Francis Jourdain summed up the situation in the March 1947 issue of *L'Architecture d'aujourd'hui*, a themed issue dedicated to interiors: "If we admit that the housing question is first and foremost a practical question governed by economics, we are better prepared to study the problem that nowadays can be posed, basically, like this: how to satisfy an ever-growing number of needs in an ever-shrinking space."[18] In their search for a solution to this problem, architects had two pertinent traditions of domestic architecture upon which they could draw: the *habitations à bon marché* (HBM) apartments, which were meant to house families hygienically and comfortably in small and inexpensive spaces, and the rationalist machines for living created by Modernists, who attempted to derive home design from physiological needs instead of from inhabitants' social status.

Prewar Precursors: HBM Architecture and Modern Architecture

From the founding of the Société française des habitations à bon marché in 1889 to the 1912 Bonnevay law, which allowed for the establishment of municipal and departmental public housing offices, the target tenants of social housing had been large working-class families. The 1913 competition sponsored by the Office public d'habitations de la Ville de Paris (OPHVP) began to elaborate distinctions within social housing when it articulated two categories of HBM: a "normal" one reserved for working-class families and another for destitute families being rehoused from slum areas.[19] By 1937, the year in which the OPHVP published its 235-page report on social housing in Paris, two more categories had been added, establishing a hierarchy of housing meant to correspond to various income levels and to the different lifestyles assumed to accompany these. The 1928 Loucheur law created the *immeubles à loyer moyen* (ILM), and in 1930 the HBMA—the "A" stood for "ameliorated"—emerged to occupy an intermediate level between the HBM and the ILM. These models were also entitled to state financing but were directed at a new population: the middle class. While the ILM sought upper-middle-class residents, the HBMA category was destined for lower-middle-class tenants like store clerks, office workers, and teachers. Thus, by 1939, housing planners' fundamental understanding of the constituency for "social" housing had evolved to incorporate not just the poor, but a much broader segment of the population. Social scientist Michael Harloe has identified "two predominant models of social housing" in Europe: mass and residual. The latter takes a "safety net" approach, providing shelter to the least fortunate in the name of social cohesion; the former fits in with welfare-state concepts of maximizing quality of life for the general population.[20] Targeting multiple income levels, mass housing thus appears to have gotten its start in France with the Loucheur law, rather than having its origins in the post–World War II housing crisis.

The Loucheur plan's target numbers are, in this sense, revelatory. Calling for two hundred thousand HBMs and sixty thousand ILMs to be constructed over a five-year period, the plan projected thirty-six thousand HBM and twenty-five thousand ILMs for the Parisian metropolitan region alone. The ratio of ILMs to HBMs rose for Paris, where it was assumed that more cosmopolitan, educated, and hygienic families could take advantage of—and could pay for—ILMs. It should be noted, however, that the lack of available funds for social housing during the 1930s meant that comparatively few new units were built. Most of the projects built were in and around Paris, and, when all was said and done, Paris ended up with fifty thousand new HBMs and twenty thousand ILMs.[21] (As Marie-Jeanne Dumont points out, this compared rather poorly with Berlin and London, which, over the same period, built 120,000 and 250,000 units of public housing, respectively.[22]) A 1936 study by the OPHVP revealed that the majority of those living in municipally funded apartments were working-class families who had three or four children, and who had previously lived in a one-room dwelling, so despite the fact that public housing planners wished to turn to a mass housing model, the core constituency of social housing—poor working families—remained at the heart of their mission.[23]

The four model plans published in the 1937 OPHVP report make it clear that public housing planners associated different dwelling practices with each class of tenants to be housed. The first type, the "Henri Becque" model (Figure 2.1), was the most elementary and was built for families

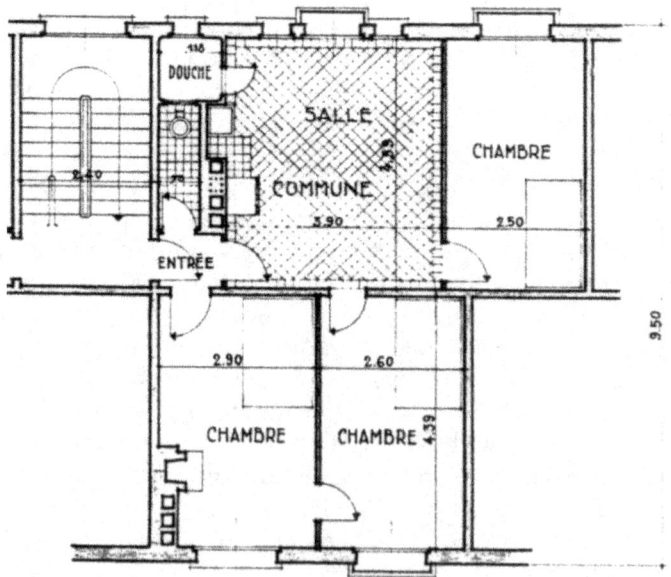

Figure 2.1. The Henri Becque model apartment. © 2014 Paris Habitat.

previously living in slums.[24] The OPHVP considered the Henri Becque model to be "trainer housing," a pedagogical interior that would teach occupants how to live hygienically. The Henri Becque was thus thought of as a transitional stage between tenements or shacks and the "normal" HBM.[25] The plan called for a *salle commune,* or common room, with kitchen facilities off to one side of that room and an adjacent shower. All three of the other main rooms were bedrooms; each one lay off of and communicated directly with the common room. The salle commune was thus literally the center of communal family life; it was kitchen, dining area, and living area. The report noted that hallways and shelving areas had been reduced to a bare minimum because they provided storage areas that might pose hazards to good hygiene if uneducated tenants filled them with dirty or dusty items. Only a small entryway remained.

Though still modest, the second category of housing, the "normal" HBM (Figure 2.2), represented a quantum leap from the Henri Becque. Besides a larger entryway and the restoration of the hall closet, this plan called for not only a separate kitchen but also a space explicitly designated as a dining room. Although denoted as *"salle à manger"* on the plan, the dining room was also clearly meant to operate as the primary locus of family activities, for the kitchen was too small for this purpose, and the other rooms were bedrooms. Moreover, the sole bay window was in

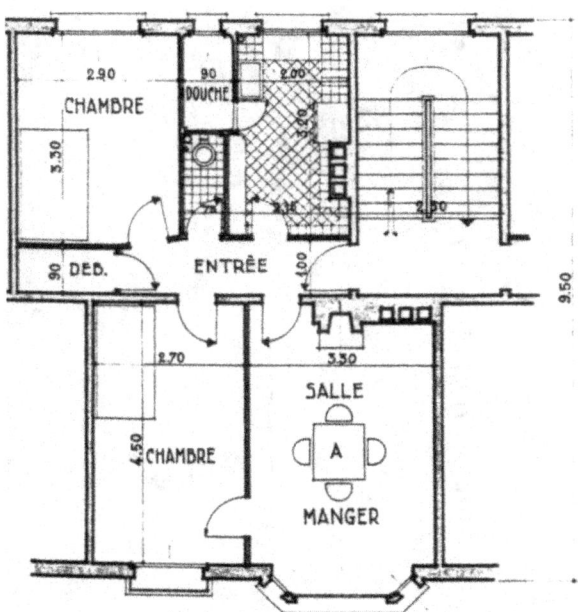

Figure 2.2. The "normal" HBM model apartment. © 2014 Paris Habitat.

the dining room, highlighting this area's role as the privileged locale for family interaction and social gatherings. The disposition of the plan established a public-private division. Though a door connected one of the bedrooms to the dining room, one could also enter the bedroom through the hallway, allowing for more privacy and setting up a public part of the home on the right and a private section on the left.

This floor plan remained nearly unchanged in the case of the "ameliorated" HBM, the HBMA (Figure 2.3). The most significant difference was the establishment of a completely separate room for bathing, which came equipped with a sink and allocated space for a bathtub and a hot water heater. All of the other rooms were larger than their HBM equivalents, and the report noted the apartment's "basic comfort," represented by the radiators in each room and a garbage chute in the kitchen. The public-private division remained the same as in the HBM plan.

The ILM plan (Figure 2.4) reflected another jump, this time from the lower middle class to the upper middle class. Two fundamental changes make this apparent: the addition of a parlor pointed to the occupants' preference for a more specialized site for receiving visitors, and the separate entrance to the kitchen from the stairwell signaled the expectation that ILM residents would have domestic help. As Monique Éleb and Anne Debarre have observed, it was the presence of a parlor that signified that

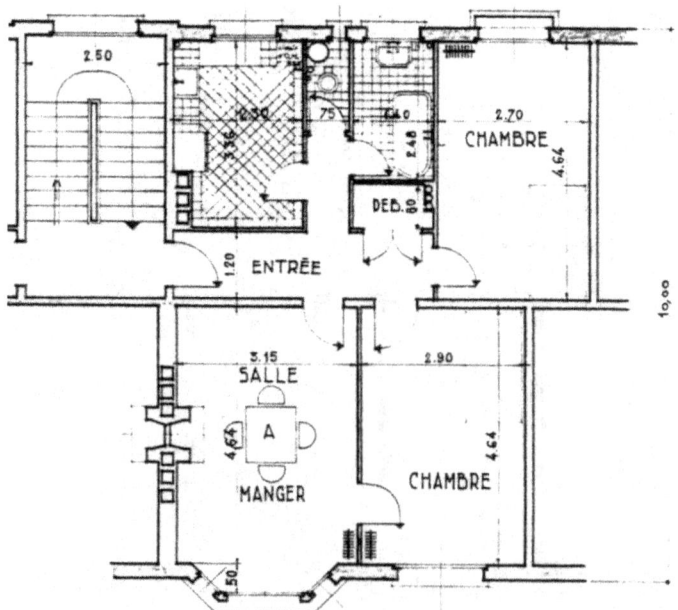

Figure 2.3. The "ameliorated" HBM model apartment. © 2014 Paris Habitat.

Designing for the Classless Society 63

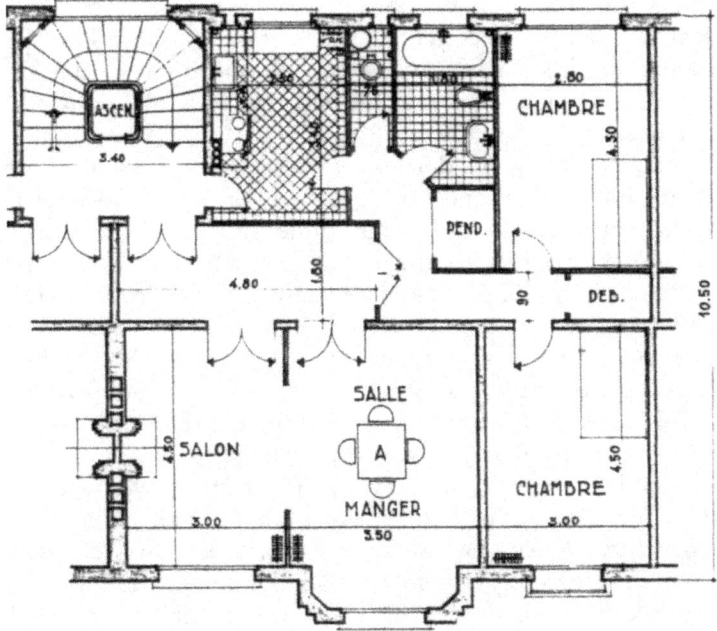

Figure 2.4. The ILM model apartment. © 2014 Paris Habitat.

one belonged to the middle class.²⁶ The bedrooms did not communicate with any other rooms, reinforcing intimacy and privacy, values that bourgeois families had associated with that space since the second half of the nineteenth century.²⁷ In accordance with the presumed higher standard of living, these apartments also had more closet space, hot running water, a full-size bathtub, and a bidet. (The photographs of the model apartment that accompanied the plan showed a piano in a corner of the parlor, as well as a sumptuously decorated vestibule.) An elevator served each floor. The ILM's name referred to the tenants' abilities to pay "average rents," and by extension, this apartment was destined for the "average" middle-class family. Yet, incorporating the latest in "modern comfort," the ILM was, really, the 1930s version of the middle-class dream home.

Social housing planners based their hierarchy of model plans upon the belief that there were classed variations in dwelling practices. Housing for the least fortunate followed a simple, self-consciously hygienic design. As one climbed the social ladder, however, the projected needs of the imagined tenants grew more sophisticated, and HBM architects attempted to address these with an increased specialization of rooms, an explicit distribution of public and private areas, and graduated levels of technical installations that reflected purported class differences in standards of bodily care. Though the provision of alternative plans seemed almost self-evident in a classed society, this was the very premise that Modernist architects sought to undermine as they attempted to elaborate a *logis nouveau*—a new dwelling—in the late 1920s and 1930s.

The development of Modernism encompassed several tendencies.[28] Most germane to understanding the genesis of French postwar architecture are the adherents to the Congrès international d'architecture moderne (CIAM) and particularly the CIAM's French branch. The first CIAM meeting was held in 1928 at patron Hélène de Mandrot's chateau in La Sarraz, Switzerland. Among the twenty-eight architects present were Le Corbusier and André Lurçat; they were joined by De Stijl architect Gerrit Rietveld and Bauhaus members Ernst May and Hannes Meyer. The De Stijl and Bauhaus movements, born at the end of World War I, shared with Le Corbusier a belief that in the wake of that war's horrors had been born an *"esprit nouveau."* The "new spirit" would advance the cause of humanism by helping to replace a civilization built on status, wealth, and appearance with a more egalitarian society. Modernists believed that a new social order, a moral imperative after the demonstration of man's inhumanity to man during the war, was now materially possible, because the Western world was entering the Machine Age. The Machine Age, as they understood it, meant that new technologies and materials, assisted by production innovations like Fordism and Taylorism, could put high-quality quotidian items within the reach of the average individual. To maximize productivity, the Modernists of the 1920s and early 30s embraced a purist aesthetic, emphasizing spare, geometric forms and the employment of building materials like glass, concrete, and steel.

Throughout the 1930s, the CIAM, which also included members from Spain, Finland, and Italy, encouraged the diffusion of ideas about contemporary architecture throughout Europe. Challenges to Beaux-Arts aesthetic principles, interrogations of the relationship of function to form, and discussions of ideal building materials began to spread even farther when the Nazis closed the Bauhaus in 1933. Ludwig Mies Van der Rohe, the Bauhaus school's last leader, emigrated to the United States, as did Walter Gropius, its founder. Hannes Meyer went to the Soviet Union for five years, then settled in Mexico. The emigration of Bauhaus architects facilitated the dissemination of Modernist design principles, which were celebrated in the United States at a 1933 exhibition at the Museum of Modern Art in New York. The exhibition provided an overview of the features of contemporary European architecture (especially as practiced by Le Corbusier and the Bauhaus) and grouped these under the rubric of "International Style."

From the outset, the Modernists stated their commitment to creating an architecture that engaged with socioeconomic factors for the general good. In the CIAM manifesto penned at La Sarraz, they affirmed, "The idea of modern architecture includes the link between the phenomenon of architecture and that of the general economic system. The idea of 'economic efficiency' does not imply production furnishing maximum commercial profit, but production demanding a minimum working effort. ... The most efficient method of production is that which arises from rationalization and standardization."[29] Yet, not only did rationalization and standardization have implications for home builders and architects, but they placed demands on inhabitants, too: "They expect from the consumer ... a revision of his demands in the direction of a readjustment to the new conditions of social life. Such a revision will be manifested in the reduction of certain individual needs henceforth devoid of real justification; the benefits of this reduction will foster the maximum satisfaction of the needs of the greatest number, which are at present restricted."[30] For the Modernists, housing was the key to the organization of a new society, in which the waste and decadence of the bourgeoisie (whose "certain individual needs" were the ones being targeted for reduction) would be eliminated and the needs and aspirations of the masses would be reckoned with.[31] A society prioritizing quality homes for the greatest number would replace a civilization that devoted more resources to monuments than to social housing. The rationalized home would break through the traditional values of domestic architecture, in which the façade was more architecturally important than the interior and a room's size corresponded to the status of the people who used it.

Creating egalitarian housing did not mean simply spatially transcribing poll results, however. Since the latter reflected merely opinions of dominant models, inventing a truly new mode of living meant that architects had to come up with an affordable solution that avoided both the barracks-like workers' housing of the nineteenth century as well as poor man's imitations of bourgeois apartments or villas. The latter would have included both HBM apartments as well as the suburbs of bungalows whose proliferation seemed to threaten the possibility for a rational urbanism. Le Corbusier insisted that the question was not simply one of making affordable housing for the poor but of getting people from *all* classes to live differently, to live *rationally*. Because its design would be based on dwelling practices and would not be in accordance with neoclassical principles of proportion or signifiers of social status, the rational dwelling would engender Rational Man (and Rational Woman). These new beings would live in harmony with nature, even in the heart of the city, and expend the least amount of labor possible in their everyday lives;

they would live simply, expressing their individuality by cultivating their minds and passions instead of by accumulating objects. It was only radical design, Modernists believed, that could provoke such a transformation.

Modernists turned to forms of transportation as inspiration for both the layout and décor of the *logis nouveau*. Automobiles signified the assembly line's potential for the democratization of luxury, while ocean liners and railroad dining and sleeping cars inspired architects by the ways in which superior organization made a small space livable. Le Corbusier exalted his own experience of a ship's cabin: "A man is happy [there], fulfilling all the functions of domestic life—sleeps, bathes, writes, reads, entertains friends, in fifteen square meters."[32] Marcel Gascoin, the man who would become the leading Modernist interior designer of the postwar era, grew up in the French port city of Le Havre as the son and grandson of sailors.[33] The organization of ocean liners made a tremendous impression on Gascoin: despite the shortage of space, every item had its place, and the overall effect was pleasing to the eye.[34] This successful manipulation of reduced quarters held great promise for the homes of the future, which would necessarily—in keeping with limited resources and the goal of satisfying the needs of the greatest number—be small.

The most fully realized vision of modern design during the interwar period could not be found in France, but in Germany, at Ernst May's *existenzminimum* apartments in the housing estates built for the city of Frankfurt. In 1929 the CIAM gathered in Frankfurt to study the housing question in more depth. May's apartments attempted to provide everything deemed necessary to dwelling in the smallest space possible. They came to be symbolized by their kitchens, designed by the Austrian architect Grete Schütte-Lihotsky. Inspired by Taylorism, Lihotsky conducted time-and-motion studies, consulted with housewives about their daily activities, and measured standard utensils in order to come up with an efficient, fully equipped kitchen. It was perhaps the *equipment* of the kitchen that was most revolutionary, for it was standard practice for renters to furnish most of their own kitchen facilities, from cupboards to stoves. Incorporating these into the kitchen design raised all of the inhabitants' standard of living equally, and mass production would make the costs lower than if each individual family had to install its own furnishings.[35]

The Frankfurt kitchen astonished by the attention to detail: flour containers were crafted from oak, thought to keep mealworms away; a slot was carved into the beechwood countertops to collect vegetable peelings into a waiting garbage can below. Lihotsky included a stool in her design, so that most work could be performed sitting. The overall surface area measured less than two meters by three and a half meters, and it was barely three meters from the stove to the dining table. The form of the kitchen intentionally mimicked that of a train's dining car. Lihotsky's kitchen communicated with the living room–dining room area by a sliding door, so that women could both supervise playing children and hide the chaos produced by meal preparation from her guests or her family at mealtime. This kitchen was promoted as the paragon of efficiency and exhibited at Frankfurt's annual international trade fair in 1927. None other than Louis Loucheur (he of France's 1928 housing law) wanted to buy 200,000 for his HBMs.[36]

May built over twenty thousand of these apartments for the city of Frankfurt at the request of the city's social democratic mayor; in general, the Weimar Republic supported Bauhaus and other Modernist initiatives, particularly in Berlin. In Austria and the Netherlands, too, Modernists architects were appointed to posts as municipal architects or given substantive housing contracts. In France, however, such commissions remained dependent upon a centralized system that awarded major projects primarily to École Nationale Supérieure des Beaux-Arts (ENSBA) graduates, and most often to winners of ENSBA's prestigious Prix de Rome competitions. These competitions took as their subjects monuments and large public works projects, not social housing, which had never been part of the ENSBA curriculum. Moreover, the government felt little pressure from below to build state-sponsored housing. Whereas, in other nations, left political parties or labor unions agitated for better-quality housing, in France, these actors instead successfully lobbied the government to maintain the tight rent controls put into place during World War I.[37] State-financed housing depended largely upon the individual initiative of directors of HBM offices. Trailblazer Henri Sellier, director of the Office Public d'Habitations du Département de la Seine, hired Marcel Lods and his partner Eugène Beaudouin (future winner of the MRU's Cité Rotterdam competition discussed in chapter 1) to build 1,200 HBM units at Drancy. The Drancy project earned acclaim for its innovative approaches to construction, but Beaudouin and Lods did not significantly reconceptualize interiors; their HBM apartments at Drancy resembled almost exactly the HBM model plan seen above, in the OPHVP report.[38] Le Corbusier remained limited to private commissions; the fifty workers' homes he built at the request of an industrialist's son at Pessac, in the Gironde, was his largest project during this period. These contracts constituted but a fraction of the projects being built in Germany or Austria. Comparatively, French Modernists had little opportunity to test their theories about urbanism and housing on the built environment during the interwar period.

Most of the French Modernists' ideas thus remained couched in magazine articles, displayed in exhibitions, and advanced in manifestoes like Le Corbusier's 1926 *Les 5 Points d'une architecture nouvelle,* in which he called for columns to raise a structure off of the ground, freeing up green space; a free interior plan; a free façade; a roof garden (more green space), and long, horizontal windows to allow a maximum of air and light to penetrate the interior.[39] These five points referenced the possibilities afforded by the development of reinforced concrete frame construction that liberated façades and interior walls from bearing a structure's weight. Le Corbusier's 1928 Maison Loucheur (Figure 2.5) attempted to put these points into concrete form for an inexpensive, HBM home. The interior featured a free plan with a central sanitary core. Open space during the day converted into private sleeping space at night with the aid of sliding doors and fold-down beds. This house was never built, but Le Corbusier's Unité d'habitation de grandeur conforme in Marseille, built after the war as an ISAI, managed to incorporate all five points.

Before moving on to the relationship of HBMs and Modernist designs to postwar ISAIs, it bears mentioning that the French branch of the CIAM, which included Lods and Beaudouin, was not the only active group of self-identified Modernists in 1930s France. At the 1929 Salon des Arts Décoratifs, a schism developed within the ranks of the Société des Artistes Décorateurs (SAD). Designers advocating mass-produced furniture and furnishings offering function and affordability found themselves at odds with the SAD establishment, which continued to celebrate the decorative aspects of ornament and to prefer artisanal craftsmanship. In 1929, the dissenters, among whom figured Robert Mallet-Stevens, Charlotte Perriand, and Francis Jourdain, founded the Union des Artistes Modernes (UAM).[40] The new members of the UAM promoted the use of industrial materials like steel and glass in home furnishings and urged that "form follow func-

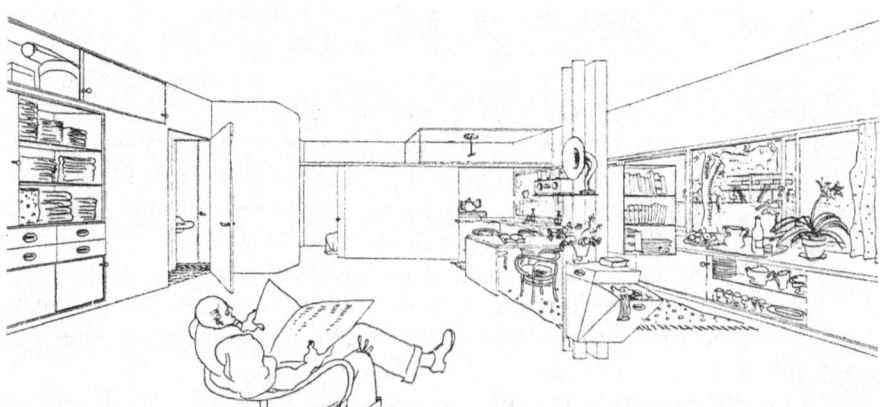

Figure 2.5. Le Corbusier's 1928 "Maison Loucheur." © 2013 Artists Rights Society (ARS), New York / ADAGP, Paris / F.L.C.

tion." United under the appellation "Modern artists," the UAM included designers, engineers, architects, and painters. In the 1930s, the UAM added Le Corbusier, Lurçat, Lods, Beaudouin, Georges-Henri Pingusson, André Hermant, and Marcel Gascoin to its ranks; the UAM thus provided cross-fertilization and a network for many of those most prominent in the development of French postwar domestic interiors.

Needs-Based Architecture and the Postwar 4P

The horrors of World War I had inspired Modernists to mobilize the epoch's "new spirit" for the reorganization of society, and Le Corbusier's famous formulation from his 1923 *Vers une Architecture*—"Architecture or revolution"—averred that social change was imminent one way or another. By the late 1940s, however, the worldwide economic depression of the 1930s and the events of World War II seemed to many to have accelerated, if not accomplished, the process of democratization, so that architects now found themselves reacting to, instead of instigating, change. Modernists shared with many others a belief that economic upheavals had influenced the social order, contributing to the "progressive impoverishment of the petty and middle bourgeoisie and a rise in the standard of living for the working classes."[41] This process had repercussions for lifestyles and hence for homes. Alexandre Persitz observed that what was taking place was "a sort of 'democratization' of the architecture of the home, which we must not underestimate the importance of on the social level."[42] His peer at *L'Architecture française,* Louis-Georges Noviant, agreed, explaining that a classless home was in the process of emerging: "Let us note that social evolution and financial leveling-out, added to the technical discoveries of our machinist epoch, have reduced the margin that once separated the worker's house from that of the bourgeois. If the latter, facing dwindling resources, attaches less importance to the secondary functions of his dwelling (external appearance, entertaining, décor...), the worker, for his part, no longer contents himself—with reason—to the simple shelter of old."[43] This was wishful thinking, particularly since the 1947 INED survey (see chapter 1) had revealed that those from "less fortunate backgrounds" thought a comfortable residence to be "inaccessible to those of modest resources."[44] Yet the notion that the blurring of class boundaries implied a corresponding homogenization of lifestyles helped architects to solve the problem of how to design a one-size-fits-all apartment when materials and resources were at a premium. Workers, deserving (if not yet seriously aspiring to) comfortably equipped and rationally designed homes, and the middle class, presumed to be shedding a too-expensive and morally suspect commitment to appearance and status, could both be satisfied by a space devoted to the fulfillment of their common needs.

In other words, if Modernist architects had once believed their task to create living spaces (and cities) that would spawn social change, now their mission had evolved into designing for the social changes already under way—in addition to the more immediate task of easing the housing shortage. Functionalism was a principle well suited to this process, for, as Persitz affirmed, "Whether it be a millionaire's residence, a bourgeois villa or a worker's house, the functional elements of the program are essentially analogous. In fact, we must create a dwelling that responds to the requirements of family life, the activities and rhythm of which no longer differ so much from one social class to another. Here Man and Child remain in the first place the measure of all things."[45] By turning to an essentialized version of families and individuals ("Man" and "Child"), Modernists evacuated class, gender, and age variations in dwelling practices from consideration in home design. Though they were aware of these (both *L'Architecture d'aujourd'hui* and *L'Architecture française* published summarized results of the INED survey in 1947), architects largely thought them to be irrelevant. No longer would homes be planned around extraneous considerations of status or even preferences; instead, they would be built, literally, to the proportions of adults and children and in accordance with the motions that these bodies performed in domestic space.

In order to design such spaces, architects had to isolate the universal needs, rhythms, and habits of family and individual life. What did they understand these requirements to be? *L'Architecture d'aujourd'hui* identified eight: hygiene, sleep, children's activities of play and homework, circulation (movement throughout the apartment), nourishment, relaxation, entertaining, and housework. *L'Architecture d'aujourd'hui*'s more moderate competitor, *L'Architecture française,* proposed nine: relaxing/cultivating one's interests; cooking, eating, sleeping, studying/playing, bathing, "W-C," laundering, and "moving around/putting away/other." For an encyclopedia of home economics and decoration, architect Pierre Sonrel recognized five needs—feeding oneself, entertaining oneself, sleeping, washing oneself, and raising children—and then suggested that these activities could be classified under the categories of "hearth" and "bed," or "day" and "night" functions.[46] Obviously, when it came to an objective determination of primary functions, the spirit of scientific law mattered more than its taxonomic letter.

Because economic shortages entailed spatial constraints, and because standardization would impose the same choice for all inhabitants of a particular apartment complex, what arose in the pages of the trade press, therefore, were various materialized versions of a needs hierarchy. If consensus reigned about the "need" for a foyer-type entrance (no matter how miniscule) and built-in shelves, other questions were not so easily resolved. Debates focused on issues of size, placement, and privacy. Should the kitchen be an eat-in one or a Frankfurt-style "laboratory" kitchen? Should it be open, allowing for the illusion of more space and not exiling the mother working within from participation in family activities and conversations with guests? Or should it be closed, to provide her with her own private space, simultaneously protecting the eyes and noses of the family and visitors from the disorder and odors of the work done there? Should the kitchen be set far from the dining area or close to it? And when it came to the dining area, where was the family going to take its meals? In the kitchen? In a corner of the living area or elsewhere? Should that living area be the largest room in the apartment? Or should some of the space allocated to the "family room" be given to bedrooms, so as to provide ample room for "individual life"? Should the living area occupy the apartment's center, to facilitate family interaction, or should it be off to one side, to allow for a separation of day and night functions? Should part of the living area be used as a bedroom or not? Where should the bathroom functions be placed? Close to the kitchen, to simplify the mass production and insertion of plumbing? Or close to the bedrooms, to maximize individual privacy? These discussions, held in pages of *L'Architecture d'aujourd'hui* and *L'Architecture française*, revealed how seriously architects were taking the problem of housing the masses.

To get some idea of how leading French Modernists answered these questions, consider the solutions proposed in the late 1940s by four of them: Le Corbusier, Marcel Lods, André Lurçat, and Michel Roux-Spitz. These architects were among the first to erect apartment complexes for the MRU's experimental ISAI program (see chapter 1). The ISAIs help us to better reconstruct how architects wrestled with the mandate of housing different clienteles in standardized homes because ISAIs, true to their name, were not for specific attribution to a particular community; instead, they existed primarily as life-size laboratories for advancing techniques of mass construction.

Le Corbusier's name is, of course, synonymous with the Modern Movement, and his Unité d'habitation de grandeur conforme at Marseille (construction began in 1946) remains one of the most visible symbols of Modern architecture. The apartment plan itself was strikingly original due to its two-story, puzzle-piece-like form. Le Corbusier used the two stories to establish a day-night separation of functions. The kitchen was primarily open, set off from the living area only by a high counter incorporating a serving hatch called a *passe-plat*. The living area, referred to by the term *séjour*, was divided into a *coin-repas* (dining corner, or dining nook) and a section dedicated to relaxation and entertainment. The floor devoted to sleeping and bathing positioned parents and their children at opposite ends, for maximum privacy. In between them were the bathroom components, as well as a sort of walk-through closet. The children's rooms were parallel, but separated by a movable partition, so that during the day, they could, if desired, be combined into a larger play area. The staircase that linked the two floors led directly from the living room–dining room area to the bathroom components, so visitors did not have to pass the private bedrooms. The Unité thus retained a commitment to open, flexible space while maintaining a public-private division within that space.

Marcel Lods was, like Le Corbusier, an ardent promoter of urban planning and mass production in housing construction. Lods, however, had followed the standard course of architectural training at ENSBA. He was less dogmatic than Le Corbusier, but Ernst May's Frankfurt apartments had made quite an impression on him. At Sotteville-lès-Rouen (construction began in 1948), Lods offered less ambitious floor plans than those found at Le Corbusier's Unité. Lods's elegant design for Sotteville[47] employed a similar division of space into day and night functions, but instead of creating two stories, Lods separated the space into two segments, using a left-right division. As in Le Corbusier's apartment, a lab kitchen lay off of the dining corner, separated only by the *passe-plat*, though Lods added a door that allowed occupants to close off the view of the kitchen from the entryway. The notion of privacy permeated the apartment: Lods placed a movable partition squarely between the day and night halves of the residence, while a second partition allowed parents to combine or separate their children's rooms. The children's rooms, while proximate to the master bedroom, did not communicate directly with it. Two balconies extended the apartment, accentuating the most important spaces in the home: the living room portion of the *salle de séjour* and the parents' bedroom. The kitchen and bathroom elements were separate, not grouped together, which underscored the day-night separation, and Lods zoned the dining and relaxation spaces of the *séjour* into the north and south areas respectively.

André Lurçat was a colleague—and rival—of Le Corbusier's in the CIAM, but in the 1930s, while working in the Soviet Union, he grew less involved in CIAM activities and closer to the Communist party. As we have seen, Lurçat played an instrumental role in the formation of the FNA and in 1945, MRU minister Raoul Dautry selected both Le Corbusier and Lurçat for his advisory committee on architecture (the Comité supérieur de l'Architecture et de l'Urbanisme), assigning the reconstruction of Maubeuge, in northern France, to Lurçat.

Lurçat also designed specific ISAI apartment complexes for Maubeuge (construction began in 1947). Lurçat's design (Figure 2.6) also employed a

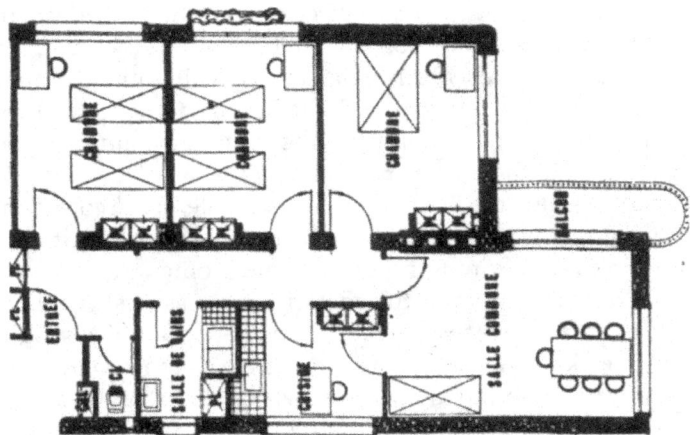

Figure 2.6. André Lurçat's Maubeuge 4P, 1947. From *L'Architecture d'aujourd'hui* 13–14 (September 1947), 135; all rights reserved.

day-night functional separation, but one marked instead by a "front" and "back" division. Like the Unité, Lurçat's apartment had a lab kitchen, but doors isolated it from the living room–dining room area, and the dining corner was placed farther from the kitchen, next to the window. The *salle commune,* or common area, was the privileged room of the apartment, not only because it was the largest, but because it opened onto the balcony. It had no communication with the bedrooms, which enjoyed maximum privacy, each linked only to the hallway. Unlike other apartment plans, however, Lurçat's led the visitor past the bedrooms and "service" areas before arriving at the reception area, revealing a less rigid preservation of the public-private distinction.

Furthest from Le Corbusier's radical interpretation of Modernism was Michel Roux-Spitz's plan for an ISAI in Nantes. Founder of *L'Architecture française* in 1942, Roux-Spitz advocated a moderate Modernism. Roux-Spitz was opposed to "skyscrapers of dwelling" like the Unité d'habitation and preferred clusters of smaller, four-story complexes, such as those he built at the Cité des Hauts-Pavés at Nantes (construction began in 1947). In Roux-Spitz's 4P, one finds another day-night separation.[48] Like Lurçat, Roux-Spitz opted for a front-back organizing principle, though he reversed the terms. Roux-Spitz also chose to separate his lab kitchen from the dining corner and the hallway with two doors. As in Lods's apartment, the principal "day" space, baptized "living-room" in English on Roux-Spitz's plan, was zoned into two areas, one for dining and another for relaxing or entertaining, and the dining area lay right next to the kitchen. Roux-Spitz proposed something different for the bedrooms, however. One children's room lay off of the master bedroom, which itself opened onto the bathroom area. This bathroom area then led into the other children's room, in a variation of Le Corbusier's plan. This alteration facilitated parents' access to younger children and allowed a modicum of privacy for older children. In another departure, the younger children's room also opened directly onto the living area.

When one considers the ISAI designs as a whole, some common aspects emerge. All four architects elected for a tiny lab kitchen (either open or closed), a living room–dining room area, and some kind of "day-night" separation. These, then, were the material expressions of the "requirements of family life." Decisions had been made: families would spend most of their waking hours at home together in the *séjour*; they would neither eat nor bathe in the kitchen; and visitors were to be as isolated as possible from sleeping areas to maintain privacy.

These design (and hence, in the architects' view, dwelling) principles based on "common needs," but which in fact drew upon middle-class uses of space, were popularized in the "Appartement idéal," a model apartment sponsored by the mass-circulation magazine *Paris-Match* for the 1952 Salon des Arts Ménagers. Designed by architect Marcel Roux, a member of the UAM and an MRU employee, in collaboration with Pierre Faucheux, the Appartement idéal (Figure 2.7) provided hundreds of thousands of French men and women with a glimpse of the model modern

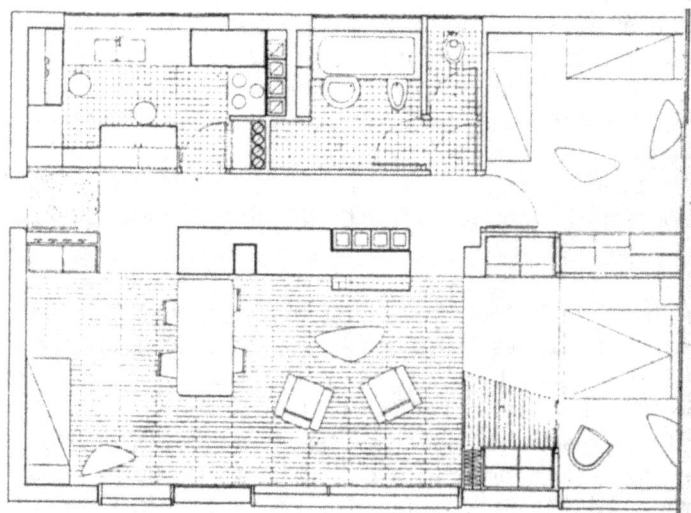

Figure 2.7. Marcel Roux and Pierre Faucheux's Appartement idéal (Appartement Paris-Match), 1952. From *L'Architecture d'aujourd'hui* 40 (April 1952), XXIII; all rights reserved.

home. In his commentary on the plan in *L'Architecture d'aujourd'hui*, Faucheux wrote that in "this 'ideal apartment' can be rationally installed everything necessary to the life of four or five people. The vital functions[49]: sleep, meals, toilette, relaxation find here their full development [*leur complet épanouissement*]. The life of the individual can be fully exercised while remaining within the bounds of family life."[50] The script for the guided visit to the Appartement idéal boasted that its three movable partitions—in imitation leather—gave the greatest comfort of all: "space at will." And, owing to its well-thought-out storage spaces, the Appartement idéal had no wasted space; that, the guide assured visitors, was its biggest secret. The lack of wasted space symbolized both perfect functionality and a purist's commitment to eliminating decadent excess.

Looking carefully at Faucheux and Roux's plan, however, one might be struck by its similarity to the highest echelon of prewar HBM housing: the ILM. Certainly Modernist design principles have been applied: rooms conform to right angles, the movable partitions give a nod to the free plans advocated in Le Corbusier's *5 Points*, and the dining room and parlor have been replaced by the living room–dining room combination. Yet, the ILM had also employed room dividers and the day-night separation of functions. The servant's entrance is absent from the small, equipped kitchen, but otherwise, the two look quite alike. Surprisingly, this resemblance provoked no comment in contemporary discussions of the Appartement idéal, either in the professional or mass media press.[51] Although designed according to functionalist Modernist principles that derived from a commitment to creating a "machine for living" that would reshape the way people from all classes inhabited homes, the postwar Modern home was not a radical remake of domestic space, but rather an imaginative edit of a prewar middle-class home.

Innovation from Above and the Art of Living

What is perhaps most interesting about this composite space, the 4P, is the way that it was described in the Modernist press. Obscuring or ignoring the similarities of some of the 4P's attributes to aspects of social housing, the Modernists' discourse expresses a subtle anxiety about forced economies and questions the ultimate desirability of the *existenzminimum* à la Ernst May. Modernists chose to extol the ways in which the new homes were perfect adaptations to changed times and to explain how a smaller, rationally organized 4P benefited a forward-thinking middle class. In essence, their presentation of the modern home grafted the values of the more radical, 1920s-era Modernism onto existing norms of middle-class living; from this hybrid, they extrapolated a universalized dwelling aesthetic that they called the art of living.

As pointed out above, the solution proposed, that of the living room–dining room area, echoes strongly the ILM's dining room–parlor disposition. Even the *coin-repas* (dining nook) shows that the middle-class home, as represented by the prewar ILM, remained the norm; it was the model to which things were added or subtracted. It wasn't so much that the *coin-repas* fulfilled the need for a place to have meals; it satisfied a middle-class preference to take one's meals outside of the kitchen. When Francis Jourdain identified the housing question as a problem of an "ever-shrinking space," the space to which he was referring was clearly not the one- and two-room dwellings that most of the urban population inhabited.

One example of the effort to understand the new home as distinctly modern and universal that ultimately reveals the middle-class leanings of the Modernists themselves, is the various names given to the living room–dining room area. On some plans, it is referred to as the *salle commune*; on others, it is called, in English, the "living room." In the information accompanying the presentation of the Appartement idéal in *L'Architecture d'aujourd'hui*, it is labeled both the *pièce du séjour* and the *salle commune*. The area quickly came to be known, as it is today, exclusively by the neologism *salle de séjour* or, simply, *séjour*. It is likely that the coining of the term *salle de séjour* to replace *salle commune* was meant to dissociate the living room–dining room area from the common room, itself associated with rural and working-class dwellings, where families spent all of their waking hours. At the very least, the neologism expressed the functions of rest and reunion and asserted that these were distinct from meal preparation, bathing, or studying.

A second instance of revisionism pertained to the origins of the lab kitchen. First brought to French architects' attention as "the Frankfurt kitchen", Lihotsky's creation was created expressly for working-class women and inspired by the desire to reduce a working mother's expenditure of energy, as well as the household's expenditures on furnishings. Yet the lab kitchen was heralded in the French architectural press on behalf of the "mistress of the house"[52] who, unable to find domestic help after World War II, was forced to do her own meal preparation. The 1947 issue of *L'Architecture d'aujourd'hui* illuminated the reasons for the disappearance of servants, explaining that industrialization had offered new and more lucrative avenues to the people who had once chosen domestic work. The editors remarked, "The number of households where all of the housework is performed by the lady of the house herself, without the help of salaried personnel, is expanding to include larger and larger strata of the population. ... It is thus logical to put the rational furnishings and equipment, which reduce the time and effort required by housework to a minimum, at the disposition of all households, at all echelons of the social hierarchy."[53] In *L'Architecture française,* Louis-Georges Noviant explained the public's preference for southern and southeastern exposures in the kitchen because the "lady of the house," now without servants, had to spend numerous hours there each day.[54] She should not also be forced to do so in a dark, somber space, he implied.

These explanations for the lab kitchen were based more on perception than fact. Though younger, single women did more often opt for factory work over domestic service, older, married women took up the slack. As they did so, they changed the nature of the work. Married women with their own households to run became *femmes de ménage,* operating on a live-out basis and replacing the live-in domestic servants who had specific roles like cook or laundress. The evolution in the character of the work was as much due to a decreased demand for live-ins among the middle classes as to the "desertion" of young girls from service. In fact, in the years from 1921 to 1951, the period when architects were commenting upon the "servant problem," there was actually an *increase* in the numbers of women working as daily maids. In 1921 there was one charwoman for every eleven live-in servants; by 1951, the ratio was one to four.[55] But the explanation offered by architects was that the lab kitchen in particular, and the scientific organization of the home in general, were mandatory in the modern home because the middle-class woman had to do the housework and cooking by herself.

This rationale for the lab kitchen was even put forth by Charlotte Perriand, the avant-garde UAM designer, who worked closely with Modernists Le Corbusier and Jean Prouvé. In 1950, she edited an issue of *Techniques et Architecture* on the theme of the "art of dwelling." Perriand explained, "With the progressive disappearance of domestic help, food preparation has naturally resumed its place within the familial community."[56] To be sure, Perriand's assertion that the servant crisis had the salutary effect of reducing the false pretense of social status and restoring the "natural" link of family unit and meal preparation was consistent with the Modernists' disdain for social artifice. Nevertheless, Perriand's explanation for incorporating the kitchen into the heart of the home, and no longer isolating it from the rest of the apartment (as had been the custom in bourgeois apartments), rested upon the assumption that the kitchen should reflect the higher social status of the woman now performing this work. This assumption is also evident in Perriand's recommendation that the lab kitchen be linked to the dining area by a waist-high divider so that the woman preparing food would not be excluded from conversation with guests at her luncheons or dinner parties.[57]

The disappearance of domestic help also functioned as a signifier of upheavals in the social order. The specter of the servant seemed to signal a bygone era and the need for new ways of dwelling. Thus, the editors of *L'Architecture d'aujourd'hui* proclaimed, "In the house of tomorrow, the position of what was the 'dining room' is quite compromised. The milieus who used it often through the last century, in accord with an abundant supply of domestic help, and in keeping with the taste for a certain scenic protocol, have given the example of abandoning this formula and are asking architects to create a *pièce de séjour* comprising an area for meals, but set up in such a way that this area is not the sole focus of the room ...."[58] Similarly, the UAM designer Marcel Gascoin noted that social relations "have lost their ceremonial character; receiving for display purposes [such as "visiting days," which took place in a parlor] once frequent, are now considerably spaced out or have taken on a greater bonhomie."[59] Marie-Anne Febvre, in an article for *L'Architecture d'aujourd'hui* entitled "The Center of Relaxation: The Salle de Séjour," added: "In the formula of the modern Habitation, the salle de séjour, which uses the space once reserved for the dining room and the parlor, creates an intimate atmosphere that is completely different than that which the juxtaposition of these two rooms offered in large interiors or than that of the implantation, in a small house, of a poorly used dining room, in which one only entered on Sundays and holidays."[60] What such comments implied was that, although the *séjour* might mirror the functions of the HBM's *salle commune*, the essence of the space was quite different. The *séjour*, these Modernists claimed, was instead a lifestyle choice, not the by-product of a taste for necessity. To hear Modernists tell it, the *séjour* was a new invention demanded from above by a forward-thinking upper middle class.

Perhaps more evocative of postwar Modernists' middle-class projections were their worries about an overly rationalized domestic space. Some fretted that the principle of rationalization might be taken too far. In 1947, *L'Architecture d'aujourd'hui* warned:

> For a number of years now, we have noticed the marked trend toward the reduction of surface area allocated to the bedroom, in favor of enlarging the *pièce commune*. The public seems to accommodate itself well to these layouts. If you follow this principle to its logical conclusion, you arrive at "cabin"-like rooms destined only to contain a bed and those elements strictly indispensable for putting away one's things. As "functional" as this solution might seem, it seems to us that it doesn't take into account man's basic psychological needs, the need to have a personal retreat, a space tailored to his aspirations and tastes. As big as the *salle commune* might be, it is a place by definition destined for "collective" activities. [...The public's taste in bedrooms] has resisted, until now, fundamental transformation. The acquisition of the "beautiful bedroom set," with a bed in the middle of the room, a night table, and an armoire, still heads the list of those just starting out. However, this is a room where, on the contrary, it would

be interesting to decorate with multipurpose elements, giving it the character of a bedroom/living room area, which would give parents the possibility of enjoying—since we lack the "offices, boudoirs and smoking rooms" of yesteryear—a room where one can live and work and not only sleep.[61]

This lengthy quote underscores the key argument of this chapter, which is that the 4P, a space imagined as the universal modern home, with roots in HBM social housing and radical interwar Modernism, in fact privileged middle-class dwelling preferences. Some postwar Modernists shied away from Le Corbusier's celebration of the ocean liner cabin, worrying that miniscule bedrooms did not allow sufficient escape from the pressures of collective living. Marie-Anne Febvre explained their point of view: "One quickly finds, in dwellings where no one has an individual center of activity (which is naturally found in the bedroom), the entry point for disorder, fatigue, a desire to flee everyday life, which causes mothers of families of reduced circumstances to become worn out and youth to be alienated from the home."[62] The obsession with meeting the needs of the individual, which permeated discussions of apartment size and layout,[63] is not one that would have troubled your average working-class family, accustomed to living in the *salle commune* (where the heat was) and willing to sacrifice space for lower rent. Clearly, it was a middle-class preference for personal space that was at stake here, and, in order to preserve this space, Febvre conjured up demons of nervous exhaustion and juvenile delinquency.

Concerns about the "missing" offices, boudoirs, smoking rooms—as well as the "missing" domestic help, the "missing" dining room, and the "missing" parlor—point to the middle-class home as the norm. The *existenzminimum* may have been fine for working-class Germans, the collective discourse of the postwar French Modernists implied, but the minimum around which the French modern home was going to be built was the minimum in which one could still live a "normal" middle-class life. In other words, if the 4P consisted of "solutions," they were solutions to the middle-class problem of "suppressed" spaces. Furthermore, despite the fact that Jourdain had claimed the housing question to be governed by economics, the postwar Modernists failed to ascribe changes in domestic space exclusively to scarce funds. Instead, they interpreted the 4P's form as evidence of transformations of the middle-class lifestyle; it was true that the transformations might be due in part to economics, but primarily, they asserted, they stemmed from the middle class's desire to disdain excessive formality and to embrace the prospect of living rationally and comfortably. It was these desires, presumably, that formed the basis for the art of dwelling.

What was the relationship of the postwar 4P to this art of dwelling? The art of living extolled a purist formal aesthetic that fit perfectly with the functionalist, needs-based architecture at the 4P's origin. As Monique Éleb and Anne Debarre have pointed out for the practitioners of Art Nouveau, the Modernists' spiritual predecessors, the art lay in simply, yet beautifully, articulating in space the needs of the individual and of society.[64] By making human needs the starting point of art, they would be valorizing nature instead of bourgeois artifice. Nearly a quarter of a century later, Charlotte Perriand rearticulated this aesthetic for a new generation, claiming that a minimalist art of living would contribute to the life of the mind, ensure peace and simplicity in everyday life, and restore human beings' relationship to nature:

> [D]o not all our efforts in urbanism and architecture tend toward the creation of a habitat that would permit man to live in harmony, isolated as much as possible [from overcrowded cities] and enjoying nature through a wide open façade, [overlooking] gardens or the sky? Tranquility of each member of the same family, a need more and more necessary in the hectic life of our century. An ambiance created by a well-conceptualized urbanism and architecture. On the inside, furnishings and equipment that create a void, emptiness.
>
> We have taken our stand: the world of knowledge is rich enough to populate our life without adding the need for useless knickknacks that would do nothing but consume our minds and our leisure hours. It is better to spend the day in the sun than to dust (with or without a vacuum cleaner) our useless objects.[65]

Her manifesto resonates with the authority of the Modernist tastemaker, having made the choices of sun, air, green space, and minimalism for all.

The art of living involved a total commitment to the spare aesthetic of modernist minimalism; the modern home did not consist solely of a rational floor plan, but also demanded built-in equipment, functional furniture, and a spare, simple décor. The modern home would not work, could not "function," if cluttered with baroque furniture; large picture windows could not bring nature into the home if obscured with heavy draperies or even traditional lace curtains. *L'Architecture d'aujourd'hui* and *L'Architecture française* renounced bulky armoires, overstuffed sofas, and copper pots demanding too much labor to polish. *L'Architecture d'aujourd'hui* praised the butterfly chair, condemning the traditional armchair as archaic: "In his hieratic armchair, the Frenchman has an uncomfortable attitude, held back as he is by a sort of respect for façade, for his dignity. Here [with the butterfly chair] one asks of the armchair the reason why it was made. The American stretches out, relaxes in every way; the flexibility of the form and of the material lends itself to movements unrestrained by any worry about decorum. Excellent method for the people of our era, obliged to take hasty—but complete—breaks."[66]

Not coincidentally, the modern art of living carved out a specialized area of expertise for architects within the contested field of housing construction. In an opinion piece that appeared in the 1950 issue of *Techniques et Architecture* edited by Charlotte Perriand, the architect André Hermant wrote:

> We know that an exact response can be given now to each demand, to each call to live better in a dwelling and in surroundings worthy of the human mind and favorable to its development [*épanouissement*]. But this call can not be heard if it is not formulated, and most people, crippled by the tasks of everyday life, caught up in the cogs of routine and prejudices, do not even suspect that part of their difficulties and fatigue comes from clutter, from disorganization, from the ugliness of a dwelling that they think normal... but which they flee as soon as they can. In every milieu, the majority is completely unaware of this art of living that is one of the conditions for *joie de vivre*. ... At school we learn math, geography, history, but the teaching of taste is absent from the curriculum; however, isn't a dubious-looking object or a questionable ambiance more haunting than a spelling error? ... It is the public that we must inform, educate, "sensitize," if we are to break the vicious circle that encloses buyers, sellers, and producers in the same rut. ... Materials and science are at our disposition. All we need now are beings capable of accomplishing the most beautiful of tasks: to fashion surroundings that are in accordance with their time and for the true happiness of all.[67]

Hermant thus claimed for architects the responsibility of shaping the aesthetics of everyday life and for teaching an appreciation for that aesthetic to the French public. In so doing, Hermant reprised the words of his fellow UAM member Jean Prouvé, who had announced five years earlier, "We must show them [the French] the home of the future and give them the idea of what it can be. We must educate them."[68] Queried about the architect's role, Marcel Lods echoed, "He must teach people how to live, because they don't know how."[69]

Architects began to redefine themselves by emphasizing their aesthetic contributions, as creators of and educators in this "art of living." As mentioned earlier, jurisdictional claims on the architect's field of competence were reshaping the field and establishing a new division of labor. As the more technical aspects of an architect's work were being dictated by state technicians at the CSTB or assumed by engineers, the architectural profession began to look to home design as its primary function. Alexandre Persitz was right when he suggested that architecture was experiencing a mutation, but rather than its field of activity becoming larger, it was contracting. Identifying themselves as the ones who would give the French renaissance its shape and content, architects became tremendously invested in the success of the rationalist, functionalist modern home.

Conclusion

In the years after Liberation, the architectural profession found itself in the process of transformation, confronted with four new circumstances. The first new circumstance involved changes in the ways of working; state oversight and competition from engineers and town planners narrowed the parameters of the liberal profession. Second, Modernism became the dominant theoretical influence, coming into the aesthetic legitimacy for which it had been fighting during the interwar period. Though Modernism encompassed multiple strains, all adherents agreed upon the desirability of streamlined forms and rationalized construction processes. On the other hand, if interwar Modernism was going to have its day in the sun, it would be in the postwar historical context; this meant that the causality of interwar Modernism's raison d'être—to revolutionize society through radical design—had seemingly been rendered moot by the depression and the war. The blurring of class boundaries that contemporaries understood to have been launched by these events put Modernist architects in the position of having to design for changes already taking place. This was particularly important because of the fourth factor, which was the novel situation of being employed by the state to build homes for "the masses," whose desires and dwelling practices varied (as indicated by the results of the INED survey discussed in chapter 1).

As Modernists began to design homes for the MRU, they attempted to solve the problem of plural preferences by turning to functionalist principles of universal needs. Yet, as this chapter has demonstrated, those "universal needs" turned out to consist largely of middle-class dwelling preferences, such as dining outside of the kitchen. Given that architects understood democratization to be bringing working-class tastes in line with middle-class norms, and not the other way around, this was entirely logical. Nevertheless, postwar Modernists' concerns about and explanations of the 4P reveal that they were confused or even ambivalent about the form that democratized housing should take.

Although they worried about the effects that forced economies might have on home design, Modernists refused to lament the 4P as a compromise between ideals and budgets. Instead, they pitched the modern home as a perfect vehicle for helping the French to adapt to a new era. When architects mobilized Modernist values of rationalism and functionalism to justify the spaces and functions "missing" from the 4P, they reinforced middle-class dwelling practices as the dominant norms for the design of the domestic interior. But even as they sought to build for a classless society, "elevating" the working class by opting for middle-class values of privacy, they also looked to reshape middle-class behavior, disposing of the "Sundays-only" parlor and its "false" concern with appearances. Consequently, neither working-class nor middle-class inhabitants recognized themselves or their lifestyle in the aesthetic of the modern home; acculturating the French to this composite space thus required architects to assume the mantle of educator. This project helped architects to carve out a new sphere of expertise within a crowded field of competence, which explains, to a certain extent, their mid-century orthodoxy with regard to the 4P.

Notes

1. Alexandre Persitz, "Habitations individuelles," *L'Architecture d'aujourd'hui* 18–19 (June 1948), 2.
2. Kopp, Boucher, and Pauly, *L'Architecture de la Reconstruction,* 91.
3. Roger Gilbert, "L'architecte devant la Reconstruction," *L'Architecture d'aujourd'hui* 1 (May–June 1945), 25.
4. The organization's name can be roughly translated as the French Society of Architects Holding Degrees from National Architecture Schools.
5. Voldman, *La reconstruction des villes françaises,* 248.
6. Pierre Claudius (Eugène Petit), "Renaissance," *L'Architecture d'aujourd'hui* 1 (May-June 1945), 6.
7. *L'Architecture d'aujourd'hui* 12 (July 1947), 4.
8. Alexandre Persitz, "À Propos de la Première Exposition de la Reconstruction," *L'Architecture d'aujourd'hui* 4 (January 1946), 64.
9. Voldman, *La reconstruction des villes françaises,* 248.
10. Kopp, Boucher, and Pauly, *L'Architecture de la Reconstruction,* 80. For more information on Lurçat, consult Jean-Louis Cohen, *André Lurçat, 1894-1970: autocritique d'un moderne* (Liège: Mardaga, 1995) and Pierre Joly and Robert Joly, *L'architecte André Lurçat* (Paris: Picard, 1995).
11. Kopp, Boucher, and Pauly, *L'Architecture de la Reconstruction,* 80.
12. For more on Roux-Spitz, see Michel Raynaud, Didier Laroque, and Sylvie Rémy, *Michel Roux-Spitz, architecte 1888-1957* (Brussels and Liège: P. Mardaga, 1983).
13. Voldman, *La reconstruction des villes françaises,* 254–55.
14. Cited in Kopp, Boucher, and Pauly, *L'Architecture de la Reconstruction,* 92.
15. Voldman, *La reconstruction des villes françaises,* 247, 258–63.
16. This is sociologist Andrew Abbott's term. See his *The System of Professions* (Chicago and London: University of Chicago Press, 1988).
17. Gilbert, "L'architecte devant la Reconstruction," 25.
18. Francis Jourdain, "Un problème à reconsidérer: L'Habitation humaine," *L'Architecture d'aujourd'hui* 10 (March 1947), 4.
19. Monique Éleb and Anne Debarre, *L'Invention de l'habitation moderne. Paris: 1880-1914. Architectures de la vie privée* (Paris: A.A.M./Hazan, 1995), 349. For more on social housing, see Roger-Henri Guerrand, *Propriétaires et locataires: les origines du logement social en France, 1850-1914* (Paris: Quinette, 1987); Jean-Paul Flamand, *Loger le peuple. Essai sur l'histoire du logement social* (Paris: La Découverte, 1989); and Dumont, *Le logement social.*
20. Michael Harloe, *The People's Home? Social Rented Housing in Europe and America* (Oxford and Cambridge, MA: Blackwell, 1995), 72.
21. Dumont, *Le logement social,* 138, 143.
22. Dumont, *Le logement social,* 143.
23. Power, *Hovels to High Rise,* 38.

24. The model was named after the plan by Jean-Georges Albenque and Eugène Gonnot, which won the OPHVP's 1913 competition for a project on the rue Henri-Becque.
25. L'Office public d'habitations de la Ville de Paris, *L'Office public d'habitations de la Ville de Paris* (Paris: L'Office public d'habitations de la Ville de Paris, 1937), 15.
26. Éleb and Debarre, *L'Invention de l'habitation moderne*, 135.
27. On bourgeois associations of the bedroom and privacy, see Roger-Henri Guerrand, "Private Spaces," in *A History of Private Life*, vol. 4, *From the Fires of Revolution to the Great War*, ed. Michelle Perrot and trans. Arthur Goldhammer (Cambridge, MA, and London: Harvard University Press, 1990), 368 and Éleb and Debarre, *L'Invention de l'habitation moderne*, 118–19.
28. On the history of the Modern movement, the canonical works include: Leonardo Benevolo, *The History of Modern Architecture*, 2 vols. (Cambridge, MA: MIT Press, 1971); Kenneth Frampton, *Modern Architecture: A Critical History* (London: Thames and Hudson, 1980); Charles Jencks, *Modern Movements in Architecture*, 2nd ed. (New York: Penguin Books, 1985); Manfredo Tafuri and Francesco Dal Co, *Modern Architecture* (New York: Electa/Rizzoli, 1986); William J.R. Curtis, *Modern Architecture Since 1900*, 3rd ed. (London: Phaidon Press, 1996); and Sigfried Giedion, *Space, Time and Architecture: The Growth of a New Tradition*. 5th ed. (Cambridge, MA: Harvard University Press, 2009). For a study of French Modernism, an indispensable reference is the three-volume series published by Picard, *L'Architecture moderne en France*.
29. Cited in Frampton, *Modern Architecture*, 269.
30. Ibid.
31. Alex T. Anderson, in *The Problem of the House: French Domestic Life and the Rise of Modern Architecture* (Seattle, WA, and London: University of Washington Press, 2006), argues that questions of dwelling also determined the entire Modernist aesthetic, lying at the origin of Modernism's tenets, materials, and forms.
32. Cited in Anatole Kopp, *Quand le moderne n'était pas un style, mais une cause* (Paris: ENSBA, 1988), 154. Note that Le Corbusier does not consider meal preparation and consumption as functions of domestic life.
33. Gascoin, a dominant figure in shaping the streamlined aesthetic of the postwar years in France, is now the subject of two recent studies: Guillemette Delaporte, *Marcel Gascoin: Décorateur des Trente Glorieueses* (Paris: Norma, 2010) and Pierre Gancey, *Marcel Gascoin: Design utile* (Paris: Piqpoq, 2011).
34. Pascal Renous, *Portraits de décorateurs* (Paris: Éd. H. Vial, 1969), 5. As an aside, one may find it ironic that the Modernists' praise of the streamlined and rational ocean liner echoes that of the Greeks. In Xenophon's *Œconomicus*, Ischomachus remarks to Socrates that a Phoenician ship is the most perfect example of order because everything has its logical place, a fact that makes the ordering both convenient *and* beautiful. Aestheticizing order, Ichsomachus prefigures the Modernists by a good two thousand years. Moreover, as Ann Bergren points out, by finding both the rule and examples of order in a choir, an army, and a ship, Ischomachus's conception of the household draws on masculine examples, thus creating a domestic sphere that echoes the male public sphere (Ann Bergren, "Female Fetish Urban Form," in *The Sex of Architecture*, ed. Diana Agrest, Patricia Conway, Leslie Kanes Weisman [New York: Henry N. Abrams, Inc., 1996], 82). The Modernists, as well as the proponents of scientific organization of the home, will do the same thing. (The reference to Ischomachus and the Phoenician ship can be found in Cannes Lord's translation of Xenophon's *Œconomicus* in Leo Strauss, *Xenophon's Socratic Discourse: An Interpretation of the Œconomicus* [Ithaca, NY: Cornell University Press, 1970], 38.)
35. At the same time, as Susan Henderson observes, Lihotsky also successfully *commodified* the kitchen, since the mass-produced Frankfurt kitchen was available for individual

purchase and installation. It even came in two alternate models for middle-class households; these were larger, to accommodate one or two servants. (See Susan R. Henderson, "A Revolution in the Woman's Sphere: Grete Lihotzky and the Frankfurt Kitchen," in *Architecture and Feminism,* ed. Debra Coleman, Elizabeth Danze, and Carol Henderson [Princeton, NJ: Princeton Architectural Press, 1996], 235.)

36. Henderson, "A Revolution in the Woman's Sphere," 238. According to Henderson, Loucheur's purchase order was canceled when the government learned that he planned to pay for the kitchens out of a war reparations account (252 n.43).
37. See Kopp, *Quand le moderne n'était pas un style,* 136–37. The effect of rent control on the housing market is also discussed in chapter 4.
38. This assessment is shared by Robert Weddle in his dissertation on Beaudouin and Lods's Drancy project, the Cité de la Muette. Weddle does acknowledge novelty in the employment of moving partitions in a portion of the apartments at Drancy. These allowed for the conversion of living space into sleeping space and vice versa. See Robert Brian Weddle, "Urbanism, Housing, and Technology in Inter-War France: The Case of the Cité de la Muette," (Ph.D. diss., Cornell University, 1998). For more on Lods, see Marcel Lods, *Le Métier d'architecte. Entretiens avec Hervé Le Boterf* (Paris: Éditions France-Empire, 1976).
39. The literature on Le Corbusier is copious. A useful English-language starting point is William J.R. Curtis's *Le Corbusier: Ideas and Forms* (London: Phaidon Press, 1994). Le Corbusier's "Five Points" manifesto was published in *Almanach d'Architecture moderne* (Paris: G. Crès, n.d. [1926]).
40. For more on the SAD, see Suzanne Tise, "Between Art and Industry: Design Reform in France, 1851-1939," (Ph.D. diss., University of Pittsburgh, 1991). For a history of the UAM, see Arlette Barre-Despond, *L'UAM, Union des Artistes Modernes* (Paris: Éditions du Regard, 1986).
41. *L'Architecture d'aujourd'hui* 10 (March 1947), 29.
42. Persitz, "Habitations individuelles," 2.
43. Louis-Georges Noviant, "Le logis d'aujourd'hui," *L'Architecture française* 111–12 (1951), 11.
44. [INED], *Désirs des Français,* 14.
45. Persitz, "Habitations individuelles," 2.
46. Pierre Sonrel, "L'habitation," in *L'Art ménager français,* ed. Paul and André Breton (Paris: Flammarion, 1952), 26.
47. This plan can be seen in *L'Architecture d'aujourd'hui* 13–14 (September 1947), 134.
48. This plan can be seen in Michel Roux-Spitz, *Réalisations,* vol. 3 (Paris: Éd. Vincent, Fréal & Cie, 1959), 9.
49. With true rationalist élan, Faucheux and Roux have reduced Sonrel's five functions to four.
50. Pierre Faucheux, "Appartement Paris-Match présenté par le Salon des Arts Ménagers et Paris Match," *L'Architecture d'aujourd'hui* 40 (April 1952), XXIII.
51. It is most unlikely that Modernist architects, in particular, were unaware of HBM architecture, especially since *L'Architecture d'aujourd'hui* had devoted a special issue to the topic in 1937 (*L'Architecture d'aujourd'hui* 5e année, 6–7 [June–July 1937]).
52. The class difference is reflected in the different terms used to describe the female in charge of the household. Where middle- and upper-class homes had the *"maitresse de maison"* — the lady of the house — working-class homes had a *"ménagère"* — housewife, though this term also included mothers employed outside the home.
53. *L'Architecture d'Aujourd'hui* 10 (March 1947), 29.
54. Noviant, "Le logis d'aujourd'hui," 16.

55. Louise A. Tilly and Joan Scott, *Women, Work and Family* (New York: Holt, Rinehart and Winston, 1978), 154; Olivier Marchand and Claude Thélot, *Le Travail en France (1800-2000)* (Paris: Nathan, 1997), 130. Tilly and Scott observe that the decline of women in live-in service during the first three decades of the twentieth century in England (a 12 percent decline) was much more marked than in France (approximately 2.5 percent) (153). As Robert Frost points out for the interwar period, the rhetorical value of claiming that one simply could not find any servants to hire had a positive effect on one's social capital without a corresponding negative effect on one's budget (Frost, "Machine Liberation: Inventing Housewives and Home Appliances in Interwar France," *French Historical Studies* 18, 1 [Spring 1993]: 114).
56. Charlotte Perriand, "La nourriture," *Techniques et Architecture* 9/10 (5 August 1950), 37. For more on Perriand, see her autobiography, *Une vie de création* (Paris: Odile Jacob, 1998) and Mary McLeod, *Charlotte Perriand: An Art of Living* (New York: Harry N. Abrams, 2003).
57. Perriand, "La nourriture," 41.
58. *L'Architecture d'Aujourd'hui* 10 (March 1947), 61.
59. Marcel Gascoin, "Le mobilier," *L'Art ménager français* (Paris: Flammarion, 1952), 48.
60. Marie-Anne Febvre, "Le Centre de détente: La Salle de séjour," *L'Architecture d'aujourd'hui* 10 (March 1947), 70.
61. "Le Centre sommeil: La chambre, son équipement fixe et mobile," *L'Architecture d'aujourd'hui* 11 (May–June 1947), 68.
62. Febvre, "Le Centre de détente," 70.
63. Indeed, references to the organization of individual life and communal life abound in architectural discourse from the late 1940s through the 1970s. To cite just one example, discussing the layout of his "Minimum Family Home in Stone," architect Paul Nelson emphasized the autonomy of the zones within the apartment, which meant that "each activity of family life can be performed easily without bothering the others" (*L'Architecture d'aujourd'hui* 13–14 [September 1947], 138). In chapter 4 we will again see home professionals' attentiveness to the needs of the individual.
64. Éleb and Debarre, *L'Invention de l'habitation moderne*, 451.
65. Charlotte Perriand, "L'art d'habiter," 33.
66. "Normes et volumes d'encombrement," *L'Architecture d'aujourd'hui* 10 (March 1947), 99.
67. A[ndré] Hermant, "Réflexions," *Techniques et Architecture* 9/10 (5 August 1950), 95.
68. Cited in Kopp, Boucher, and Pauly, *L'Architecture de la reconstruction*, 88.
69. Cited in Paul-Henry Chombart de Lauwe, *Famille et habitation*, vol. 1 (Paris: CNRS, 1959), 192.

Chapter 3

THE SALON DES ARTS MÉNAGERS
Teaching Women How to Make the Modern Home

> *If the household arts establish the rules for homemaking, if they thus dictate, to some extent, social mores, they have no intention of limiting themselves to domestic materialism. They also aspire to goals of an incontestable purity.*
> —Paul and André Breton, Salon des Arts Ménagers executives, 1952[1]

"Every means of propaganda and activity must be undertaken to give the Frenchman the taste and desire for bright, sunny, practical, and comfortable housing," exhorted engineer and social reformer Daniel Parker in 1945.[2] Other contemporary observers agreed that the first step in improving family life and the housing problem was educating the French about the need for hygienic housing.[3] The Salon des Arts Ménagers (SAM), an annual exhibition that ran from 1923 to 1983, fulfilled this role with brio, becoming an evangelist for modern homes. Indeed, no history of domestic space in France during the Trente Glorieuses would be complete without an account of the Salon des Arts Ménagers.[4] Linked in the French popular imagination with a dream world of shiny, new appliances, the SAM was actually more of an institution than an exposition. Acting as publisher, consumer advocate, art patron, interior decorator, and home economics instructor, the Salon[5] offered a forum to and coordinated the efforts of architects, appliance manufacturers, decorators, home economists, furniture-makers—anyone who had anything to do with the art of living. The SAM sought to bring the best of modern life into the home and in so doing modeled the perfect housewife it hoped to inspire women to become.

Previous commentators on the Salon have emphasized its role in helping France transition into a consumer society.[6] Robert Frost has argued that the projections of a mechanized future presented at interwar Salons prepared the French for the massive and rapid changes they would experience during the modernization project of the Trente Glorieuses. Martine Segalen has suggested that the SAM was a critical motor for growth, driving spending and thus contributing to the economic miracle of the postwar period: "Under the cover of home improvement, the family was invited to spend and was thus burdened with the responsibility of economic development."[7] However, to understand the Salon's message of home improvement as simply a "cover" for economic recovery is to fail to take seriously the SAM's crusade to raise the prestige of the domestic sphere and to miss some of the implications of its celebration of the modern home. This chapter thus turns the spotlight on the ways in which the Salon articulated a powerful domestic ideal. This domestic ideal, into which consumerism was woven, linked the Modernist functionalist aesthetic to domestic space and identified the modern home as the primary source of personal fulfillment and family unity.

While the Salon did not play a great role in the design and layout of the modern home, it had a large part in its diffusion as a normative model for which families should strive. In addition to encouraging a public reluctant to spend its budget on housing or furnishings to do just that, the SAM served to acculturate the French to the forms and ideology of the modern home. The Salon was the place where many of the French saw, for the first time, the new homes of the MRU's experimental programs, Modernist architects' formulations for the one-size-fits-all home, the slender forms of modern furnishings, and the electric offerings from manufacturers like Arthur Martin and Moulinex. The Salon also merits our attention because of the ways in which the SAM self-consciously embraced its pedagogical mission; its raison d'être was to persuade the French to invest—for moral as well as for financial reasons—in home improvement. The Salon directed this message at both men and women in gendered ways. It hoped to convince the former that modernizing one's home would yield more pleasure than purchasing an automobile or a television or spending one's free time at cafes. Addressing women, the SAM reified a wife's responsibility for homemaking by explaining how the modern home would reduce expenditures of her time and effort. Overall, the SAM put the onus on women of all classes to modernize, by purchasing modern furniture and new appliances, by implementing more efficient methods of housekeeping, or, preferably, by doing both.

This chapter narrates the origins of the Salon des Arts Ménagers in the interwar period and locates its attempt to integrate technology into the domestic sphere in a familialist effort to keep educated middle-class women from abandoning their homes in search of professional opportunities. The second section considers how the SAM expanded its structure and enlarged its audience after the war to include working-class and rural families in its pedagogical efforts. The third segment zooms in on the way the Salon linked the modern home to women's maternal and familial responsibilities, and especially to her labor. The final part considers the postwar Salon's Modernist aesthetic as an inalienable aspect of the domestic ideal. As we shall discover, at both the prewar and postwar SAMs, old pronatalist concerns and conceptions of gender roles met new materials and aesthetics in the service of the "family home," the privileged site for personal happiness.

The Origin and Mission of the Prewar Salon des Arts Ménagers

The Salon des Arts Ménagers was born at the crossroads of hygiene and technology. It was not an entrepreneur who launched the first Salon, but an inventor. The SAM was the brainchild of Jules-Louis Breton, a fascinating figure. Born in 1872 to a bourgeois family from the north of France, Breton became radicalized during his student days, as he was training to become a chemical engineer. A supporter of Socialist activist and politician Édouard Vaillant, Breton cofounded the Étudiants socialistes révolutionnaires internationalistes de Paris; because of his political writings, Jules-Louis Breton was the first to be prosecuted under the first "loi scélérate" of 1893. In 1898, Breton entered political life as a Socialist deputy, and by the beginning of World War I, Breton was also putting his scientific vocation to work as undersecretary of state for inventions. (His office dealt with inventions concerning national defense.) The inventions office, after the war, became the Office national des recherches scientifiques et industrielles et des inventions (ONRI), better known today as the National Scientific Research Center (CNRS).[8] (The CNRS is similar to the National Science Foundation in the United States, but much broader in scope.)

Breton was also interested in questions of social reform and pronatalism. In 1920, Breton became the first minister of hygiene and social welfare in prime minister Alexandre Millerand's cabinet. As minister, he put together a national council on fertility and created the Médaille de la Famille Nombreuse, an award for mothers of large families, which earned him the nickname "The Birthrate Minister." He also worked with Henri Sellier and Louis Loucheur to try to ease the interwar housing crisis. During this period, he met Paulette Bernège, the foremost French expert on the scientific organization of the home, and Breton became convinced that technology had as much place in the home as it did on the battlefield.[9] His first exhibition, the Salon des Appareils Ménagers, was sponsored by ONRI and featured new prototypes of household appliances designed for well-to-do households. In 1926, the Salon became the Salon des Arts Ménagers and began to broaden its horizons. Bernège organized a week of home economics education in 1927, and the architecture journal *L'Architecture d'aujourd'hui* began sponsoring a yearly exhibit called L'Exposition de l'habitation in 1934.[10]

As Martine Segalen, Robert Frost, and Ellen Furlough have conclusively demonstrated, the first SAM exhibitions targeted a largely upper-middle-class audience, offering a means of salvaging and signifying elite social status during economically difficult times. Labor-saving appliances, the Salon intoned, offered households a way to economize (by eliminating servants) while simultaneously demonstrating modernity through the acquisition of the latest technology; scientific organization of the home promised to maximize all of a family's resources, including each member's leisure time. A concern for bourgeois standards of taste can be found in the SAM's ambivalence toward mass-produced furniture and other items of home décor. As it celebrated "mechanical servants," the Salon's displays of fine art and antiques confirmed that the latter were compatible with the tasteful contemporary home.

Segalen, Furlough, and Frost also agree that the SAM tailored its messages to women, whose traditional roles and feminine essence were in the process of being redefined. Confronted with the new cultural figures of the American feminist career-woman, or *la garçonne,* the cigarette-smoking free love advocate, the women who went to the Salon found themselves invited to pursue an alternative path, that of the domestic engineer.[11] The SAM combined Bernège's emphasis on the scientific organization of the home with its presentation of state-of-the-art mechanized mother's helpers to place modernity squarely within the domestic sphere, thereby offering a way for enlightened and educated women (in particular) to be modern without abandoning their domestic responsibilities.

At the same time, Breton attempted to ease any potential aesthetic qualms about the introduction of machinery into the home by describing the activities of the domestic engineer as "arts ménagers," a neologism integrated into the Salon's title in 1926. It is interesting that, at a time when domestic Taylorism was gaining ground in France through the efforts of Paulette Bernège, especially as a means of giving women professional status within the domestic sphere, the existing nineteenth-century appellations—*économie domestique* and *science domestique*—would be replaced by "arts ménagers." Women were thus to be engineers, financial managers, *and* artists, a prescription for multitasking that would appear to subvert household appliances' labor-saving potential. The Salon tried to counter that interpretation by linking these activities together as a single vocation, that of the homemaker; in the Salon's pedagogical formulation, homemaking was the perfect marriage of art and science.

In its efforts to maintain the middle class's standard of living and to encourage women to embrace their vocation as wives and mothers, albeit as "modern" ones, the prewar Salon worked to "preserve particularities" of gender and class, as Ellen Furlough has put it.[12] Jules-Louis Breton, in spite of his Socialist predilections (although by the mid 1920s, he had aligned himself with the more moderate Radical-Socialists), offered an exposition that was primarily aimed at bourgeois women in bourgeois homes. Breton's Salon complemented his other efforts in the pronatalist and familialist realms, blending an understanding of the French family as the basic unit of a healthy society with an interest in using technology within the domestic sphere to maintain and protect that unit.

The Structure and Activities of the Postwar SAM

When the SAM recommenced its exhibition in 1948, the organization was under the sole stewardship of Jules-Louis's son Paul, who had been general commissioner of the SAM since 1929; Jules-Louis had died in 1940. Paul had trained as an engineer at the École Nationale des Arts et Métiers and was a member of the UAM. Through his work with the prewar SAMs, Paul Breton had become well known as an expert at mounting large-scale exhibitions and had coordinated Modernist architect Paul Nelson's Techniques américaines de l'habitation et de l'urbanisme exhibit in the summer of 1946. He also enjoyed a reputation as an expert on home furnishings and design. In 1951, Breton was asked to head up the Household Equipment Commission at the CSTB. This committee examined and approved sanitary and kitchen apparatuses for the MRU.[13] In 1955, Paul Breton took over the presidency of the Association for the National Campaign in Favor of Construction and Housing, a group that sponsored traveling exhibitions about domestic space.[14] The same year also witnessed the publication, under his editorship, of the enormous *La Civilisation quotidienne*, the fourteenth volume of the *Encyclopédie française*. He was elected president of the French Design Council in 1969. To a large extent, Paul Breton alone determined the goals and mission of the SAM, and when he retired in 1977, the Salon only lasted six more years.

Paul Breton recognized that the postwar SAM would have to address the changes that were taking place in the realm of housing and interior decorating. Where the SAM had once been the innovator with regard to modernizing domestic space, the Salon now had to integrate and curate changes initiated by others. The mechanized bourgeois apartment celebrated by the prewar SAM as the ideal home could no longer represent the modern home, for it was clear from the scale of the housing crisis and from the first MRU experiments with modern housing that the home's form was going to change as much as its equipment. Furthermore, the emerging Modernist functionalist aesthetic privileged mass-produced items on the basis of their egalitarian qualities—as long as they were beautifully designed. In society at large, too, there were changes that would affect the SAM. Like the Modernist architects described in chapter 2, Breton understood contemporary democratization as a blurring of class boundaries, and, for Breton and his brother André (a Socialist parliamentary deputy like their father), this meant an expansion of the Salon's target audience: "Henceforth, household arts are no longer the privilege of an aristocracy. They are expanding to address all classes. They are adapting themselves to all milieus."[15]

In order to ensure that the Salon that could speak to all of the changes that were affecting domestic space, Paul drew upon his contacts with MRU representatives, UAM designers and architects, and home economists from the UNCAF.[16] In concert with these participants, he added even more stands and events to the Salon's annual exhibition, which took place in Paris over a two- (and eventually three-) week period at the end of February and beginning of March each year. During this time, the paying public could examine new home furnishings and household products, including everything from plumbing fixtures to detergents. In 1948, 1,200 presenters demonstrated their wares in the Grand Palais. Other elements of the annual exhibition included the *Fée du Logis* (Ideal Homemaker) competition for the best housewife, introduced by UNCAF in 1949. The Exposition de l'Habitation returned in 1950. The MRU prepared a stand publicizing its efforts in reconstruction and urbanism, and the Foyer d'Aujourd'hui (Today's Home) demonstrated the latest in home furnishings. The UAM offered a stand called Formes Utiles (Useful Forms), which boasted the most efficient—and therefore beautiful—designs for everything from sinks to dishware. Attendees could watch films or sit in on talks, given on the theme for the day, such as Coal, Electricity, Sanitary Equipment, Color, or Reconstruction.[17] In 1949, visitors could listen to the MRU minister himself, Eugène Claudius-Petit, speak on construction and housing. In 1950, Paulette Bernège lectured on the topic, "If Women Made Household Appliances." If they chose, visitors could also have a meal in the restaurant, where the menus featured different regional cuisines.

The annual Salon was thus a major event. It was widely advertised at town halls, police stations, Parisian open-air markets, and post offices, and on subways, buses, and commuter trains. Department stores began to time white sales to coincide with the dates of the Salon, and the mass media devoted pages and airwaves in February and March to the novelties introduced at that year's Salon.

Who came to the Salon? Attendance was impressive: in 1948, over 795,000 attended, and by 1950, over a million tickets were sold. The number of visitors per year would not dip below one million until 1972.[18] Even the French president made an appearance; in the rare years when he was unavailable, a high-ranking minister or two would take his place. Although in the first years after the war, men composed the slight majority of visitors (54 percent men and 46 percent women attended the 1948 Salon), by 1957, surveys showed a predominantly female public (61 percent). It is difficult to determine a class breakdown of the women who attended the SAM, because entry polls grouped all unwaged women together as "no profession," whether they came from middle- or working-class households. Wage-earning women were counted as members of their profession, whether civil servant or factory worker. A very rough estimate puts general attendance at about 25 percent upper-middle-class, 20 percent middle-class, 20 percent lower-middle-class, 10 percent working-class, and 3 percent rural visitors; the rest were mostly trade professionals mixed with a smattering of artisans and retirees.[19]

The Salon's public was overwhelmingly Parisian. Discounts were offered on train fares to encourage more visitors from outside Paris, but the number of provincial visitors only rose by 7 percent in a decade. To further diffuse its message, therefore, the SAM sponsored mini-exhibitions in large provincial cities like Toulouse, Marseille, Reims, Metz, Nantes, Dijon, and Bordeaux; these presentations lacked the scale and regularity of their Parisian parent, however. When the Salon was not in session, its influence could be felt, or at least read, in a monthly magazine, *Arts ménagers*, launched in 1949. The SAM even had its own press, the Éditions du Salon des arts ménagers, which published works such as Caisse d'Allocations Familiales home economist Marie-Louise Cordillot's *Cours ménagers* (Home Economics Courses). In 1952, the publishing house Flammarion published the Salon's definitive statement, called, simply, *L'Art ménager français*. An impressive tome of nearly 1,300 pages, this book aimed, like its older competitor, the *Larousse ménager*, to guide women in all aspects of creating and caring for a household. It opened with architecture and decoration and extended through child-rearing, sewing arts, cooking, and household management.

Martine Segalen has placed the SAM at "the hub of a complex network of relationships between industry, social policies, government, designers, and other normative institutions," and the SAM's incorporation of all of these groups of actors into its mission manifested its ambition to attract a larger segment of the population.[20] Above all, the postwar SAM sought to improve living conditions for an imagined average French family, and it shared this objective with the MRU. Both entities believed, following in the footsteps of nineteenth-century social reformers like Jules-Louis Breton, in the moral power of decent homes to guarantee social peace and family unity. As French President Henri Queuille, opening the Salon in 1949, declared:

> The SAM does not content itself with presenting the solutions of home appliances only as improvements in their material and economic aspects: its educative task encompasses the spiritual life of the home. ... The social reach of such an education should not be underestimated. *Thanks to well-being at home, the yearning for happiness that is a legitimate motivator of man in his daily endeavors is largely met.* The improvement of the home is the best vindication of the will to work and the attraction of the *home* [in English] is the condition for healthy and comforting leisure pursuits.[21]

The MRU relied on the SAM to cultivate the public's desire to invest in housing. Though the ministry's new homes guaranteed access to modern comfort in the form of showers and central heating, the MRU could not also undertake the renovation of existing housing stock. The government did establish, in 1945, the National Home Improvement Fund (the Fonds National de l'Amélioration de l'Habitat, or FNAH) to grant small home improvement loans, but, first, people had to be persuaded to renovate and modernize. The MRU aimed to accomplish this goal by diffusing the message that happiness was inextricably linked to home improvement.

In 1951, Breton felt obliged to remind the government of the Salon's role in its modernizing drive when the Salon was in danger of losing some of its time in the Grand Palais to the Salon de l'aéronautique. In protest, Breton drafted a long memo to the government, emphasizing the Salon's pedagogical function: "The Government is applying a social program. It wants to ensure home renovation and to satisfy the need for comfort. It is striving to encourage an active and persevering will [to better one's home] in all classes of society. Only an education that is unceasingly pursued over a long period of time responds to this governmental focus. By universal consent, it is at the Salon des Arts Ménagers that this education is lavished."[22] Breton reminded the government that the Salon was not only a marketplace, but a school, and, on the basis of his memorandum, his plea for more time met with success.

In order to encourage a mass taste for home improvement, it was vital that consumers have access to affordable furnishings and equipment. For the first few years after Liberation, the only things to sell were the concepts of modernity and plenty. Vendors in the late 1940s often showed only prototypes of what would be made once their factories could start up production again, and even those few customers with sufficient disposable income had to wait anywhere from six months to two years for their orders to arrive.²³

Breton campaigned for collective and concerted action on the part of industrialists in order to develop the appliance market. In 1953, Breton helped Bernard Verriès form the Syndicat national de l'équipement de cuisine (National Union of Kitchen Equipment, or SNEC) whose members included twelve of the largest manufacturers of kitchen elements. By coordinating production and markets, the Syndicat could increase profits while bringing prices down on its offerings.²⁴ Breton motivated manufacturers with profits but also exhorted that they take action as part of their civic duty. In an address to the SNEC, Breton urged: "There is cause to establish materials that respond to the needs of the average household, which for mass production is not at all utopian, since the costs of this would correspond to larger sales. This is, for the kitchen installer, the way of prosperity, it will be also the highest justification of his social mission in the universal race to happiness that we are currently experiencing and in which we must all participate as best we can."²⁵ The domestic ideal—and the democratization thereof—was not just something the SAM preached to housewives, therefore, but also to trade professionals; the notion that everyone had the right to the fulfillment created in and by the "happy home" permeated the postwar social imaginary.

The paternalism of a Salon that sought to improve daily life for ordinary people extended into consumer protection. The SAM mounted campaigns and competitions for the adoption of norms and standards for a variety of household products. The Bretons were behind the 1926 creation of the Association française de normalisation (AFNOR), a standards organization that set up protocols for the fabrication and usage of a gamut of products. Some of these norms became obligatory; both French and foreign refrigerators and gas ranges, for example, had to be AFNOR-certified in order to be sold in France. Such consumer advocacy was itself part of the Salon's mission and lasted throughout the SAM's lifetime; as late as 1969, Breton initiated a competition for the best user's manual for a household appliance.²⁶

Breton used competition to stimulate large-scale mass production of modern furniture, too. In 1951, he created the René Gabriel prize, named after the pioneering designer who had passed away the previous year. Because mass-produced furnishings still lacked the prestige of finely crafted, artisanal work, the 100,000-franc prize was meant to encourage top designers to compete in this arena. The prize continued to be awarded over the course of the next thirty years.

Breton also served as a liaison between designers and retailers. For example, the Modernist designer Charlotte Perriand recalled in her memoir that not only did Breton get the women's magazine *Elle* to sponsor her designs for a Japanese-style model home shown at the 1957 Salon, but he also arranged for the popular department store Galéries Lafayette to purchase the entire collection after the Salon's closing.[27] Lesser-known decorators lamented high participation fees that they felt excluded new talent from exhibitions, but Breton, a member of the UAM, worked tirelessly to promote the new style in furnishings.

Though each group of actors used the Salon to promote its own agenda, Breton tried to establish mutually beneficial relationships among these groups and also sought to use Salon visitors' preferences as market research for housing, design, and appliance professionals. For instance, in his capacity as head of the Household Equipment Commission at the CSTB, Breton initiated the establishment of guidelines based on both technical research and user surveys that were to be used by architects and industrials when building homes.[28] And, after a 1949 model home exhibit, at which visitors had completed thousands of surveys, Breton forwarded the results to his friends at *L'Architecture d'aujourd'hui* to publish, so that urban planners and architects might know what people wanted. (Or did not want, as in the case of collective laundry facilities, universally rejected by respondents.) In this sense, the Salon gave credence to the needs and desires of inhabitants, as defined by—and not for—the latter.

Dream Homes and Women's Work

As industrialists, designers, and architects presented new products and forms for literal and figurative consumption, Breton selected the most state-of-the-art projects to publicize as spectacles. Flashy, sensational exhibits, promoted on the radio and in newspapers, would attract a paying public, and Breton hoped that, once in the door, people might also stop to examine colorful mixers, learn about new cleaning products, or attend a lecture. Breton counseled exhibitors to make their stands as attention-grabbing as possible. In April 1951, he held a meeting with the organizers of the MRU pavilion, noting the poor attendance at their stand that year. Sensitive to visitors' preferences, he explained, "In the future, what you need is a general theme and, rather than presenting a series of unrelated projects, only a few well-explained plans should be proposed for the public's attention."[29]

As the 1950s progressed, Breton developed a formula of linking a popular magazine's patronage to an ideal dream home. In 1952, *Paris-Match* presented Marcel Roux's Ideal Apartment (see chapter 2), and in 1955, *Paris-Match* and *Marie-Claire* cosponsored the Electric House. The following year the magazines presented a house composed entirely of glass and steel, but this "Luminous House" was upstaged by *Elle*'s offering, the Plastic House, an innovative home made completely of plastic, which shocked visitors with its snail-like shape. Pierre Lazareff, head of the daily *France-Soir*, wrote of the Plastic House: "The appearance of the first house made entirely of plastic is comparable to the advent of print. The latter allowed the reproduction and diffusion of human thought, which is the source of civilization. This house will allow man—by the reproduction and mass distribution of a residence within his reach—to resolve the problem of family life, an essential step on the road to individual happiness, which is the goal of civilization."[30] Such grand futurist visions guaranteed visitors, and the SAM turned a profit each year.[31]

Yet, according to the accounts he penned of each year's SAM, Breton measured the scale of the Salon's success by the number of visitors, not by the profits made. For Breton, each attendee represented a pupil, and the goal was to teach as many students as possible. (Breton meant students in the literal as well as figurative sense. The Salon offered discounts for teachers bringing schoolchildren on field trips to the SAM.) If Breton employed a showman's tactics and plotted the Salon's growth, it was all to benefit the Salon's educative mission. Dream homes not only drew in visitors, but they offered a vision, as articulated by Lazareff, of a life in which health and happiness were guaranteed. While all-electric or all-plastic homes might lie years in the future, the rest of the Salon, by contrast, implicitly suggested to visitors that the happiness that such dream homes promised could be theirs in the present if they simply followed the Salon's advice and equipped their homes elegantly and efficiently.

The Salon took for granted that men were ultimately in charge of making large purchases (such as appliances or furniture) and deciding when to renovate heating and sanitary installations, but it also assumed that women played a significant role in leading them to these decisions and in allocating the budget for household expenditures. One issue of *Arts ménagers* describing that year's Salon illustrated its pages with photographs of a woman leading her husband around by the elbow or begging him on bended knee to buy her heart's desires. The text, narrated in the husband's voice, detailed the powers that his wife held over him: seduction, enchantment, laughter, but the "power that she deploys with the most mastery is purchasing power."[32] Confronted with explicit competition for household resources from automobiles, televisions, telephones, and other attractions of modern life, the Salon focused part of its pedagogical task on selling Mrs. Consumer, as it were. It lobbied women at all rungs of the social ladder to recognize the urgent need for home improvement; it tried to convince them not only that they deserved low maintenance, easy-care modern furniture and labor-saving home appliances, but that these were absolutely essential to the health, safety, and happiness of their families.

The Salon, no less than the MRU or Modernist architects, preached the gospel of rationalization. The following advice offered by the home furnishings store Logis moderne to SAM visitors epitomizes the fetish for planning and the rationalist zeitgeist of the 1950s: "Proceed methodically. Reflect in advance upon what particularly interests you. On this basis, establish a pathway [through the Salon] and follow it as much as possible. Begin by visiting the stands showing the kind of products you would like more information on. Don't lose time uselessly, and set an approximate schedule, in order to have, from your first visit, an impression of the whole."[33] Every object within the home was to be chosen and every action performed in the interest of economy, whether the savings be that of space, time, or effort. Economy did not mean doing without, however, and the SAM endeavored to identify for its public which products and practices were indispensable to modern living. While women were urged to acquire refrigerators or space-saving bunk beds for their children, they were also entreated, for instance, to dispose of their armoires. Critics complained about the "extra" work it took to clean these large pieces, especially since built-in shelving made them, from a functionalist perspective, redundant.

The modern home encompassed more than efficient furnishings and mechanical servants. The ambiance of the interior needed to be just right. Interiors had to be simultaneously comfortable and relaxing *and* lively and cheerful. One of the novelties introduced by the Salon during the 1950s was the explosion of bright color into domestic space. With the advent of new production techniques and materials, color became imperative in home decor. That bible of home economics, *L'Art ménager français*, offered a chart of complementary colors and advice on implementing color within the home. In 1952, the manufacturers of kitchen elements debuted countertops in turquoise and pale green Formica, and Philips's pink refrigerator (complete with a built-in radio in the door) was not far behind. Colorful furniture, appliances, and tabletops served both affective and rational functions; the combination of objects provided decoration without the accumulation of "useless" items like souvenirs, tchotchkes, or knockoff paintings.

The official endorsement of color had larger implications. Showing colorful kitchens at the Salon signaled the beginning of an end to the ideological dominance of hygienicism as the ultimate standard for homemaking. No longer did kitchens have to be hospital-white to spot the first sign of dirt and preempt the spread of disease. Instead, the technology of range vent hoods, which would whisk away greasy fumes, would permit a new standard, one of comfort and cheer, to emerge as the ultimate measure of a happy home. The shift to color also suggested a transition from universal standards to possibilities for individual expression. Tastemakers now encouraged families to mix and match colors to reflect their unique preferences and personality instead of outfitting their kitchens with spotless tiles and white appliances. The move away from white not only promoted a consumption mentality, therefore, but it also indicated the demise of a universal standard—hygiene—in favor of individuality and self-expression.

For the SAM, the advantage of rationalization was to promote well-being by maximizing repose. Rationalization was useful not as economy for economy's sake, a sort of moral austerity, but for minimizing the labor associated with maintaining a household. As the Breton brothers wrote in their manifesto, the household arts must "dominate the difficulties of a breathless epoch: for men and for women, too, leaving the home for work or busy with children, time is lacking, as is replacement help."[34] In the "breathless epoch" characterized by the "race to happiness," it was now the speed of change, not 1920s-style feminism, that appeared to threaten the rituals and the integrity of the middle-class family. For middle-class women, the Salon promised, just as it had in the prewar period, that the household arts would make their responsibilities within the domestic sphere pleasurable accomplishments in which they could take pride.

Though the reference to "replacement help" clearly indicated that the SAM was addressing its middle-class audience, the SAM also invoked the household arts as a means to a healthy, comfortable home that would ease the hardships of less fortunate women, protecting their children from illness and keeping their husbands at home. When Paul Breton inaugurated an exhibition of "Domestic Comfort and Equipment" in Marseille in 1956, he proclaimed the goal of the household arts to be "happiness at home, family health, the reward of women and mothers too long burdened with household chores, the abolition of slavery, freedom for mothers loaded with endless repetitive and tedious tasks.... Thanks to the kind of exhibits that we have just inaugurated, mirth, happiness, bloom, sun, and health will now penetrate, for the children's joy, into homes that until now were dark and forlorn."[35] Such rhetoric, as well as that in his remarks to the kitchen installers about their "social mission," locates Breton among the social reformers of his father's generation. Proselytizing for the domestic ideal, Breton believed that a clean, efficient home would elevate those who dwelled within and secure the foundations of family life.

Though women from working-class or rural households could not immediately acquire the labor-saving devices that were the cornerstone of the Salon's promise, rationalizing their movements or decorating with color were improvements women could make immediately with little expenditure. "All" that was required was effort—and a willingness to implement without improvisation the Salon's lessons. A 1950 issue of *Arts ménagers* featured a woman who had written in to share her experiences renovating an old kitchen in a rural home and to show off her new, modern kitchen. When the magazine ran photographs of the new kitchen, it also took the opportunity to inform its readership of the eight "errors" the homemaker had made, including "the dish dryer too exposed to view."[36] In the SAM's eyes, a woman was a foot soldier, not a general, in the battle to modernize the home, and the SAM wasted no energy trying to seduce her with sophisticated messages into modernizing. It simply, almost naïvely, told her what was expected of her.

It was the SAM's desire to teach women how to be happy—and better—housewives and mothers that made the participation of the home economists and the UNCAF representatives as essential to its success as the contributions of Modernist furniture designers or appliance manufacturers. In fact, right after the war, Paul Breton had been working toward the creation of a "French Institute of Household Arts and Domestic Economy." His plan never came to fruition, but the Salon consistently integrated lessons in home economics and parenting into its expositions and into *Arts ménagers*. The enormously popular Ideal Homemaker competition, for example, was not only about efficient homemaking, though participants were quizzed in written and oral exams about the best way to arrange items on a shelf, to clean a kitchen, or to get stains out of wool.[37] It was also about raising a family. In 1952, for example, competitors had to be able to identify signs of good health in a ten-month-old infant, to suggest ways in which to deal with a child who lied, and to explain how to "inculcate orderly habits in a child."[38] Given that the only candidates eligible for participation in the competition were teenaged girls enrolled in home economics courses (in both public and private schools),[39] this knowledge was understood to form the foundation for their future as modern mothers.

The Ideal Homemaker was the professional housewife par excellence. In March 1956, during the final phase of the national competition, attendees could watch a short play called "Rendez-vous chez Chrysale"; in the style of a Molière farce, the comedy took place in 1672 at the home of Chrysale, a "bon bourgeois," whose daughter was getting married that day. After a long elegy to various household items like plates and chairs, Chrysale predicts:

There will come a time when our learned women
will perform without shame the tasks of servants.
When no one will want to leave to other people
the care of looking after and nurturing her children.
When men, finally, before marriage
will be better informed about a household's needs.
Of a thrifty woman, they will understand the worth,
and will all want to have a Fairy [*Fée*] at home.[40]

The play didactically promotes the Salon's overarching message to both men and women, which was that the modern home was an important place for women to work, and that women who invested their time and energy (as well as any available financial resources) into homemaking could consider their efforts to be on par with those of any other professional. In this sense, the postwar discourses of the SAM offered a hybrid vision of modern womanhood, marrying the 1920s vision of the housewife as scientific home engineer to the older, nineteenth-century image of the "angel of the household," who was the moral and spiritual center of the home.

Women of all classes, therefore, had something to learn at the Salon. Martine Segalen has observed that consumer society requires education in order to develop the market for goods. Consumers must be convinced that inherited expertise has been made obsolete by new items; further, they must be made to believe that the novelties are indispensable and taught how to employ them.[41] Home professionals perceived habit to be Public Enemy Number One in the fight for modernity, and they worked hard to persuade women that, in the new France, their traditional realm of activity demanded new methods—and supplies. *Les Arts Ménagers*, a book by economist Jean Fourastié and his wife Françoise, argued that women themselves were hampering the development of the modern home by their inefficient habits and old-fashioned preferences. In the book's preface, the Fourastiés proclaimed: "At the same time that we want the men responsible for the development of the French economy to understand the social importance of the household arts, we want this little book to help women to rationally examine their work and to thus be able to maximize their limited resources." The authors then went on to encourage women to abandon their predilections for copper pots, which were no longer useful because they required too much work to polish, and parquet floors, which were only desirable in the *séjour* and should be replaced with linoleum in other rooms for easy upkeep.[42] As new materials like linoleum or Formica, or new goods, like electric ranges or frozen foods, appeared on the market, the Salon vaunted the ways in which these would improve and simplify women's lives. In so doing, they integrated innovative goods and novel practices into the traditional understandings of women's responsibilities. Embracing the new would put a woman on the path to domestic success. In Breton's formula, happiness in the domestic sphere was inextricably bound to the expenditure of energy: to successfully make the modern home, "all" women needed was a "taste for action, the longing to improve, the revolt against habits that level and make ugly."[43]

Paradoxically, as others have noted,[44] the labor-saving promises of household technology and rationalization thus depended for fulfillment upon an increased expenditure of women's time and energies, at least in the initial stages of a woman's apprenticeship in modern homemaking. A woman had to apply herself to learning new ways of working, implementing new products into her routine, and meeting the revised standards for housework. While washing machines, central heat, and refrigerators did provide real relief from onerous or time-consuming household tasks, discussions about easing women's burdens guaranteed that modern men would not be tasked with doing laundry in a washing machine or preparing dinner on an electric cooker. Although some men had participated and continued to participate in the work of the household, contemporary discourses construed this as "helping" women, whose primary responsibility it was to maintain the home. As the appliance manufacturers had observed, "[T]he woman, the mother, the housewife will never be able to forget that there is laundry to do, food to prepare or store, that the dishes pile up after meals, that one has to clean, dust, warm the place, and even save some time for relaxation. And this is fortunate. These occupations often deemed mundane have their root in the familial cell."[45] In other words, it was the very fact of women's housework and homemaking that kept the family together. If the postwar Salon departed from its prewar predecessor by expanding its vision to include working-class and rural families, it remained committed, in the interest of promoting the nuclear family, to preserving a gendered division of labor in the home.

Teaching Taste

Though the Salon was engaged primarily in cultivating a thirst for home improvement and renovation in the French, it also strove to impart a taste for the art of living to families of all income levels and class backgrounds. Breton faced a particular challenge, however, in presenting the new aesthetic as developed by Modernist designers and architects. First, the Salon had to convince the middle classes that a home based upon rationalist and functionalist design was elegant, distinctive, and the most fitting expression of their lifestyle; second, it needed to persuade working-class and rural families that aesthetics in general were as important to home improvement as indoor toilets and labor-saving devices. What motivated the Salon to accomplish these tasks was the belief, shared with the Modernist architects, that democratization meant that lower-class households aspired to social mobility and wanted the same things out of life as did their middle-class compatriots.

The SAM was aware that the modern home, marked by flat roofs or the new arrangement of rooms prevalent in the ISAI's 4Ps (see chapter 2), needed to be sold as much as the appliances that would go in it. To do so, it presented its visitors and readers with an ideology that privileged the natural and the biological and linked these inextricably with beauty. For example, in *L'Art ménager français,* architect Pierre Sonrel wrote that "we can be assured that our new abodes, as surprising as they may look to us sometimes, will be beautiful and agreeable to live in because they will be perfectly adapted to our essential human needs."[46] Similarly, the streamlined, spare forms of modern furniture, particularly when constructed from unfamiliar materials, had to be marketed. As we saw in chapter 2 with the example of the butterfly chair, advocates of the new aesthetic celebrated such furnishings on the basis of their ergonomic suitability to life as it was really lived. Modern furniture, in this interpretation, represented the triumph of authenticity over the deceptions of artifice. Hence, Breton argued that mass production was no longer a threat to good taste: "The mass-produced object does not bear the ugliness of useless, artificial, and overcharged objects.... A good piece of furniture, even mass-produced, is nowadays the fashion for everything that carries rational qualities as opposed to the defective Henri II cabinets, false Louis XV armchairs, and Renaissance cupboards with sculpted ornaments."[47] Imitations were not only more difficult to clean, but inherently dishonest. Consumers, he claimed, would be better off with simple, useful pieces that embraced the future instead of trying to mimic the past.

Meanwhile, the SAM lectured lower-income women about the importance of taste and the need to incorporate the new styles into their modest homes. "In spite of its apparent resignation, the soul is secretly hurt by the lowering vulgarity of things," Breton warned.[48] He fused the art of living to the duties of parenthood, declaring that furniture and other household goods must be chosen with care, for "they will give children the taste for the beautiful or the habit of ugliness."[49] An appreciation for art and culture was one of the traditional values that Breton thought the family was responsible for passing on, and the Salon's insistence that art accompany industry into the home reflected this. As families waited for Breton's (and others') efforts to lower the costs of mass-produced furniture to bear fruit, he hastened to assure them that they could beautify their homes right away with minimal expenditure: "Painting, wallpaper, clear [sic] curtains and light screens, such are non-costly artifices and pleasant decorations. Moreover a few flowers, a potted plant can animate most graciously the sternest homes. What is important is not so much the financial means. Is it necessary to have a large sum of money in order to decorate with exquisite taste a very modest home?"[50]

In fact, it was. Logis 49 ("The '49 Dwelling") was a model home whose presentation exposes SAM's aesthetic agenda. Logis 49 had its origins in "Logis 48," an exhibit prepared by the Parisian-area family allowances office (the Caisse centrale d'allocations familiales de la région parisienne, or CCAFRP) in the summer of 1948. Describing the exposition in a feature in the UNCAF's monthly publication, *Informations sociales*, the organizers clarified that the purpose of the exhibit was not "to present the ideal home of tomorrow, but to propose different means of making the best out of a minimum of habitable space—30 square meters for six people, which is too often the lot of today's families."[51] The exhibit and accompanying booklet aimed to offer a viable solution for families of very limited means to live efficiently and as comfortably as possible; they attempted to encourage rational living by proposing furniture that performed more than one function or that could be folded up out of the way or hidden. Logis 48 was decorated with items that the father of the family could build himself; the CCAFRP gave measurements for each piece as well as information about the materials, costs, and time needed to construct each item. Unwilling to put comfortable living off into the future—even a foreseeable one—the CCAFRP took a realistic approach to working-class families that emphasized inhabitants' agency in the here-and-now.

The imagined inhabitants of the Logis 48 were a family of six, composed of a mother and father, two young boys, and two babies. In the *séjour* (Figure 3.1) was the parents' bed, which doubled as a sofa during the day. Superposed twin beds slept two boys at night and also served as daytime seating areas; they were separated from the parents' bed in the evenings by a folding screen. In the dining area, a bench held toys inside and sat children at the dinner table. Captions accompanying the exhibition read, "The centralization of work precludes useless steps and gestures" and "Good hygiene is necessary for health"; these slogans spoke to the functionalist and hygienicist concerns of the CCAFRP's social workers and home economics instructors.

A year later, a feature in *Le Décor d'aujourd'hui* (Today's Décor) introduced the "Logis 49," a creation "inspired by" the CCAFRP's exhibit and which had been featured at that year's SAM. The article's author, Maurice Dufet, explained that the CCAFRP's home economics department had

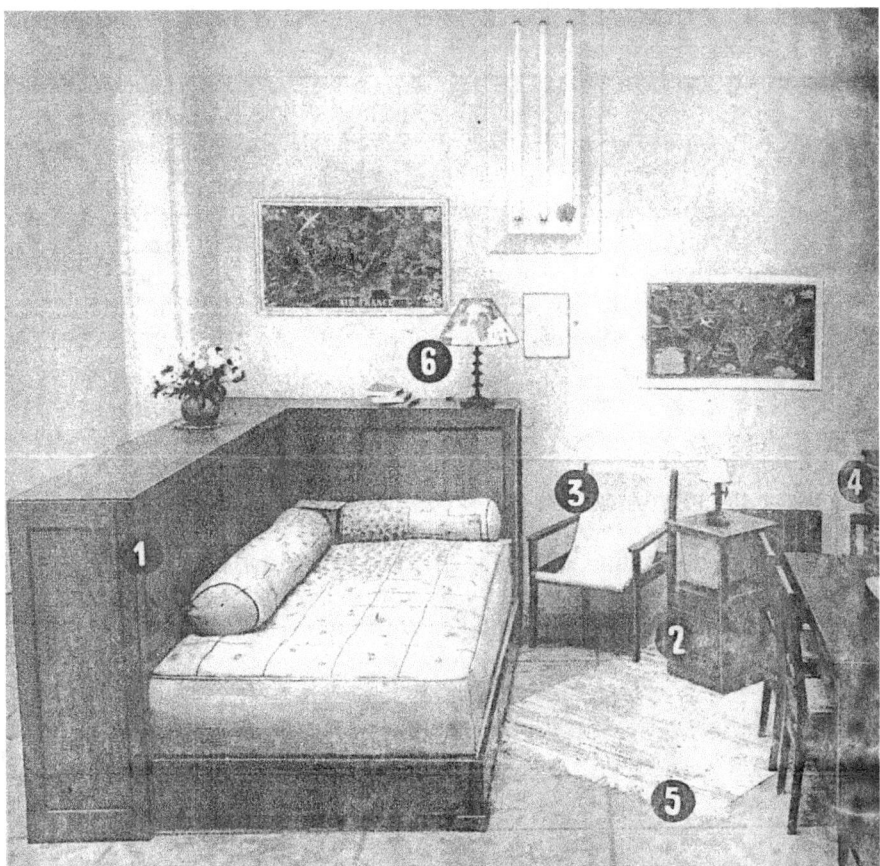

Figure 3.1. Photo of living room from the CCAFRP's Logis 48 exhibit, 1948. From Le Logis 48 brochure, 2 (Brochure is addendum to "L'Amélioration de l'habitat," *Informations Sociales* 19 [1 October 1948]); used with permission.

wished to illustrate, in built form, the conclusions of their technical studies of housework. That form needed to be considered not only in the light of ease, affordability, and convenience, but also had to be beautiful. "For that," Dufet explained, "it was necessary to ask a master of contemporary decorating for help."[52] In reality, the path to Logis 49 was not quite so straightforward.

Paul Breton had originally contemplated including Logis 48 in the 1949 SAM exhibition. He sent Jacques de Brunhoff, the director of *Le Décor d'aujourd'hui,* to see the exhibit at the CCAFRP's headquarters. In a letter to Breton, de Brunhoff wrote, "I could not hide my disappointment in noting that the exhibition, as marked by good intentions as it may be, had been created without the assistance of any of the masters who have been studying these difficult problems for years, problems to which this exhibit only offers, in my opinion, a timid and mediocre solution."[53] He opined that Logis 48 could only be shown at the Salon des Arts Ménagers if it were reworked by a decorator. Thus in 1949, Logis 49, created by Breton's UAM colleague Marcel Gascoin, appeared at the Salon. (It also later appeared in Paris at the town hall of the 15th *arrondissement*.)

The projected residents of Logis 49 (Figure 3.2) were a family of eight: two parents, an eighteen-year-old boy, two girls of twelve and eight, two young boys of six and four, and an infant. Several changes indicated that this family enjoyed a better socioeconomic situation than their Logis 48 predecessors. The furniture was to be purchased, not made at home, and the article in *Décor d'aujourd'hui* included the prices for specific items. The *séjour* no longer did double duty as a sleeping area; instead, the model apartment featured four bedrooms: a master bedroom for the parents and infant, a girls' room, a room for the younger boys, and a separate room for the oldest boy. Logis 49 thus assured the centers of individual activity that Marie-Anne Febvre had informed readers of *L'Architecture d'aujourd'hui* to be crucial for familial solidarity (chapter 2). The oldest boy's room included a desk, because he "needed to work in peace."

Figure 3.2. Photo of living room shown at SAM's Logis 49 exhibit, 1949. From Maurice Dufet, "'Logis 49'," 33; all rights reserved.

Since the school-leaving age until 1955 was fourteen years of age, it was clear that this eighteen-year-old doing his homework must have belonged to a family who did not need his salary to make ends meet. In other words, the residents of Logis 49 were no longer the CCAFRP's constituency, and the do-it-yourself approach that the CCAFRP had recommended to working-class families had been definitively rejected by the SAM as tasteless. The mass-produced designer creations lauded by the SAM were to be interpreted as infinitely preferable to *bricolage*; without the former, the home could not be wholly modern.

Indeed, there was a decidedly middle-class flavor to the democratic home. The Fourastiés' recommendation that labor-saving linoleum be used in all rooms *but* the *séjour*, where the parquet would still require waxing, the elimination of Logis 48's sleeping area from the living room of Logis 49, the "error" of exposing the dish dryer to public view: these lessons reinforced housing professionals' efforts to ensure that the aesthetic of the democratic home was not that of the lowest common denominator. Maintaining middle-class norms meant the rejection of multipurpose or labor-saving solutions already devised by real families facing constraints of time or budget. Preserving the parquet in the *séjour*, making sure that families had a dining area outside of the kitchen, featuring only award-winning furnishings by top Modernist decorators: these were all ways of protecting a French art of living, ensuring that rationalism for its own sake didn't strip the modern home of its charm or elegance. In establishing a design threshold, proponents of the modern home could, in the words of industry and energy minister Jean-Marie Louvel in the Salon's 1953 program, maintain the "French tradition of always combining aesthetics and progress."[54]

The art of modern living was therefore not as accessible as Breton claimed. Was it still attractive? Did the SAM win many converts to its vision of the modern family home? It is difficult to determine to what extent the Salon's audience embraced the new aesthetic. In 1957, for example, more people visited the antiques stands than Charlotte Perriand's Japanese House. And the departmental delegate from the Pas-de-Calais observed that, although Marcel Roux and Pierre Faucheux's "Ideal Apartment" for *Paris-Match* (see chapter 2) piqued visitors' curiosity, many expressed a desire to see a "less luxurious" model apartment that might be more in line with their pocketbooks. Moreover, the delegate noted that, on the whole, Parisians seemed more open to trading space for comfort (symbolized, for example, by the fully equipped lab kitchen), but provincial visitors preferred larger spaces to central heating or indoor plumbing.[55] It was precisely such preferences that the SAM, along with the MRU and Modernist architects, hoped to modify.

Though they did not adopt aesthetic counsel, product recommendations, or technical lessons uncritically, Salon visitors and *Arts ménagers* readers, regardless of class background, did look to the Salon for advice and information. Entry polls revealed that, in any given year, approximately one-fourth of the Salon's attendees came in search of specific information about a particular product or furnishing. Further, some people did eagerly embrace the SAM's presentation of the modern home; the archives of the SAM (and the MRU) are filled with letters from people inquiring where they could purchase the bunk bed, the kitchen cabinets, or even the model homes that had been displayed at the SAM. Departmental agents for the MRU staffing the ministry's stand at the 1952 Salon reported that Salon attendees constantly asked them for lists of approved manufacturers of prefabricated homes or recommendations about furniture and appliances; these visitors did want to invest in home improvement. The admission statistics alone testify to the public's interest; in 1950, for example, the SAM had over 1.1 million paying visitors, in spite of a mass transit strike. But while the SAM hoped to teach women the art of modern living, the lecture that attracted the most visitors each year was on flower arranging. This may have been disappointing to the designers of Formes Utiles, for example, who hoped to impart a taste for the spare forms and lean aesthetic of Modernist design, but it proved that women agreed, at least to a certain extent, with the Salon's assumption that a warm and artful ambiance could foster happiness at home.

Conclusion

If the interwar Salon des Arts Ménagers aimed to integrate technology and rationalization into the middle-class home, the postwar Salon aspired to disseminate new conceptions of home to an enlarged constituency. The new, modern home, the postwar Salon claimed, looked unlike either the working class's cherished bungalow or the middle class's urban apartment, and the Salon tried to convey to its public that it was precisely the unusual forms of new housing that permitted modern homes to guarantee happiness and self-fulfillment to all members of society.

Articulating this message, the Salon acted in concert with the MRU and Modernist architects, explaining to the French why new model homes were superior to familiar types of housing, and not simply the result of "making do" in times of scarcity or the "taste of necessity."[56] The SAM also asserted that home improvement was necessary to both family unity and personal success, establishing a domestic ideal around a vision of domestic space as the center of the nuclear family within which each member would be able to maximize his or her potential or *épanouissement*. The domestic ideal, promoting both individual and familial comfort and happiness, advanced the idea among the public that these were reasonable expectations for all French citizens.

This focus on the home that ignores the role of community action and civic relationships in an individual's life resonates with Kristin Ross's treatment of domesticity as an element of the "privatization of everyday life," and Elaine Tyler May's work on domestic "containment" in 1950s and 1960s United States.[57] Women who had once worked in factories or for the Resistance or brought in harvests during wartime, now, despite having acceded to the franchise, were asked to devote their energies not to serving the government, but to serving modernization via home improvement. For if the SAM celebrated a domestic ideal that found the modern home to be the primary source for personal development, family unity, and individual happiness, it reminded women that the home could only be such a site if created and maintained through their labor and enlightened consumption. That the SAM played such a key role in diffusing the norm of the perfect housewife, as exemplified by the Ideal Homemaker competition, can be seen in the fact that it was chosen as the site of a sit-in in 1975 by the Mouvement de Libération des Femmes (MLF) and the Mouvement pour la Liberté de l'Avortement et la Contraception (MLAC). The MLF and MLAC protested against the norm of individual washers, dryers, cookers, and dishwashers that ensured that women's work-weeks were always longer than men's, and they demanded collective facilities that would release women from their individual responsibilities for housework.[58] Though their demands went unmet, it is due, at least in part, to the efforts of these feminists that, as Segalen asserts, "the discourses of the SAM began to seem terribly old-fashioned,"[59] revealing as they did a paternalist and patriarchic vision of the modern home.

Nevertheless, during the 1950s the activities of the SAM spoke to the importance of the home in the national modernizing project. To be sure, this derived in part from the economic implications of home improvement; the purchase of both large and small consumer goods, furniture, paint, windows, and the like would certainly drove economic growth. Yet it would be a mistake to interpret the Salon's role solely as a motor for the development of consumer society. The Salon was about more than maximizing GDP; it was also about the revolutionary concept that one could maximize personal happiness. As the furniture store Logis moderne's slogan succinctly put it: "Modern home, joyful home; modern home, happy home." The Bretons' desire to better house the French, to have the French literally live better—more hygienically, more efficiently, and more beautifully, in planned communities and with more affordable options, put the SAM at the nexus of complex relationships between women and men, producers and consumers, and state officials and private actors. The Salon, more than any other actor, took on the role of evangelist, sermonizing to the French that modernization began at home. In so doing it added its voice to a chorus that increasingly sung the praises of the modern home as a privileged site for personal happiness.

Notes

1. Paul and André Breton, "Manifeste de l'art ménager," in their *L'art ménager français* (Paris: Flammarion, 1952), 13.
2. Daniel Parker, *La Famille en face du problème du logement* (Paris: Éditions Sociales Françaises, 1945), 37.
3. See Watson, "Housing Policy," 43; Bertheim, "Housing in France," 62.
4. Due to the war, the SAM did not take place during the years 1940 to 1947.
5. Because of the extensive activities pursued by the organizers of the Salon des Arts Ménagers in the domain of home improvement—activities that included but were not limited to the annual exhibition—I will generally refer to the SAM as an actor, but it was also, obviously, a site.
6. These include: Robert L. Frost, "Machine Liberation: Inventing Housewives and Home Appliances in Interwar France," *French Historical Studies* 18, 1 (Spring 1993): 109–30; Ellen Furlough, "Selling the American Way in Interwar France: *Prix Uniques* and the Salons des Arts Ménagers," *Journal of Social History* 26, 3 (Spring 1993): 491–520; Martine Segalen, "The Salon des Arts Ménagers, 1923-1983: A French Effort to Instil the Virtues of Home and the Norms of Good Taste," *Journal of Design History* 7, 4 (1994): 267–75; and, for the postwar period, Claire Leymonerie, "Le Salon des arts ménagers dans les années 1950: Théâtre d'une conversion à la consommation de masse," *Vingtième Siècle* 91, 3 (2006): 43–56 and Rebecca J. Pulju, chapter 5 of *Women and Mass Consumer Society in Postwar France* (Cambridge: Cambridge University Press, 2011). The primary work of substance on the SAM is Jacques Rouaud's two-volume history/memoir of the Salon, *60 ans d'arts ménagers* (Paris: Éditions Syros Alternatives, 1989/1993). Rouaud joined the SAM administration in 1960 and took over as its commissioner general after the resignation of Paul Breton, who had held the position since 1929.
7. Segalen, "Salon des Arts Ménagers," 268.
8. This and the following biographical information comes from Justinien Raymond, entry on Jules-Louis Breton in *Dictionnaire biographique du mouvement ouvrier français*, ed. Jean Maitron, vol. 11 (Paris: Les Éditions ouvrières, 1973); Furlough, "Selling the American Way," 503; Segalen, "Salon des Arts Ménagers," 269; and Jacques Rouaud, "L'esprit Arts ménagers," in *Les bons génies de la vie domestique*, exhibition catalogue (Paris: Éditions du Centre Pompidou, 2000), 51-58. For more on Breton, see the recent biography by Christine Moissinac and Yves Roussel, *Jules-Louis Breton, 1872-1940: un savant parlementaire* (Rennes: Presses universitaires de Rennes, 2010).
9. For more on Bernège, see Clarke, "L'organisation ménagère comme pédagogie."
10. Rouaud, "L'esprit Arts ménagers," 52–53.

11. For more on *la garçonne* and other tropes of interwar womanhood, see Mary Louise Roberts, *Civilization Without Sexes: Reconstructing Gender in Postwar France, 1917-1927* (Chicago: University of Chicago Press, 1994).
12. Furlough, "Selling the American Way," 511.
13. From the summary of the SAM's activities in 1951; yearly descriptions of and press releases for each year's SAM are available in AN, CAC 19850023/4.
14. This traveling exhibition was part of a campaign to increase awareness about desirable forms of housing. It involved the MRU, Gaz de France, Électricité de France, Charbonnages de France, Crédit Foncier de France, Fédération Nationale de l'Habitat, the Sous-comptoir des entrepreneurs, and the Société centrale immobilière de la Caisse des dépôts et consignations. The exhibit offered both films and a model apartment furnished by award-winning decorators. Approximately 13,000 to 20,000 people across France saw this exhibit each year. Documents pertaining to this group can be found in AN, CAC 19850023/121.
15. Paul and André Breton, "Manifeste de l'art ménager," 9.
16. The UNCAF was the national organization put into place as part of the welfare state in 1945 in order to oversee distribution of family allowances.
17. The titles of SAM lectures provide a nice sense of the evolution of everyday life. As time passed, the subjects of talks shifted from reconstruction to "Frozen Foods [1965]," "The Place of the Television in the Household [1965]," "Plastics and Food Products [1970]," and "Communication in the Couple: Divorce [1975]."
18. Admissions totals taken from yearly press releases reporting on the SAM, which are available in AN, CAC 19850023/4.
19. Admissions statistics here and following are derived from three entry polls: one conducted in 1948 by an organization called ETMAR, entitled *Les visiteurs vous parlent*, and two performed by the Contact-Express company in 1957 and 1961. They are located in AN, CAC 19850023/19. The socioprofessional breakdown is further complicated by the fact that the Etmar and Contract-Express groups did not use the same categories of classification.
20. Segalen, "Salon des Arts Ménagers," 267.
21. Cited in Segalen, "Salon des Arts Ménagers," 271–72. My emphasis.
22. "Le Salon des Arts Ménagers, aura-t-il lieu en 1951?" 2, in AN, CAC 19850023/4. The SAM had its habitual run that year at the Grand Palais, but Breton's ambitions for the Salon meant that it eventually outgrew the Grand Palais. In 1961 it moved to the Centre national de l'industrie et des techniques at La Défense.
23. The SAM was, for all intents and purposes, only open to French products until 1961. That year, the SAM became the Salon international des arts ménagers. Before 1960, customs regulations and protectionist quotas kept other European appliances out of France, but the 1957 Treaty of Rome had elaborated a three-year time period for phasing out the quotas and reducing duties. This launched a stiff competition in the refrigerator market between France and Italy, especially, known as the "affaire du froid."
24. "500 numéros de l'Officiel," *L'Officiel hebdomadaire de l'équipement ménager* 500 (September 1977), special issue: *Livre d'or de l'électroménager européen*, 108.
25. Cited in a brochure for a store called "Logis moderne," brochure 2 (dated February 1955), n.p.
26. Rouaud, *60 ans d'arts ménagers*, vol. 2, 163.
27. Perriand, *Une vie de création*, 278.
28. From the summary of the 1951 Salon in AN, CAC 19850023/4.
29. From minutes of meeting between MRU and Paul Breton, 17 April 1951, AN, CAC 19770660/7.

30. Rouaud, *60 ans d'arts ménagers,* vol. 2, 46.
31. This profit, in keeping with Jules-Louis Breton's wishes, continued to go into the coffers of the CNRS.
32. Jacques Bodoin, "Les Arts Ménagers," *Arts ménagers* 183 (March 1965), 114. Along similar lines, *L'Express* advised its female readers interested in acquiring household appliances to "let your husband talk about the mechanics [of the item] with the salesman, that way he'll have the impression that he's buying something for himself instead of doing it for you" ("Quelques conseils pratiques," 8 March 1957, 32).
33. "Logis moderne" brochure 2 (February 1955), n.p.
34. Paul and André Breton, "Manifeste de l'art ménager," 11. Segalen cites the date of this manifesto, incorrectly, as 1960. It appeared at least as early as 1952 and may have been delivered earlier as a speech.
35. Segalen, "Salon des Arts Ménagers," 271. Unfortunately, this citation is given in English without a reference to the original, but I am almost certain that "bloom" here is a translation of *épanouissement* and would be better rendered as "fulfillment."
36. "C'était une vieille cuisine," *Arts ménagers* 8 (May–June 1950): 20–25.
37. The hype surrounding each year's Ideal Homemaker was comparable to that given to the crowning of Miss America (particularly during the 1950s and 60s). The Homemaker was profiled in national and regional newspapers and interviewed on the radio.
38. "Le IVe Concours national d'Enseignement ménager," *Informations sociales* 4 (15 February 1952): 237.
39. According to Claire Duchen, home economics courses, originally the exclusive domain of working-class and rural girls, began to attract more and more middle-class girls in the postwar period (*Women's Rights and Women's Lives,* 82).
40. René Mongé, *Rendez-vous chez Chrysale,* a verse play performed on 3 March 1956 for the final competition of the eighth Concours national d'enseignement ménager (Paris: UNCAF, 1956), 18.
41. Segalen, "Salon des Arts Ménagers," 268.
42. Jean and Françoise Fourastié, *Les Arts Ménagers* (Paris: PUF, 1950), 12.
43. Breton, cited in Segalen, "Salon des Arts Ménagers," 273.
44. The canonical work on this dismal phenomenon is Ruth Schwartz Cowan's *More Work for Mother: The Ironies of Household Technology from the Open Hearth to the Microwave* (New York: Basic Books, 1983).
45. "25 ans d'évolution technologique et de progrès technique continus," in *L'Officiel hebdomadaire de l'équipement ménager* 500 (September 1977), special issue: *Livre d'or de l'électroménager européen,* 43.
46. Pierre Sonrel, "L'Habitation," *L'art ménager français,* 42.
47. Cited (in English) in Segalen, "Salon des Arts Ménagers," 273. A better translation would be "fake Louis XV armchairs."
48. Ibid.
49. Paul and André Breton, "Manifeste de l'art ménager," 13.
50. Cited (in English) in Segalen, "Salon des Arts Ménagers," 273.
51. "L'Amélioration de l'habitat," *Informations Sociales* 19 (1 October 1948), 1191.
52. Maurice Dufet, "'Logis 49': Une réalisation de Gascoin, suscitée par la 'Caisse centrale d'allocations familiales de la région parisienne'," *Le Décor d'aujourd'hui* 50 (1949), 35.
53. Jacques de Brunhoff, letter to Paul Breton, 17 June 1948, in AN, CAC 19850023/118.
54. Cited in Pulju, *Women and Mass Consumer Society,* 190.
55. See reports from the MRU's Délégation départementale du Loiret agents, dated 1 and 2 April 1952 and the report from the MRU agent from the Délégation départementale du Pas-de-Calais, dated 29 March 1952. All can be found in AN, CAC 19770660/7.

56. The phrase is Pierre Bourdieu's from *Distinction: A Social Critique of the Judgement of Taste* (Cambridge, MA: Harvard University Press, 1984), chap. 7.
57. See Kristin Ross, *Fast Cars, Clean Bodies: Decolonization and the Reordering of French Culture* (Cambridge, MA: MIT Press, 1995) and Elaine Tyler May, *Homeward Bound: American Families in the Cold War Era* (New York: Basic Books, 1999).
58. Rouaud, *60 ans d'arts ménagers,* vol. 2, 162.
59. Segalen, "Salon des Arts Ménagers," 268.

Part II

Mass Homes for a Changing Society

Chapter 4

HOUSING FOR THE GREATEST NUMBER
The Housing Crisis and the Cellule d'Habitation, *1953–1958*

> *Thus, as a phenomenon of compensation, the home and the family, at the moment when an anonymous world reduces them to their vital dimensions, make up for it by the breadth of their horizons.*
> —Architect Pierre Sonrel, 1955[1]

In January 1953, few could have predicted that the next twenty-four months would leave indelible and significant marks on the French urban landscape. Geopolitics and governmental crises dominated newspapers and parliamentary debates: the government of premier Antoine Pinay had just fallen, victim of the bitter struggles over the European Defense Community and the prospect of a pan-European military that would include an armed Germany. France's war in Indochina and the problems of the French Union also figured prominently in the nation's concerns. One might be forgiven for thinking that the government had its hands full with foreign policy. Nevertheless, scholars of French housing concur that the years 1953 and 1954 mark a turning point for state-funded housing projects.[2] During these two years, the focus of the Ministry of Reconstruction and Urban Planning turned from reconstruction to new construction. As it did so, it moved from the phase of experimentation that had characterized the MRU's early years, under ministers Raoul Dautry and Eugène Claudius-Petit, toward a commitment to a single vision of modern housing. Over the course of the 1950s, in response to the persistent housing crisis, the state mobilized financial, judicial, legislative, and technical apparatuses in order to produce large quantities of housing. Advocating mass production of construction elements and rationalization of building procedures, the state increased its financial investment in housing while simultaneously enlarging its role in determining the form of the final product, marginalizing the contributions of architects. Out of this process arose the clusters of apartment complexes known as *grands ensembles*, which still dominate metropolitan French landscapes.

This chapter looks first at the details of the housing crisis and links these to the ministry's choice of the *grand ensemble* as the predominant form of urban domestic space. Faced with the realities of the housing crisis, the ministry introduced "urgent" and "transitory" forms of public housing, establishing a hierarchy based on both total surface area and the degree of "comfort," as defined by technical installations and equipment. The second part of the chapter identifies the ways in which the shift toward "statistical architecture" — a term used by Bruno Vayssière to characterize the ministry's decision to favor designs and construction processes that minimized the time and cost of construction while maximizing output — changed domestic space. As we shall see, the procedures and regulations adopted by the state to stimulate construction also discouraged architectural innovation, fixed the dimensions and distribution of apartment plans, and whittled away increasing amounts of an apartment's inhabitable area.

Interestingly, rather than seeing in these changes a lesser version of the ideal modern home, many housing professionals trumpeted the virtues of the mass home, arguing that the *"cellule d'habitation,"* the standardized building block of the *grand ensemble*, was uniquely capable of guaranteeing personal happiness, and therefore worthy of both individual and collective investment. The third section of the chapter relates the advice the French gave and received regarding how to inhabit the *cellule* in order to maximize their satisfaction. Housing officials and architects argued that size did not matter in the rational, functional home: the well-planned layout of the average apartment would not only assure tranquility and family unity but save time and energy by minimizing the space requiring upkeep. Residents had a role to play as well, however; in order to render their homes fully functional, they were urged to invest in modern-style furniture and home appliances. The former would save space, while both would reduce labor. The combination of the functional floor plan, streamlined furnishings, and state-of-the-art appliances were supposed to yield the maximum from the minimum. This was the very essence of scientific management, and, in the *cellule* of the *grand ensemble*, rationalization, originally imported into the domestic sphere in the interwar period by architects, engineers, and home economists, finally reached its apex.

The Housing Crisis and the Rise of the *Grand Ensemble*

The dominance of the *grand ensemble* model can only be understood in the context of the acute housing crisis that still plagued France in the 1950s.

By 1954, 96 percent of the housing stock predated 1949; well over half of it dated before 1915, and more than a third had been erected before 1871.[3] The 1948 law on rents, which had unblocked rent controls (in exchange for the creation of housing allocations), aimed to spur private investment in housing, but by the end of 1953, less than 170,000 new units had been built without some form of state aid. The MRU's budget in 1948 had been 181 billion (old) francs; by 1952, that figure had grown to 400 billion.[4] However, as we saw in chapter 1, most of the state-financed efforts during this period prioritized reconstruction over new construction. Even where funding existed for new construction, the lack of necessary materials and skilled workers continued to hamper the industry; many of these resources had been diverted to the principal sectors of industry prioritized in the Monnet Plan. Consequently, the pace of production was slow; from 1944 to 1953, the state funded or helped to fund an annual average of only 22,000 new units, and total new construction averaged about 46,000 units per year.[5]

Both the mass press and architectural journals often observed that France still trailed behind construction efforts in Great Britain and, more rankling, West Germany. Between 1949 and 1951, these nations had built 885,000 and 591,000 new housing units, respectively, while France's output added up to an anemic 290,000.[6] This was due to structural, financial, and political factors. For example, in Britain the housing shortage dominated electoral campaigns in the elections of the late 1940s and 1950s in a way that it did not in France. Second, Britain turned to local municipal authorities, who had been accustomed to overseeing substantive numbers of social housing projects during the interwar period and were thus more prepared to launch new construction programs than the young MRU offices. West Germany, like the United States, placed more of the onus for new construction onto the private sector than did France, encouraging individuals and companies to build via tax breaks and other financial incentives. Moreover, West Germany did not have to contend with the financial drain of colonial and military engagements.[7] France had been fighting the Viet Minh in Indochina since 1946, a war that did not end until 1954. Independence movements in Tunisia and Morocco also depleted French manpower and resources during this period.

Demographic shifts continued to affect housing availability. The baby boom, immigration, and rural exodus put particular pressure on urban centers: between 1946 and 1954, the total French population grew by 2.3 million, while cities grew by 2.4 million. People crammed into any available form of housing: besides apartments (some shared with family or friends) or bungalow-style homes on the outskirts of towns, urban families also frequently lived in furnished rooms, and, as we saw in chapter 1, some still inhabited the shacks or wooden provisional barracks erected for disaster victims and laborers during and after the war by the MRU. (One suburban Parisian cluster of "temporary" shelters housing 83 families wasn't demolished until 1964.[8]) By 1954, over 14 million people lived in congested conditions. The situation was particularly acute in the capital, where 40 percent of Parisians suffered from an overcrowded home environment, and for working-class families, who composed 67 percent of the 14 million total cited above.[9] In the Parisian region alone, a survey of three thousand wage laborers revealed that 30 percent of them—and a full 50 percent of those younger than thirty-five—were looking for new places to live.[10]

While overcrowding remained the statistical index of poor housing, even those who did not have to inhabit cramped spaces still lacked many of the comforts that we now associate with an average home. According to the 1954 census, 38 percent of households did not have running water, 73 percent did not have a toilet in the home interior, and 90 percent had neither a bathtub nor a shower on the premises.[11] A 1955 national survey on housing, which, unlike the census, excluded farmers and agricultural workers, found that 31 percent of the non-rural population went without running water and 87 percent without a bathtub or shower. A greater number, though, had toilets inside their homes, though 46 percent still did not.[12] These statistics fared poorly in comparison to the United States and Great Britain. In England and Wales, the 1951 census revealed that only 38 percent lacked a fixed tub or shower in the home interior, while only 22 percent lacked an indoor flush toilet. In urban areas in the United States, by 1950 merely 13 percent did not have exclusive access to a toilet, while 17 percent of urban homes did not have a fixed shower or bathtub.[13]

Clearly, France remained "backward"; not much progress had been made on the comfort front since 1946, despite the creation in 1945 of the National Home Improvement Fund (FNAH), which granted home improvement loans at low interest rates.[14] In 1955, the SAM magazine *Arts ménagers* ran a feature entitled "I'm Modernizing My Apartment." It showed the renovation of a three-room flat in a central Parisian apartment building; five people, including Geneviève Dangles, a designer trained at the prestigious Arts Décoratifs institute, lived in the apartment. Before the renovation, the apartment had a parlor, a kitchen, a dining room, and one bedroom; because the flat housed three generations, however, two of the rooms served as bedrooms, with the young parents sharing a room with their child. Although the apartment had a rudimentary toilet, it had only one sink, in the kitchen, and no bathing facilities, nor any heating facilities beyond a large stove. The renovated apartment had a shower, a bathroom sink, radiator heat, a *séjour,* and two bedrooms. The article began by explaining that "one could not consider this apartment as a model one, and without the housing crisis, its occupants never would have undertaken such renovations."[15] To contemporaries, then, the housing crisis was not only a problem of homelessness or of overcrowded, working-class tenement housing—though it was that, too—but also a problem of inadequate, decidedly unmodern living conditions that extended across the nation and from one class to another.

Compared to apartments like the Dangleses', the Logeco housing created by Pierre Courant in the early 1950s *did* shine as model modern homes. In January 1953, Courant, an Independent known for his budgetary expertise, took the helm of the MRU from Eugène Claudius-Petit. By June of that year, following the resolution of another governmental crisis, both minister and ministry had changed, as new premier René Mayer named Maurice Lemaire, a Polytechnique engineer and member of the Union Républicaine d'Action Sociale Party, to head the rechristened Ministry of Reconstruction and Housing (Ministère de la Reconstruction et du Logement, or MRL). However, during Pierre Courant's brief six-month tenure, he had put into place several mechanisms whose impact on French housing would be significant. Adopting Claudius-Petit's proposed benchmark of 240,000 new housing units a year, a goal that would be integrated into the Second Plan (Deuxième plan de modernisation et d'équipement, the successor to the Monnet Plan), Courant acted to accelerate mass production in the construction industry. The measures he implemented are collectively known as the Courant Plan, which had three primary components. The first of these, and the one most pertinent to this chapter, was the creation of the "logements économiques et familiaux" (economical family homes), a unit known as the Logeco. Logecos were homes based on *plan-types,* model plans approved by the housing ministry and designed to facilitate mass construction. To procure land on which to build Logecos, the second element of the Courant Plan involved a law expanding the application of eminent domain to allow the state to expropriate territory for use by developers. Finally, to stimulate construction, the state would grant bonuses and favorable loan terms to builders using the model plans. To finance this aid package, the third aspect of the plan entailed the promulgation of a law requiring businesses with more than ten employees to contribute 1 percent of their total salaries to the state; this measure became known as the "1 percent *patronal.*"[16]

The Logeco model plan system aimed not only to spur industrialization of construction, but also to simplify the regulatory processes involved with building homes. Individuals who purchased and built from a model plan would be eligible for the same state aid that private companies or public HLM offices received. However, the Logeco program limited an individual's options. A family of three might have wanted to select a three-bedroom model plan, anticipating, perhaps, the eventual sheltering of elderly parents or future siblings for their only child, but regulations would have only permitted them to build a two-bedroom home if they wished to qualify for Logeco aid.

By June 1953, two books of model plans had been published; one was for detached homes, duplexes, and row houses, largely intended for use in small provincial towns, and another contained the plans for large apartment complexes, destined for urban and suburban areas. In November of the same year, the ministry devised a process whereby private companies could also propose a model plan for endorsement by its regulatory commission; if approved, a company could build according to its own model plan or sell copies of its plans to others.

Whereas in the late 1940s and early 1950s, the workers known as the Castors had built their own homes with sweat equity, model plans gave new financial incentives to individuals and local building societies. A nonprofit federation of building cooperatives known as Baticoop tried to maximize private housing initiatives. Using model plans, Baticoop chapters expanded construction, growing from the twelve thousand homes built by Castors between 1948 and 1952 to five thousand to ten thousand units built annually under Baticoop's auspices in the 1950s and 1960s. These units represented approximately 20 percent of all of the Logecos built in France.[17]

Accelerating the productive capacity of the housing industry at large was going to take time, and the particularly brutal winter of 1953–1954, marked by freezing temperatures and inclement weather, overshadowed the public sector's efforts to ease the housing shortage. Those inhabiting shacks and provisional barracks suffered enormously. At the end of December 1953, the MRL proposed an amendment to the construction budget to build emergency housing for homeless families and those living in shantytowns, but the amendment was rejected by Parliament. Then, in January 1954, right outside of Paris, a baby died from exposure to the freezing temperatures; the infant's parents, lacking the funds to rent a room, had taken to living in an abandoned bus. Less than a month later, a woman who had been evicted from her home froze to death on the Boulevard Sébastopol in Paris. The following day, the charismatic priest, former Resistance fighter, and ex-parliamentary deputy Abbé Pierre took to the radio airwaves to rally the French to the aid of the homeless in his still-famous "appel," or call: "My friends, help!" Abbé Pierre called for immediate donations of blankets and tents. (A rough parallel for this event in the twenty-first century would be the national mobilization of donations and offers of lodging in the United States after Americans, horrified, witnessed the plight of Hurricane Katrina victims on television.) After working to establish several emergency shelters and relocate homeless families in the short term, Abbé Pierre began a private HLM company. Charitable donations flowed in, including contributions from a program sponsored by the laundry detergent Persil. For every box top sent in during the "Fortnight of Solidarity," Persil donated ten francs to Abbé Pierre's Emmaüs foundation, which ultimately collected 27 million francs for the homeless.[18]

The media kept its spotlight on victims of the housing crisis. In March 1954, *Le Monde* published the account of a mother of three young children who committed suicide by gassing herself; she had been living with her husband and children in a tiny one-bedroom apartment for four years. The note she left behind to her family explained that, with her death, "the four of you will have more room."[19] The cumulative effect of these *fait divers* galvanized public opinion and put pressure on the state to allocate more funds to construction. Shamed into action by the private-sector efforts of Abbé Pierre to house the French, and sensitive to the public outrage accompanying the constant media accounts of the tragedies of homelessness, the government sponsored two measures to escalate production of new housing during the spring and summer of 1954. First, the state moved from simply lending money to public HLM offices, private entities, or cooperatives to becoming a developer itself. On 11 June 1954, largely at the instigation of François Bloch-Lainé, the former Inspector of Finances and at that moment director of the Deposits and Consignments Fund (Caisse des dépôts et consignations, or CDC), a public financial institution charged with the safeguard of public funds, the state created the Société Centrale Immobilière de la Caisse (Central Realty Company, or SCIC) as a subsidiary of the CDC. The SCIC, a public real estate company, turned the state into the largest housing developer in France; over the course of four years the SCIC broke ground on more than 60 percent of the public housing projects in Paris.[20]

The arrival in power of Pierre Mendès-France gave further impetus to an expansion of construction. During the governmental crisis in June 1953, when Parliament failed to approve any of the president's candidates for premier and the nation spent five weeks without a government, Pierre Mendès-France (known, like JFK and FDR, as PMF) nearly won investiture. His famous speech—"To govern is to choose"—won many adherents but failed to garner enough votes due to opposition to his foreign policies, particularly his desire to withdraw French troops from Indochina. By May 1954, however, the Viet Minh's dramatic defeat of the French army at Dien Bien Phu swung French opinion toward pulling out of Indochina, and the popular leader known as PMF finally won the premiership. In his investiture speech, having earlier invoked France's lag with regard to construction in Germany, and thereby contextualizing the slow pace of construction as yet another instance of French "decline," PMF asserted: "We must build, because the physical and moral health of workers and their families, as well as the mobility of the workforce, are indispensable to the functioning of our productive capacity. We must build because it would be inadmissible if the housing crisis were to remain unresolved and a whole generation were to be abandoned to discouragement, or even revolt, because it had to renounce the humble ideal that is the creation of a household." Increasing exports and construction, PMF then claimed, would serve national independence in the first case and social peace in the second.[21] PMF's speech reprised Liberation-era arguments that housing was inextricably linked to production, social reproduction, and the nation's moral health.

After having rejected the MRU's budget amendment at the end of 1953, in 1954 Parliament allocated an additional 10 billion francs to construction.[22] Yet this victory came at a cost: the fracturing of the Liberation-era promise of comfort for all. For, along with larger, and more direct, state investment in housing, the MRL now opted to produce a more minimal version of HLMs. In March 1954, it added a new category of housing, the "logement économique de première nécessité"[23] or LEN, to the HLMs and the Logecos. Similar to the bare-bones housing constructed on a smaller scale by the MRU to house those being relocated from slums in 1951 and 1952, LENs provided neither central heat nor hot water and were smaller than HLMs, but they did include bathroom and kitchen sinks, as well as indoor toilets and showers. By fall 1954, the LEN (now renamed "logement économique normalisé" or "standardized economical housing") had been incorporated into a program called Opération Million, which called for the construction of housing units for 1 million francs (approximately $2,860 in 1954), within a one-year time frame. Housing design again depended on the outcome of an MRL-sponsored competition, called Conception-Construction, whose goal was to yield even more model plans, this time to develop the mass production of the most basic level of public housing. Between the summer of 1955, when the winners were announced, and the end of 1957, the winning plans had been used in fourteen French departments and amounted to nearly twelve thousand units. In the spring of 1955, the LEN were joined by the "logement populaire et familial" or LOPOFA, which were slightly better equipped.

Both LENs and LOPOFAs were destined for the rental market, and they could be had at lower rents than could HLMs. After the passage of the 1948 law removing rent controls, even HLM rents had been climbing steadily, making them less affordable for working-class families, particularly those unaccustomed to allocating much of the household budget to rent.²⁴ The 1955 national housing survey found that, with regard to their proportion of the population at large, middle managers and salaried employees were overrepresented in HLMs, though wage laborers remained the highest percentage overall of total HLM inhabitants. The survey also discovered, however, that almost twice as many blue-collar workers lived in furnished rooms as in HLMs; the number was about even for salaried employees, but middle managers were over five times as likely to live in an HLM than in a furnished room.²⁵

The introduction of LENs, LOPOFAs, and Logecos to HLMs meant that social housing began to return to the articulated hierarchy of prewar HBM housing (see chapter 2). Just as the Henri Becque–style apartment had been designed for families unaccustomed to living hygienically, so too did the LENs reflect the presumption that families moving into them from slum housing would fail to use or even ruin unfamiliar elements like elevators, hot water heaters, automatic garbage disposals, or thermostats. Thus, for the LENs, MRU officials recommended that only hookups for hot water heaters be provided, so that residents could install them on their own if they so desired.²⁶ Discourses prevalent at the Salon des Arts Ménagers about lessening women's burdens had been eclipsed at the ministry by a desire to house everyone as soon as possible.

Indeed, LENs and LOPOFAs derived from the aim of replacing the provisional barracks built by the MRU whose upkeep was now becoming quite costly, but whose residents had nowhere else to go.²⁷ For such families, even the LENs, with their sinks and tubs, represented a step on the road to the modern home, particularly in contrast to the conditions in unrenovated private apartments, shabby furnished rooms, and shantytowns. Jacques Dreyfus, who worked in the 1950s and 1960s as an engineer for the CSTB, later interpreted indoor plumbing, the lower limit of comfort, as the state's effort to inculcate a taste for modern living, to teach inhabitants to need what they didn't know they wanted, and thus, eventually, to be willing to pay higher rents for better equipped spaces.²⁸ In this sense, LENs and LOPOFAs were "starter homes", training the French to dwell in modern ways.

Given that the housing ministry had opted, in the interest of accelerating mass production, to reduce both the size and the standard of comfort of some of its housing, it seemed self-evident that the more one could save on land and infrastructure expenditure, the more homes one could build for the available amount of resources. Building high-rise and long, thin strips of housing—the collective housing system known as "towers" and "bars"—thus came to seem like the obvious solution to the housing crisis. Towers and bars could be built on relatively small parcels of land, unlike the larger swaths necessary for tract developments of detached homes. Furthermore, the construction processes involved facilitated the multiplication of units. The *grand ensemble* was made possible by a system of construction whereby cranes and materials could be moved along a railway line built on site (called the *"chemin de grue"*), which determined the rectilinear aspect of most housing projects. With media publicity and public pressure percolating about unhealthy, overcrowded living conditions, and with housing finally acknowledged as a priority of modernization in the Second Plan, whose production targets were set at 240,000 units annually for the years 1954 to 1957, "urgency and cheapness took priority over everything else."[29]

Figuratively speaking, the ground had been prepared for the shift to dense models of collective housing at the very beginning of the 1950s by Eugène Claudius-Petit's endorsement and celebration of modern housing projects like Le Corbusier's Cité Radieuse in Marseille and Eugène Beaudouin's Cité Rotterdam in Strasbourg (see chapter 1). Architect Eugène Beaudouin had completed the eight hundred housing units called for in the Strasbourg program in a year and a half, delivering the complex exactly on time to the prefect of the Bas-Rhin.[30] Such efficiency impressed administrators and housing professionals. Furthermore, as heralded by Claudius-Petit and other Modernists, the *grand ensemble* appeared to offer a morally superior approach to urban planning and housing. In other words, the *grand ensemble* was understood to be a new alternative to the anarchic collection of shacks and bungalows that had sprung up in the interwar period. When asked, decades later, why planners elected for the *grand ensemble* over the individual detached homes for which the majority of the French had expressed a preference in the 1947 INED survey (see chapter 1), François Bloch-Lainé replied that they had based the decision upon their own prewar experience: "We criticized the proliferation of suburban bungalows, where life did not appear to us to be *a priori* more joyful than in tall apartment buildings. ... The people of my generation were impressed by his [Le Corbusier's] sketches of the Cité Radieuse as a reaction against the disorder and clutter of urban space."[31]

Though the turn to Logeco model plans had impinged upon their freedom to innovate, Modernist architects shared this vision of collective housing as morally superior to individual detached homes. André Hermant, echoing the claims of his peers who had argued the aesthetic merits of standardized architecture a decade earlier, proclaimed: "In this unified framework [of identical *grands ensembles*] individual freedom and fulfillment [*l'épanouissement*], in the familial environment, will be protected, because the unity of language, a condition of harmony, does not exclude— on the contrary—the variety of expression. ... And so much the better, for the best human development, that the diversity of personalities manifests itself by aspirations, by a culture, by individual activities, instead of by an artificial and illusory originality, affirmed by extravagant and excessively personalized homes."[32] Hermant's objection to "excessively personalized" homes rejected the notion of domestic space as a commodity or signifier of lifestyle; anonymous spaces would, if anything, encourage the individuals who dwelled within to develop their minds, to exercise their creativity, to focus on their literal selves instead of their façades.

Modernist architects like Hermant thus embraced the *grand ensemble* with high hopes and few complaints. Two years after his former partner Eugène Beaudouin had completed the Cité Rotterdam, Marcel Lods led the construction of a project more than twice its size: 1,500 Logecos, begun in 1955, dispersed in a series of five-story buildings at Marly-le-Roi, on the western outskirts of Paris. In 1955 and 1956, Émile Aillaud began to assert his place in the suburban Parisian landscape with 1,656 apartments at Les Courtillières at Pantin, featuring seven towers and a long, undulating bar called "The Serpent"; he also launched the 1,500-unit Cité de l'Abreuvoir in the neighboring commune of Bobigny. Bernard Zehrfuss oversaw the erection of the two tremendously long bars of Haut-du-Lièvre, outside of Nancy in 1956: 3,388 units, predominantly HLMs, housed 12,500 people. The previous year, Henri Delacroix and Clément Tambuté had begun the famous four thousand HLMs at La Courneuve and, with Roger Boileau and Jacques-Henry Labourdette at the architectural helm, the SCIC broke ground for the epic mass production of Sarcelles. These enormous projects got underway with the help of a 1955 law, which accrued even more power to the state; it mandated that the housing ministry—instead of a municipal authority—could grant a building permit if it was for a housing complex of 250 or more units.[33] In the same year, the state reinforced its commitment to the high-rise formula by increasing by 5 percent the maximum allowable cost of each LOPOFA or HLM if the units were to be part of a complex with more than five inhabitable stories.[34] Such directives and incentives added up to a clear mandate for collective housing.

The sea change was reflected in the cover of the *Petit Guide du Logement*, a brochure issued by the National Building Federation and the FNAH to educate readers about building and renovating their homes and to increase awareness of opportunities like the housing allocation, the FNAH, and the Logeco. In 1950, the brochure's cover featured children playing on the patio of their Noisy-le-Sec-style bungalow, a one-story, reinforced concrete prefabricated unit with a pitched, tiled roof. Their mother, smiling, leans out of the window, whose shutters are flung open, and trees, grass, and bushes can be seen to surround the patio. At the beginning of the 1950s, such prefab homes symbolized modern lodgings; by 1957, however, despite the fact that the guide contained essentially the same information found in its predecessor, this time a looming, ten-story *grand ensemble* was chosen to grace the *Petit Guide*'s cover. In front of the complex, there were some bushes and a single tree. A few windows were open, but no humans were evident, although a couple of cars could be seen parked in front of the complex. The changing iconography of the modern home marked the housing ministry's definitive vote for collective housing and encapsulated the swiftness with which, once will and funds had been established, the ministry and the government moved.

The *Cellule d'Habitation*

André Hermant's analogy of the relationship of the linguistic system to self-expression hints at a perceived need to soothe worries about the loss of individuality in the *grand ensemble*. The standardized, repetitive façade of the *grand ensemble* was unfamiliar and off-putting to the French, and so Pierre Agard attempted to allay fears about the new form in the intellectual journal *Esprit*, using a metaphor the French were sure to appreciate: the *grand ensemble*, he observed, comprised "veritable tiny houses incorporated into a vertical structure, like so many different bottles in the same wine rack."[35] As architects intoned time and again, at the heart of the apartment complex, indeed, of the successful urban plan, was the apartment. The apartment was the "cell," the core element that composed the floors that composed the buildings that composed the projects that composed the residential section of the planned city. Like a biological cell, the *cellule* apartment was the building block of the *grand ensemble* body. It was also where the "different bottles" would be able to develop their individuality to the fullest, a privileged site for *épanouissement*. (Though it seems unbelievable, the jailhouse connotations of the word "cell" went unmentioned.)

The first book of Logeco model plans was published in June 1953 with a preface by minister Pierre Courant. Anticipating the objections of architects to further constraints on the free exercise of their profession, Courant wrote, "Great freedom subsists, moreover, since the model plans impose neither the exterior architecture nor a single mode of construction, but limit themselves to specifying the interior dispositions of the premises with the normalization of a certain number of accessory elements like communicating doors."[36] Courant was unwittingly challenging a basic tenet of Modernist architecture by reassuring architects that their contribution to Logeco design, in a sense, was the composition of a beautiful façade, traditionally a hallmark of an architect's talent and thus a symbol of the bourgeois Beaux-Arts system against which Modernists had rebelled. The micromanagement of the interior demonstrates the state's interest in the home as a vector for modernization, but its position on apartment complexes also points to its desire to use domestic architecture as a vector of renewal and rebirth. Adrien Spinetta, the ministry's director of Construction, who introduced the term "*grand ensemble*" in an issue of *L'Architecture d'aujourd'hui*, thus rendered the architect's task in more flattering terms, appealing directly to the architect's conception of his vocation: "The use of norms [of surface area and equipment established for the *grand ensemble*], the repetition of forms do not at all contradict freedom of expression. It is not sufficient to give a roof to each French family; what shelters the family and what surrounds it must contribute to the elevation of the human being."[37] As we saw in chapter 2, Modernists proposed that it was precisely in designing a domestic space that would promote individual self-fulfillment within the framework of a standardized structure that the architect would be able to display his artistic competence and genius.

Out of hundreds of projects, the MRU committee selected the works of twenty-seven architects for the first two books of model plans; the majority were Modernists, including Héaume, Persitz, and Zehrfuss, all winners of previous MRU competitions (see chapter 1). Model plans were evaluated on the basis of a ten-page document, which specified floor plan dimensions and guidelines for distribution and "habitability." Overall, plans were judged based on their applicability as a model, their functionality, and their aesthetic qualities.

The MRL conceived of the *cellule* essentially as a cluster of specialized rooms linked together with two principles in mind: "The relative position of rooms must satisfy a double condition: (1), reduce to a minimum the routes taken most frequently by the occupants inside the home; (2), assure to family life the potential for gathering at certain times (meals, communal entertainment) and for isolation at other times (nighttime activities, bathing, absorbing work)."[38] The instructions for evaluating prospective model plans called for the proximity of the kitchen and the *séjour* (note how quickly the term has been adopted; terms like "living room" and *salle commune* have been left behind) and for a dining nook in the *séjour*. They also mandated the independence of bedrooms; at most, bedrooms could only open onto the *séjour*. The *salle d'eau* (a space for laundering and bathing, separate from the toilet) had to be proximate to both the kitchen and the bedrooms, while the toilet had to be in its own tiny room; moreover, it could not lie off of any other room other than the living room–dining room area. The directives continued to discourage the creation of any space that might resemble a Sundays-only-style parlor, "although this tendency [of space usage by inhabitants] is widespread."[39] Suspicious of solutions that seemed to work only on paper, the MRL began to micromanage the design of model plans, specifying that architects should ascertain that the door to the toilet was not positioned in such a fashion that a "brusque" opening might cause an accident; furthermore, they should ensure that "essential" pieces of furniture could be placed in the rooms, tracing these onto the plan with their exact measurements.[40] Architects, in the face of such specificity, might have been surprised that even the façade of the apartment complex had been left to their discretion.

Two years later, in October 1955, Roger Duchet (founder of the Centre National des Indépendants, a liberal right political party), who had taken up the MRL portfolio in February 1955, dealt a further blow to architects by issuing a decree creating the National Construction Regulations (Règlement de la construction), complemented in November and December by the Handbook of Minimum Technical and Functional Instructions (Cahier des prescriptions techniques et fonctionnelles minima, or CPTFM). The CPTFM applied to two categories of rental HLMs in apartment complexes, the HLM A (also known as the LOPOFA) and the HLM B ("regular" HLMs). In the interest of further simplifying the planning and construction of HLMs, these regulations fixed everything from thermal requirements to minimum electrical requirements to the ceiling heights (2.5 meters). The instructions regarding room size and layout most constrained architectural innovation. Master bedrooms had to be at least nine square meters; other bedrooms (presumably for children) could be as small as seven square meters. The toilet could neither open off of the kitchen nor lie off of any of the main rooms, including the *séjour*.

Between Logeco model plans, Opération Million model plans (many of which were also used for the construction of LOPOFAs), the National Construction Regulations, and the CPTFM, architects who were interested in social housing found that the housing ministry and the SCIC had largely resolved the fundamental questions of the "cell" for them. When Jean Prouvé, the engineer from Nancy who had built a modern prefabricated home at Noisy-le-Sec (chapter 1), did try to come up with an imaginative solution to the housing crisis, he collided with a system that had already decided upon the "one true way" to build quickly and cheaply. At the request of Abbé Pierre, Prouvé had designed a freestanding, prefabricated house that could be erected in a mere four days. Outside the 1956 Salon des Arts Ménagers, where the stars of the show were the sensational, snail-shaped Maison en plastique and the gleaming Maison lumineuse made entirely of steel and glass, Prouvé's Maison des jours meilleurs (Better Days House, Figure 4.1) stood humbly on the Quai Alexandre III.

Calculated to fall within the surface area requirements of the Courant Plan and costing 1.5 million francs, the house met the guidelines of the Logeco program. Its design eliminated hallways completely and used a free plan around a central core, itself a prefabricated element containing

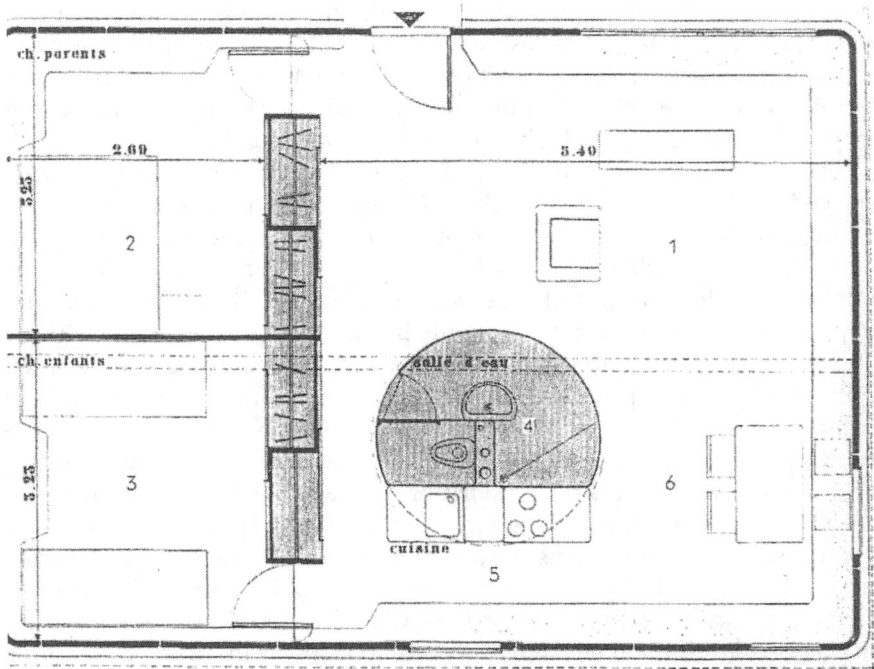

Figure 4.1. Floor plan of Jean Prouvé's Maison des jours meilleurs, 1956. © 2013 Artists Rights Society (ARS), New York / ADAGP, Paris.

the kitchen, toilet, and bathing apparatuses. Room dividers doubling as closets and shelving and an interior ledge running the entire length of the house and serving as a space for storage and seating reduced furniture needs to a minimum. Upon seeing the Better Days House, Le Corbusier called it "the most beautiful home that I know, the most perfect means of habitation, the most perfect built object."[41] Prouvé, well aware that the cost of land in and around urban centers precluded an official policy of developments composed of freestanding houses, had wisely drawn up plans for the adaptation of the model for four-story or taller apartment buildings.

In the end, only three prototypes of the house were produced. The technical services of the MRL refused to approve the house as a model plan because of the central position of the kitchen and sanitary elements.[42] The 1955 National Construction Regulations prohibited such a disposition, and although the CSTB had the power to grant exceptions to the rule, they rarely did so. They thought the layout unhygienic because neither the kitchen nor the sanitary installations would have access to light or direct ventilation via windows. Moreover, from the MRL's viewpoint, the position of the kitchen and bathroom in the midst of the living area was thought to detract from the aesthetic quality of the family room. It is noteworthy that norms, these ostensibly technical determiners, existed to protect not only contemporary notions of hygiene, but also a certain dwelling experience in keeping with elite conceptions of tastefulness.

The example of the Better Days House demonstrates how even experienced housing professionals like Prouvé, who had been trying for two decades to combine techniques of mass production and Modernist principles to create livable, low-cost housing, ran up against a system of administrative, technical, and financial limitations that could dam rather than promote innovation. Complaints began to appear frequently in the architectural press, blaming the government, builders, and an uneducated public and press for precluding architects from finding the highest quality solutions to the housing crisis. Architects chafed, too, at the primacy of the technical services and what they saw as a campaign to replace architects with engineers.[43] As Bernard Zehrfuss later admitted, innovation in the arena of domestic space was no longer at the top of the architect's agenda: "You had to play the game, because the goal was to improve construction techniques. The point was to meet criteria of economy and speed."[44] Despite Spinetta's affirmation that the architect would be free to exercise his *métier* within the *grand ensemble* format, ever-proliferating constraints meant that this was far from the truth.

Zehrfuss was not paranoid. François Bloch-Lainé of the CDC and his director of the SCIC, Léon-Paul Leroy, had repeatedly reminded concerned parties that "use value" was the key determining factor and that "aesthetic considerations" would have to take a backseat.[45] Upon taking the helm of the SCIC, Leroy, an engineer, had toured the MRU's experimental projects and a number of modern housing complexes in Scandinavia, but he had little use for Modernist architects like Le Corbusier and refused to appoint design experts to oversee the work of the individual architects hired by SCIC, much to the chagrin of the housing ministry. The confidence the SCIC had in its own processes and values and its disdain for notable Modernists of the day appalled former minister Eugène Claudius-Petit. He reproached Leroy at a meeting in 1957, complaining that the SCIC and the SCET (the Société centrale pour l'Équipement du territoire, the SCIC's partner agency charged with land use management), would produce only a "dehumanizing urbanism that neglects architecture in favor of profit."[46] Like Zehrfuss, Claudius-Petit saw clearly: one of Leroy's explicit objectives was to reduce architects' scope and autonomy, which Leroy saw as driving up costs and slowing down production.[47]

Indeed, the SCIC systematically ramped up production. Historian Paul Landauer cites the example of the community of Mourenx, in the

Pyrénées. Where Jean Maneval, the first architect assigned to the project, had planned for five groupings of three hundred units to promote community spirit and identification with the neighborhood, Philippe Douillet, who took on the project at Léon-Paul Leroy's request, replaced that plan with three groups of nine hundred units. The definition of the community took second place to the "familial sphere of the apartment," and the SCIC could offer 2,700 of Douillet's units to the rental market, nearly double that of Maneval's original plan.[48] Clearly, the fears and protests of Modernist architects were not unfounded, and Claudius-Petit's objections fell on deaf ears, as the SCIC continued to pursue "housing for the greatest number." Examples like these serve to remind us that Modernists are not always the villains of the postwar housing story; they, too, fought to protect the quality of the dwelling experience for the pioneers moving into mass modern homes. The roles were shifting and changeable: housing heroes became ogres, and enemies of the people's housing morphed into their champions over the course of the Trente Glorieuses.

Inside these apartments, the net effect of model plans, their accompanying specifications, the ministry's regulatory mechanisms, and SCIC's entry into the mass construction business was the creation of a floor plan that remained, for all intents and purposes, fixed for a decade. The quintessential 4P as "cellule d'habitation" appeared thousands of times over in the *grands ensembles* of the 1950s and 1960s. Consider two typical examples of floor plans for four-room "cells" (Figures 4.2 and 4.3):

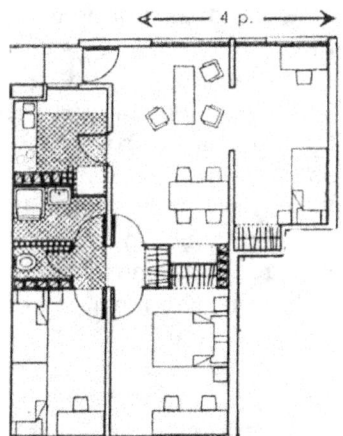
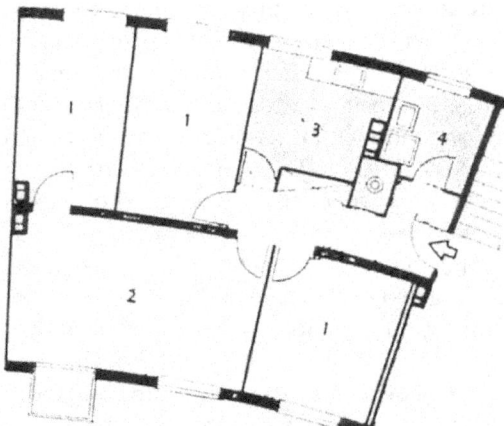

Figure 4.2. Georges Candilis and Guy Brunache's Opération Million plan. Used with permission from Takis Candilis.

Figure 4.3. Émile Aillaud's plan in a "bar" at the Cité de l'Abreuvoir, Bobigny. Used with permission from Fabio Rieti.

The plans shared—with countless others—a number of common features. Hallways have been eliminated or reduced to a bare minimum, although all retain a tiny, token entryway, thought to be necessary to help residents and visitors transition from public to private space. The apartments have laboratory kitchens, and the largest space is the living room–dining room area. The "services" of corporeal care and meal preparation are clustered together; one no longer finds the bathrooms in one section of the apartment and the kitchen in another, as in Roux-Spitz's Nantes apartments or those of Marcel Lods in Sotteville (see chapter 2). This has, in the case of the three-bedroom apartments, decimated the tidy distribution of the floor plan into "day" and "night" functions. While the two-bedrooms were often able to retain this separation, the addition of a third bedroom usually required that at least one bedroom open onto (or, in the case of simpler plans, be carved into a section of) the living room–dining room area. To preserve intimacy, none of the bedrooms communicated with each other.

This functional "cell" changed little to house larger families, adding on more bedrooms and another bathroom sink if the apartment was five rooms or larger. The kitchen stayed the same, since, as André Hermant explained, the nature of the work performed within did not change, whether the family consisted of two or of eight individuals.[49] This was not, actually, true, and in practice, the laboratory kitchen deprived the housewife from getting much assistance with meal preparation from other family members. The relentless focus on the individual eclipsed alternative visions of family life and rhythms. In any case, few apartments capable of housing eight people were included in most apartment complexes. Logecos ran, in general, from one to four bedrooms, with a concentration of two- and three-bedrooms, and in December 1955 Duchet's regulations limited the average apartment size in any one apartment complex to 3.5 rooms, excluding studios. Five- and six-bedroom apartments were rare, reflecting a common belief that children should share rooms and a new mentality that an ideal family size was three (or four, maximum) children. Housing design helps us to see that pronatalist policies were not intended to encourage some families to have many children but to support a majority of families to expand from one or two to three or four children.[50]

While the layout of the cell became more fixed, its size did not. As the 1950s progressed, the inhabitable surface area of apartments shrank. The table below illustrates the changes. The 1953 move to statistical architecture resulted in the slashing of surface areas, and Logeco size restrictions produced a scenario whereby an individual family building its own Logeco and benefiting from state subsidies could be living in a smaller home than a family of the same size renting an HLM apartment.

Table 4.1. Evolution of Surface Area Allowances for Public Housing, 1947–1955 (measurements given in square meters)

	1947 HBMA*	1951 HLM†	1953 HLM	1953 Logeco	1955 Lopofa	1955 HLM B
2P	44–50.6	40.5–49.5	34–45	34–45	34–39	39–45
3P	57–64.9	54.2–62.7	44–62	44–57	45–51	51–57
4P	71–80.3	64.6–74.8	53–74	53–68	55–61	61–70
5P	86–96.8	77.9–90.2	63–90	63–82	65–73	73–85

* HBMBs were allotted two more square meters each.

† This category covers HLMAs and HLMBs; while the measurements were now the same for both categories, HLMBs came with central heating.

Sources: Arrêté, 19 December 1947, "Arrêté fixant les caractéristiques auxquelles doivent satisfaire les immeubles construits au titre de la législation sur les habitations à bon marché" (CAC 771096/1); Arrêté, 4 May 1951, "Arrêté fixant les caractéristiques auxquelles doivent répondre les ensembles construits au titre de la législation sur les habitations à loyer modéré" (CAC 771096/1); Arrêté, 17 March 1953, "Caractéristiques auxquelles doivent répondre les logements économiques et familiaux" (*Journal Officiel*, 18 March 1953, 2562); Arrêté, 30 December 1953, "Normes des maisons construites dans le cadre de la législation sur les habitations à loyer modéré et les plafonds de prêts susceptibles d'être accordés par l'État pour ces opérations" (Magri, *Logement et reproduction de l'exploitation,* 200); Arrêté, 23 November 1955, "Normalisation des caractéristiques techniques des habitations collectives à loyer modéré à usage collectif" and circular of 29 November 1955, "Circulaire 55-155 relative à la normalisation des caractéristiques des habitations collectives à loyer modéré à usage collectif. Cahier des prescriptions techniques fonctionnelles minimales. *Journal Officiel,* 18 December 1955 (both published in Journal Officiel, *Habitations Collectives à loyer modéré à usage locatif: Normalisation des caractéristiques* [Paris: Impr. des Journaux officiels, 1955], 1).

In 1955, Duchet did raise the minimum norms slightly, but the maximum norms shrank dramatically. The evolution in the kind of modern home that the ministry hoped to provide to the citizens of the Fourth Republic can be seen by comparing the 1947 and 1955 norms. The 1955 version of the "best" HLMs, the HLMB, was now smaller than its HBMA predecessor, marking the shift from utopia to reality. In 1946, MRU director of Construction André Prothin had determined space to trump technical installations and labor-saving devices when it came to inhabitant comfort, but by 1955—in the race to build "quickly and cheaply," in Bloch-Lainé's words[51]—the equation had been reversed.

Despite continued assaults upon their ability to freely design interiors, many architects endorsed the *cellule* as the mode of housing most appropriate to modern life. Waxing sociological in the *Encyclopédie française* volume on "La civilisation quotidienne (Everyday Civilization)," which appeared in 1955, architect Pierre Sonrel located the origins of the size and shape of the modern home in the larger transformations that had taken place in French society. According to Sonrel, the growth of interest in activities such as scouting reflected urban inhabitants' desire to escape the dirty, overcrowded, chaotic city. The modern home served the human urge to commune with nature by replacing tenement walls with large picture windows and inviting the outside in via balconies and terraces. Concurrently, the emergence of more casual social mores in the aftermath of World War I changed the purpose of the home, which was no longer supposed to operate as a signifier of social status. The modern home could—and should—be reduced to a functionalist minimum because excess space itself had become useless; the proliferation of rooms and the ability to house large quantities of ornamental possessions ran counter to the democratization of the good life sought for postwar France. Moreover, Sonrel opined, space was less necessary because migration for education and work had stripped households down to their nuclear-family cores. As nuclear families turned away from their extended family support networks and toward the public sphere of the welfare state for family allocations and Social Security, they needed less space in the private sphere; the large picture window, opening onto the world outside, symbolized all these changes.[52]

The Art of Living "Smally"

In 1950, in a "Que sais-je"[53] volume on the domestic arts, Jean and Françoise Fourastié observed, "Although most French people, by education and tradition (because they visited Versailles in their youth), remain sensitive to the charm of large spaces, they are, little by little, letting themselves be converted to the comfort of limited space."[54] Like Sonrel, the Fourastiés identified space with habit and redefined small spaces as both more comfortable and more suited to modern times. While conscious that economies of time and funds trimmed meters off of the *cellule* and reduced the full repertory of its comfort, architects, housing officials, and modernizers like Fourastié nevertheless celebrated the tiny cell as a modern home on the basis of its well-thought-out design. They believed that, ultimately, size was not very important. Not only did the zoning of rooms ensure that all of the functions of daily life could take place, but the activities to be performed within would proceed relatively undisturbed due to the felicitous distribution of spaces within the cell.

One of the ways that the modern mass home was understood to be an improvement on its rural predecessors, for example, was in its ability—in theory—to give each member of a nuclear family some privacy. Anne-Marie Raimond gushed in a 1955 *Elle* article describing the Maison Heureuse (the "Happy House"), an apartment designed by the young architect Claude Parent, who had briefly worked with Le Corbusier, to fit within the Logeco surface area requirements: "You will want to live in the 'Happy House' because it is designed for a harmonious family life. You can have mood swings, your husband can isolate himself to read or work, your children can play completely freely without, at any moment of the day, bothering anyone else."[55] It was in the name of the individual's total freedom that the architect André Hermant argued against the MRU's policy of reducing hallways to a minimum in order to maximize room size. He explained, "The bedroom, even so small [as six square meters] remains a site of solitude, the private domain of a single individual. ... A larger bedroom runs the risk of being shared, with all that the constraints and annoyance that sharing implies."[56] The modern home's success was to be evaluated on the basis of its capacity to allow the *épanouissement*, or the full development, of the individual's mind and body, and tranquility and privacy were understood to play a role in that process of development.

If individual inhabitants were to be the key beneficiaries of the modern home, they had a role to play in its actualization. The state and the architect could not create the modern home alone. As we saw in chapter 3, the Salon des Arts Ménagers (SAM) attempted to impart each year to its visitors that "users" of a modern home must complete their interiors by purchasing new furnishings and appliances and implementing modern methods of home economics. Other actors joined the SAM, seeking to instruct residents how to contribute to the national project of modernization. Throughout the 1950s, and consistent with the production of ever-shrinking apartments, magazines and books dedicated to homemaking and decoration educated readers in the art of living "smally." For example, a 1953 issue of the upper-middle-class publication *Maison et jardin* ran a feature illustrating how chic Parisians used minimalist furnishings to create more space in their tiny Parisian apartments.[57] In 1958, Gisèle Boulanger published *L'Art de s'installer* (The Art of Making a Home), a guide to interior decoration. She condemned the armoire, explaining that it was archaic in the modern home: "The large antique armoire is no longer conceivable in our cramped apartments—and moreover the rooms of our apartments no longer applying to the same purposes as old homes did, one had to invent other pieces of furniture. Our living-room, this parlor-office-dining room, and sometimes bedroom, called for the hybrid furnishing which can be bar, shelving unit, bookcase, desk, china cabinet, and linen cabinet."[58] Magazines and newspapers were filled with advertisements featuring just these kinds of multitasking furnishings, especially sofa beds. Boulanger would have approved of a piece being advertised by the Établissements Roche in the March 1955 issue of *Arts ménagers*: a combination sideboard, bar, bookshelf, and desk that even included a table that slid out at dinnertime.

To "convert" the French "to the comfort of limited space," to use the Fourastiés' phrase, the MRL also began a more formal public relations campaign. Speaking in April 1955 to a group of decorators, Roger Duchet announced his intention to create a public relations campaign, which would, "via exhibitions, the press, cinema, show the public the possibilities that are at their disposal—of which they are unaware—and teach them how one can live better in a small but logically organized dwelling, than in one that is cluttered up with large, bulky furnishings."[59] Three months later, a travelling exhibition left Paris for the provinces with this goal in mind. Spearheaded by the SAM's Paul Breton, the exhibition was produced by the National Campaign for Construction and Housing, an association coordinating the efforts of the MRL, the SCIC, the Crédit Foncier, the Fédération Nationale de l'Habitat, and the utility companies. Featuring a mobile home that represented a two-bedroom Logeco, decorated with mass-produced furniture designed by award-winning decorators, the exhibition traveled to the provinces, where it was visited by thousands, who stepped into the tiny apartment, received leaflets and brochures, and watched films produced by the ministry and the utility companies.[60]

Though requests for building permits increased in towns where the exhibition had stopped,[61] it is less clear that the lessons in interior decoration succeeded. In a March 1955 issue of *Paris-Match* that displayed their offering at that year's SAM, the state-of-the-art Maison électrique, the Galéries Barbès, a chain of furniture stores, ran an advertisement recommending an "English style" décor; they showed knock-off Chippendale chairs and a loveseat that clearly could not double as a bed or anything else.[62] Galéries Barbès was an enormously popular store with fairly affordable prices, and they allowed customers to spread out payments over two years. In 1953, the Galéries Barbès catalogue hawked bedroom suites with large armoires, and most of its pieces were heavy, resting on the floor and made of thick pieces of oak. None were made from metal. By the end of the 1950s, however, the tastemaking efforts of Breton and his colleagues in the Union des Artistes Modernes had begun to permeate major retailers and manufacturers. The 1958 Barbès catalogue pushed TV tables, metal furnishings, and furniture raised up from the floor by spindly legs. Bedroom suites still featured armoires, but the contemporary versions of these were streamlined and also raised up off of the ground, allowing for a perception of space and airiness. Such furniture unintentionally mimicked the form of Le Corbusier's Unités d'habitation, raised up on pilotis.

While public officials and Modernist decorators led the campaign against bringing large and heavy pieces of furniture into the petite cell, they had no such qualms about encouraging the purchase of large appliances, like refrigerators and washing machines. But, as the 1950s progressed, the Liberation-era dream of providing public housing with fully equipped kitchens dissipated as budgets became tighter and the expectations of what equipped meant evolved. The MRU tried to advance industrialization of kitchen counters and cabinets in order to install these, along with kitchen sinks, in public housing projects. In 1952 André Prothin, as director of Construction, contracted with the Saint-Laurent kitchen furnishings company to install nearly 7,500 HLM kitchens in six cities, and in 1954 Adrien Spinetta, his successor, organized a contest for these, where projects were evaluated by the CSTB and selected by HLM builders in sixteen cities throughout France, including Le Mans, Le Havre, Lille, Marseille, Nantes, Orléans, Rennes, and Roubaix.[63]

The "need" to incorporate labor-saving appliances into the home interior grew as its livable area shrank, for these would complete the functionality of the *cellule* and hence fully realize its modernity. Moreover, collective facilities like laundromats were rare in *grands ensembles*. Not only would they add to the total cost of project construction, but both public officials and architects were familiar with UNCAF survey results that indicated that over three-quarters of apartment complex residents did not want to share washing machines with their neighbors. Reasons for this included a concern about the loss of autonomy with regard to arranging one's household tasks (if access to the washing machines depended upon a fixed, appointed time) and a worry that the shared machines might be a source of conflict between neighbors.[64] The solution opted for most often was to provide the option for individual installation of things like refrigerators and hot water heaters by supplying the necessary hookups and by allocating space within the kitchen and the bathroom for appliances. It was fully expected that people would acquire appliances, even if it took time for them to acquire the "taste" for convenience; the guidelines for designing Logeco model plans indicated tersely that "space for a refrigerator is useful."[65]

Housing professionals had every reason to suspect that appliances would enter en masse into individual "cells." Between 1954 and 1960, the number of households owning washing machines rose from 8.4 percent to 24.4 percent; those owning refrigerators increased from 7.5 percent to 25.8 percent. Television also began to make inroads; only one percent of households possessed one in 1954, but 13.1 percent did by 1960.[66] The presumption that each home would be—eventually—equipped with a complete array of modern conveniences was reflected in the 1955 national housing survey that only recorded inhabitants as having access to "comfort" if that access was exclusive.[67] This reflected a normative assumption that the democratization of comfort should proceed on an individual basis, household by household, even for families dwelling in collective housing. Put another way, it did not count as comfort if it had to be shared.

In 1957, close to 71 percent of households did not have full access to comfort, for they did not own any of the aforementioned appliances.[68] Several obstacles separated the consumer from the goods. First was cost. Throughout the 1950s, when other newspapers ran features in February and March of each year exclaiming over the labor-saving and aesthetic qualities of that year's offerings at the Salon des Arts Ménagers, the daily of the French Communist Party, *L'Humanité*, could be counted on to calculate for its readership how many hundreds of hours the average worker would need to put in to afford these. In order to help consumers take home some of these devices, in 1957 some lenders established a "household equipment" loan. Available from certain local family allocations offices, the Union coöpérative de crédit ménager, or, for civil servants, the Caisses de Crédit municipal, these loans were offered at half, or even less than half, of the rates offered by commercial credit lenders.[69]

A second obstacle, at least to the accumulation of appliances, was that apartments and houses were not always outfitted with an optimal level of electricity. Most households had just enough wattage to power small household appliances like table lamps, irons, and radios. It was not until 1963 that the nationalized utility Électricité de France began a long campaign called the "Compteur bleu" initiative. "Compteur bleu" aimed to increase the power available to each home from one kilowatt to six kilowatts in cities with more than two thousand people, a change that, in conjunction with the decrease in tariffs on imported appliances mandated by the 1957 Treaty of Rome, caused the market for appliances to take off.[70] During the 1950s, however, the availability of electrical power was limited, if it was available at all: a cartoon in *France-Soir*, with the caption "Home from the Salon des Arts Ménagers," showed a farmer's wife beating her laundry by hand in the basin of a newly purchased washing machine. Her husband comments, "Those machines must be practical ... when you have electricity."[71]

Though the cartoon made a valid point, it was not clear that the rural wife really would have bought a washing machine at the SAM, for farming families were always in the lowest percentage of households owning appliances. This was in part due to a lack of disposable income, but it also stemmed from a perception that, in fact, washing machines and the like simply were not necessary. Alongside consumers hoping to purchase labor-saving devices, particularly in the 1950s, there was also a population that was skeptical of their need for them, such as older women who had long since determined for themselves the most efficient ways to accomplish their household tasks. Publicity campaigns, sponsored by manufacturers and disseminated in the women's-interest press, attempted to counter misconceptions and potential misuse of appliances. Some thought washing machines were unhygienic, and *Elle* chastised its readership for believing erroneously that the mechanics of a washing machine ruined clothing fibers, asserting that belief to be "absolutely false."[72] A marketing study for refrigerators noted that people, even those who already owned refrigerators, were not sufficiently aware of the ways in which the appliance could cut down on the time spent shopping for groceries. Moreover, 23 percent of owners turned them off during the winter. The study also found that 57 percent of refrigerator owners bought units too small to really be "rational" and, if they had to do it over again, they would buy a larger unit. This led the researchers to conclude that people quickly developed the "need for cold," and they suggested that appliance distributors might try renting refrigerators or even loaning them out free for a short time in order to cultivate this need among larger swaths of the population.[73] As late as 1960, readers of *Arts ménagers* were being educated on how to store various types of food in a refrigerator and how a refrigerator could save trips to the market.[74] These messages seemed to be most effective for the middle classes, white-collar workers, and employees in the service sector, for censuses and surveys showed that they proportionally purchased appliances more quickly and in greater numbers than their counterparts in the bourgeoisie, in the working class, or in the agricultural professions. Regional factors could also play a role, however: washing machines tended to be purchased most by those dwelling in medium-sized cities, where there were fewer laundromats; those in the warm South of France bought refrigerators before their northern neighbors did.[75]

Although in 1957, as indicated above, almost 71 percent of households lacked a washer, refrigerator, or television, *L'Express,* during that year's Salon des Arts Ménagers, took the opportunity to sponsor a roundtable debate around the question, "Does the washing machine spin in the direction of History?" Observing that in two years, the amount that the French had spent on household appliances had nearly doubled, the magazine wondered how the accession to comfort would change the individual's relationship to society. The participants, who included sociologist Edgar Morin, political scientist Charles Morazé, women's rights activist Colette Audry, and Edmond Lisle, of the Centre de recherches et documentation sur la consommation (Center for Research and Documentation on Consumption), attempted to identify the implications of the developing mass consumerism on the family and social structures. Participants debated whether labor-saving devices threatened a woman's sense of self: Audry interpreted the rise of household technology as a sign that women's time was finally beginning to be seen as equal in value to men's, whereas Morazé saw appliances as alienating women from their inherited expertise; Lisle concluded that the debate for or against mechanical servants was irrelevant to working-class women, who needed to be liberated from the burden of the second shift.

L'Express also asked, "Can a man who has a refrigerator make a revolution?"[76] That is, would the democratization of comfort take the steam out of labor unions' political demands or kill more ambitious proposals for the redistribution of wealth by fobbing off the masses with televisions and washing machines? Morin conceded that workers in the 1950s were more interested in working overtime in order to gain a higher standard of living than in reducing the length of their work-weeks. Moreover, buying items on credit accentuated this trend and made workers more dependent on their jobs. Nevertheless, all of the participants granted that improvement in the material conditions of everyday life should not be denied to people who had suffered the hardships and scarcities of war; a certain austerity might be ideologically desirable, but it was not pragmatic, and it was not fair. By the end of the debate, *L'Express* acknowledged that the postwar period had seen the development of a right to happiness, and, invoking the domestic ideal, *L'Express*, too, linked personal happiness to the home.

Conclusion

Just as in 1953 and 1954, geopolitics and parliamentary convulsions made for prominent headlines in 1957 and 1958. In 1957 France had taken a decisive step toward Europeanization by ratifying the Treaty of Rome. While tying itself more closely to Europe, France questioned its relationship to its colonial holdings and to the status of Algeria. Indeed, the bitter Algerian war spawned a governmental crisis that overshadowed those of the early 1950s, one that brought down the Fourth Republic in May 1958. By June 1958, Charles de Gaulle had been voted full powers to form a new republic and to draft its constitution. Yet, even as it careened from one political crisis to another, France had made some headway in resolving the housing crisis, and thus a summer 1958 issue of *Elle* magazine could accompany a young housewife into her new home in Sarcelles. Though its physical footprint had shrunk, and the ministry had shifted from a period of eclecticism to a commitment to the *grand ensemble*, the pro-family, democratic narrative of the modern home sketched out in the Liberation years remained unchanged.

In August 1958, writing for *Elle* under the pseudonym Stanislas Fontaine, Albert Palle accompanied a certain Yvette Sarton as she moved into Sarcelles. Palle was a novelist, former Resistance fighter, and a journalist colleague of intellectuals Jean-Paul Sartre and Raymond Aron. Madame Sarton had waited five years to be allocated an HLM apartment, living, with her husband and two children, in a one-room apartment in the village of "old" Sarcelles. The author condemned the "sad piles of houses that compose the towns that we've been building for the past 150 years" and rejoiced that the Sartons "only have to go two kilometers in order to leave the past and enter into the future."[77] Fontaine, who had written for *Combat*, was full of praise for the SCIC and the state for the huge undertaking at Sarcelles. He compared the state's actions favorably to those of the local notables he accused of building only token pockets of new housing, just enough to prove to voters that they were addressing the housing crisis. In reality, Fontaine charged, these municipal authorities stopped short of really resolving the crisis for fear that housing the masses would shift their communities' voting patterns to the left.

Elle readers who sought such improvement in their lives learned that anyone who worked for a company that directed its 1 percent *patronal* to the CDC could apply to live at Sarcelles. Successful applicants would be able to brag, like the Sartons, of having a bathroom—"still a rarity in France," lamented Fontaine. He also recounted Madame Sarton's pleasure at finding a rubbish chute in the apartment, affirming for readers that women's burdens had not been forgotten in the rush to statistical architecture. Moreover, women would find that "entry into the new apartment brings a real fulfillment [*épanouissement*]. They discover the traditional—but for them new—activities of a housewife. For some of these young women, who have lived years in a furnished room or who were crammed in with their children at their in-laws', moving day is the real beginning for their marriage."[78] Fontaine thus reprised the leitmotifs of the Liberation generation of planners: improved health for children "in the countryside," stable marriages, and the paradoxical goal of more leisure for the women who would embrace modern housewifery.

Even as the size of the *cellule* shrunk, then, housing professionals continued to invoke the domestic ideal, trumpeting the functional modern home's unique ability to deliver comfort and independence to each member of a nuclear family—as long as she or he knew how to artfully inhabit it. Fortunately for Sarcelles residents, they had their own teachers in the complex; residents could take advantage of on-site, drop-in childcare while they met with home economics advisors. On the day of Fontaine's visit, a Madame Battaglini was getting help making curtains and borrowing a sewing machine while her two children played at the day care center.[79]

In 1958, therefore, architects, housing officials, and many observers could still see in the *cellule d'habitation* and its "shell", the *grand ensemble*, the brave new world of domestic space. Pierre Sonrel proclaimed that the home was the "only milieu capable of responding to the totality of a person's needs and of helping him find his equilibrium in the general rhythm of the world."⁸⁰ Fontaine agreed, but lest he be accused of rose-colored glasses, he acknowledged "difficulties" like the old-fashioned, tacky sideboards and armoires that did not mesh at all in the new apartments. The ideal, Fontaine, remarked, would be for new residents to bring nothing other than the pair of boots needed to traipse through the fresh mud of ongoing construction.⁸¹ His observation underscores the desire to embrace only the new, to leave the past behind. In so doing, of course, the 1950s *cellule* demanded that, in order to extract the maximum from one's *existenzminimum*—the essence of rationalization—one had to buy something new. Ironically, modern homes relied on consumption in ways that reinscribed difference and compromised prewar modernism's egalitarian objectives.

For all involved, embrace of the mass home involved compromise. Modernist architects saw their vision of collective housing triumph as the dominant form of urban domestic space, but this was at the cost of further encroachments upon their sphere of jurisdiction. The housing ministry compromised, too, having to scale back its ambitious, egalitarian program of spacious, one-size-fits-all modern homes envisioned in the late 1940s and introducing instead a hierarchy of housing based on gradations of size and comfort. Yet "statistical architecture" also resulted in production output that exceeded the targets specified in the Second Plan. By 1957, the annual rate of housing units being constructed was 270,000, and the ministry could point to concrete evidence of its efforts to ease the housing crisis.⁸²

Whether the French who moved into the *grands ensembles* had to compromise depended on how poorly they had been housed before they arrived and to which kind of housing—Logeco, LEN, HLM, or *cité d'urgence*—they had been assigned. Certainly, in the short term, most of the modern home's new tenants found that their apartment fostered an immediate improvement to their everyday lives, and this was just the sort of individual satisfaction that the *cellule*'s creators envisioned and privileged, even as they glossed over the need for community and social life. Yet, at the dawn of the 1960s, a crop of surveys—particularly those conducted by a new actor, the urban sociologist—began to put into question the very functionality that was supposed to be the hallmark of the modern home, and it is to those critiques that we now turn.

Notes

1. Pierre Sonrel, "Les nouvelles habitudes domestiques," *La Civilisation quotidienne*, ed. Paul Breton, vol. 14 of *L'Encyclopédie française*, ed. Gaston Berger (Paris: Société de gestion de l'Encyclopédie française, 1955), 14.24-25.

2. See, for example, CREPAH-GERASE, *Conditions et évolution de la production architecturale dans l'habitat social* (Paris: Secrétariat de la recherche architecturale, 1982); Kopp, Boucher, and Pauly, *L'Architecture de la reconstruction*; Flamand, *Loger le peuple*; Voldman, *La reconstruction des villes françaises*; Anne-Marie Fribourg, "Évolution des politiques du logement depuis 1950," in *Logement et habitat. L'état des savoirs*, 223–30; and Tellier, *Le temps des* HLM. CREPAH-GERASE and Kopp, et. al. emphasize the poverty of architectural innovation due to administrative constraints, while Fribourg, Voldman, and Tellier focus more on the role of the state in financing new construction.
3. Clanché and Fribourg, "Grande évolution du parc et des ménages depuis 1950," 85.
4. Newsome, "Struggle for a Voice," 94.
5. Ibid., 172.
6. "La Construction en France et à l'étranger," *L'Architecture d'aujourd'hui* 44 (September 1952), XXI.
7. Harloe, *The People's Home?*, 282, 337–39; Power, *Hovels to High Rise*, 179–83, 187.
8. Geneviève Michel and Pierre-Jacques Derainne, *Aux Courtillières: Histoires singulières et exemplaires* (Paris: Créaphis, 2005), 33.
9. All of the statistics in this paragraph hail from Voldman, *La reconstruction des villes françaises*, 322 and 344.
10. Cited in Pulju, *Women and Mass Consumer Society*, 101.
11. Clanché and Fribourg, "Grandes évolutions du parc et des ménages depuis 1950," 85.
12. Institut National de la Statistique et des Études Économiques [INSEE], "Une enquête par sondage sur le logement (octobre 1955)," *Études Statistiques* (April–June 1957): 38, 40.
13. Data comes from the report of the Population and Housing Division of the U.S. Bureau of the Census, "United States Summary," part 1 of vol. 1, *General Characteristics*, in *Census of Housing: 1950* (Washington, DC: U.S. Government Printing Office, 1953), 32 and figures derived for Britain from statistics in David Kynaston, *Austerity Britain* (London: Bloomsbury, 2008 [2007]), 592.
14. Newsome, *French Urban Planning*, 85.
15. "Je modernise mon appartement," *Arts ménagers* 63 (March 1955), 125.
16. The phrase means "the employers' 1 percent." This law was modeled on a similar mechanism devised by the Comité national interprofessionnel du logement (CNIL), a federation born in the interwar period. The regional CILs (interprofessional housing committees) grouped employers and their employees into private construction initiatives dedicated to the creation of workers' housing (Voldman, *La reconstruction des villes françaises*, 341).
17. Michèle Attar, Vincent Lourier, and Jean-Michel Vercollier, *La Place de la forme coöpérative dans le secteur de l'habitat en France* (Paris: Éditions du PUCA, 1998), 21.
18. Rouaud, *60 ans d'arts ménagers*, vol. 2, 27.
19. "L'Activité de l'Abbé Pierre," *Le Monde*, 2 March 1954, 7.
20. Newsome, *French Urban Planning*, 109.
21. Pierre Mendès-France, *Gouverner, c'est choisir* (Paris: Julliard, 1953), 36–37.
22. Roger-Henri Guerrand and Roger Quilliot, *Une Europe en Construction. Deux siècles d'habitat social en Europe* (Paris: La Découverte, 1992), 178.
23. "De première nécessité" translates as staple or vital; the implication is that this housing is a basic need for sustaining life.
24. As we saw in chapter 1, by 1948, the average renter devoted a mere 1 to 2 percent of his income to rent.
25. [INSEE], "Une enquête par sondage sur le logement," 38, 40.
26. In a memo to the minister of the MRU regarding the LEN's predecessor, the *logement économique de relogement*, Adrien Spinetta, then working for the department responsible

for new HLM construction, proposed, "With regard to the provision of hot water, this seems desirable as a general rule. But one may worry that certain families, who are little-evolved or of a suspect morality, will not use or will damage the apparatuses of hot water production" ("Note pour Monsieur le Ministre," no date [circa 1950], AN, CAC 19771096/1).
27. Jean-Claude Croizé, "Normes et maîtrise du coût de la construction (1945-1980)," vol. 4 of "Politique et configuration du logement en France (1900-1980)" (Ph.D. diss., University of Paris X-Nanterre, 2006), 88.
28. Jacques Dreyfus, *La Société du confort* (Paris: L'Harmattan, 1990), 110.
29. François Bloch-Lainé, *Profession: Fonctionnaire. Entretiens avec Françoise Carrière* (Paris: Seuil, 1976), 137.
30. Voldman, *La reconstruction des villes françaises*, 388–90.
31. Thierry Pacquot, "François Bloch-Lainé," *Urbanisme* 284 (September–October 1995): 7.
32. André Hermant, "Les conditions générales d'un logement," *La Civilisation quotidienne*, ed. Paul Breton, vol. 14 of *L'Encyclopédie française*, ed. Gaston Berger (Paris: Société de gestion de l'Encyclopédie française, 1955), 14.28-10.
33. Mission Mémoires et identités en Val de France, *Les Carreaux 1955-1963: Naissance d'un grand ensemble en banlieue parisienne* (Villiers-le-Bel: Communauté d'agglomération Val de France, 2006), 28.
34. "Normalisation des caractéristiques des habitations collectives à loyer modéré à usage collectif," Arrêté du 23 novembre 1955, published in Paris as a separate pamphlet called *Habitations collectives à loyer modéré à usage locatif* (Paris: Journal Officiel de la République Française, December 1955).
35. Pierre Agard, "L'Unité de résidence," *Esprit* 21 (October–November 1953): 600.
36. Ministère de la reconstruction et de l'urbanisme, *Logements économiques et familiaux. Plans types: logements individuels* (Paris: MRU, 1953), n.p.
37. "Les grands ensembles," *L'Architecture d'aujourd'hui* 46 (February–March 1953), 24.
38. This directive comes from an internal memo of the Groupe Technique Central of the MRL's Direction de la Construction: "Plan d'examen des projets sous l'aspect qualité de l'habitat et de l'architecture," AN, CAC 19771096/1, 2.
39. Ibid., 4.
40. Ibid., 5.
41. Cited in Rouaud, *60 ans d'arts ménagers*, vol. 2, 28.
42. Catherine Coley, *Jean Prouvé* (Paris: Centre Georges Pompidou, 1993), 54; Dominique Clayssen, *Jean Prouvé: l'idée constructive* (Paris: Dunod, 1983), 80.
43. Token examples during these years include *L'Architecture d'aujourd'hui* 48 (July 1953), VII, *L'Architecture d'aujourd'hui* 54 (May–June 1954), V, and *L'Architecture d'aujourd'hui* 65 (May 1956), V.
44. Jean Balladur, Bernard Zehrfuss, and Bruno Vayssière, *Jean Balladur, Bernard Zehrfuss: le 7 février 1991* (Paris: Éditions du Pavillon de l'Arsenal, 1998), 54.
45. Paul Landauer, "La SCIC, premier promoteur français des grands ensembles (1953-1958)," *Histoire urbaine* 23 (December 2008): 76.
46. Pouvreau, *Un politique en architecture*, 172.
47. Landauer, "La SCIC, premier promoteur," 75.
48. Landauer, "La SCIC, premier promoteur," 79–80.
49. Hermant, "Les Conditions générales d'un logement," 14.26-7.
50. Popular opinion seemed to agree. In a survey inquiring about the ideal number of children a couple should have, those who believed that two or four was the best number fell between 1947 and 1955, while those who thought that three was ideal rose during the same period (Henri Bastide and Alain Girard, "Attitudes et opinions des Français à l'égard de la fécondité et de la famille," *Population* 4–5 [July–October 1975]: 698).

51. Bloch-Lainé, *Profession: Fonctionnaire*, 136.
52. Sonrel, "Les nouvelles habitudes domestiques," 14.24-5.
53. The "Que Sais-je?" series is a sort of "pocket encyclopedia" that features inexpensive, slim volumes written by experts offering a layperson's introduction to the current scholarship or thinking on a topic.
54. Jean and Françoise Fourastié, *Les Arts ménagers* (Paris: PUF, 1950), 12.
55. Anne-Marie Raimond, "Au Salon des Arts Ménagers *Elle* expose la Maison Heureuse qu'elle a construite pour vous," *Elle* 480 (21 February 1955), 34. In subsequent issues of the weekly, Raimond detailed how readers could buy the Logeco plans directly from the architect or purchase a Happy House through the intermediary of the Société Générale Foncière. Several of these Logecos were built in the greater Parisian area.
56. Hermant, "Les Conditions générales d'un logement," 14.26-5.
57. "Sous le signe de l'espace réduit," *Maison et jardin* 3, 14 (April–May 1953).
58. Gisèle Boulanger, *L'Art de s'installer* (Paris: Hachette, 1958), 184.
59. *Cahiers du Ministère de la Reconstruction et du Logement* 5 (May 1955), 124.
60. See documents pertaining to the Campagne Nationale en Faveur de Construction et de Logement in AN, CAC 19850023/121 and "Inaugurée hier à Paris, l'Exposition de la Construction visitera les principales villes de France," *France-Soir*, 24–25 July 1955, 6E. The Association for the Campagne Nationale en Faveur de la Construction et du Logement met until May 1966, when it was absorbed into the public relations department of the MRL's successor, the Ministère de l'Équipement.
61. Newsome, "Struggle for a Voice," 227.
62. *Paris-Match* 309 (26 February–5 March 1955), 26.
63. On the contract with Saint-Laurent, see Rouaud, *60 ans d'arts ménagers*, vol. 2, 64 and for the ministry-sponsored kitchen element contest, see the documents pertaining to the "Consultation nationale" in AN, CAC 19771133/01, especially the meeting minutes of 6 July 1954.
64. *L'Architecture d'aujourd'hui* 29 (May 1950), XVII.
65. Groupe Technique Central of the MRL, Direction de la Construction, "Plan d'examen des projets," 6.
66. Marie-Claude de la Godelinais and Gérard Lang, *L'Équipement des ménages en biens durables au début de 1976*, #213 of the Collections de l'INSEE, série M, #55, November 1976 (Paris: INSEE, 1976), 21.
67. [INSEE], "Une enquête par sondage sur le logement," 36.
68. Ibid.
69. "Le prêt à l'équipement ménager," *L'Express*, 8 March 1957, 34.
70. Rouaud, *60 ans d'arts ménagers*, vol. 2, 167 and "25 ans d'évolution technologique et de progrès technique continus," *L'Officiel hebdomadaire de l'équipement ménager* 500 (September 1977), special issue: *Livre d'or de l'électroménager européen*, 45.
71. Rouaud, *60 ans d'arts ménagers*, vol. 2, 129.
72. "Comment choisir, acheter, amortir, entretenir vos machines ménagères," *Elle* (21 February 1955), 61.
73. *Le Marché du réfrigérateur ménager* (Paris: Comité d'action pour le développement de l'intéressement du personnel à la productivité des entreprises, 1955), 21–29.
74. Christiane Cossus, "Opération réfrigérateur," *Arts ménagers* 127 (July 1960): 20–23. Cossus was head of the Household Appliance information "hotline" at Électricité de France.
75. See INSEE, "Équipement ménager 1957," *Bulletin hebdomadaire de statistique* 557 (17 January 1957) and Godelinais and Lang, *L'Équipement des ménages en biens durables*. Family size was another variable in the acquisition of appliances. For example, larger families purchased washing machines before smaller ones did, a purchase often enabled by fam-

ily allocations; this possibility has been famously satirized by Christiane Rochefort in *Les Petits Enfants du siècle,* her 1961 novel about a young girl living in a new HLM in Bagnolet (Paris: Éditions Bernard Grasset, 1961).
76. "La machine à laver tourne-t-elle dans le sens d'histoire?" *L'Express,* 1 March 1957, 14.
77. Stanislas Fontaine [Albert Palle], "Une ville est née," *Elle* (28 August 1958), 37.
78. Fontaine, "Une ville est née," 66.
79. Ibid., 40.
80. Sonrel, "Les nouvelles habitudes domestiques," 14.24-7. André Hermant concurred, refuting even the possibility of restoration by vacation, since automobile traffic returning home reversed any possible relaxing effect produced by the countryside (a phenomenon familiar to twenty-first-century New Yorkers returning to the city on a Sunday evening); a tranquil balance could only be obtained in the well-designed, functional home ("Les conditions générales," 14.26-5).
81. Fontaine, "Une ville est née," 66.
82. Harloe, *The People's Home?,* 322.

Chapter 5

"WHO IS THE AUTHOR OF A DWELLING?"
From User to Inhabitant, 1959–1961

> [T]he architect draws up plans in a functional manner in order to respond to needs. Each part of an apartment has its function. But to which needs does it respond? If these needs are defined only in the architect's studio or in the administration's offices, they have a good chance of not really being the needs of families.
> —Sociologist Paul-Henry Chombart de Lauwe, 1959[1]

Journalists and sociologists have been writing about the *grands ensembles* since the 1950s, but now that well over half of a century has passed since the first *grand ensemble,* the Cité Rotterdam, sprung up in Strasbourg, historians have begun to turn their attention to the *grands ensembles* as an object of study.[2] One of the features that this history, in its current incarnation, recaptures is the sense of uncertainty and hope that infused the creation of this new form of habitat. François Bloch-Lainé, the SCIC's president, emphasized the fact that both the state and the architects involved in public housing during the 1950s and 1960s were "beginners"; neither had much experience in matters of domestic architecture before the war.[3] Minister of Construction Pierre Sudreau, in a 1961 interview, worried (correctly, as it turned out) about the new terrain they were charting: "[T]he rhythm of modern progress is so rapid, so rapid that, when all is said and done, we don't know if the new towns of which we are so proud right now, these new neighborhoods, won't be very quickly out-of-date in twenty years."[4] Though the *grand ensemble* had become the dominant form of urban housing in the 1950s, the feeling of experimentation still permeated planning and policy circles. At a CSTB working group for the improvement of floor plans, Gérard Blachère, the center's head, described the process of housing the masses as "putting people in different kinds of apartments and seeing how they react."[5]

In 1959 and 1960 two sets of widely publicized results from this monumental experiment provoked a reconceptualization of both the modern home and its occupants. In the years between 1953 and 1959, the MRL's policy of building according to model plans had, for all intents and purposes, put an end to discussions of interiors in both mass market and professional publications. In 1959, however, the housing ministry itself put the question of the ideal modern home back under the microscope with its "Appartement référendum," a model apartment designed according to the wishes and practices expressed by women in interviews and surveys. Built according to women's feedback, a full-scale model of the Referendum Apartment appeared at the 1959 Salon des Arts Ménagers, and the ministry encouraged visitors to add their voices to the referendum by filling out an evaluation of the model.

The second event that allowed inhabitants' voices to be heard by housing professionals was the publication of the two-volume *Famille et habitation,* a scholarly work by a group of urban sociologists led by Paul-Henry Chombart de Lauwe. The first volume appeared in 1959; drawing upon the social scientific literature about homes over time and across cultures, it attempted to offer an interdisciplinary view of housing issues. The second volume, published the following year, focused on three apartment complexes belonging to the first generation of *grands ensembles* and offered the most in-depth study of residents in public housing to date.

This chapter examines the content of these resident critiques, looks at the changes in home design that they sparked, and argues that these changes reflect a reconceptualization of both domestic space and the people who dwelled within by the housing ministry and by some architects. The Referendum Apartment and *Famille et habitation* suggested that the small *cellule,* predicated on functionalist principles and designed to impart the art of living to its occupants, was failing in its mission. Residents were not only not using their homes in the manner that architects had anticipated, but the former also resented the ways in which standardized 3Ps and 4Ps thwarted their own dwelling preferences. Moreover, the results intimated that the state's wager had not paid off: although new residents of HLMs and Logecos appreciated the technical accouterments of the modern home, such as indoor plumbing and central heating, comfort was a necessary but not sufficient condition of resident satisfaction. The French housed in HLMs were not embracing the *cellule* as their modern dream home.

Why not? Functionalist conceptions of domestic space had held that residents were *usagers,* users who had certain basic needs that the 3Ps and 4Ps would meet and whose practices could be shaped by the space. The surveys and studies demonstrated definitively that residents had—and continued to have—their own ideas about how to live. Recognition of this fact entailed a new understanding of residents as inhabitants, actors in domestic space, along with the realization that functionalism needed to be defined from below, not from above. The chapter concludes with a retrospective look at the encounters of some first generation *grand ensemble* dwellers with their modern mass homes. If they found that less had been delivered than tastemakers and proponents of the domestic ideal had led them to expect, many inhabitants also enjoyed their entry into modern comfort, created satisfying homes, and fashioned new social networks.

The *Appartement Référendum*: What Women Want

With the birth of the Fifth Republic in 1958 came another new name for the housing ministry: urging Charles de Gaulle to turn toward the future of France, his choice for minister, Pierre Sudreau, suggested that the organization should henceforth be known as the Ministry of Construction (MC), not Reconstruction.[6] Sudreau, born in 1919, was from a bourgeois family, although the death of his father contributed to a difficult childhood. He was a great friend of Antoine de Saint-Exupéry, and, after studies in law and political science, Sudreau joined the French Resistance as part of the Brutus Network. He was captured and sent to Buchenwald. At Liberation, Sudreau joined the Interior Ministry, then became prefect of the Loir-et-Cher, invented the sound-and-light shows for chateaus, and, in 1955, took the position of commissioner of construction and town planning for the Parisian region. Created in 1955 and affiliated with the Département de la Seine, this regional post was designed to ensure that the efforts to solve the housing crisis would not run counter to decentralization initiatives. Sudreau's success as commissioner led President Charles de Gaulle to appoint him the new Fifth Republic's housing minister.[7]

While commissioner, Sudreau had coordinated the erection of *grands ensembles* with the urbanists in charge of regional planning and had worked closely with the SCIC. In 1957 he instituted a committee to study life in the *grands ensembles.*[8] Drawing its membership from residents' associations, this committee embodied Sudreau's pragmatic belief that the success of *grands ensembles* would depend upon resident buy-in. Upon becoming minister in June 1958, Sudreau expanded his efforts in the realm of housing and took the idea of democratic participation a step further by giving women a voice in the evaluation and planning of domestic space. The last person to look for women's input in housing design had been André Lurçat in 1951, during the jury examinations of the Cité Rotterdam contest submissions (see chapter 1). His suggestion had lain dormant until Sudreau's arrival at the housing ministry.

In search of a capable spokesperson for French women, Sudreau turned to Jeanne Picard. Picard had a long career representing working-class families. At the age of eighteen, she founded the first group of Young Female Christian Workers (Jeunesse ouvrière chrétienne féminine, or JOCF) in her parish in 1928, after having worked as a bookkeeper in a factory in Clichy, northwest of Paris.[9] Picard rose very quickly through the ranks of the JOCF and took over as the permanent president of the organization, but only after working for three months in metallurgic factories around Paris in order to gain a more substantive understanding of young female factory workers' needs. During World War II, she married and began a family, eventually bearing four children. She pursued her activism by joining the Mouvement populaire des familles, a Left Catholic familialist group, and established organizations to train young women to be mother's helpers for working-class families.[10] In 1953, she joined the administrative council of the Union nationale des associations familiales (National Union of Family Associations), the state's key consultant on questions pertaining to the family, and the prestigious consultative body, the Conseil économique et social (Economic and Social Council), serving the latter as a lobbyist for families. By 1958, Picard had spent three decades working with and for working-class women and their households, and it was the needs of this population, for whom the HLMs were officially intended, that Sudreau hoped to ascertain when he appointed Picard a ministry representative.

Picard's first task was to survey families in new HLMs about their homes, and she visited approximately three hundred households. When asked specifically about their interiors, occupants complained about the absence of entryways, the lack of separation between the kitchen and the living room–dining room area, the absence of privacy for the bedroom integrated into the *séjour*, picture windows that were too large (entailing further lack of privacy and costly expenditures for window treatments),[11] and rooms whose walls, broken up by windows, radiators, doors, and closets, left few options for furniture placement. They also objected to poor soundproofing, cheap fixtures, and wall and floor coverings that were difficult to clean.[12]

Apprised of these criticisms, Sudreau invited Picard to assemble a team to form policy recommendations to improve resident satisfaction. Picard joined with three home economics institutes and organizations (the Association pour la Diffusion des Techniques Ménagères, the Centre d'Études

des Travaux Féminins, and the Institut Français d'Information pour l'Économie Ménagère) and consulted with nearly thirty different women's groups. The groups ranged from war widows' associations to groups for female small-business owners and included leagues of women doctors, organizations for female university graduates, women factory workers' associations, and groups for single mothers. Their collective membership, Picard boasted, represented 3 million French women. Out of these consultations arose a new model home. Picard tapped the MC's house architect, Marcel Roux, to give form to the women's recommendations, and the ministry decided to show a life-size model of the unit at the 1959 Salon des Arts Ménagers. In order to maximize the extent to which the remodeled *cellule* could be representative of the average French person's dwelling preferences, the MC decided to survey SAM visitors on their reactions to the space; moreover, the plan, photos, and description of the apartment were widely published, and readers (particularly those from the provinces who rarely visited the SAM in person) were encouraged to send in their comments as well, making the apartment a "referendum" on the present and future of public housing.

The Referendum Apartment was a 4P and bore many of the marks of Modern architecture. Marcel Gascoin had decorated the model home, and hostesses for the guided visit of the apartment noted that it did not suffer from "useless" or "outmoded" furnishings. They reminded visitors that the *séjour* had "definitively dethroned" the conventional dining room. As had been the case with the 1955 Happy House (see chapter 4), here too, one of the vaunted advantages of the Referendum Apartment was its ability to provide separate domains for children and parents. Because the entire space had been planned so that the children could work and play in their rooms without being disturbed or disturbing their parents, the tour guides claimed that the apartment would preserve intimacy and calm nerves.[13] In understanding the home as a site for tranquility and individual privacy, the Referendum Apartment offered continuity with past model modern homes shown at the SAM.

There were, however, some significant changes. First and foremost, Picard's team had increased the overall, inhabitable surface area of the apartment by approximately twelve square meters, well exceeding the MC's existing maximum norm of seventy square meters for a typical HLM 4P. In and of itself, this change represented a critique of the MC's policies, a critique rendered explicit by Picard's call for an official change in norm regulations.

If the *séjour* followed Modernist orthodoxy, the kitchen, on the other hand, represented heresy. Picard's apartment featured a large, eat-in kitchen (Figure 5.1). At twelve square meters, the Referendum Apartment

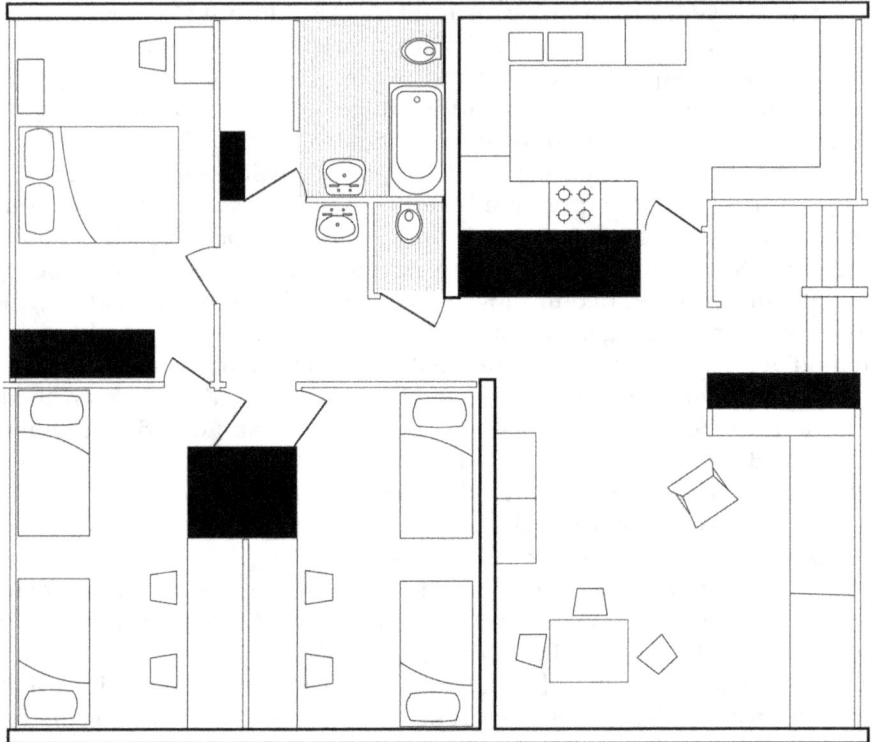

Figure 5.1. The *Appartement référendum*, 1959. Author's rendering, based on the original by Marcel Roux.

kitchen reflected the reality that families routinely dined there. Picard's team rejected the lab kitchen, where families did not have the option of having even informal meals like breakfast. Nevertheless, Roux retained the lab kitchen's rationalizing principle of reducing energy expenditure in meal preparation by placing the dining section of the kitchen off to one side of the room. In effect, he simply placed the dining nook found in *séjours* to the other side of the U-shaped lab kitchen.

Other changes included bedrooms that were separate from the *séjour* and designed to accommodate the size and placement of the traditional furniture that families owned (although an armoire was conspicuously absent from the décor of the Referendum Apartment at the SAM). The master bedroom connected to one of the children's rooms, and a long hallway and entryway restored independent circulation. A second sink facilitated morning and bedtime preparation for the family of six for whom this 4P was designed. Some of the changes seemed minor, but reflected major improvements in daily living from the point of view of those surveyed: a small bathtub replaced the shower stall ubiquitous in social housing, twice as many electrical outlets appeared in each room than called for in the CPTFM, and high-quality plumbing fixtures ensured that the comfort for which public housing had become famous would not require frequent repair.

The public took the referendum literally, and thousands offered their evaluation of the space. SAM visitors filled out surveys, and letters poured in to Picard at the ministry. Letter-writers noted that they had heard Picard on the radio or had seen the apartment in *Elle, Paris-Match,* or *Arts ménagers* magazine. They suggested adaptations for rural homes or proposed adding a play space for young children; a couple of writers recommended the inclusion of a "nice mirrored armoire" in the master bedroom. Others signaled their approval by simply wondering how they could acquire the plans for such a home or more information on the fixtures and furnishings featured in the Referendum Apartment. Comments and questions appear to have been taken seriously, with someone (most likely Picard herself) penciling reactions and notes in the margins.[14]

One group unanimously voted no on the referendum. Architects and designers, while concurring that the MC should increase the norms for surface area, rejected Picard's model. *Techniques et architecture* devoted an entire issue to a reconsideration of the *cellule* in the spring of 1959 and featured a spread on the Referendum Apartment, but added that, while HLM tenants had every right to complain about the lack of space, poor soundproofing, and faulty materials, these deficiencies were due to the administration, not to architecture; moreover, the problems occupants reported with ventilation, the editors claimed, demonstrated that the former simply did not know how to use their new spaces.[15] Some had a more violent reaction. Ionel Schein, architect of the futuristic Plastic House that had caused a sensation at the 1956 SAM, drafted a five-page letter to Jeanne Picard. He rejected the very premise of the Referendum Apartment and railed against its traditional corridor and eat-in kitchen:

> The public can not do this work and neither can three million women, even though they are users [of the spaces]. You don't go to the doctor to have him sign a prescription that you've written yourself … It's the same for a dwelling! … As soon as one enters [the Referendum Apartment], one is surrounded, in a hostile manner, by long walls and closed doors. There are not only unwanted visitors in a dwelling! How will a child evolve in such an environment? Have the three million mothers thought of *that*? But they haven't even thought of themselves! The problems of the kitchen, the dining area, and the living room have been thoroughly analyzed for over forty years by those who have been fascinated from the beginning by the question of the organization of the home with respect to new modes of living.[16]

Even Marcel Roux, the architect who had drawn up the Referendum Apartment blueprint, distanced himself from the project: "The plan presented here puts feminine aspirations into concrete form, but it should not be considered an ideal apartment, neither from an architectural point of view, nor from my own."[17] Architects and designers interpreted Picard's proposal—which rejected the lab kitchen, reestablished a corridor at the heart of the apartment, and used several sizes of windows (anathema to advocates of standardization)—as a referendum on the whole of modern architecture and the art of living that it was meant to inspire. After the housing ministry's turn to model plans in the early 1950s, which challenged the architect's raison d'être, the ministry's decision to incorporate women's feedback directly into home design seemed to represent a further blow to the architectural profession and a roadblock to the Modernist project to remake the French home.

Thus, the following year, in a more constructively critical vein, the Syndicat des Architectes de la Seine, an architectural collective led by Jean Balladur, a member of the Resistance and follower of Le Corbusier, exhibited a rebuttal apartment called the "Essai d'habitation évolutive (Experiment in Adaptive Housing)" at the SAM. The authors of the project attempted to accommodate inhabitant preferences in a more Modernist form, one that they imagined would represent progress and not simply reconstruct traditional interiors in a smaller space.

The plan for evolutionary housing identified a static floor plan as the real source of resident dissatisfaction. For the SAS, when domestic space could not evolve with the arrival of more children or with the different needs children had as they grew, then frustration with the space was bound to result. SAS therefore proposed a central service core, around which a number of moving partitions articulated rooms (Figure 5.2). By moving the partitions, residents could change room size and also attribute room usage as they wished. Believing this design to be an elegant and satisfactory response to the needs of inhabitants, the SAS appealed to Sudreau for state sponsorship of the Essai d'habitation évolutive at the 1960 SAM, but Sudreau replied that the ministry had already accorded its patronage for the 1960 exhibit to Picard's follow-up project, the Maison familiale (Family House), a detached home version of the Referendum Apartment.[18]

The Essai elicited praise, however, from those proponents of Modern architecture who had rejected the Referendum Apartment. In *L'Architecture française,* a feature on the Essai claimed that the model's high quality proved architects' superior expertise when it came to housing design. Françoise Choay, the architecture critic, praised it in *France-Observateur,* and L. Veillon-Duverneuil penned two glowing reviews in *Combat* and

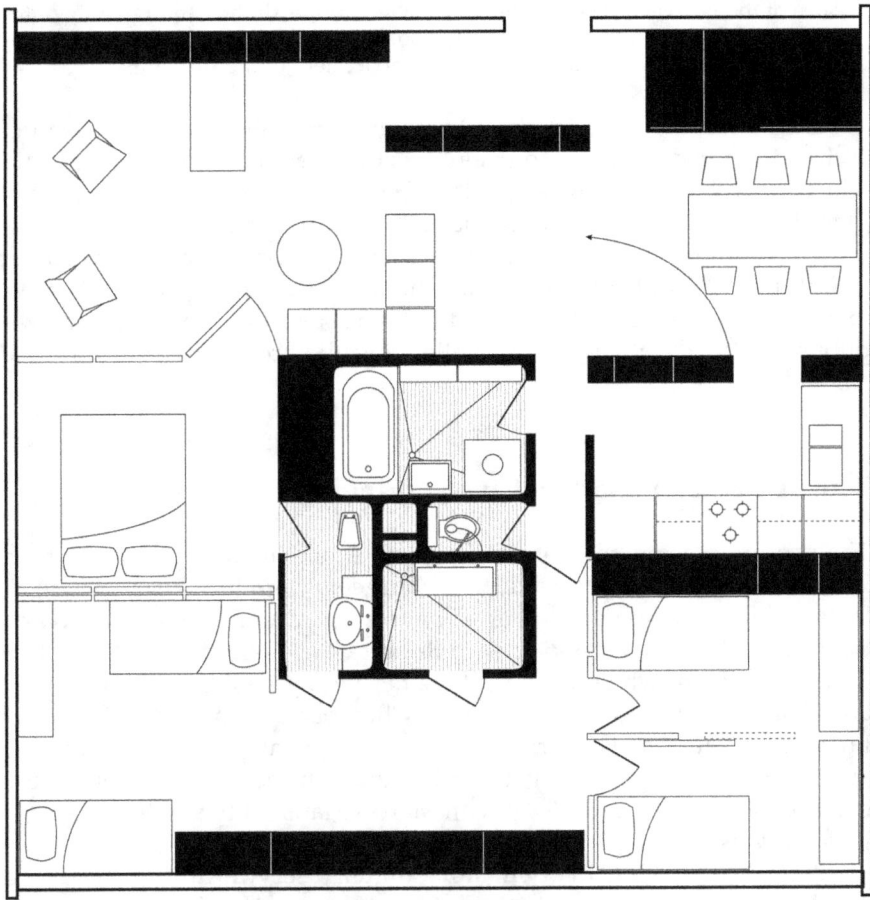

Figure 5.2. The *Essai d'habitation évolutive*, 1960. Author's rendering, based upon the original by the Syndicat des Architectes de la Seine.

the *Revue de l'ameublement et des industries du bois,* a trade publication. In the *Combat* piece, Veillon-Duverneuil belittled the participatory aspect of Picard's model:

> Last year, a charming learned assembly of matrons, all housewives, right-thinking and well-intentioned, in response to the ridiculous vague impulses of one amongst them, presented a "referendum" apartment, which seemed at the same time—we can say it now—both a practical joke and a do-it-yourself home! ... Architects, who, when these ladies permit them, also deal with questions of housing, reacted individually and collectively within their professional organizations. They reacted discreetly, as well-bred men. Courteous and gallant, they were careful not to upset this witty bevy of delightful little faces (delightful, but

sure of themselves!). They gathered together, modestly, and thought—men too have such ideas!—that perhaps they, too, by joining forces, who knows? they could present on the cours de Selves the apartment of their dreams.[19]

Veillon-Duverneuil and Schein both underscored the architects' expertise and undermined women's contributions by referring to them in sarcastic, sexist, and condescending terms. They reproduced the original position of interwar Modernists, who had rejected popular demands and desires as the basis for determining the optimal form of mass housing (see chapter 2). Yet their attempts to marginalize the women's contribution ultimately failed when urban sociologists, led by Paul-Henry Chombart de Lauwe, published *Famille et habitation*, challenging the architects' authority and competence.

Paul-Henry Chombart de Lauwe: Bringing Class Back In

The son of an army colonel, Paul-Henry Chombart de Lauwe was born in 1913 into a "half-aristocratic, half-bourgeois" family, whose fortune allowed him to pursue a number of interests, including flying and painting.[20] At 20, he began working with Robert Garric's Catholic organization Équipes sociales, which brought together young people from the upper and working classes in study groups; Chombart de Lauwe worked with Équipes sociales for six years.[21] When he was twenty-one, he spent a year at ENSBA, studying painting and sculpture, but soon dropped out to undertake the study of ethnology with Marcel Mauss at the Institut d'ethnologie in Paris.

After first fulfilling his obligatory military service during the 1930s, at which time he befriended the urbanist Robert Auzelle, Chombart de Lauwe joined the French leadership school at Uriage in 1940 and then the Resistance; he also flew for the Royal Air Force. It wasn't until Liberation that Chombart de Lauwe was able to begin building his academic career in earnest. Appointed a researcher at the CNRS, he also founded the Social Ethnology Group at the Musée de l'homme to study aspects of working-class life, and he invited Auzelle to join this group. In 1950, Chombart de Lauwe began work on a study of Paris as social space, published in 1952 as *Paris et l'agglomération parisienne*. Combining ecology, history, demography, sociology, and ethnography, his project centered on the anthropology of Parisian neighborhoods, with particular attention paid to the needs of working-class communities. Chombart de Lauwe had trouble getting CNRS funding for the project, because, as Claude Lévi-Strauss informed him, it would not be considered ethnology since it focused on the

French. Nor, however, could Chombart de Lauwe's work qualify as sociology: Chombart de Lauwe's thesis advisor, Georges Gurvitch, warned him that his intellectual approach exceeded sociology's disciplinary boundaries. Seeking support for what he called "social ethnography," Chombart de Lauwe eventually received funding for his study of Paris from Eugène Claudius-Petit at the MRU, to whom he had been introduced by Auzelle. The difficulty Chombart de Lauwe encountered obtaining institutional support for his work signaled to him early on that he would have to make explicit its unique contribution to scholarship and to contemporary society.

For the administration, an organization devoted to sophisticated analysis of working-class populations was a welcome associate, offering expertise to technocratic offices lacking the resources to acquire such knowledge on their own. After obtaining sponsorship from Claudius-Petit at the MRU, in 1955 Chombart de Lauwe garnered a commission from the CSTB to study three new HLMs in the Parisian area. In the fall of that year, his newly formed group for applied research, the Center for the Study of Social Groups (Centre d'études de groupes sociaux, or CEGS), conducted interviews at apartment complexes in Aubervilliers, Villeneuve Saint-Georges, and Argenteuil to isolate sources of resident satisfaction and dissatisfaction. The results of the study appeared in the *Cahiers du CSTB* in 1957 and were well-known at the housing ministry; Jeanne Picard even drew upon them for her Referendum Apartment.[22] With regard to interiors, the CEGS team learned that HLM inhabitants wanted eat-in kitchens, rooms sized in such a way that standard furniture[23] fit the space, and an end to the practice of placing a bedroom in an alcove or off of the *séjour*. Parents who had children of different sexes wanted to be able to put them in separate bedrooms after the age of eight.[24] These findings prefigured the results of both the Referendum Apartment and the second volume of *Famille et habitation*.

By the time the first volume of *Famille et habitation* appeared in 1959, Chombart de Lauwe had added two more works to *Paris et l'agglomération parisienne* and the 1957 article published by the CSTB. The CEGS performed another study of public housing in the Bordeaux metropolitan area, which appeared in the November 1958 issue of the *Cahiers du CSTB*, and in 1956 Chombart de Lauwe completed *La Vie quotidienne des familles ouvrières* (The Everyday Life of Working-Class Families), which examined the consumption patterns, social life, and time management of working-class men and women. Cumulatively, these projects, most of which built on in-depth interviews with residents, suggested that inhabitants of public housing had needs that architects and policymakers had not been able to identify and that user surveys and quantitative measures alone could not relate. In other words, Chombart de Lauwe claimed for urban sociologists the ability to distill residents' fundamental requirements and expectations from their discrete complaints about small room size and poor soundproofing. Thus, from the empirical reporting of inhabitants' satisfactions and dissatisfactions in the 1955 study of the HLMs in the Parisian region, Chombart de Lauwe isolated a resident's ten needs and aspirations. These were: (1) space; (2) the ability to organize and appropriate space; (3) the independence of groups of persons inside the housing unit; (4) rest and relaxation; (5) separation of functions; (6) well-being and freedom from material constraints; (7) intimacy of the family unit; (8) prestige; (9) ability to adapt the layout and organization of space to family structures; and (10) social relations outside of the home.[25] What the mass of complaints demonstrated was that the standardized *grand ensemble* 4P, as it existed in 1955, satisfied only partially some of these conditions, while precluding the possibility of realizing the others.

Chombart de Lauwe believed the notion of aspiration to be key to his contribution to housing design. In his view, architects' understanding of functionalism focused too much on physiological needs, such as meal preparation and consumption, sleeping, or shelter from temperature extremes, while arbitrarily determining residents' psychological needs, like intimacy. Dwellers expected their homes to fulfill other requirements, and these expectations, or aspirations, encompassed both the psychological (the affective role of furniture and its placement, for example) and the material (space to place a future purchase of an automobile or refrigerator). As long as these aspirations remained unknown and hence unfulfilled, the individual liberty that the 4P was supposed to guarantee remained only an "illusion"; moreover, Chombart de Lauwe presciently observed that contemporary aspirations were tomorrow's needs and warned builders, planners, and architects that they dismissed these at their own peril.[26]

The first volume of *Famille et habitation* attempted to trace the broad outline of the evolution of family structures and home design as societies moved from preindustrialization to industrialization and studied more closely the housing crisis in contemporary France, with a focus on the problems and dangers of slum housing and overcrowding. Drawing upon past studies and the recommendations of optimal surface areas developed by the Union Internationale des Organismes Familiaux at its 1957 conference in Cologne (subsequently known as the Cologne norms), Chombart de Lauwe's team recommended that policymakers allow at least fourteen square meters per person in an apartment. Otherwise, they warned, dissatisfaction would inevitably result. They also asserted a "critical threshold" of eight to ten square meters per person, below which serious psychological disturbances threatened family unity.[27]

The second half of the first volume sketched a brief history of functionalism in architecture and, in an effort to identify contemporary trends in architecture, contained interviews with a dozen leading architects and designers of the day, including Michel Bataille (a colleague of Jean Prouvé), Michel Écochard (famous for his work in Morocco), André Wogenscky (Le Corbusier's partner), Bernard Zehrfuss, André Hermant, Charlotte Perriand, Georges-Henri Pingusson, and Marcel Lods. Acknowledging the vanguard position of Le Corbusier in the architectural field, a separate section addressed his work and opinions.

This survey of Modernist architects is perhaps one of the most valuable contributions of Chombart de Lauwe's work for the twenty-first-century scholar of French modernism or domestic architecture. His team asked the architects questions that went straight to the heart of the debates that had filled the pages of the professional press since the interwar period. The interviewers asked architects to take a position on collective versus individual housing, the eat-in kitchen, the place of aesthetics in architecture, and the relative importance of the *cellule* in a *grand ensemble*'s site plan. Zooming in on the subject of their inquiry, the interviewers also posed specific questions about domestic space for families. What did the architects see as the particular needs of families, and how did they integrate these into their designs? What accommodations did they design for children within a home? What should be a family's role in the elaboration of an apartment plan?

With regard to this last question, virtually all of the architects were skeptical about the contributions families could make regarding the equipment and layout of their homes. Echoing Ionel Schein's analogy to physicians, André Wogenscky argued for the architect's absolute expertise: "Their [families'] attitude vis-à-vis the doctor is different: when they consult him, they explain what they are feeling, but they don't dictate the medicine that they should take. It's the opposite with architects. Women, in particular, are astonishing, they describe exactly what they want. Naturally, the architect should take people's desires into account, to the extent that their opinions seem justified to him."[28] Women's "astonishing" input clearly counted for little in architects' minds. Their position derived from sexism, classism, and a sentiment that women, as homemakers whose expertise and preferences drew from inherited knowledge and local norms, were responsible for perpetuating the very dwelling practices that the Modernists aimed to eliminate. Bataille articulated his colleagues' view when he replied that "families think they have opinions, but they really only have habits." André Hermant conceded that families could have some freedom as to the equipment and organization of their apartments, but only under the architect's guidance or tutelage. Most agreed with Wogenscky that families should be permitted to arrange their furniture how they liked, even if they made "errors." But only the furniture. Pingusson summed up their general position, posing the rhetorical question: "Should we be democratic and follow the desires of families, who have confused ideas based on what they have always seen, or should we advise them, orient them in an imperative fashion toward the norms of the new way of living?"[29]

Having opted for the latter, architects were willing to wait residents out. Resident dissatisfaction, as transcribed by the CEGS studies, for example, made little impact on these architects' beliefs about good design. Rather than accept that "the customer was always right," the architects surmised that users had not yet learned their lesson. Rural or working-class dwelling practices that deviated from the new art of living simply had not been exposed long enough to the spaces designed to eliminate them. In other words, resistance to residents' input did not only stem from the perception that their professional competence was being threatened. It also originated in the belief that there was a teleology of dwelling, and that architects, through good design, could—and should—educate users in the art of living for the greater good of sociocultural progress. On this basis, Pingusson justified the spatial tyranny of the lab kitchen: "I'm for the lab kitchen, one should not be able to have a lot of people in there, [the lab kitchen] is the exact opposite of the peasant kitchen, the hearth around which the family gathers, where you have the radio, and the laundry drying… This is a way of being together, but in a place where you shouldn't be. I consider the trend of confusing the kitchen with the living/dining area to be a fleeting one. It's both an American-bourgeois and a French-peasant tendency, one that I judge to be a backward step for the art of dwelling and a social decline."[30]

The first volume of *Famille et habitation* concluded with a vivid critique of such pedagogical architecture. Chombart de Lauwe accepted Modernists' claim that modern architecture distanced itself from its Beaux-Arts antecedent because human needs—not abstract aesthetic principles or concerns about social status—governed design. Yet the questions posed by Chombart de Lauwe's team exposed architects' tendencies to identify those needs in an individual, unscientific, and arbitrary manner. Hence, in Chombart de Lauwe's opinion, modern architecture was unable to satisfy what was, in fact, a complex plurality of fundamental requirements. He argued that only methodical observation by social scientists could accurately designate, categorize, and rank the needs—and aspirations—of *all* classes of families.[31]

Such methodical observation was the subject of the second volume of *Famille et habitation*, which brought the voices of residents onto the page. The households of workers, salaried employees, and managers, teachers, and civil servants contributed their evaluations of life in Le Corbusier's Cité Radieuse in Nantes-Rezé (a version of the Unité d'habitation at Marseille), in Jacques Carlu's Cité de la Benauge in Bordeaux, and in Robert Auzelle's Cité de la Plaine, in the Parisian suburb of Clamart. In the second volume, Chombart de Lauwe emphasized the novelty of mixed classes inhabiting one apartment complex and stressed the specificity of needs and aspirations, which varied not only by class, but by age, gender, family size, religion, and other variables. He observed that, since needs were socially constructed, it followed that the reception of new HLMs, designed for a single set of requirements, would vary as well as inhabitants transitioned from one form of housing (shared urban apartment, condemned tenement, or rural freestanding house, for example) to their modern mass homes.[32]

In response, Chombart de Lauwe's team set out to identify, categorize, and measure changes in individuals' and groups' behavior, satisfaction, and expectations as a result of living in modern social housing. Over 80 percent of families expressed satisfaction with their new apartments, but when residents were asked to decide whether they were "very happy" or "happy and not more," only 20 percent of middle-class residents claimed to be very happy, whereas between 40 and 42 percent of workers and lower-middle-class occupants, respectively, opted for this evaluation. The majority of families (93 percent) had modified their apartments in some fashion, confirming the need to appropriate space and demonstrating that the apartments rarely operated as anonymous machines for living. Chombart de Lauwe's team also discovered that over 50 percent of fathers spent more time at home since their families had moved into the HLMs, and that workers did so in a higher proportion than the other two groups. (More than likely, this phenomenon had much to do with the fact that working-class men were now far from familiar urban gathering spots like cafés, and many didn't own automobiles. Once they returned home from work, men found fewer social distractions in the *grand ensemble* community.) Researchers also found that men helped more with housework, though the chores that they assumed varied by class (working-class fathers assisted with cooking and shopping, while the manager/civil servant group helped with the dishes).[33]

Other findings exposed the difficulty of life in the *grands ensembles* when apartments suffered from overcrowding, when the housing projects lacked certain collective facilities, such as childcare centers and spaces for adolescents,[34] or when they were far from shops and served infrequently by mass transport.[35] The study of the Cités Radieuse, de la Benauge, and de la Plaine led to a series of recommendations for urban planners, architects, and policymakers. In order for different classes to successfully inhabit the same apartment complex, Chombart de Lauwe asserted, it was imperative to use the highest quality soundproofing, to design hallways in such a way as to facilitate anonymous comings and goings, to permit the development of residents' advocacy groups, and to incorporate the feedback of these groups into the day-to-day administration of the *grands ensembles*. Chombart de Lauwe was the first to say outright that the post-Liberation dream of the one-size-fits-all democratized modern home was, in fact, a dream. He thought the goal of mixing classes to be, in general, a novel and positive one (comparing it to efforts to "force blacks and whites to live together" in the United States), but he warned that, without sufficient attention to sociological differences in dwelling practices, *grands ensembles* would only aggravate the tensions between the classes and groups who lived within them.[36] The middle classes might disparage those who hung their laundry on the balconies; working-class inhabitants might come to hate their more fortunate neighbors, who could afford the streamlined furniture, televisions, and cars that made *grand ensemble* living more enjoyable.

In general, apartments fared better in residential evaluations than did the *grands ensembles* as a whole. Yet, the improvements that inhabitants suggested for their domestic spaces sound familiar. Chombart de Lauwe summarized these in his conclusion to the second volume: "Renters do not like having a bedroom right off of the living room. On the other hand, they often would like a hallway that facilitates the isolation of the other rooms. Finally, a larger kitchen permitting family dining is desired, particularly by working-class and lower-middle-class households."[37] In other words, the residents of these three new complexes approved—indirectly—the Referendum Apartment.

Architects, Engineers, and State Planners React

Having sponsored the Referendum Apartment and recruited Chombart de Lauwe for one of his *grand ensemble* working groups,[38] it is not surprising that Sudreau was receptive to reports of inhabitant preferences. The MC implemented a number of changes that responded to residents' concerns. Most significantly, Sudreau revised the size requirements for state-funded housing. In April 1960, the MC raised the minimum surface area norms for Logecos (although the maximums remained the same), and in 1961, the maximum surface areas norms for normal HLMs increased. Moreover, acknowledging that technical comfort did not compensate for small spaces, even among the least fortunate classes, the ministry made the regular HLM norms universally applicable to all categories of HLMs.

This included the new category of housing called the *programmes sociaux de relogement* (social relocation programs, or PSR), designed for housing tenants of slum housing; PSRs replaced LOPOFAs, but they would henceforth be equal in size to ordinary HLMs.[39] On the other hand, the fact that it took until 1963, and the tenure of the next minister, Jacques Maziol, to raise the minimum surface norms for the HLMs tempered the achievements of Sudreau's administration with regard to satisfying public demand. The table below summarizes the content of these amendments.

Table 5.1. Evolution of Surface Area Allowances for Public Housing, 1954–1963 (measurements given in square meters)

	1955 Logeco	1960 Logeco	1955 HLMB	1961 HLM/PSR	1963 HLM/PSR
2P	34–45	39–45	39–45	39–50	42–50
3P	44–57	51–57	51–57	51–63	55–63
4P	53–68	61–68	61–70	61–77	66–77
5P	63–82	73–82	73–85	73–93	80–93

Sources: *Habitations Collectives à loyer modéré à usage locatif: Normalisation des caractéristiques* (Paris: Journal Officiel de la République Française, December 1955), 1; Arrêté, 14 April 1960, "Caractéristiques des logements économiques et familiaux" (*Journal Officiel* 15 April 1960, 3524); Arrêté, 24 May 1961, "Caractéristiques des habitations à loyer modéré à usage locatif" (Magri, *Logement et reproduction de l'exploitation*, 203); Arrêté, 13 October 1963, "Caractéristiques des habitations à loyer modéré à usage collectif" (Magri, *Logement et reproduction de l'exploitation*, 204).

In addition to augmenting the surface area of the apartments, Sudreau proceeded to improve their quality. The Handbook of Unified Minimum Technical and Functional Instructions (Cahier des prescriptions techniques et fonctionnelles minimales unifiées, or CPTFMU), issued by Sudreau in June 1960, eliminated differences in the quality of equipment, fixtures, and materials employed in the different categories of HLMs.[40] The CPT-FMU spoke directly to criticisms highlighted by Picard and Chombart de Lauwe by stipulating that kitchens could no longer open onto the *séjour* (except for studio and one-bedroom apartments) and implicitly endorsed the eat-in kitchen by specifying a minimum combined surface area for the kitchen and living room–dining room area of twenty-one square meters. (The *séjour* retained its status as the most important room in the home, however, since it had to measure at least twelve square meters.)

Other improvements included an increase in the amount of storage space in HLMs. Henceforth, closet space and shelving in any unit had to total at least 4 percent of the inhabitable surface area, and all new construction (except near the Mediterranean) had to offer central heating.

Moreover, the minimum temperature of a heated apartment rose from 12 degrees Celsius (53 degrees Fahrenheit) in the bedrooms and 16 degrees (60 degrees) in the *séjour* to a consistent 18 degrees (64 degrees) throughout the entire apartment.[41] Ideas about what constituted comfort—and what higher rents entitled residents to—were evolving as France entered the second half of the Trente Glorieuses.

Norms of privacy and intimacy were changing, too. HLM offices altered their attribution regulations to allow a couple with two young children to rent a 4P if the children were of different sexes; previously, they would have been placed in a 3P. This policy change recognized two realities. First, it accepted parental desires to segregate children of the opposite sex. Second, it acknowledged that, while in theory, the family would have been reassigned a larger apartment when the children grew old enough to merit separation, in reality, HLM waiting lists were so long that families who would have preferred to move into larger quarters did not always get the opportunity to do so. The policy change attempted to ease, if not completely prevent, HLM overcrowding.[42]

In addition to these modest responses to the residential critiques relayed by Picard and Chombart de Lauwe, the construction ministry assisted attempts to prolong the life of the Referendum Apartment. With the benefit of state funds, a private HLM company built over 400 "referendum apartments" at Thiais, in the southern suburbs of Paris.[43] Also, reincarnations of the Referendum Apartment appeared at both the 1960 and 1961 SAMs. As mentioned above, Picard showed the Family House, essentially the Referendum Apartment in detached house form, at the 1960 SAM. The National Building Federation, which had cosponsored the Family House, received approval from the MC to use a modified version of the plan as a Logeco model plan. In 1961, *Arts ménagers* magazine exhibited the "Prefab Apartment," another design based on the Referendum Apartment.[44] It was built by the Société d'Études et de Réalisation de Procédés Économiques de Construction (SERPEC), a conglomerate of the largest construction companies. As had the National Building Federation, SERPEC received Logeco model plan certification.[45] Now the ministry's model plans included not only those designed by modernist architects but those incorporating residents' preferences.

Cumulatively, these changes did not amount to a revolution in social housing, and one should not overestimate their significance; the extended life of the Referendum Apartment did not signal an end to technocratic modernist home design. But they did represent a shift in ministerial outlook. Modification of the *cellule*'s floor plan and an increase in surface areas reflected the seriousness with which the ministry took the findings of Picard and Chombart de Lauwe and suggested a real willingness to incorporate some resident desires into policymaking.[46] Where a minister like Claudius-Petit had cherished Modernist housing as a vehicle for his vision of future French grandeur and had therefore endorsed Modernists architects' top-down approach to shaping domestic space, the next generation of leaders, personified at the MC by Sudreau, sought out inhabitant input. Confronted directly with resident discontent, and wanting to maintain the *grand ensemble* as the predominant form of urban housing, Sudreau's decision to modify aspects of the *cellule* to maximize "customer satisfaction" reflected a less ideological, more pragmatic approach to the provision of housing. It thus signified an end to the ministry's attempt to shape the way French people lived.

The endorsement of the eat-in kitchen in the Referendum Apartment and the exhortation to architects to allow space for inclusion of "traditional" furniture amounted to official recognition of Chombart de Lauwe's argument that class mattered at home. At the same time, the ministry's efforts to reduce the normative differences between varieties of public housing by creating one set of spatial and equipment norms illustrates its desire to maintain the Liberation-era ambition of raising the standard of living for all citizens by improving their domestic spaces. Chombart de Lauwe's work tolled the death knell for the one-size-fits-all 4P as an ideal modern home, but—and this is important—it did not lessen the ministry's commitment to providing the French with a minimum level of comfort, and to revising official conceptions of that minimum as the nation's material situation improved throughout the 1950s and 60s.

Another official initiative to incorporate French inhabitants' expectations and dwelling preferences took place in the belly of the technocratic beast: the CSTB. In a 1961 issue of the CSTB's journal, Jacques Dreyfus and Jean Tribel published an article entitled, "The Housing Cell: Analysis of Its Problems; Search for New Solutions."[47] Dreyfus was, at this time, a head engineer for Ponts et Chaussées and in charge of the CSTB's Service des études fonctionnelles (Office of Functionality Research). Tribel was an architect who served as an advisor to the CSTB. With another architect, Georges Loiseau, Tribel had won a 1959 SCIC competition to design a *grand ensemble* and, in 1960, had cofounded a collective of leftist architects, engineers, and designers known as the Atelier d'urbanisme et d'architecture (AUA). Together, Dreyfus and Tribel set out to determine the design implications of Chombart de Lauwe's research.[48]

As their point of departure, they took from Chombart de Lauwe the principle that family structures—not an idealized art of living—should be at the center of a needs-based functionalism. Moreover, they emphasized that these family structures changed over time. The question they then set out to answer was: how could an apartment designed for a family with four young children still be suitable when those children reached adolescence? If the previous conception of inhabitants' needs attempted to reconcile privacy (of the individual) with intimacy (of the family as a whole), a refined understanding of needs based on sociological studies led to the isolation of the requirements of groups within the family. Dreyfus and Tribel commented wryly, "The picture of the large family gathered together in the *séjour*, the father reading and the mother performing some household task (sewing, for example), while an older child does his homework and the young ones play on the floor with blocks is somewhat idyllic."[49] Families did not spend all of their waking time at home in the living room–dining room area, so they needed more space elsewhere in the home to accommodate the different requirements of parents, older children, and younger children. Dreyfus and Tribel argued that parents had to maintain prestige in the eyes of their children in order to reinforce parental authority; they thus needed a separate, master bedroom apart from the *séjour*, a space larger than other bedrooms to symbolize their primacy in the family unit. Smaller children had to have room to play, so Dreyfus and Tribel recommended play spaces outside of shared bedrooms for the young ones. Adolescents, on the other hand, wanted to entertain their friends separately from family activities; Dreyfus and Tribel explained that small but autonomous bedrooms fit older children's needs better. The focus on teenagers reflected both demographic and cultural phenomena: by 1961, the children of the baby boom were in their teens, and the large cohort of adolescents provoked anxiety about their specific activities, ranging to concerns about rock and roll music to worries about juvenile delinquents and youth gangs.[50]

Dreyfus and Tribel also turned to sociology to debunk the belief that comfort could compensate for small spaces, asserting that the sociological evidence definitively demonstrated that if a space was overcrowded, elements like central heating, hot running water, and sanitary installations did not rule out occupant dissatisfaction.[51] They noted that families seemed to need more differentiated spaces, like hallways, children's playrooms, and laundry rooms. They set out to determine the minimum dimensions by which a *cellule* would need to be increased if its floor plan incorporated more specialized spaces, even if the functions of these were reassigned by the household as its needs changed over time.

Indeed, a second key insight from Chombart de Lauwe's work that Dreyfus and Tribel wanted to disseminate was the idea that architectural definitions of function did not match inhabitants'. Throughout the article, they emphasized the gap between architectural conceptions of family life and the reality as exposed in surveys and studies. The clash was particularly apparent in the realm of furnishings. Dreyfus and Tribel informed architects that homes were rarely furnished as architects imagined when they were designing apartment layouts; moreover, inherited and traditional furniture fulfilled an affective function that architects ignored. They claimed that buffets and dining room suites symbolized the family's social standing, while the bedroom furniture (which often included the mirrored armoire that letter writers to Picard had suggested for inclusion in the Referendum Apartment) helped to differentiate the parents' bedroom from the others, reinforcing their "prestige" in the eyes of their children.[52]

In order to maximize occupant satisfaction, Dreyfus and Tribel urged architects to reconcile themselves to a seemingly imperfect functionalism. Of the armoire they wrote, "If we want to accelerate the apparently desirable disappearance of this bulky and expensive piece of furniture, it follows that we must include a closet in [the master bedroom], while giving users the possibility of putting an armoire in there. Unfortunately, a waste of space results."[53] In proposing this seemingly inefficient but transitional solution, Dreyfus and Tribel explicitly affirmed the Modernist premise that a modern art of living entailed spare and streamlined furnishings. Like architects, they seemed confident that inhabitant preferences would eventually catch up with those of Modernist tastemakers; the latter simply needed to be more patient. Dreyfus and Tribel did not question key aspects of the Modernist vision of domestic space. In another example, they tried to reassure architects that residents with eat-in kitchens would not waste precious space by turning their living areas into Sundays-only parlors. In the authors' view, this was unlikely to happen because of the public's increasing acquisition of televisions, which families tended to place in the *séjour*.[54]

Furthermore, their creation of autonomous zones for older and younger children outside of the *séjour* followed a Modernist trend of preserving the living room–dining room area for adult activities. Presenting the Essai at the 1959 SAM, the SAS had argued that one of the advantages of their floor plan was its independent circulations, which kept traffic within the home from disturbing those at rest, either the "relaxation of the parents in the *salle de séjour* or the sleep of a little one in his bedroom."[55] The very function of the *séjour* had originally been as the primary site of family interaction and the production of family unity; now architects were exiling children to their own rooms or to playrooms. This concern for the prestige, privacy, and relaxation of the parents, apart from their children, supports Kristin Ross's assertion of the growing importance of the couple in postwar France. Ross cites sociologist Edgar Morin's contemporary observation: "The totality of affective attachments, which were previously diffused in a number of interfamilial relations, ... now tends to become concentrated in the couple."[56] A mentality privileging the couple apart from their children also reflected the decline in pronatalist activism. As Antoine Prost points out, by the beginning of the Fifth Republic, the goals of the pronatalists had been met, and Rémi Lenoir notes that the family allocations portion of the Social Security budget had declined from 40 percent in 1949 to almost 29 percent in 1960.[57]

In the second part of their article, Dreyfus and Tribel laid out six different "examples of non-traditional solutions," each accompanied by a chart listing the advantages and disadvantages. Their model plans juggled evolving and differing needs by incorporating children's play areas, privacy for parents, "boxes" for adolescents, where they could entertain friends or just be alone, and sliding doors on the eat-in kitchen, to offer residents the option of closing the dining space off from the *séjour* or leaving it open. Some of these dispositions appeared in later HLM buildings, attesting to the article's influence (see chapter 6).

The CSTB's "The Housing-Cell" and *Techniques et Architecture*'s issue on "Housing: Conception-Equipment" thus brought interiors back onto the pages of the architectural press. The fact that the reexamination of the *cellule* was often accompanied by critiques (ranging from mild to severe) of architects refueled architects' conflicts with state planners. When SAS put forth the design for its "Essai d'habitation évolutive," a laundry list of complaints about the administrative regulations that constrained innovative architectural solutions accompanied the plan. Written by SAS members Rémy Le Caisne and O. Lesné, the protests condemned, for example, the regulation enforcing ceiling heights of two and a half meters, which kept architects from proposing two-story apartments like those found in Le Corbusier's Unité d'habitation, or the prescription against bedrooms smaller than nine square meters, "when all the foreign countries have adopted bedrooms of five and six square meters."[58] Even the Essai's central service core, reminiscent of that employed by Jean Prouvé in his Better Days House (see chapter 4), represented a challenge to policymakers, since this disposition was still prohibited by the CPTFMU, a proscription of which Dreyfus and Tribel approved in their article.[59]

Some architects did not reserve their enmity for the state alone. As the Chombart de Lauwe interviews had shown, many architects believed families themselves—with their "bad habits" and "peasant tendencies"—were partly to blame if their homes weren't satisfactory. Speaking at the Salon International de la Construction et de l'Équipement in 1959, Jacques-Henry Labourdette, one of Sarcelles' architects, lashed out at residents: "If it is true that our apartments are sometimes imperfectly completed, conversely, people, generally, live quite poorly. And when we see the manner in which nicely finished apartments are found after six months of inhabitation, we are absolutely sick at heart. ... Sometimes it happens that we provide unpainted apartments in order to reduce the cost price. A few months later, the walls still haven't been painted but are covered with stains. On the other hand, the occupants have bought, on credit, a car and a television."[60] For Labourdette, inhabitants' use of credit seemed to reveal the moral failings that made them poor tenants. He did not see that residents might have been willing to go into debt to buy automobiles and televisions because these were necessary if one was to live in *grands ensembles* far from mass transportation, work, movie theaters, or cafés. Modernist architects like Pingusson and Labourdette took the position that the *cellule could* be an ideal home, if completed by its occupants with the furnishings and appliances that would make it fully functional. If residents failed to do so, dissatisfaction with their domestic space was their own fault.

A new generation of architects was beginning to dissociate itself from its Modernist forebears, however. In 1956, at the CIAM's tenth congress, Georges Candilis had been among a group of younger architects who had interrogated the premises of the Charter of Athens, challenging Modernism's abstract functionalism and urging a more humanistic approach to architecture and urbanism. It was, in fact, Candilis's call for an adaptive apartment that would take into account individual familial contexts that inspired the form of SAS's Essai d'habitation évolutive. SAS's Jean Balladur, born in 1923, and the AUA's Jean Tribel, born in 1929, belonged to a cohort that included Tribel's colleagues in the AUA, Paul Chemetov (b. 1928) and Jean Deroche (b. 1931), as well as Jean Renaudie (b. 1925), Michel Andrault (b. 1926), Pierre Parat (b. 1928), and Jacques Bardet (b. 1928). All had learned architecture from masters like André Lurçat, Marcel Lods, and André Hermant, but they were a generation removed from Modernism's interwar origins. By 1960, Modernism had won its battle for legitimacy in architectural circles, and the society whose needs a functionalist architecture was designed to fulfill was still changing, as Dreyfus' and Tribel's reference to the implications of television indicated.

"Putting People in Different Kind of Apartments and Seeing How They React"

As mentioned at the outset of this chapter, the past decade has been a fruitful one for the historiography of the *grands ensembles*. As certain buildings or whole complexes have been demolished or renovated, researchers, often working for local municipalities, have been active compiling memories from the first and second generations of *grand ensemble* inhabitants. Although the problems with using memories as evidence are well known,[61] testimonials from residents provide additional materials that help us to reconstruct "how it felt" to live in a new *grand ensemble*, without the filter of a Chombart de Lauwe concerned explicitly with policy recommendations. In other words, recent oral histories and interview projects allow twenty-first-century historians to get at the second half of Gerald Blachère's description of Trente Glorieuses housing policy: "putting people in different kinds of homes and seeing how they react." How did residents react? What did they think about their homes? Did they construct modern lives for themselves in mass housing?

Two recent oral histories, Geneviève Michel and Pierre-Jacques Derainne's *Aux Courtillières: Histoires singulières et exemplaires* and Sylvain Taboury and Karine Gougerot's *Billardon, Histoire d'un grand ensemble,* are particularly helpful for providing a wealth of first-person material describing life at two *grands ensembles*: Émile Aillaud's Les Courtillières (see chapter 4), and a fourteen-story "bar" of 250 apartments at the Cité Billardon in Dijon, designed by architect Pierre Beck and built between 1953 and 1955. Billardon was followed in 1956 and 1957 by two neighbors, the similar though somewhat more spartan bars, Epirey and Les Lochères. All three bars were ultimately demolished: Epirey in 1992; Lochères in 2000, and finally, the "Dijonnaise Cité Radieuse"—as it was described at its inception—in 2003. Taboury and Gougerot's collection serves as a sort of wake for Billardon, with both former and longtime residents recounting their memories of the complex. *Aux Courtillières* was written in conjunction with a massive rehabilitation project undertaken by the city of Pantin to preserve Aillaud's efforts, and, in so doing, to recall what worked, and what did not work, for neighborhood residents. Together, the collections allow us to draw upon the collective experiences of Parisian and provincial *grand ensemble* dwellers, and they merit our attention, especially because these complexes were put less frequently under the media's microscope than was their infamous peer, Sarcelles. Through these oral histories, therefore, we can therefore get at a certain quotidian, non-sensationalized experience of life at a new *grand ensemble*.

Reading these collections, we learn that Chombart de Lauwe and Blachère were correct to note the novelty of the social mixing taking place in *grands ensembles*. What accounted for such diversity? Heterogeneity stemmed especially from the different vectors of apartment attribution. Buildings proximate to one another might have been built by different public companies. "The serpent," also called "the noodle," at Les Courtillières, for example, was built for SEMIDEP (Société d'économie mixte immobilière interdépartementale de la région parisienne), whereas Pantin's HLM public housing office built the complex's nine blue, thirteen-story towers. Builders, ministries, and municipalities divvied up the units of a *grand ensemble*; typically, a municipality had the right to disburse 10 percent of a *grand ensemble*'s apartments to local residents, and, as apartments became available, officials allocated them according to a list kept at the town hall. Eager home-seekers often signed up on multiple lists in different suburbs or *arrondissements*, hoping their number would come up somewhere. It was not rare to wait years prior to receiving an allocation, as was the case for Geneviève Legrand, who had waited six years for an attribution.[62] Local companies could sponsor employees for apartments through the 1 percent patronal contributions, and a number of Courtillières residents mentioned that this was the route that they had taken to new homes.[63] Local family allowances offices were able to allocate a certain number of apartments and often prioritized large families living in severely overcrowded apartments or furnished rooms. Finally, particular ministries might be given access to a ration of apartments. The Ministry of Overseas France lodged a number of its repatriated staff at Les Courtillières, while career military had priority at Billardon, as did employees (primarily teachers but also other educational staff) of the National Education ministry. Residents observed that they really did have neighbors from all walks of life. At Les Courtillières, industrial designers, photographers, CPAs, typographers, and publishing industry employees mixed with mechanics, office workers, salespeople, and factory foremen. Billardon housed many career military officers, but also pipefitters, postal carriers and clerks, journalists, electric company employees, nurse-midwives, lab technicians, police inspectors, and a driving school instructor. Because Billardon's first floor included eight shops, the shopkeepers who lived above their businesses were neighbors with their customers. Residents recalled their interactions with the baker, dry cleaner, grocers, hairdresser, and news agent, and one of the grocers extolled his twelve years at Billardon as the best in his professional life, before he began to lose business due to the rise of big box stores like Carrefour.[64]

There was also some ethnic diversity in the first generation of *grands ensembles*. True, as we have seen, architects and planners' imaginary residents of the modern 4P were primarily white, French, nuclear families, but the realities of attributions were somewhat more complex. Families of foreigners were only eligible for an HLM attribution if they had been in the Hexagon for at least ten years and had children, and even then, a cap limited the number of foreign nationals in any given HLM to 6.5 percent of the available units.[65] Algerians, on the other hand, were housed by SONACOTRAL, an organization created in 1956 and headed by none other than Eugène Claudius-Petit. For those fortunate enough to escape shantytowns, SONACOTRAL built barracks for single workers and housed families in prefabricated transitory housing known as *cités de transit*. Yet, worried about the social and political pitfalls of ghettoization,

SONACOTRAL and public housing authorities settled on a de facto quota of 15 to 20 percent Algerian families per *grand ensemble*. Integrating Algerian families, authorities believed, would speed their assimilation into French culture and dilute any tendencies toward political separatism. At the same time, limiting the Algerian population within any given apartment complex would, it was hoped, protect public authorities and Algerians themselves from hostility from poorly housed native French families, while assuring a conflict-free social environment for building managers.[66]

The *grands ensembles,* as spectacles of "ultramodernity," lent themselves easily to caricature: those who focused on their social repercussions painted a picture of apartment complexes that housed only white nuclear families whose middle-class fathers commuted hours to work, whose lonely stay-at-home mothers stared despondently out of their shiny picture windows, and whose bored children roamed the estate grounds looking for trouble. Yet, at Billardon, for example, at least one of the career military officers to whom an apartment had been attributed was a woman. The building also housed Moroccan *tirailleurs,* whose 5th regiment was garrisoned in Dijon from 1955 to 1965. At Les Courtillières, one family was headed by a married couple of white physical education teachers, and their neighbors were Algerians whose family received an apartment attribution because the father was part of the corps of workers who had built Les Courtillières. The apartments may have been standardized, but the residents certainly were not.

What residents did often have in common were their reactions to the new homes. New residents were nearly always struck by the large size of the rooms. At Les Courtillières, those moving in used words like "marvel" to describe their impressions of their homes and joked about getting lost in their multiple-room apartments.[67] Marie-Louise Courdemanche recalled that she had previously been living in a furnished room sublet from an aunt, and that she had had to send her newborn son to a wet-nurse because there was no heat in the apartment.[68] Similarly, Viviane Belhassen spoke of a night prior to moving into her *grand ensemble* when her parents had to turn two of their children over to child welfare services because there were too many of them for their rented room.[69]

It was the same story in Dijon. Before moving into Billardon, Raymond and Aline had been living in a small house without heat. The only running water was in the courtyard, and it often froze. In 1956, coal was hard to come by, and the couple requested permission from the local authorities to gather wood from the nearby forest. Even with fires from the wood and kindling they scavenged, however, the home only reached a temperature of 55 degrees, and they had a six-month-old baby. When they arrived at Billardon, Aline wept. There were bright, well-lit rooms and hot running water. "It was paradise," Aline exulted.[70] It is worth noting that theirs was no story of rural poverty: Raymond was an agronomist specializing in viticulture who had been transferred from Montpellier to a laboratory in Dijon. Like residents of Les Courtillières, Billardon residents also used the word "palace" to describe their new homes.[71]

It is impossible to overstate the novelty of and gratitude for indoor toilets. In their former apartment, Jean-Claude and Nicole's toilet was twenty yards from their building; another resident named Jean-Claude was overjoyed about his new flush—instead of a Turkish—toilet.[72] Monique, who moved into Billardon in 1965, related that her previous home, in an old Dijonnaise apartment building, only had a toilet on the first floor, a smelly locale housing all of the garbage cans for the building. Monique had no nostalgia for the "old days": "Young people simply can't imagine it. When I hear my son-in-law tell me, 'It's much harder now for young people to start out, than for you,' I say, 'You have *no* idea what you're saying! You don't know what we endured.'"[73] Jean-Claude, who had been living in a *chambre de bonne* with his family, observed, "It was great progress," and Jacques explicitly linked "comfort" and "progress."[74] These inhabitants located their residential pasts in a "before," subscribing to a teleology of dwelling that validated the state's efforts to modernize everyday life for the French.

Yet the shared relief and gratitude at having found a personal solution to the national housing crisis did not blind residents to imperfections in their homes. At the Courtillières towers, the prefabricated panels used in their construction had been imperfectly joined, so water entered many of the apartments.[75] Geneviève Legrand complained that the care taken by the Courtillières' management to protect building amenities meant that they took elevators out of service when families moved in, so that boxes and furniture did not damage the elevators; unfortunately for Legrand, she was moving into an eighth-floor apartment.[76] Other imperfections, while disappointing, practically required a household to appropriate its space, as inhabitants adapted interiors to their preferences. Wanda Maggio and Lucette Magnon, at Les Courtillières, each told of their shock when they first saw the completely bare, unpainted walls of their new homes.[77] Residents at both Billardon and Les Courtillières papered the walls to their liking, but did so at their own expense. Since their apartments lacked the interior doors or accordion walls that would allow residents to adapt space to their needs, renters at both complexes installed partitions, creating a "real" dining room, indicating a separation between an alcove bedroom and the living room, or putting up a curtain to close off the kitchen.

Lucette Magnon recalled her frustration when, two months prior to moving in to her apartment at Les Courtillières, she bought a washing machine, only to discover that there was no place to plug it in in her new home. Her husband ultimately managed to rig up something in the bathroom, but the absence of appropriate outlets was bizarre, she observed, because washing machines, while not ubiquitous, were not exceptionally rare in 1958.[78] Magnon's astonishment reveals her expectation that the modern *grand ensemble* should incorporate state-of-the-art interiors, an expectation nourished by the mass press and the Salon des Arts Ménagers. Her surprise was echoed by Frederick Rose, the prominent New York builder and developer. Rose had built two thousand units of publicly funded Mitchell-Lama housing in New York for middle-income families, and he visited *grand ensemble* HLMs in Paris and Tours in 1962 as part of the United Nations Economic Commission for Europe's Housing Committee. Critiquing the lab kitchen's exiguousness, he also disparaged the lack of electrical outlets, noting that in some apartments he saw five extension cords plugged into one outlet.[79] Interiors "lagged behind the times," according to Rose, because they failed to accommodate or anticipate the appliances that drove the modernization of the household. Clearly, the "learned assembly of matrons" knew what they were doing when they demanded more outlets in the Referendum Apartment.

Inhabitants' appropriation of space was not always limited to the interiors. At Billardon, for example, renters took care of the hallways and kept the rubbish chutes tidy.[80] This appears to have been standard operating procedure in the first generation of mass social housing, and Monique, a mother of four who had moved to Billardon after her husband died, remembered the tensions that arose at another HLM building after she had had twins and failed to contribute to the upkeep of the public spaces: "When I had the twins, I barely had time to think of the staircases, I had to drive my older children to school, to take care of my girls [the twin babies], all that... And then one day, [my neighbor] let me know that there was dust in the staircase, and that I should really do the staircases—I told her that the stairs came second, and then, well, there you go, we were off."[81] Previously quite social, after that experience Monique made a deliberate effort to keep to herself at Billardon.

Other aspects of *grand ensemble* life also impaired the individual freedom that architect André Hermant had promised the modern home would maximize. Les Courtillières banned pets, for example, and at Billardon, residents earned a reprimand from the building manager if they left a baby carriage in the hallway outside of their door.[82] Children who grew up at Billardon and Les Courtillières remembered the efforts they made to avoid getting in trouble with building superintendents for playing where they shouldn't or running on lawns not intended to be playgrounds. At Les Courtillières, management prohibited the following: keeping bicycles or children's scooters in the apartment; running a business out of one's home; washing or hanging laundry in the kitchen or living room; beating rugs on the terraces except at particular times; and leaving one's front door open. Housewives could only receive deliveries before 11:00 AM in the winter or 10:00 AM in the summer.[83] Could one ever feel completely free or at home in such a milieu?

And what did these residents make of their social lives at Billardon and Les Courtillières? Much of the received knowledge about *grands ensembles* suggested that residents were bored and lonely. "Life Boring for French in a Suburb," the *New York Times* reported in 1962; women were reputedly prone to nervous depression—the infamous "Sarcellitis"—caused by a "crushing sense of isolation."[84] Yet the lived experience of both former and longtime *grand ensemble* residents as recorded by interviewers suggests that satisfying or rewarding social experiences could be had ... to the extent that one wanted them. For every Monique who retreated into her interior, there was also a Paulette who reported enjoying "Friendship Hours," during which she and her neighbors would get together, knit, exchange recipes, and have *les Tupéroirs,* Tupperware parties.[85] Nicole at Billardon called her years there (1966–1974) the "belle époque," because of the close and long-lasting friendships she made with other mothers at the playground.[86] At Les Courtillières, which did not have the on-site shops that Billardon did, a grocer brought his truck to the apartments' parking lot, and standing in line allowed shoppers to get to know one another; renters also mentioned socializing at the twice-weekly farmer's markets.[87] Parent-teacher associations were a significant source of social interaction at the complex, and the PTA organized theater excursions and cinema nights for adults and children.[88] While there was much less PTA activity at Billardon, there, for residents who had not come from the greater Dijon area and therefore had no family or friends in the region, social organizations formed based on professional contacts or even on geographical origin. Natives of the Lorraine region or of the Saône and Loire department would get together, welcoming new arrivals and planning outings.

Other initiatives included the youth center at Les Courtillières, which later became "La Maison de tous," "Everyone's Center." Geneviève Legrand reported how, in the late 1960s and early 70s, she and her family went to the center three times a week; she did gymnastics, yoga, and pottery, while her husband took photography and her daughter played checkers; others, like Danielle Souriau and Ludovic Binet, recalled feeling aloof from the center but had friends elsewhere with whom they did things.[89] On-site or proximate places of worship contributed opportunities for sociability at both *grands ensembles,* particularly during festivals. Children at Les Courtillières would go to religious services with friends. Viviane Belhassen extolled the joys of multiculturalism: "We were Jewish, and there were lots of Muslim or Catholic families. We had the impression that this diversity was a plus for the children. When it was a holiday for us, our friends came over. When it was Ramadan or other holidays, we went to our friends', we also went to their ceremonies. ... I went to catechism not to know the word of God but to be with my girlfriends."[90] Haïet Cherbal, a Parisian Muslim, also went to catechism with her Catholic best friend: "When she went, I went. I never left her side!"[91]

Some initiatives, like the Maison pour tous, were later additions to the *grand ensemble* community, but, for the first generation of inhabitants, consumer goods also proved to be a unifying device. Because each household did not yet have a television, those who did would invite neighbors to watch something, such as a rugby game, and guests would bring treats to share. Those with cars would give a lift to a neighbor. At Les Courtillières, about thirty families belonged to the "Association populaire familiale," which purchased a portable washing machine for members to share, as well as a floor waxer; the association also bought meat in bulk from a Parisian butcher for member families.[92] Viviane Belhassen recalled how the neighborhood's social worker assisted Belhassen's mother by lending her a portable sewing machine for two weeks; regular contact with that social worker meant that she was almost part of the family; "we could easily talk to her about our problems."[93]

Mutual aid knitted some families together. Besides an evening in front of the television, a car ride, or the proverbial cup of sugar, neighbors lent each other a few francs when needed. They took turns watching each others' children. Because Pantin was not far from Paris, women may have also at times done what certain Sarcelles mothers had arranged: the latter profited from informal babysitting exchanges to go to Paris for window-shopping or to see old friends and family from the neighborhoods they had left behind.[94] Undoubtedly, this was not true of all families; if for some the *grand ensemble* felt like a village or a family, for others it was less social. As Jean-Claude observed, "It's true that we would never have gone to ask the young engineer for the electric company if we could watch TV at his place. There was a hierarchy forming at that time.[95] Rhythms, ambiance, and modes of sociability could vary from one building to the next and from one *grand ensemble* to another. Billardon was "more social" than its neighbors Les Lochères and Epirey, while Buildings A and B in the Serpent were known to be a bit more couth than Building C.[96]

Indeed, what arises from these collections of memories is the sense of how the *grands ensembles* differed as a residential experience from one building to another, from one resident to another. Certainly these are selected accounts, by people who agreed to give interviews in the first place, and who could be found, and so on. Nevertheless, the lived experience—of those who left and those who stayed—points to the plural and multidimensional aspects of residents' reception of the *grand ensemble*. By and large, residents found life in their *grand ensemble* satisfying, even if it meant getting used to surveillance by management, creating new social networks, and adapting to the lack of soundproofing. Those who left report having done so most often for professional opportunities or to obtain more spacious apartments as their families grew. Others stayed put, retained by solidarity with their neighbors and their relatively low rents,[97] until the twenty-first century, when public officials decided to rehabilitate or raze residents' mid-century mass homes.

Conclusion

The year 1959 marked another turning point in the history of French postwar domestic architecture: as a result of the conflicts within the CIAM at the 1956 Bridgewater congress, the Modern Movement was declared officially dead at its eleventh and final meeting in the Netherlands in 1959, the same year as the presentation of the Referendum Apartment and the publication of the first volume of *Famille et habitation*. In 1959 these projects exposed the dream of the one-size-fits-all ideal home as an illusion. The state's choice of small but comfortable homes did not guarantee resident satisfaction, and Modernist efforts to inculcate an art of living were foundering on the rocky shores of sociological differences in dwelling practices. For architects, this failure was a bitter pill to swallow; some blamed an oppressive administration and recalcitrant users, arguing that more time was needed to change old-fashioned ways of dwelling. Other, younger, architects began to reevaluate the design tenets of domestic architecture in order to accommodate change and diversity within the home.

Sociological studies had unearthed dissatisfaction with life in the *grands ensembles*; tenants complained about noise and the lack of services. In 1959, the media publicized these critiques and added their own; writing in *France-Observateur*, Françoise Choay condemned huge apartment complexes as "rabbit cages," while the title of André Remond's four-part series on life in the *grands ensembles*, "Building F, Staircase 75, 8th floor, Door 6," dramatically encapsulated for *Libération* readers the purported anonymity of that existence.[98] Novelist Christiane Rochefort described the *grand ensemble*'s monumental aspect in a fictional account: "The new [housing] blocks were more and more inhabited. One block completed, and, hup, they filled it. I saw them being built. Now they were nearly full. Long, high, placed on the plain, they made you think of boats. The wind blew on the plateau, between the houses. I liked to walk by there. It was big, and beautiful; and terrible. When I passed close by, I thought that they were going to fall on me. Everyone seemed miniscule, and even the [low-rise] blocks of our Cité [of HLMs] next to them seemed like toy blocks."[99] Yet the administration was not willing to give up on the *grand ensemble*, which still seemed the best way of meeting the continued demand for housing. In 1960, according to the daily *Le Figaro*, there were 800,000 to 900,000 candidates for HLMs in the Parisian region alone.[100] Clearly, the shift to standardized and mass produced housing was succeeding on the supply side: 1959 saw the erection of a record-setting number of 275,000 new units funded with state aid, and more homes had been built between 1958 and 1960 than in the years 1953–1957 combined.[101] Sudreau's working groups on improving life in the *grands ensembles* illustrate the ministry's commitment to making this relatively new form of housing work. If tweaking elements of the apartment would ensure greater satisfaction with collective housing, state planners were willing to sacrifice the interior as a vehicle for promoting sociocultural change.

Concordant with the reevaluation of the model 4P was a reconceptualization of its occupants. The emergence of urban sociologists as experts on residential needs meshed well with the demands of a technocratic state devoted to planning. Work like Chombart de Lauwe's prompted housing professionals to attribute more agency to residents. His reports of their actual behaviors and practices—as well as the oral histories of complexes published nearly half a century later—revealed that people were inhabitants, actively contributing to home creation, and not simply users passively consuming a product. Architects were slower to grant this point. Designing homes in strict accordance with resident preferences represented another jurisdictional claim on their professional competence.

Yet Chombart de Lauwe's basic challenge to functionalist Modernists—*whose* functions?—did not fall on deaf ears, resonating especially with the younger generation of architects. The concerns of the latter illuminate for twenty-first-century eyes what was felt to be changing: the couple displacing the family as a key social unit; the development of needs and aspirations specific to adolescents; increasing value given to individual privacy. Of course, the architects interviewed in *Famille et habitation* did not abandon their pedagogical agendas overnight. But projects like the SAS's Essai, with its moving partitions, or Dreyfus and Tribel's solutions, with their additional, unattributed rooms and eat-in kitchens, proved that at least some architects were learning to allow families some choices about how to inhabit their spaces instead of educating them in the art of living. They were learning to allow them, in other words, to become modern in their own ways.

Notes

1. Paul-Henry Chombart de Lauwe, et al., *Famille et habitation*, vol. 1, *Sciences humaines et conceptions de l'habitation* (Paris: CNRS, 1959), 19.
2. It is not surprising that attempts to write a history of the *grands ensembles* that did not demonize their creators originated in architectural circles. Architect Bruno Vayssière's book, *Reconstruction-déconstruction: le hard French ou l'architecture française des trente glorieuses* (1988), was the first to attempt a history of the *grands ensembles*, a history that was revisionist with respect to orthodox journalistic and sociological evaluations that condemned this form of collective living. In Joseph Abram's survey of modern architecture, he cites Henri Caracos, the former mayor of Sarcelles, who asserted that the first generation of Sarcelles inhabitants was quite pleased with the *grand ensemble* as a form of housing. It was, rather, the lack of mass transit, shops, schools, and other "collective equipment" that impoverished their daily lives and contributed to the unhappiness sensationalized as the disease "Sarcellitis." (*L'Architecture moderne en France*, vol. 2, 137). For historiographical treatments of the *grands ensembles*, see Christine Mengin's "La solution des grands ensembles," *Vingtième siècle* 64 (October–December 1999): 105–11; a special issue on the history of the *grands ensembles* in *Urbanisme* 322 (January–February 2002); and Annie Fourcaut, "Les premiers grands ensembles en région parisienne: ne pas refaire la banlieue?" *French Historical Studies* 27, 1 (January 2004): 195–218. With Frédéric Dufaux and Rémi Skoutelsky, Fourcaut published an extensive bibliography of primary sources: *Faire l'histoire des grands ensembles. Bibliographie 1950-1980* (Lyon: ENS Éditions, 2003). Dufaux and Fourcaut also edited a comparative treatment of *grands ensembles* around the world in the collection *Le Monde des grands ensembles* (Paris: Créaphis, 2004).
3. "François Bloch-Lainé," interview with Thierry Pacquot, *Urbanisme* 284 (September–October 1995): 7.
4. Sudreau was interviewed in 1961 on the television program *Faire face*; cited in Fourcaut, "Les premiers grands ensembles," 216.
5. Minutes of the meetings of the working group on "l'étude de l'amélioration des dispositions des logements," 30 September 1957 and 18 February 1958, AN, CAC 19770775/4.
6. Pierre Sudreau, *Au-delà de toutes les frontières* (Paris: Odile Jacob, 1991), 98.
7. Sudreau, *Au-delà de toutes les frontières*, 31, 44, 95, 97, 107. Christiane Rimbaud has published a biography based on interviews with Sudreau: *Pierre Sudreau: Un homme libre* (Paris: Le Cherche Midi, 2004).
8. Fourcaut, "Les premiers grands ensembles," 214.
9. The biographical information about Picard comes from Picard's book, published under her maiden name: Jeanne Aubert, *JOC, qu'as-tu fait de nos vies?* (Paris: Éd. Ouvrières, 1990), 201 and from Geneviève Dermenjian's brief account at http://www.femmeset associations.org/biojaubert.htm (consulted April 2004; site now discontinued but Dermenjian's notice has been republished at http://www.ajpn.org/personne-Jeanne-Aubert-Picard-656.html).
10. For more on Picard, the JOCF, and the Mouvement populaire des familles, particularly with regard to social Catholic ideas about workers' housing, see W. Brian Newsome, "French Catholics, Women and the Home: The Founding Generation of the Jeunesse ouvrière chrétienne feminine," *Historical Reflections* 37, 1 (Spring 2011): 18–44.
11. Dissatisfaction with large picture windows turned up notably in a later study of residential experiences with Modernist architecture. In 1969, Philippe Boudon interviewed occupants of Le Corbusier's 1926 group of workers' homes at Pessac (see chapter 2). By 1969, Boudon found that over half of the homeowners had shortened the windows, covering up parts of them so that the remainder resembled standard-sized windows,

which extended interior wall surfaces for furniture placement. (See Philippe Boudon, *Pessac de Le Corbusier* [Paris: Dunod, 1969], esp. 71–72.)
12. See "Nos desiderata en matière de logements," AN, CAC, 19850023/120 and "L'enquête de Mme Picard," *Techniques et Architecture* 19, 2 (March–April 1959), 114.
13. Script for "visite guidée," AN, CAC, 19850023/120.
14. These letters can be found in AN, CAC, 19850023/120.
15. "L'enquête de Mme Picard," 114.
16. Ionel Schein, letter to Jeanne Picard, 16 February 1958, AN, CAC, 19850023/120.
17. "Points de vue des architectes," *Techniques et architecture* 19, 2 (March–April 1959), 114.
18. Pierre Sudreau, letter to Jean Balladur, 2 February 1960, AN, CAC, 19790660/11.
19. L. Veillon-Duverneuil, "Les cloisons de l'appartement de demain seront mobiles," *Combat*, 22 February 1960, 8. See also his "Le Syndicat des Architectes de la Seine réagit contre l'appartement de 'ces dames' présenté en 1959," *Revue de l'ameublement et des industries du bois* 2 (February 1960): 35; Françoise Choay, "Un appartement sur mesures," *France Observateur* (25 February 1960), 15–16; and "Essai d'habitation évolutive," *L'Architecture française* 211–12 (1960), 112.
20. The biographical information about Chombart de Lauwe in this section is taken from André Grelon, "In Mémoriam. Paul-Henry Chombart de Lauwe, 1913-1998," *L'année sociologique* 49/1999 (1): 7–18 and Paul-Henry Chombart de Lauwe, *Un anthropologue dans le siècle: entretiens avec Thierry Pacquot* (Paris: Descartes & Cie., 1996), 157, 181–82.
21. François Bloch-Lainé had also joined Garric's Équipes sociales as a youth. It is noteworthy that a number of the key players in the history of housing—Picard, Chombart, and Bloch-Lainé—had been active in Catholic activist groups in the interwar period. The prominence of social Catholics in housing policymaking confirms the observations made by Philip Nord in *France's New Deal* that Catholics were key to the remaking of France after World War II.
22. W. Brian Newsome, "The 'Apartment Referendum' of 1959: Toward Participatory Architecture and Urban Planning in Postwar France," *French Historical Studies* 28, 2 (2005): 342.
23. By standard furniture, Chombart de Lauwe meant not the lean, modern pieces whose dimensions architects fit neatly into their blueprints, but the larger, traditional-style items that poorer families were likely to have received from family members or purchased themselves at popular furniture chain stores like Galéries Barbès. In his study on working-class families, Chombart de Lauwe revealed some of his own "half-aristocratic, half-bourgeois" taste when he lamented that working-class families "are often unconscious slaves to commercial publicity, the lack of practice in choosing things on their own makes them easy prey. '[The Galéries] Barbès' and 'Lévitan,' the manufacturers heard most often on the radio, unload into workers' homes mass-produced furniture which definitively removes any personal cozy note from the household's décor." (Paul-Henry Chombart de Lauwe, *La vie quotidienne des familles ouvrières* [Paris: CNRS, 1956], 87).
24. Paul-Henry Chombart de Lauwe, "Le logement et le comportement des ménages dans trois cités nouvelles de l'agglomération parisienne," *Cahiers du Centre Scientifique et Technique du Bâtiment* 30, cahier 257 (October 1957): 13–52.
25. Chombart de Lauwe, "Le logement et le comportement des ménages," 51.
26. Chombart de Lauwe, *Famille et habitation*, vol. 1, 212.
27. Ibid., 108.
28. Ibid., 191.
29. The three citations in this paragraph come from Chombart de Lauwe, *Famille et habitation*, vol. 1, 188, 190.

30. Ibid., 178.
31. Ibid., 212.
32. Chombart de Lauwe, *Famille et habitation*, vol. 2, *Un essai d'observation expérimentale* (Paris: CNRS, 1960), 11, 13–14.
33. Chombart de Lauwe, *Famille et habitation*, vol. 2, 82, 92, 167, 267.
34. Volume 2 of *Famille et habitation* included two chapters on young people, one examining their needs within the home and one looking at their presence in the *grand ensemble*'s larger community.
35. Because collective facilities like schools, post offices, and shops fell outside of the MC's aegis, new housing complexes often opened their doors to residents well before construction had begun on the other projected elements of a site plan. In May 1957, the mayor of the Parisian suburb of Villiers-le-Bel issued an ordinance prohibiting developers from allowing families to take occupation of newly completed apartments if the construction of *grand ensemble*'s schools was not also complete (Mission Mémoires et identités en Val de France, *Les Carreaux 1955-1963*, 29). Actions like these point to the pressure *grands ensembles* put on local officials, who had the responsibility of responding to citizens' concerns but who lacked the mandate to rectify problems caused by centralized authorities.
36. Chombart de Lauwe, *Famille et habitation*, vol. 2, 15.
37. Ibid., 267.
38. Chombart de Lauwe participated in the working group for "improving apartment layouts." See minutes of their meetings in AN, CAC, 19770775/4.
39. Because PSRs had lower construction budgets, however, the only way that builders could satisfy the improved norms was to build PSRs on cheaper land, land that was generally found at a greater distance from the urban center and hence less desirable. See Magri, *Logement et reproduction de l'exploitation*, 210, and Dreyfus, *La Société du confort*, 113.
40. The prescriptions were "unified" with respect to their predecessor, the CPTFM of 1955, because they applied to all housing built in part or wholly with state financial aid, instead of only to HLMs. The specifications referred to in this paragraph are taken from the text of the CPTFMU, which was published in the *Journal Officiel de la République Française* (3 July 1960): 6039–49.
41. An August circular attempted to alleviate some of the budget constraints on PSR builders by permitting doorless storage spaces, less storage space, and cheaper floor coverings, but the other amendments stood.
42. André Remond, "Les Trois Souhaits des Locataires et Candidats des H.L.M.," *Libération*, 28 May 1959. One of these candidates appears in Chris Marker's film, *Le joli mai* (1963); interviewed in May 1962 in front of her slum housing, she reports joyfully that she has finally been assigned a 4P after seven years of waiting.
43. "Thiais: Groupe d'H.L.M.," *Techniques et Architecture* 24, 1 (November 1963): 116; Anne-Marie Pajot, "Mode d'emploi pour un H.L.M. 4 pièces," *Arts Ménagers* 171 (March 1964): 210–14.
44. Anne-Marie Pajot, "L'Appartement préfabriqué," *Arts Ménagers* 136 (April 1961): 226–32.
45. See Newsome, "Struggle for a Voice," 301–4.
46. The ministry was not interested in more than periodic empirical reports of resident feedback, however. An internal memo from André Trintignac, who worked for the MC's regional planning office, recommended that the ministry reject Chombart de Lauwe's proposal for a six-year grant to conduct "pure" research, arguing that six years was too long a time period and that this kind of research was unlikely to provide any applicable insights (memo dated 21 July 1959, AN, CAC, 19770775/4).

47. Jacques Dreyfus and Jean Tribel, "La Cellule-logement: Analyse des problèmes; recherche de solutions nouvelles," *Cahiers du CSTB* 48, cahier 382 (February 1961): 3–56.
48. According to Chombart de Lauwe, he was good friends with Tribel (*Un anthropologue dans le siècle*, 197) and Tribel's article with Dreyfus for the CSTB cited five of Chombart de Lauwe's published works as the basis for their study (20).
49. Dreyfus and Tribel, "La Cellule-logement," 23.
50. The years 1958 through 1960 especially saw copious media attention given to youth issues. Richard Ivan Jobs discusses rising concerns about juvenile delinquency in books like Jean Chazal's 1958 *L'Enfance délinquante*, published in the popular Que sais-je series by PUF (Presses Universitaires de France) and articles such as *Elle*'s 1958 feature, "Why Are Adolescents Becoming Murderers?" See Jobs, *Riding the New Wave: Youth and the Rejuvenation of France After the Second World War* (Stanford, CA: Stanford University Press, 2007), esp. chap. 4.
51. Dreyfus and Tribel, "La Cellule-logement," 19.
52. Ibid., 23, 28.
53. Ibid., 32.
54. Ibid., 21.
55. "Essai d'habitation évolutive," *Arts ménagers* (April 1960), 85.
56. Ross, *Fast Cars, Clean Bodies*, 127–33, quotation from 127.
57. See, respectively, Antoine Prost, "L'évolution de la politique familiale de 1938 à 1981," *Le Mouvement social* 129 (1984): 15 and Rémi Lenoir, "Family Policy in France Since 1938," in *The French Welfare State: Surviving Social and Ideological Change*, ed. John S. Ambler (New York: NYU Press, 1991), 159.
58. Cited in François Choay, "Un appartement sur mesures," 16.
59. Dreyfus and Tribel, "La Cellule-logement," 21 n.1. Gérard Blachère, head of the CSTB, exemplified the engineer's remove from the problems of HLM administration a few years later, when he called the "evolutionary apartment" a "mistake" in his manual for construction professionals, *Savoir Bâtir*: "If the composition of the family changes, the solution is to move" (Gérard Blachère, *Savoir Bâtir: Habitabilité, durabilité, Économie des bâtiments* [Paris: Éditions Eyrolles, 1971 (1966)], 34).
60. J.-H. Labourdette, taken from the minutes of a roundtable held 18 March 1959 at the Salon International de la Construction et de l'Équipement at the CNIT (La Défense), AN, CAC, 19790660/2.
61. See Alessandro Portelli, "The Peculiarities of Oral History," *History Workshop Journal* 12, 1 (1981), 96–107; Alice M. Hoffman and Howard S. Hoffman, "Reliability and Validity in Oral History: The Case for Memory," in *Memory and History: Essays on Recalling and Interpreting Experience*, ed. Jaclyn Jeffrey and Glenace Edwall (Lanham, MD: University Press of America, 1994), 107–30; Ronald J. Grele, "Oral History as Evidence," in *Handbook of Oral History*, ed. Thomas L. Charlton, Lois E. Myers, and Rebecca Sharpless (Lanham, MD: AltaMira Press, 2006), 43–104; Paul Thompson, *The Voice of the Past: Oral History* (Oxford: Oxford University Press, 2000 [1978]), esp. chap. 4.
62. Michel and Derainne, *Aux Courtillières*, 90. Legrand notes that she had signed up on several lists to maximize her chances of procuring an apartment.
63. Michel and Derainne, *Aux Courtillières*, 47, 90, 96.
64. Sylvain Taboury and Karine Gougerot, *Billardon, histoire d'un grand ensemble* (Paris: Créaphis, 2004), 267.
65. Ralph Schor, *Histoire de l'immigration en France de la fin du XIXe siècle à nos jours* (Paris: Armand Colin/Masson, 1996), 214. For more on the housing of immigrants, see Vincent Viet, "La politique du logement des immigrés (1945-1990)," *Vingtième siècle* 64 (October–December 1999): 91–103 and Amelia Lyons's dissertation, "Invisible Immigrants:

Algerian Families and the French Welfare State, 1947-1974" (Ph.D. diss., University of California, Irvine, 2004), esp. chaps. 3 and 4.
66. Lyons, "Invisible Immigrants," 219–22.
67. Michel and Derainne, *Aux Courtillières*, 81, 119.
68. Ibid., 47.
69. Ibid., 63.
70. Taboury and Gougerot, *Billardon*, 206–9.
71. See, for example, Taboury and Gougerot, *Billardon*, 306.
72. Ibid., 305, 185.
73. Ibid., 283–84.
74. Ibid., 185, 138.
75. Michel and Derainne, *Aux Courtillières*, 21, 118–19.
76. Ibid., 91; see also 118.
77. Ibid., 59, 96.
78. Ibid., 60.
79. "Builder Assays Suites in France," *New York Times*, 13 October 1963, 6R.
80. Taboury and Gougerot, *Billardon*, 148, 186, 310.
81. Ibid., 303.
82. Michel and Derainne, *Aux Courtillières*, 82; Taboury and Gougerot, *Billardon*, 147.
83. Excerpts from original guidelines in Michel and Derainne, *Aux Courtillières*, 82, 91.
84. Newsome, *French Urban Planning*, 2.
85. Taboury and Gougerot, *Billardon*, 145.
86. Ibid., 307–8.
87. Michel and Derainne, *Aux Courtillières*, 39, 83.
88. Ibid., 41.
89. Ibid., 92, 75, 103–4.
90. Ibid., 64.
91. Ibid., 84.
92. Ibid., 40.
93. Ibid., 64.
94. "Formidable pour les Enfants," Document 25 of Mission Mémoires et identités en Val de France, *Textes et images du Grand ensemble de Sarcelles, 1954-1976* (Villiers-le-Bel: Communauté d'agglomération Val de France, Mission Mémoires et identités en Val de France, 2007), [n.p.].
95. Taboury and Gougerot, *Billardon*, 140, 192.
96. Taboury and Gougerot, *Billardon*, 211; Michel and Derainne, *Aux Courtillières*, 72, 106.
97. In 1960, by way of example, monthly rent at Les Courtillières cost 130 francs for a two-bedroom apartment and 212 francs for a four-bedroom duplex (Michel and Derainne, *Aux Courtillières*, 138). The average salary for a (male) executive in 1960 was 2,284 francs a month, while a middle-manager or *cadre* earned 1,170 francs, and an entry-level male employee brought home 633 francs each month. Figures are derived from Christian Baudelot and Anne Lebeaupin, "Les salaires de 1950 à 1975," *Économie et statistique* 113 (July–August 1979): 15–22.
98. Françoise Choay, "Cités-jardins ou 'cages à lapins'?" *France-Observateur*, 4 June 1959; André Remond, "Bâtiment F, Escalier 75, septième, porte 6," *Libération*, four-part series beginning 27 May 1959.
99. Rochefort, *Les Petits Enfants du siècle*, 14.
100. "La Vérité sur les HLM," *Le Figaro*, 20 April 1960, 10.
101. Roncayolo, *Histoire de la France urbaine*, 646.

Chapter 6

BEYOND THE FUNCTIONALIST CELL TO THE URBAN FABRIC, 1966–1973

> *The architecture of a detached home (individual habitation), as good as it may be, no longer is of any interest if it doesn't include the potential for integration into an urban fabric, or if it does not provoke the creation of a new fabric. The development [l'épanouissement] of family life, its freedom and its personality must find their place in collective association, that is, in an urban framework.*
> —Architect Georges Candilis, 1968[1]

The year 1966 was one of French unilateralism on the world stage: President Charles de Gaulle withdrew French forces from NATO's integrated military command and evicted NATO from its Parisian headquarters. This action followed on the heels of France's refusal to sign the nuclear test-ban treaty agreed to by Great Britain, the United States, and the USSR, and its first of two vetos of Great Britain's bid to join the European Common Market. Such policy decisions demonstrated de Gaulle's "third way" at work and characterized the president's attempts to negotiate a path for France—and a role for the French in Europe more broadly—between the "Anglo-Saxons" and the Soviets.

The search for a "third way" distinguished Gaullist domestic policies, too. Eschewing free-market capitalism *à l'Américaine* while rejecting Communist-style state planning, de Gaulle continued the *dirigiste* planning that had guided the French economy since the late 1940s. At the same time, as Julian Jackson has noted, de Gaulle worried about the alienation of modern man and the dignity of the individual.[2] Humanist concerns coupled with a desire to stave off social conflict led him to call for *participation*. At first, participation referred only to the association of workers and management in decisions about profit-sharing and working conditions; yet, in the context of the social movements of the late 1960s, *participation* evolved into a general belief that individuals should have more decision-making power in shaping the institutions that touched their lives, in arenas such as work, education, and community affairs.

As Gaullist policymakers sought to define a French "third way," one marked by de Gaulle's concerns with both grandeur and a humanist modernization, planners, architects, politicians, and sociologists also struggled to identify the best path forward for housing design. The proliferation of social science research, much of it financed by the state, spoke to a common desire to understand the effect of the new *grands ensembles* on social relations. For whom did this new way of life work? What effect did it have on the working class? On women? At the same time, other social changes called into question received ideas about the "consumers" of public housing: the emergence of a new social group called *cadres,* a class of junior executives and managers made possible by the democratization of education and the expansion of the tertiary sector; the documented fact of married women working outside the home in increasing numbers; the repatriation of French Algerians settling in mainland France after the end of the French-Algerian War in 1962; and a new wave of immigration that included North Africans and Portuguese workers. What kind of homes, in what kinds of developments, could best serve these populations? How should housing address growing concerns about urban life and the social relations produced by cities and suburbs?

Thus, while de Gaulle was busy expelling NATO, housing professionals in 1966 turned their attention to two events of some significance in the realm of housing: the publication of a sociological study called *Les Pavillonnaires* (The Suburbanites), which examined residents of single-family bungalows, and the launch of Villagexpo, a state-sponsored model development of single-family homes. The new focus on the detached home signaled a change in the debate over how the French ought to dwell. From disagreements about the site of the dining area or the need for a long hallway as an artery of distribution, the debate shifted to the form that state-sponsored housing should take: collective or individual? The *pavillon* (generally understood to be a modest, often bungalow, or cottage-style, home) or the large apartment complex? The housing question, in other words, evolved from concerns about its prompt provision and ideal floor plan to discussion of its proper place in the urban landscape. This was in part due to the fact that by the mid 1960s the housing shortage had begun to ease; over 400,000 new units became available in 1965 alone.[3] Moreover, in 1966, the administration fused the construction ministry with the ministry of public works and transportation to create a ministry of infrastructure, the Ministère de l'Équipement (ME). This reorganization reflected the state's decision to improve the planning and management of urban France. Falling under the purview of a secretary of state, housing could no longer be considered, as it had been in the early days of the *grand ensemble*, as an entity apart from its environs.[4] Yet how, exactly, did *homes* fit into urbanization? Throughout the 1960s and early 1970s, the ministry offered several responses to this question, returning to the eclecticism and experimentation that had characterized Raoul Dautry's MRU.

As it did so, it met with disapproval from the architectural community. The complex relationship (described in chapter 5) between the state's housing initiatives, the contributions of urban sociologists, the representations and expressions of popular preferences, and the priorities and projects of architects became even more complicated during the second half of the 1960s, a moment of political, social, and ideological turmoil worldwide. This chapter unpacks what was at stake for the shapers of domestic space in the tussles between state planners and architects during this period and reveals how these actors continued to try to shape social relations through home design. In particular, they sought to answer two questions born of the burgeoning *grands ensembles* and the emerging consumer society: what is the relation of the individual to the community, and what role does collective housing play in that relationship?

As we shall see, new personnel soon reversed the ministry's longstanding aversion to individual houses, but planners did not view this shift as incompatible with planned urbanization. On the contrary, by sponsoring research into innovative ways of building and grouping single-family homes, housing ministry officials hoped to find their own version of a "third way" between the disorderly interwar *lotissements* and wasteful American-style suburban sprawl. Further, despite a change in policy, continuity reigned insofar as the state retained its role as the nation's number one housing developer.

Modernist architects, on the other hand, unilaterally rejected the detached home in favor of collective housing. Their objections will be traced to two related sources: a revised understanding of dwelling that included an individual's interactions with the "urban fabric," and a renewed anxiety about the future of the profession. Both sentiments had been fed by the work of urban sociologists, who were simultaneously studying the relationship of city dwellers to their neighborhoods and the unanimous French preference for the *pavillon*.

This time, architects' customary complaints met with fresh overtures from a ministry willing to explore alternatives to the model plan and the *grand ensemble,* and the third section of the chapter looks more closely at the changes that were made to interiors. Though the Referendum Apartment did not come to dominate, the plans that garnered state sponsorship acknowledged, to a greater or lesser extent, the occupant's agency in creating a home. By the beginning of the 1970s, the functionalist cell—as developed, advocated, and constructed over the course of nearly twenty-five years—had fallen out of favor with architects and state planners alike, and sociologists' focus on individual agency and aspirations in homemaking challenged the premises of standardized housing. Planners, builders, and designers wondered: how could home design maximize residents' appropriation of space? Was the individual home necessary, or would an "individualized" home, one that could be personalized, suffice?

Urban Zones and Suburban Developments

To understand the issues at stake in the debate over individual versus collective housing, it helps to return to the beginning of the Fifth Republic. As we saw in chapter 5, construction minister Pierre Sudreau launched several initiatives to improve the everyday lives of *grand ensemble* occupants, establishing commissions to study their problems, amending surface area norms, and streamlining administrative procedures to speed construction and improve the quality of the physical plant. Up until 1958, the focus had been primarily at the level of the apartment, but proposals to improve the home began to appear more frequently in concert with attempts to build communities around the *grands ensembles.* Studies like those conducted by Chombart de Lauwe for the CSTB had concluded that the most serious problem with *grands ensembles* was the dearth of services; when complexes lacked nearby commercial establishments, schools, and opportunities for employment, dissatisfaction simmered, resident turnover was high, and a "dormitory city" was born.

To ameliorate this situation, the state created the *zones à urbaniser par priorité* (high priority zones to urbanize, or ZUP), at the end of 1958. The MC had the power to designate ZUPs throughout the nation, placing their planning under the coordination of the local prefect, who was then authorized to expropriate the land necessary for the erection of housing and accompanying infrastructure. This element of ZUP policy aimed to guarantee enough territory to complement *grands ensembles* with the collective facilities deemed crucial to their success. The most celebrated and ambitious ZUP plan, Toulouse-Le Mirail, designed by the team of Georges Candilis, Alexis Josic, and Shadrach Woods, called for, among other facilities, four stadiums, eight pools, five markets, twenty-three shopping centers, four high schools, and five cinemas to animate life in the 23,000 new housing units.[5]

A second goal of ZUP policy was familiar: maximize productivity and further industrialize construction. Where the Logeco program had tried to do this through preapproved model plans, the ZUP approach went a step further by limiting an operation to a single team—composed of one developer, one builder, and one architect—for an entire ZUP. No longer could a housing site have three different *grands ensembles* designed by separate architects, built by several builders for multiple developers. At minimum, each ZUP had to include at least five hundred housing units, but the ZUP formula facilitated real mass construction, and most ZUPs provided thousands of dwellings. During the decade that the program existed, approximately 200 ZUPs comprised over 2 million housing units, and nearly 45 percent of these units were rental HLMs.[6] At Toulouse Le Mirail, over 75 percent of the housing was to be HLMs.[7] By 1970, more than 41 percent of workers lived in housing built since 1949, compared with 26.5 percent in 1963. The figure was even higher for middle management and white-collar workers, who often found it easier to pay HLM rents than did working-class families. In 1963, over 38 percent of the middle class lived in new housing, but by 1970 more than 61 percent did.[8] The ZUP formula allowed the state to quickly reach, and then exceed, its goal, specified in the Third Plan, of 300,000 homes a year.

Some of those entering ZUP homes had come from inner-city slums. At the 1958 Salon des Arts Ménagers, the MRL had announced a program to eliminate dilapidated, unhealthy housing. The MRL displayed a map of the 450,000 substandard housing units in the Hexagon; nearly half were in the Paris metropolitan area.[9] The need to relocate residents of slum housing close to their jobs in Paris, as well as the demographic evidence that showed that Paris's rate of growth had increased exponentially since 1954[10] made the downsizing of Paris—one of the ministry's aims since the 1947 publication of Gravier's *Paris et le désert français*—impossible. Moreover, Charles de Gaulle's inclination to celebrate Paris as a symbol of French grandeur led him to sponsor a number of new public works projects and renovations in Paris *intra muros*.[11] What the Gaullist planners chose to do, therefore, was to pursue a policy of urban renewal and regional expansion (elaborated under the aegis of the Délégation à l'aménagement du territoire et à l'action régionale [Delegation for Territorial Planning and Regional Action, or DATAR], formed in 1963) as well as concerted planning and development of the Paris metropolitan area.

A vast program to restructure Paris and its surrounding communities got underway in the 1960s. A first step was the 1961 creation of the District de la région of Paris, with one of de Gaulle's trusted favorites, Paul Delouvrier, at its head. The reorganization would follow the principles outlined in the Plan d'Aménagement et d'organisation générale (Land-Use Management and General Organization Plan, or PADOG). In 1965, the publication of the Schéma Directeur d'Aménagement et d'Urbanisme (Master Plan for Territorial and Urban Planning), a document that revised and completed the PADOG, called for the creation of *villes nouvelles*, based on the model of the British "new towns" or "satellite cities." Unlike most ZUPs, designed to complement and interact with a city center, the purpose of the villes nouvelles was to siphon off some of the population of the largest French cities, with Paris first and foremost among them. In 1966 the District became simply the Region of Paris, with eight *départements*. Overall nine new towns arose from scratch, including five dispersed throughout the Parisian départements: Cergy-Pontoise, Évry, Marne-la-Vallée, Melun-Sénart, and Saint-Quentin-en-Yvelines.[12]

The early and mid 1960s, then, saw an intense effort to plan and manage French urbanization via ZUPs, new towns, and the designation of certain regional cities as *métropoles d'équilibre*, or sites for the relocation of certain scientific, academic, and industrial entities from Paris. This last initiative, which ultimately fell short of planners' expectations, aimed to advance the program of *aménagement du territoire*, or reorganization of the Hexagon, which had been one of the housing ministry's objectives since the tenure of Eugène Claudius-Petit. Yet with the arrival of Jacques Maziol at the helm of the Construction Ministry (MC) in 1962, another of the ministry's longstanding goals—the development of collective housing—would be put into question.

Unlike his predecessor, Sudreau, a pragmatist whose politics leaned slightly left of center, Maziol, a Gaullist party loyalist from Toulouse, agreed with many of his government colleagues that the state should begin to assume less of the financial burden involved with the construction and management of social housing. To do so, Maziol looked to the individual homes for which French had so often stated their preference. After a decade of the ministry's commitment to *grands ensembles*, Maziol began planning a "Salon de la maison individuelle" (Single-Family Home Show) at the end of 1964. The exposition was to consist of a number of houses built in a single development, and the MC launched a competition for both the development's site plan and for the homes to be included therein. The site plan would be a key factor in the exhibition, since it was precisely the principle of the *planned* subdivision that would permit the state to pursue a policy of individual home construction without running the risk of either the haphazard growth of poorly built shacks that characterized the interwar *lotissements* or the heavy infrastructure demands of

American-style suburbs, whose sprawl failed to facilitate any feeling of community or solidarity.

The "salon-village," called "Villagexpo," opened to the public on 23 September 1966. Developed by the Société Coöpérative d'H.L.M. de l'Île de France and placed at Saint-Michel-sur-Orge, a suburb south of Paris, Villagexpo aimed to show that planned, subsidized housing developments could put individual homes within the reach of average French families. This message was crafted to appeal to the prosperous segment of the working class, as well as to potential middle-class homeowners. Young Modernist architects Michel Andrault and Pierre Parat had won the competition for the site plan, which featured a pentagon-shaped green commons (and an exhibition hall/restaurant); from its center radiated lanes and places, where over twenty building companies had been invited to contribute groups of five to ten houses apiece. Built in 110 days, the homes' construction emphasized prefabrication and mass production. Some homes were freestanding; others were duplexes or row houses; nearly three-quarters of the 186 houses featured single-story plans, which echoed the traditional disposition of the *pavillon*. Despite their variety, the homes were part of a whole thanks to the feature of the central commons; this commons signified that this subdivision had a heart, as it were, and would therefore differ markedly from the winding, aimless rows of America's Levittowns.

Roland Nungesser inaugurated the life-size exhibition. Nungesser was the secretary of state for housing, a post created in 1966 with the reorganization of the ministry to include infrastructure. Nungesser, the former head of the District de la région de Paris, was an advocate of detached homes, believing, like Maziol, that they would help reduce state expenditures in the domain of home construction because individuals would be more willing to assume some of the costs involved. In 1963, as Maziol was planning the Salon de la maison individuelle, Nungesser had organized a contest to encourage research into new ways of grouping single-family dwellings. In 1965, he founded the Association nationale pour la maison familiale (National Association for the Single-Family Home) to push for their construction. In his inaugural address, Nungesser dismissed worries about suburban sprawl by arguing that individual homes had their place in the "operational urbanism" of ZUPs. Inserted judiciously into planned communities, single-family dwellings would "break with the monotony of the ZUPs," and Nungesser recommended that they should constitute 20 to 30 percent of the housing units in any given ZUP. He claimed, "Combined harmoniously with the densification of the ZUP center(s), which bring the concentration propitious to the animation necessary to any urban life, [detached houses] will permit the reconstitution of the sociological and urbanistic structures of the cities formed by history." He added that a policy of individual houses would also permit the preservation of architectural regional traditions.[13]

This was a new voice from the halls of state policymakers. Nungesser's references to regionalist style and the organic formation of cities over time broke with the resolute modernism of Eugène Claudius-Petit and even with the more pragmatic approach of a Pierre Sudreau, who had been reluctant to integrate the past into formulations of the future. Nungesser's desire to preserve regional architectural styles also suggested the end of regionalism's association in France with Vichy and Marshal Pétain. But Nungesser reassured his audience that the state was not now swinging entirely toward the other pole of reconstituting turn-of-the-century rural villages; each ZUP would feature only a specific percentage of individual homes. Put another way, individual homes would not replace ZUPs; the former would be only one aspect of the latter. Moreover, by putting emphasis on planned groupings of individual homes, Nungesser indicated that his office opposed a policy favoring acres of costly tract housing. The unspoken part of this promise to integrate individual homes into ZUP communities, of course, was that only home-seekers with savings and stable incomes would be able to move into such houses. This would leave the *grand ensemble* apartments as the sole option for less fortunate families and reproduce the classed housing of the historical city.

Over 175,000 people visited Villagexpo between September and November 1966 (after which the purchasers of the model homes moved in). The ministry ordered surveys of nearly all involved, including the visitors, the residents as they moved in, and the residents one year later. Visitors were asked to rank their favorite homes, and the number one choice was a home by Balency and Schuhl, whose floor plan derived from the Referendum Apartment (see chapter 5).[14]

Surveys also revealed, though, that the exterior form of the home weighed more in people's estimations than did the floor plan. Preferring pitched roofs to flat ones and single-story homes to two-story versions, over 40 percent also refused or disapproved of Villagexpo's duplexes and row houses, suggesting potential roadblocks to the ministry's policy of searching for innovative compositions of single-family homes.[15] In general, residents disliked row houses and duplexes because they felt that sharing a wall or two with neighbors diminished the privacy and freedom that they attached to the concept of the home. The land upon which a detached home sat thus offered a buffer from neighbors that many found desirable. It also provided space for gardening and puttering about, whereas the green spaces surrounding duplexes and row houses at Villagexpo, for example, were communal, thwarting opportunities for such outdoor activities.

Nevertheless, the feedback was sufficiently encouraging to confirm Nungesser's decision to extend Villagexpo into a second phase of 200 more homes at the Saint-Michel-sur-Orge site and to authorize a series of Villagexpos in the provinces. Villagexpos took place in Bordeaux, Lille, Nantes, Marseille, and Toulouse in 1967 and 1968. The ministry's desire to avoid American-style suburban development even led it to exclude the Phénix company from the provincial Villagexpos, despite the fact that the Phénix homes had ranked second in popularity with Saint Michel-sur-Orge visitors. (Indeed, the Maison Phénix company is still a leading provider of prefabricated homes in France today.) Yves Aubert, the director of Construction, explained, "The Villagexpos' objective is to show what the Administration wishes to see happen technically, architecturally, and urbanistically in the field of individual homes. It must be acknowledged that M. Pux's [the head of Phénix] conceptions are rather opposed to ours because he is an avowed partisan of the suburban system [that is] so deplorable in all respects."[16]

Aubert's distaste for the "deplorable" suburban system may have been fueled by the success that a certain American interloper was enjoying with well-heeled families in the Paris metropolitan area. In October 1965 none other than William J. Levitt, the developer of the American Levitttowns, opened a model block of single-family homes in the town of Le Mesnil-Saint-Denis, eighteen miles west of Paris. Levitt, wanting to recoup some of the profits that had been lost by Levitt and Sons in the United States after the company went public in 1960, found France to be a promising market, as it was comparatively lacking in single-family homes.[17] In 1961, 78 percent of Great Britain's housing stock consisted of single-family homes, while Germany's detached homes composed 49 percent of its stock; France lagged behind with a mere 32 percent, and most of the French single-family houses were in rural areas, far from employment opportunities.[18] By the mid 1960s, detached homes made up only approximately 20 percent of new construction in France.[19]

At the same time, the mayor of Le Mesnil-Saint-Denis, Raymond Berrurier, who was also vice-president of the national council of mayors, wanted to avoid the invasion of *grands ensembles* like those he had seen spring up in nearby Trappes. Like Nungesser, Berrurier, a notary, was a proponent of single-family homes, and he had created a local Castors association to facilitate home ownership. Berrurier saw in Bill Levitt's initiative a means of staving off the urbanizing forces of the PADOG and DATAR. Not far from the local château, now serving as Le Mesnil-Saint-Denis's town hall, Levitt's development—Les Résidences du Château—sold out in five weeks.[20]

On the basis of his development's success, Levitt received permission to exhibit two model homes at Villagexpo, but was not allowed to participate in the exposition's competition because the cost of his homes failed to come in under the limits established for the competition. Indeed, Levitt's French homes cost more than twice as much as his American ones. (This was largely due to the French aversion to wood-frame homes and to a demand for finishings in tile, stucco, and masonry, as well as the need for plumbing in both the W.C. and the bathroom.) Levitt France explicitly targeted the *cadre* population, and one had to be well-off to buy a home since mortgage policies favored those who had accumulated capital. Unlike the first generation of Levitt homes in New York, which required a minimal down payment (or none, for veterans) and could be had in a rent-to-own capacity, the French were subject to more stringent conditions. By 1965, French households aspiring to purchase a home had to offer a down payment of 35 percent of the purchase price and were accorded only a ten-year mortgage (though this later evolved to include fifteen- or twenty-year options), whereas Americans had only to put 5 percent down and could obtain thirty-year mortgages.[21] Prices at the Residence du Château ranged from 108,000 francs to 165,000 francs at a time when the average executive was earning 39,958 francs annually, the typical *cadre* brought in 19,603 francs a year, and the mean yearly income for salaried employees was 11,086 francs.[22]

Those who could afford a Residence du Château moved right in, and for the most part, confessed to journalists that they didn't mind the lack of a fence or hedge between lawns; indeed, the virtues of moving into a turn-key home where even the light bulbs had been provided thrilled these homeowners.[23] Levitt moved on to build a new development near Lésigny, not far from Orly airport, then developed several other suburban Parisian neighborhoods, adding, all told, five thousand homes to the French housing stock before Levitt France closed its operations in 1981.

It was not just Americans who were building private subdivisions. Charged with reconstructing refineries after the end of World War II, oil company executive Jacques Riboud had, like Raoul Dautry in the course of his work for the national railway earlier in the century, become preoccupied with questions of workers' housing. By the end of the 1950s, Riboud had created his own building company, Jacques Riboud Créations urbaines; with architect and town planner Roland Prédiéri, Riboud developed sites in the suburbs to the north and west of Paris and in western France, not far from Nantes. Also like Dautry decades earlier, Riboud found an inspiring guide in Ebenezer Howard and his garden cities, and Riboud believed that Howardian subdivisions could be just as cost effective as Le Corbusier's Cités radieuses. Moreover, for Prédiéri and Riboud, suburban developments facilitated social integration better than urban apartment complexes; whereas in the city, people clung to anonymity when in such close quarters, passing each other only briefly on a landing or in an elevator, suburban neighbors outside weeding or going to work in the morning would chat more often. The key to social mixing, asserted Prédiéri and Riboud, was mixed housing, by which they meant not communities composed of single-family homes and apartment complexes, but housing of greater or smaller square footage, on lots of different sizes.[24] Prédiéri and Riboud thus addressed one of the key questions being debated by housing professionals and sociologists: if everyone agreed that social integration was a civic good, how might it best be achieved?

Prédiéri had studied with Auguste Perret and Marcel Lods, and though he came to champion a more traditional aesthetic than theirs, he still combined it with a concern for thoughtful urbanism; Riboud published his and Prédiéri's ideas in his 1961 book, *An Experiment in Provincial Urbanism* (*Expérience d'urbanisme provinçal 1961*). When Riboud launched a subdivision called "La Haie Bergerie" in Villepreux, about fifteen miles west of Paris and just north of Levitt's Résidences du Chateau in Le Mesnil-Saint-Denis, he marketed La Haie Bergerie's homes as a departure from the status quo: "There is no suburban cottage [*pavillon de banlieue*] in the common sense of the term at La Haie Bergerie, but individual homes [*maisons individuelles*], which is not the same thing."[25] It was important to dissociate suburban developments from the "pavillon"; if the French were going to rethink housing, innovators had to sell planners on a "third way." Builders like Riboud and Levitt believed that the *nouveaux villages* would reconcile the desire for an individual home with an economy of resources based on shared infrastructure. What also made the nouveaux villages new was their recognition of the implications for home life of transformations like the rise of the automobile and the spread of television.

Other social changes, like those the state-built mass home had wrought in social relations, further prepared the ground for the ministry's turn to single-family home policies. A survey commissioned in 1967 by the ME's construction department from the Centre d'études des équipements résidentiels (Center for the Study of Residential Facilities, or CEDER) reported on social life in the *grands ensembles*. The survey's authors found that their population sample had a "dependent mentality with respect to the common weal. This mentality comes from the fact that everything has been conceived of, planned for, decided and organized by the developer and the state; the facilities, run by social workers and educators, are considered as instruments of assistance. Whence a passive or [welfare] recipient sort of attitude."[26] In the "anarchic" suburbs and villages of the Belle Époque and the interwar period, on the other hand, there had been no single authority figure against whom disgruntled residents might channel their discontent. The CEDER report observed that *grand ensemble* residents might have no less individual initiative than traditional suburbanites, but the latter had manifested no sentiment of dependency.[27]

Of the 175,000 housing units it had built by the mid 1960s, SCIC retained management responsibility for 95,000 of them.[28] SCIC's rent increases, policies on stroller storage and the hanging of laundry, unilateral decisions on heating charges: all of these fed into an image of a stern father to be rebelled against. Hoping to stave off mounting waves of dissatisfaction and conscious of the ramifications of mass rejection of the *grands ensembles*, in 1964 SCIC sponsored yet another study, this time into the possibilities for resident participation. This study, the Sérieyx Report, observed that "the individual relationship that, according to the law, is the only link between the landlord and the tenant, is no longer a suitable framework for the new administrative and human reality of the Grands Ensembles."[29] The report's authors therefore recommended participation in the form of elected residents' councils that would have consultative power in the arenas of rent, common charges, and collective cultural facilities. Different associations—some religious, some political, some simply of residents—had the right to propose delegates to these councils.

As architectural historian Kenny Cupers has shown, SCIC's interest in incorporating resident participation into the administration of *grands ensembles* was neither deliberately cynical nor an attempt to maximize democracy. It was a means of securing buy-in from residents to improve *grand ensemble* management, and as such, adhered to the technocratic logic of expertise that characterized Trente Glorieuses France.[30] As it happened, local municipal authorities soon eclipsed and usurped the residents' councils; the former had greater sway over *grand ensemble* developers because they could withhold building permits, sponsor countervailing town planning documents, and influence *grand ensemble* populations through specific apartment attributions. Efforts like the SCIC's to minimize resident protests and increase agency in the interest of better management amounted only to what Alain Touraine has called "dependent participation": "A man is alienated when his only relationship to the social and cultural directions of his society is the one the ruling class accords him as compatible with the maintenance of its own dominance. Alienation means canceling out social conflict through dependent participation."[31] Historian Rod Kedward has used this expression to describe de Gaulle's presidency,[32] and the appellation fits here, too, for the state was still determined to retain control of housing development, and, in the process, through arms like the SCIC, developed a paternalist relationship with *grand ensemble* tenants.

Throughout the 1960s, the construction ministry, then its successor, the MEL,[33] began diversifying the kinds of housing that would be built with state assistance, hoping to reduce the state's investment in housing by encouraging owner-occupation. At the housing ministry, researchers in the construction office hypothesized that an increasing number of women in the workforce meant that couples could be expected to acquire homes within a decade or so of marriage.[34] Would these young households seek to buy an apartment in the city, in a *grand ensemble,* or a detached home in a suburban development? Within the framework of ZUPs, new towns, and regional planning, state policymakers sought to improve the lot of *grand ensemble* dwellers while simultaneously searching for ways to integrate individual homes into urban settings. The eclectic approach hailed back to the days of Raoul Dautry and testified to the state's efforts to attack the housing problem on several fronts at once.

Jacques Riboud's Creations urbaines ultimately built over nine thousand homes, and Levitt France had built five thousand. Despite the fact that they were not alone among private building societies (California builders Kaufman and Broad infiltrated the Parisian housing market in 1969 and had become the largest developer of single-family homes in France by 1972), if the French were going to get the detached homes for which they supposedly pined, much more had to be done to make these affordable on a mass scale. The ministry's openness to an inclusive policy that would encourage individual as well as collective housing grew when Albin Chalandon, a powerful Gaullist banker and industrialist of renown, took over as minister in 1968. In the spring of 1969, Chalandon, an advocate of privatization and competition, ordered an international contest for 200,000 detached homes, hoping to spur advances in their construction; these homes, relying heavily on prefabrication, became known as "chalandonnettes." By 1970, the General Planning Commission had concluded that the biggest chance for true innovation in the building industry lay in the domain of detached homes, observing that the maximum productivity for on-site construction of collective housing had been achieved.[35]

The state's multipronged attack on the housing question spoke to a growing preoccupation with planning and managing urbanization, for by the mid 1960s, the "urban question" took center stage. The demographic pressures on urban centers had increased. In 1962, over 2 million *rapatriés* from Algeria settled into France's large cities, and the second half of the 1960s saw over a million and a half young people—the baby boom children—begin to enter the work force. Most sought employment in these same large cities, posing a serious challenge to public authorities trying to control the growth of metropolitan areas.

It was not clear that more *grands ensembles* were the answer to the urban question. Despite Sudreau's efforts, the *grands ensembles* were decreasing in popularity. There were fewer Stanislas Fontaines singing their praises, and, after an initial period during which residents expressed pleasure with novel accouterments of comfort, some subsequently became disillusioned with long commutes, scarce collective services, or lack of soundproofing and isolation that left life in the *grand ensemble* a bit too communal of an experience. The turnover in housing projects fed officials' concerns about the "ultramodern"[36] *grands ensembles* as new sites of social segregation.

Together, these factors provoked investigation into the role of the city in everyday life, an inquiry that featured prominently in the events of May 1968. Scrawled onto the walls of the Odéon in Paris during May were the words, "We refuse to be HLM-ized, Sarcellized, indoctrinated."[37]

The Myth of the *Pavillon* and the Crisis of Architecture

Given the media's tendency throughout the 1960s to publish each and every survey and opinion poll that revealed the unanimous preference of the French for the *pavillon,* state officials—Maziol, Nungesser, and Chalandon, in particular—might have been surprised by the hostility with which the press greeted their efforts to make such homes more affordable. But from Villagexpo to the chalandonnettes, journalists decried a policy that promised to further marginalize the poorer members of French society. Though Villagexpo-style homes and chalandonnettes received state funding, it was clear who would be living in the 20–30 percent of individual homes in a ZUP and who would be living in the 70–80 percent of that ZUP's *grands ensembles.* The turn toward the detached home seemed to the public to cater only to *cadres,* those white-collar managers and junior executives whose housing preferences Fifth Republic policymakers had begun to address directly with the introduction of the *immeubles à loyer normal* (ILN) in 1961. ILNs could exceed the set maximum cost price for an HLM by 10 percent, and their surface area could be larger than either the PSRs or the HLMs.[38] Housing for *cadres* was seen by many as the nail in the coffin for the democratized modern home of the postwar era. *Le Monde* noted succinctly that only a minority would be able to live in detached houses, and the left-leaning *Le Nouvel Observateur* chastised Chalandon for ignoring the housing needs of those in slums, the elderly, and immigrant workers; even pro-Gaullist *Le Figaro* conspicuously failed to express support for the policy.[39]

Some viewed the state's new commitment to individual homes as a defeat for urban planning. In a front-page article for *Combat,* Rémy Belhomme wrote that the "multiplication of Villagexpos would be, in fact, after the *grands ensembles,* the demonstration of a new cancer of urbanism."[40] Journalists lamented what appeared to them to be a return to the unplanned suburbs of the interwar period; they also castigated the French public, who continued to express a desire for the *pavillon*, for fueling the state's "anti-urban" plan. The same *Nouvel Observateur* piece that criticized Chalandon reminded its readers that the French even disapproved of row houses and duplexes; the latter wanted "a *real* bungalow, with a little yard, boundary hedges, little walls, a gravel path... Nothing that would go in the sense of a somewhat revolutionary conception of communal life, of a collective rapport which would shake up the old social structures." *Le Monde* also disapproved of Chalandon's "reactionary urbanism," calling the French preference for the bungalow a "negative choice" against the "ugliness of the *grands ensembles*, poorly built, poorly located, and poorly equipped."[41]

Urban sociologists, too, worried about a possible return to the *pavillon*. Sociologists knew that both the French Communist Party and the trade union federation advocated rental housing as best for workers' standard of living. Since the state-sponsored policy of detached homes was predicated on property ownership, *grands ensembles* remained the most abundant source of quality rental housing. Moreover, though Marxist sociologists like Henri Lefebvre observed the potential for atomization of the working class in "classless" *grands ensembles*, his research revealed that class solidarity remained intact when *grands ensembles* were located proximate to a factory or industrial site, as he found in his study of Mourenx, in southwest France.[42] Meanwhile, social Catholic sociologists, such as Chombart de Lauwe, remained optimistic that *grands ensembles* could be engines of social solidarity. Across the ideological spectrum, as Susanna Magri has found, urban sociologists—whose research was often commissioned by the state—scorned the bungalow as too individualistic, too petit-bourgeois, and wholly unmodern.[43]

Architects concurred wholeheartedly with this assessment. This chapter's epigraph comes from a 1968 article Georges Candilis penned for *L'Architecture d'aujourd'hui* entitled "The Myth of the Individual Habitat." In part, Candilis opined, the detached home was a myth because it was simply irrelevant in the context of a modernizing, urbanizing France. For architects, the future was unrelentingly urban. It was a belief in the complexity and richness of an individual's interactions with the city that had originally prompted Candilis and Team X to protest in 1956 against the abstract functionalist zoning mandated by the Charter of Athens. Their dedication to re-creating the fertile structure of street life built upon Chombart de Lauwe's observations of working-class neighborhoods and was subsequently fed by works like *Rénovation urbaine et changement social* (Urban Renewal and Social Change), Henri Coing's 1966 study of the impact of slum clearance on social networks.

Candilis's colleague, Pierre Parat, writing with Charles-Henry Arguillère in the same 1968 issue of *L'Architecture d'aujourd'hui*, titled a tirade against the single-family home, "'The Individual': Dream, Nightmare, Trends." Parat and Arguillère argued in their piece that, although the penurious economic circumstances leading to the development of the *grands ensembles* had eased, it was critical that public authorities not fall into the trap of the "*pavillon* nightmare."[44] Moreover, they saw in the inner-city riots taking place in the United States a harbinger of what Villagexpos could lead to. With the advent of suburban housing developments, and the subsequent "white flight" to these, American urban centers had become marked by social segregation and had seen their financial resources depleted. Why should France pursue such a policy now, they suggested, when even the Americans were beginning to see the ominous side effects of suburban tract housing?[45]

Like *Le Monde*, architects understood the French preference for the bungalow to be a negative vote against the mediocrity of the *grands ensembles* rather than a pure yearning for the form and lifestyle of the *pavillon*. This was the other reason that the detached home was purportedly nothing but a "myth"; it was no more than the expression of, a reference to, an archetype of dwelling. Some blamed the policy of model plans for producing general frustration with the *grand ensemble*. Curator Maurice Besset opened his survey of "New French Architecture" with a scathing critique of the *cellule*.[46] Besset agreed with Dreyfus and Tribel and the SAS (but was less optimistic than these actors about the possibilities for the *cellule*'s salvation), objecting to the "dead-end" of a floor plan that locked a family into one stage of its trajectory. Candilis, in an interview he gave in the mid 1960s, concurred. Further, he flatly rejected both Chombart de Lauwe's evidence of sociological differences in dwelling practices, as well as his predecessors' interpretative metaphors of "different bottles in one rack" or "different words in one grammar." He denounced the 4P: "Cell-types, produced ad infinitum, lead people to live in the same way, accentuate uniformity, and bring *inside their homes* the spirit of repetition, anonymity, and dullness."[47] Besset and Candilis each emphasized the need to reconceptualize the apartment itself, since the collective habitation was "the only formula admissible" for what they both called the epoch "of the greatest number."[48]

There was some sociological evidence for the assertion that the *pavillon* was a myth or a negative choice. In 1967, Paul Clerc published *Grands ensembles, banlieues nouvelles: enquête démographique et psycho-sociologique* (Grands Ensembles, New Suburbs: A Demographic and Psychosociological Study), an analysis of over 2,500 households in fifty-three *grands ensembles* spread across metropolitan France.[49] Interviewed in the spring of 1965, a full 88 percent of residents ranked their home as acceptable, satisfactory, or very satisfactory. But Clerc also discovered that 82 percent would have chosen a detached home if the costs were the same. Probing this preference further, he asked questions about how long people planned to stay in the *grands ensembles,* how much more of their budgets they would be willing to spend to own a *pavillon,* and how much longer a commute they would accept to live in one. Over half planned to stay a while, and only a third did not, although some of the latter had no concrete or immediate plans for departure. Furthermore, Clerc found that the projected increases of commuting time and personal investment were negligible and would not, in reality, be sufficient to own a bungalow. It was this evidence that made Clerc's argument more convincing, and he could then conclude that the *pavillon* was therefore primarily a "symbol" of independence and personal freedom.[50]

A 1969 MEL-commissioned study of five thousand young couples resulted in parallel findings. Asked to choose in principle between a single-family home and an apartment in a *grand ensemble,* 68 percent of five thousand young couples opted for the former; however, a full 77 percent would consider buying a co-op in a *grand ensemble* if the complex had high-quality schools, day care, sports facilities and the like. Because most of the young couples interviewed comprised dual-income families, the report proposed that collective housing responded better, in fact, to the realities of young women's lives; on-site day care would facilitate women's work outside of the home, which would in turn maximize household affluence. Financial well-being would give couples the freedom to have as many children as they wished, since they would not need to limit family size for fiscal reasons.[51] It was clear that the state, despite nods to single-family homes, was reluctant to abandon *grands ensembles.* Like the old *Ladies Home Journal* column, "Can This Marriage Be Saved?" the proliferation of these and similar state-sponsored studies in the second half of the 1960s suggests that state policymakers were scratching their heads and asking themselves a similar question: can the *grand ensemble* be saved?

Was there any way to reconcile collective housing and the myth of the *pavillon*? In a much-cited 1966 work, sociologist Nicole Haumont had deserted the legions of her colleagues researching the *grands ensembles* and went to study those already living in bungalow-style detached homes. For *Les pavillonnaires: Étude psycho-sociologique d'un mode d'habitat* (The Suburbanites: A Psychosocial Study of a Mode of Dwelling), Haumont interviewed nearly two hundred *pavillon* households (as well as seventy apartment dwellers) in eight towns and suburbs and attempted to identify what inhabitants found so compelling about the bungalow. The majority of those she interviewed were working-class families (35 percent), while salaried employees (13 percent) and *cadres* (17 percent) composed the two next largest groups surveyed.[52]

Haumont's thesis revolved around the idea of *chez soi*, or the feeling of being "at home." Like Chombart de Lauwe, Haumont believed that one could only feel at home through the successful appropriation of space, but she added to his proposition by arguing that inhabitants adapted spaces to their needs according to shared "cultural models." Haumont derived the cultural models from two key dichotomies to which her interviewees referred as they described their homes: public and private, and order and disorder. The *pavillon* engendered a feeling of being at home because, through its arrangement of indoor and outdoor areas, it allowed for dwelling according to public-private and order-disorder norms. People felt at home when they could maintain orderly public spaces (like the front yard and the living room) and hide private spaces where disorder may or may not reign (like the kitchen, bedroom, and cellar or workshed). These findings led Haumont to reaffirm the absolute necessity of a kitchen that could be shut off from the rest of the space and an entryway that obstructed one's view of the living room area, so that unexpected visitors would not be able to see any untidiness or private activity taking place in the *séjour*.

Though Haumont proposed that the norms of privacy and order were shared cultural models, she also allowed for sociological variation, explaining that members of different classes did not always identify the same rooms or areas as public or private. However, since most subjects employed the public-private distinction to describe how they inhabited their houses, one could reliably identify this dichotomy as a shared norm or cultural model. Haumont also submitted that the appropriation of domestic space was gendered. While a woman made an area her own through decorating and housework, a man tended to transform a site through *bricolage*, or puttering about. Not only did men appropriate space by putting up wallpaper or painting cabinetry, but they also worked in the vegetable garden or built small pieces of furniture in their basements or sheds, which functioned as their private spaces. From this vantage point, the *pavillon* was superior to the 4P *cellule*. If the latter had been conceived with women's housework in mind, architects had only envisaged it as a site of repose and relaxation for men, as their escape from the world of work. Therefore, the only private space for men in the *cellule* was in the master bedroom, hardly an ideal locale for repairs or gardening.

Haumont did not advocate a new housing policy focusing on the mass production of bungalows. Rather, she hoped to understand what continued to make this form of housing so attractive to the French and to use those findings to improve apartment complexes; *Les Pavillonnaires* brims with explicit recommendations for architects designing HLMs. Yet, like Chombart de Lauwe, Haumont did not shy away from critiquing architects. In an article entitled "Habitat and Cultural Models," published in the *Revue française de sociologie* in 1968, Haumont asserted that sociological studies demonstrated that housing was not the, or even a, motor for social change. At most, homes could either slow or accelerate access to certain lifestyles. Haumont concluded that the role of architect was to "adapt the habitat to lifestyle transformations by taking into account the cultural models that govern the organization of space."[53]

Haumont's challenge to the pedagogical and social power of domestic space amplified other public interrogations of the architect's purpose. Media indictments of architects purportedly responsible for mediocre housing projects had not abated, and the state's support for individual homes threatened to reduce the architect's role in building modern France to nothing. In the context of the nearly universal condemnations of experts and challenges to traditional institutions that characterized the late 1960s, as well as of specific critiques of mass housing, the intellectual journal *Esprit* published a special issue in 1969 whose theme was the "architect, urbanism, and society"; the lead article was sociologist Raymonde Moulin's provocatively titled, "Do We Still Need Architects?"[54]

In addition to their unanimous rejection of detached homes, architects reacted to critiques of the profession by challenging in turn the obstacles that they believed to be impeding their best efforts: developers, contractors, an uneducated public, but most of all, the state.[55] Both Candilis and Parat reprised the now-familiar complaint about excessive and oppressive government regulations. Parat recommended the reduction of the number of examining committees, who seemed to work at cross purposes, and called the state's many requirements and specifications arbitrary and absurd.[56] André Hermant, who was by this time one of the elder statesmen of Modern architecture, continued to defend architecture from its critics by noting in the 1969 issue of *Esprit* that "[n]ot only is 60 percent of construction done without recourse to architects, but the 40 percent that remains is so subject to the imperatives of regulations, to commercial and financing requirements, that the intervention of architects is, most often, reduced to a rescue attempt, rather than a creation."[57]

Within the profession, Modernists and their young students again took up their condemnation of formal architectural training. Although a course on sociology had been added to ENSBA's program in 1967, the continued stress on the Grand Prix de Rome as the pinnacle of an architect's education undermined any orientation toward social housing.[58] Not once had public housing been a subject of the Prix de Rome competition, and in 1966 both professors and students began protesting in favor of a curriculum whose projects and examinations were "based in reality."[59] When the events of May 1968 began, ENSBA students joined the rest of the Parisian students taking to the streets to protest against capitalism, imperialism, authoritarianism, and positivism. The ENSBA students boldly announced the dissolution of both the Ordre des architectes and the École itself. By 22 May a number of architects joined them, including the Modernist author of the two enormous bars of the Haut-du-Lièvre *grand ensemble* (see chapter 4), Bernard Zehrfuss, who declared, "The 'Movement' born in the month of May 1968 from the will of architecture students and some architects is as important, and even goes further than, the Charter of Athens."[60] While the Ordre des architectes survived, the shakeup and reorganization of the former ENSBA provoked a more general identity crisis, and culture minister André Malraux cancelled the Grand Prix de Rome. Even the General Planning Commission noted in its 1970 pamphlet on housing that the profession seemed uncertain about its purpose. Given the significant claims made upon the architect's jurisdiction by large construction companies and engineers, perhaps architects could compensate by developing their capacities as urban planners, the Commission suggested.[61]

The May Events in France were not limited to architecture, of course, and the upheavals in architecture were not limited to France. Across the globe, young architects were interrogating the relationship of the individual consumer citizen to the urban and the architect's role therein. In Italy and in England radical collectives like Archizoom and Archigram proposed utopian urban landscapes that sought to undo Corbusian rationalism by privileging the cultural implications of consumerism or technological developments as the starting points for urban architecture. In the United States Robert Venturi published *Complexity and Contradiction in Architecture,* wherein he argued for the "honky-tonk" element in architecture and encouraged acceptance of a popular vernacular, asking, "Is not Main Street almost all right?"[62] Venturi thought that architects should limit themselves to tweaking the environment with their constructions, not insist upon blank slates. Two years later Venturi followed up his 1966 manifesto by seeking to embrace the commercial in a seminal article written with Denise Scott Brown and published in *Architectural Forum*: "A Significance for A&P Parking Lots, or, Learning from Las Vegas."[63] Back in France Hungarian-born "paper architect" Yona Friedman had been, since 1958, arguing for a flexible architecture that could operate as a superstructure above the existing city. In books like *L'Architecture mobile* (published in 1958 and reprinted in 1970) and works like his Spatial City, Friedman argued for temporary constructions into which inhabitants might build their own homes. Though Venturi was against the kind of megastructures endorsed by Friedman, both agreed that individuals acted in complex and sometimes irrational ways and hence no amount of sociological study and no unitary aesthetic could shape residential behavior in a way to make a single form of architecture suitable to all. The starting point could no longer be needs based on biology, but flexibility, pluralism, evolution: principles that would maximize individual freedom, one of the central calls of the 1960s youth movement.

Meanwhile, in the realm of policymaking, the larger political turmoil and social upheaval of May 1968 provoked several responses from the administration with regard to housing design and construction. First, the government approved the dissolution of the ENSBA and authorized the school's decentralization into new "pedagogical units" (*Unités pédagogiques*), attached to the culture ministry. The ZUP policy also came up for revision, since it had proven less than successful at quickly providing adequate collective services for ZUP populations. As historian Rosemary Wakeman demonstrated with the example of Toulouse-Le Mirail, after the initial blaze of glory in which Candilis's project began, a host of problems impaired the full actualization of Le Mirail, including lack of access roads to connect the ZUP to old Toulouse; competing commercial interests that impoverished the planned shopping center; difficulties with contractors; and land prices that chipped away at the project's budget.[64] Though Le Mirail was unique in scope, its fate was not uncommon. ZUPs had become legendary for their monotonous appearance and minimal services, and their poor reputation added to the public's perception of large apartment complexes as anonymous dormitory cities. Thus, in 1969, as Chalandon was attempting to launch a new wave of individual home construction, collective housing received a third shot in the arm, as the ZUPs, which had been designed to rescue the *grand ensemble* as a viable form of housing, evolved into ZACs: *zones à aménagement concerté*. "Concerted development" involved replacing the single team in charge of developing a ZUP with several groups whose activities would be overseen by the responsible prefect. Presumably, the diversification of actors involved in creating a concerted urban zone would provide a more richly textured living environment, while the prefect's coordination would preclude the haphazard provision of collective services that characterized the first generation of *grands ensembles*.

The MEL also began to address the charge that its own administrative policies were holding back true innovation. In 1969, the MEL promulgated a new version of its *Règlement de la construction* (National Construction Regulations), which superseded those of 1955. Among other changes, the new regulations removed the prohibition against putting the kitchen in the center of an apartment and eliminated the stipulation that each apartment have a double orientation.[65] The 1969 version of the construction rules provide evidence of an ideological shift: formerly precluded on the basis of hygienic concerns, the changes reflected a new way of thinking about the home that placed confidence in technology to compensate for nature. Mechanized ventilation systems and sufficient electrical power to provide constant artificial light could offset a lack of fresh air and sunlight.

In 1971, Robert Lion (director of Construction from 1969 to 1974), agreeing, in part, that the MEL was slowing innovation in building, developed a program called Plan Construction with Paul Delouvrier's support. Plan Construction financed research by teams of architects and builders in order to foster the elaboration of new systems of home construction. The program sponsored built projects, known as Réalisations Expérimentales, as well as two contests, Modèles Innovations and the Programme Architecture Nouvelle (PAN).[66] Lion hoped that Plan Construction would not only help eager young architects excluded from contracts by a rigid system but also catalyze further development of the construction industry, which had been prioritized in the Sixth Plan.[67] These experimental projects were part of a "policy of models," intended to inspire, though not demand, imitation by other builders and architects; Lion's approach thus differed from the more heavy-handed mechanism of the Courant-era model plans. By the end of 1974, approximately 5,500 experimental housing units at twenty-eight different sites had been built under the aegis of the Plan Construction, the great majority of which were social housing in the form of rental HLMs. Ten sites were in the greater Parisian region, and the rest were scattered around the provincial periphery, proximate to cities like Toulouse, Aix, Angers, and Rouen.[68]

Initially reluctant to adopt Lion's ideas, Chalandon was eventually won over to the Plan Construction and research into "a habitat of quality."[69] What nourished his support was increasing evidence that some of the detached houses built with state aid were beginning to show the same rapid degradation of the interiors as were some of the *grands ensembles*. In 1971, after the newspaper *L'Aurore* published an exposé of the problems plaguing Villagexpo homes, a "mission control" team went to examine them; on the basis of owners' complaints about condensation, mold, heating problems, and cracked paneling and flooring, the committee recommended that the CSTB reexamine the construction processes of one-third of the building companies represented at Villagexpo.[70] Chalandonnettes fared no better, becoming synonymous with shoddy construction and cheap materials.

Even before doubts surfaced about the quality of mass-produced detached homes, the state had begun to encourage architects in their search to find the "third way" alternative to both the *grand ensemble* and the *pavillon*. In 1967, the Délégation générale à la Recherche Scientifique et Technique (Directorate-General for Scientific and Technical Research, or DGRST) ordered further research into the development of "intermediary habitat."[71] The first example of this form of housing can be traced to the work of Jacques Bardet, the architect who had won Nungesser's 1963 contest for groupings of individual homes in the Parisian region. Breaking with the rectilinear form of the *grand ensemble* and taking the housing unit as a building block to be assembled in various permutations, rather than as bricks stacked one atop another, intermediary habitat tried to reconcile, in Bardet's words, the "imperatives of density" with a "relative individualization."[72] Research efforts went into the study of "assemblages," methods of juxtaposing and superposing apartments in order to produce a feeling of independence and privacy for those who dwelled within.

Since Bardet had won the District de la région de Paris competition, in 1968 the SCIC financed 163 of his homes as ILNs in the Parisian suburb of Val d'Yerres. Key to Bardet's design was the addition of a terraced patio equal in size to the *séjour*. This large extension was meant to give residents a feeling of privacy, since the homes were not only superposed, but also juxtaposed, in an attempt to avoid neighbors on either side.[73] As Haumont had written, "What the neighbor can see is destructive of *chez soi* [feeling at home] and what he causes to be heard by signifying his presence is equally destructive of *chez soi*. The neighbor should therefore not see or be heard."[74]

The idea of the intermediary habitat found favor in both state and architectural circles. In 1967, the DGRST gave Andrault and Parat, who had won the contest for the site plan at Villagexpo, a contract for a housing development based on a pyramid-like structure of juxtaposed homes. This form was later reproduced as the winning entry in the 1973 Modèles Innovations competition for homes in the new town of Évry. In 1969, Jean Renaudie developed an HLM complex at Ivry, which featured star-shaped *cellules*, with angled interiors and terraces. As the publicity for the completed Évry apartments, which emphasized the generous terraces with differing views, observed, with a perhaps unintentional double entendre: "There is no longer only one way to see the city." It continued: "Each according to his mood, his means of locomotion, his route, discovers space and composes it to his liking."[75] Like state planners, a number of architects were realizing the importance of the individual and were struggling to reconcile social integration with individual preferences, aspirations, and freedoms.

Intermediary habitat projects all sought to square what Parat and Arguillère called the "contradictory needs of isolation and contact" of residents with the "necessary high density" of the urban.[76] In so doing, intermediary habitat seemed to provide an answer to the many problems plaguing the architectural profession: it demonstrated the architect's competence and utility, offered an alternative to suburbanization, and, by attempting to comply with dweller preferences for privacy, proffered evidence of architects' willingness to integrate inhabitant concerns into their designs for living. Projects like Renaudie's and Andrault and Parat's promised to satisfy popular demands with regard to housing, while mobilizing the architect's technical expertise, maintaining state control over new construction, and privileging urban development over purportedly atomistic suburban developments.

Back at the housing ministry, 1972 saw Olivier Guichard relieving Chalandon at the helm of the MEL (once again reconstituted, the portfolio had become the unwieldy-sounding Ministry of Land Use Management, Facilities, Housing and Tourism [Ministère de l'aménagement du territoire, de l'équipement, du logement et du tourisme]). Once minister, Guichard took the dramatic step of putting an end to the *grands ensembles* in his famous "Guichard Circular" of March 1973. Henceforth, in cities with less than fifty thousand inhabitants, a housing project would be limited to one thousand units; in larger cities, two thousand was the maximum (which was still quite large). Defending his decision before the National Assembly, Guichard lamented the social segregation endemic to both ZUPs and suburban developments. Reprising the urban ecology arguments of 68ers, he argued that the city was a microcosm of the national community, the site and symbol of a unified nation where all classes could live harmoniously. Each and every person had a "right to the city," he claimed, invoking the title of Marxist sociologist Henri Lefebvre's popular book of 1968. Guichard explained: "Right to the city because the city is a value, because the city, a work of civilization, is civilizing in return. Right to the city rather than to the four walls of a home: that is to say right to a certain type of social life where the exchange is richer. Right to the city for everyone, since urbanization is a generalized phenomenon that is encompassing the rural world."[77] If Liberation-era housing professionals had seen the one-size-fits-all functional dream home as a vehicle for and emblem of social health, by 1973, denunciation of the *grand ensemble* forced their successors to reject the domestic ideal, crossing the threshold to celebrate the urban fabric, whose crowded, bustling streets would be the threads weaving the nation together.

Yet, despite his left-leaning rhetoric, Guichard caught as much heat from the media as had his predecessors Chalandon, Maziol, and Nungesser. As contemporary leading dailies across the political spectrum observed, the timing of the Guichard Circular was suspect: coming on the heels of the 11 March runoff elections, during which the Gaullist coalition lost 190 seats, journalists—even at *Le Figaro*—suspected that the end of the *grands ensembles* and the condemnation of social segregation was really a move to dilute concentrations of leftist voting enclaves.[78] Since 1965, when the municipality of Sarcelles elected a Communist mayor for the first time in its history, the potential for *grands ensembles* to become hotbeds of Communist or Socialist voters had been a worry; indeed, in the recent legislative elections, it was in districts housing *grands ensembles* that the Gaullists had suffered the largest losses.[79]

Moreover, Guichard came under attack for what observers understood to be the state's attempt to exit the social housing development scheme. Workers still wanted affordable rental housing, and they were now accustomed to looking to the state for its provision. The relatively low rents allowed workers and their families a certain quality of life and freed up any disposable income for vacations, consumer goods, entertainment, or other discretionary expenditures. According to *Libération*, 80 percent of those under 35 years old wanted more social housing, not less, and the rents at *grands ensembles* were "significantly lower" than elsewhere.[80] Young people, it appeared, were still willing to cede their right to the city in exchange for their right to inexpensive modern suburban housing.

From the Functionalist Cell to the Personalizable Apartment

In 1964, the last Exposition de l'Habitation was held at the Salon des Arts Ménagers. After the SAM moved in 1961 from the Grand Palais in the heart of Paris to the Modernist-designed Center for New Industries and Technologies in the newly created business district of La Défense and opened its doors to international purveyors of appliances, sinks, and linoleum, the annual show began to take on a less pedagogical and more professional mission. The last model homes had been showcased in 1962; the subsequent two Expositions de l'Habitation devoted themselves to merely educating visitors about the finer points of heating and plumbing installations. Annual attendance still ran over 1 million until 1972, but the visions of modernity to be glimpsed at the SAM were less spectacular.

Did the absence of dream homes at the 1960s SAMs signal tastemakers' satisfaction with the functionalist three-bedroom apartment as the ideal mass home? Not at all. Though debates about the shape towns should take and the future of the profession had largely driven research on the *cellule* off of the pages of the architectural press, domestic space did not remain frozen in the shape of the Courant-era 4P model plan. Indeed, against a backdrop of debates about the role of the architect, sociologists' evidence of class-based variations in dwelling practices, and discussions of the urban future, a number of architects took Candilis and Besset's suggestions and rethought the interior in the late 1960s.

As we saw in chapter 5, by pointing to its failure to function in response to diverse dwelling practices, Chombart de Lauwe tolled the death knell for the functionalist interior, and the 1960s and early 1970s witnessed its passing. In the mid 1960s, following in Chombart de Lauwe's footsteps, Nicole Haumont challenged Modernist architects' functionalism: "If we consider isolated needs, we obtain a high rate of satisfaction, and we arrive at the conclusion that the construction program is a good one. It seems, however, that the general need of 'dwelling' is not satisfied, since the inhabitant refers contradictorily to another housing model that hovers like a bird of ill omen over the creations of modern architecture [i.e., the *pavillon*]."[81] Haumont's colleague at the Institute of Urban Sociology, Henri Raymond, refined her critique by urging architects to think of spaces not as places where abstract biological and psychological needs were fulfilled, but as sites of practices. These practices could vary somewhat, but only within the parameters of established cultural models (like those Haumont had identified in *The Suburbanites*), allowing for some extrapolation to a model plan.[82] The changes in the 1969 National Construction Regulations reflected this reconceptualization of space, putting an end to the state's procedure of specifying minimum surface areas for each room. If rooms were no longer perceived as only fulfilling a particular need or set of needs, then an apartment could be conceived more holistically. The elimination of the one-room-to-a-function design tenet would facilitate individual appropriation of space. Maximizing individual adoption and embrace of interior space might then permit a continuation of a policy of high-density collective housing projects, since residents would, in a sense, take "ownership" of their homes, and satisfaction with the *grand ensemble* formula would increase.

Evidence of the beginning of the functionalist 4P's end can be found in *Histoires de cellules,* a study of apartments performed in 1972–1973 by an interdisciplinary group of researchers and administrators working for the Region of Paris. The research group interviewed architects and residents of six new Parisian apartment complexes that had opened to occupants between 1967 and 1969. The research group noted that, "although aided by the Administration," they had difficulty identifying apartments that "went beyond the ordinary."[83] The six projects examined in depth included two ILNs (one of which was Bardet's La Nérac), two HLMs, and two co-op properties. One of the HLM *cellules* studied belonged to a *grand ensemble* designed by Georges-Henri Pingusson for the ZUP of Bures-Orsay. It retained all of the elements of the functionalist 4P. The dining area was in the *séjour,* next to the kitchen, no hallway facilitated distribution, the "services" (bathroom, kitchen, and toilet) were grouped into a "water block," and one bedroom, while not lying directly off of the *séjour,* lay far from the other bedrooms, decimating the day-night separation of the living space. Moreover, Pingusson had chosen this plan despite the fact that working-class families dominated the complex.

The other projects did not mimic Pingusson's pure functionalism, however. Most of the architects had attempted to incorporate some of the sociological evidence published over the last decade into their designs. Michel Andrault and Pierre Parat's cooperative apartments for the ZUP of Sainte-Geneviève-des-Bois invoked some of the recommendations published by Dreyfus and Tribel in 1961 (see chapter 5): play space for children could be found in the center of the apartment, off of the *séjour*; the kitchen included a nook for meals; and the bathroom was far from the kitchen. Moreover, the need for privacy could be met by the doors allowing the *séjour* to be shut off from visitors' view or from the noise of children in the play area. To take another example, at the second HLM, at Bagnolet, Paul Chemetov and Jean Deroche's floor plan (Figure 6.1) separated the bathroom areas from the kitchen and offered a polyvalent area that could be subdivided in several ways to encourage individual appropriation of space.

Despite these responses and adaptations of the *cellule*, the authors of the *Histoires de cellules* study did not evaluate the architects' efforts with enthusiasm. Their report noted that, lacking any direct input from residents of their apartments, architects tended to arbitrarily select which of the occupant preferences and practices they would choose to accommodate.[84] Some architects, claimed the research team, made selections based on their own, internalized hierarchy of values. Others grounded their choices in ideology, like Pingusson, who, true to form, continued to justify his lab kitchen: "To eat next to a sink or a garbage chute is a loss of human dignity."[85] Bures-Orsay residents, however, did not feel like they lived with dignity in their apartments, even if they contained dining nooks; they experienced their homes as another form of class oppression. "The architect couldn't care less, because it's for workers."[86]

It was not just dominant ideas about spaces that sociologists sought to change, therefore, but also reigning interpretations of the respective roles of architects and occupants in the production of space. The urban sociologists who studied interiors spent much of the 1960s and early 1970s begging architects to acknowledge

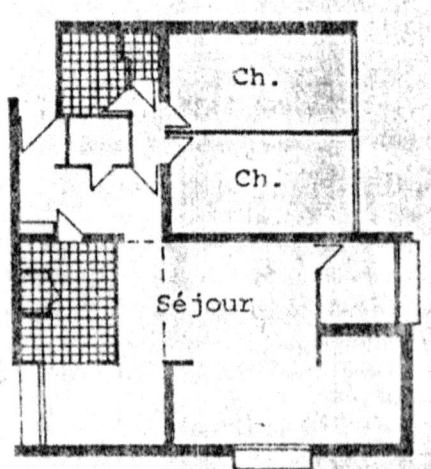

Figure 6.1. Plan by Paul Chemetov and Jean Deroche. © 2014 Artists Rights Society [ARS], New York / ADAGP, Paris.

that inhabitants were the primary agents involved in creating a home. To argue that architects could not impart a lifestyle via a *cellule*'s four walls, Nicole Haumont turned to Henri Coing's 1966 book, *Urban Renewal and Social Change*. In his study of residents of the renovated 13th *arrondissement,* Coing found that those who had been rehoused in better living conditions outside of their former neighborhood did not universally embrace their new surroundings. Whether or not occupants enjoyed their new "modern lifestyle" (meaning one centered around their apartment in accordance with the domestic ideal) depended on two factors: (1) whether they had sufficient disposable income to furnish their new dwellings in a fashion similar to their neighbors' homes, thus giving them a feeling of equality and belonging; and (2) whether they had a preexisting desire for social mobility that had been hitherto thwarted by the slum-like conditions of their former environment. Residents who met neither of these conditions resented their new surroundings and mourned their old lifestyle and former patterns of sociability.[87]

Such variables were obviously beyond the reach of architects, which is why sociologists strained—repeatedly—to get them to understand the limits to housing's pedagogical power. Raymond tried to make this point clearer by distinguishing the habitat from the lodging or apartment. In other words, architects were responsible for designing the material space of the housing unit, but dwellers created the *home*. Raymond asserted that mid-century functional housing had failed to produce Rational Man. Studies showed that inhabitants had not abandoned their armoires as directed, and if families tended to gather in the *séjour* after dinner, it was because that was where the television was, and not because they were inspired by the zoned areas for relaxation, reading, or sewing that the architects had created for this space. Furthermore, the tastemakers of the feminine press had embraced the Referendum Apartment's eat-in kitchen, a choice reflecting a dwelling practice that the Modernist architects interviewed for Chombart de Lauwe's *Famille et habitation* had roundly condemned. To the editors of the middle-class *Elle* and even the more bourgeois *La Maison française,* the eat-in kitchen appeared as the sign of the more relaxed, open society clamored for during the social unrest of the late 1960s. *La Maison Marie-Claire* observed that the kitchen was "no longer a laboratory, but a living area where we can take real pleasure in dining."[88]

Like the planners charged with orienting housing policy in the late 1960s and early 70s, architects designing new interiors were struggling at this moment to make sense of the larger social changes, intended or coincidental, accompanying the explicit national project of modernization. During the first decade of the Fifth Republic, real wages began to increase by about 3.6 percent annually, sparking a surge in consumerism.[89] This was the moment when families began to acquire appliances and leisure goods in great numbers, and modern comfort finally entered homes on a large scale. By 1968, only 9 percent of homes lacked running water, and, whereas in 1954, only 10 percent of homes had had an indoor toilet and a shower or tub, by 1968, 41 percent did. (This figure rose to 65 percent in 1975.)[90] Between 1957 and 1968, the number of households owning a refrigerator skyrocketed from 17.4 percent to 72.5 percent, those owning a washing machine leapt from 17.6 percent to 49.9 percent, and the number of televisions in French homes increased from 6.1 percent to 61.9 percent.[91] The purchase of these consumer items was evidence that the French agreed with the tastemakers of the Salon des Arts Ménagers and the mass press: the home was indeed worthy of their investment. In a relatively short period of time, modern conveniences had moved from luxuries to everyday items.

Sometimes in order to afford more such items, larger numbers of married, middle-class women entered the workforce and further increased household buying power, as we saw earlier. Women were choosing to bear fewer children during the 1960s, and pronatalism had faded from the political agenda.[92] The changes in women's lives and in family structure had implications for the "universal rhythms of family life" around which the functionalist 4P had been designed (see chapter 2). Contemporary journalists pronounced that young women were rejecting the prospect of being "only a housewife."[93] The 1950s domestic ideal of the home as the key site for individual happiness and family unity—privileged by virtue of its central heating and ultra-efficient "domestic engineer"—was becoming dated, especially in the context of the 1960s youthquake.

Another question facing architects, then, was how to take these large-scale social changes into consideration when designing interiors for mass housing. Some accepted the sociological critique that placed boundaries on their aesthetic vision. These architects extended the social doctrine of participation, which had been promoted and celebrated during the events of May 1968, into domestic space. To facilitate resident participation in dwellings, architects designed a number of variations of the Essai d'habitation évolutive's open and adaptable plan (see chapter 5). Replacing functionalism with flexibility as the first principle of good design, these architects experimented with do-it-yourself prefabricated house kits, "personalizable" plans enabling occupants to change even the apartment's orientation, and fully open, loft-style plans. All of these projects explicitly acknowledged inhabitants' agency in the making of a home.[94]

Other architects, reacting to the professional identity crisis that had been exacerbated by sociologists, claimed more for their roles. Jean Renaudie, architect of the intermediary habitat project at Ivry, wrote, "It is prudent to question the established criteria that currently determine what is good and what is bad in apartments and promote a good conscience [for the architect] by claiming to build on what the 'users' want. ... Understanding, in architecture, is not simply obeying established criteria and putting them into material form. It is to make speak what has heretofore been silent; it is to add to what we believed we knew."[95] For Renaudie, if the architect's purpose no longer was to educate users in a modern art of living, only architects, and not engineers or even sociologists, possessed the ability to design an ideal home that would exist in symbiosis with a changing world. Like his interwar Modernist forebears, Renaudie affirmed the architect's role as visionary, rejecting a professional identity that demoted the architect to scribe.

This was not simply egotism on Renaudie's part. Designing for the future was also what, particularly in the form of its Plan Construction, the state was asking architects to do. For example, in the instructions for its 1971 competition for Évry 1, a group of housing units in the new town of Évry, entrants read first: "Meal preparation primarily takes place in the kitchen, the key room of the home, where the lady of the house reigns. In fact, isn't this reign rather too often a modern form of slavery?" After posing this rhetorical question, the instructions indicated that "those who conceptualize the home, those in charge of floor plans must think of the woman who spends so much time among the four walls of her kitchen." Yet five pages later, the instructions noted: "Due to the evolution of lifestyles and notably the evolution of family life and the role of women, a new conception of the home imposes itself. The family is ceasing little by little to control a certain number of functions, like material protection, education, economic activities, and meal taking. Women are more and more liberated from housework, and they work outside the home."[96] Such contradiction—were women still spending all day in the kitchen or weren't they?—reflected confusion about the changes taking place in gender roles and family structures. Asking architects to envision the ramifications of contemporary and future social transformations and to design interiors accordingly rendered the existing sociological data about dweller preferences somewhat irrelevant.

This did not imply, of course, that the architect needed to ignore all of those preferences. In his building at Ivry, Renaudie tried to facilitate the appropriation of space by providing several different kinds of floor plans (to avoid the feeling of the repetitive model plan), within which numerous niches and angles produced polyvalent areas that inhabitants could adapt to their needs. A survey of the building's residents noted that, in

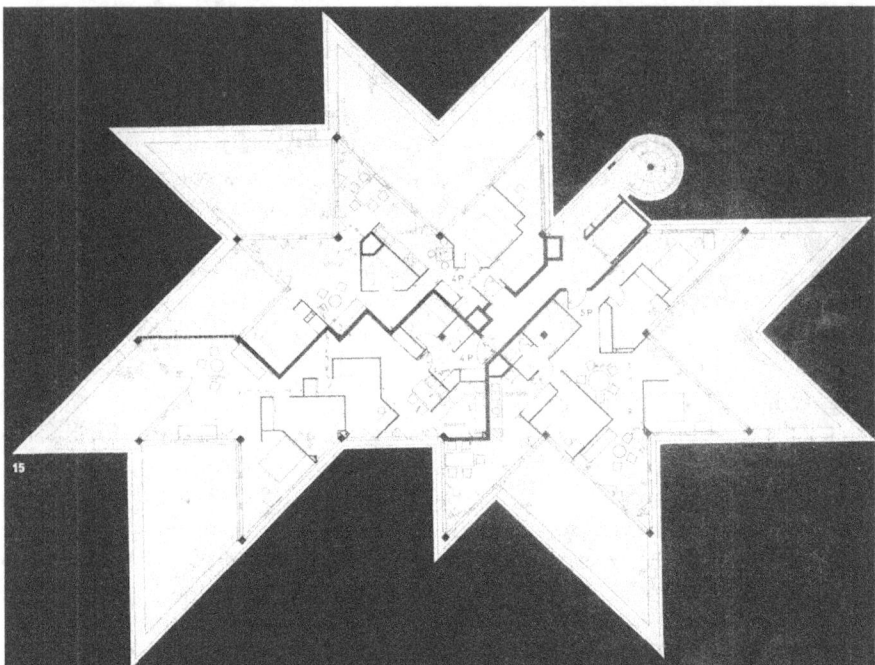

Figure 6.2. Two 4Ps and a 5P in Jean Renaudie's apartment complex in Ivry (used with permission).

fact, residents, after an initial reaction of surprise, seemed to adapt well to their apartments' unusual shape, finding it easy to furnish and decorate according to personal choices.[97]

The functionalist 4P box was becoming a relic. Under the influence of urban sociologists, a more holistic view of domestic space as more than a series of rooms fulfilling specific needs provoked reconceptualizations of the home's purpose. The *cellule* changed in a variety of ways, depending on an architect's understanding of inhabitants' roles, as well as of his own. Whether the architect felt like a visionary anticipating the future or a public servant participating with "the people" in home design, the democratized dream home in the guise of a one-size-fits-all apartment yielded to a proliferation of plans designed not only to permit but to promote individual appropriation of space.

As historian Kenny Cupers points out, this focus on the individual not only sprang from the democratic impulse championed by leftists during May 1968, it also acknowledged the rights of the consumer.[98] At the same time that housing professionals strove to identify the relationship of domestic space to the urban, they were also beginning to understand the role that homes played as differentiated commodities used to create and signify lifestyles. Researchers studying consumer behavior from 1959 to 1968 observed in 1970 that spending on home furnishings had risen much more quickly than expenditures for entertainment outside the home (restaurants, cinema, etc.), from which they deduced a new "preference for a lifestyle centered on the home."[99] That same year, the General Planning Commission's housing committee reported on the "increasing direct" link between home and lifestyle: "Hence the possibility to lead the lifestyle of one's choice—expression and condition of personality—appears to be an increasingly recognized demand, and claimed as the social groups reach a sufficient economic and cultural level."[100] While homes had long served as indicators of social status and signifiers for bourgeois families, two decades of propaganda promulgated by state officials, architects, tastemakers, and housing reformers celebrating the domestic ideal as the key site for individual happiness and self-actualization seemed to have hit its target: increasing numbers of households were choosing to identify with their homes and to invest in them, even as family life evolved within the interior to accommodate married women's paid labor, television, and youth culture.

Conclusion

State initiatives "giving the people what they want" in the shape of the Villagexpo and *chalandonnettes* prompted a strong reaction from architects, who rejected the detached home on both ideological and professional grounds. The debate that ensued focused on the pros and cons of collective housing, with the result that the research on interiors that had fueled so many of the discussions of the modern home largely disappeared from the radar screen. Nevertheless, architects did not abandon their efforts to define how the French should dwell. Where their Modernist forebears had drawn plans calculated to produce Rational Man (see chapter 2), the architects of the late 1960s and early 1970s oriented their projects, like the intermediary habitat, toward the definition of an Urban Man. Though numerous architects attempted to incorporate some popular preferences into their designs, it was only insofar as these preferences remained consistent with their vision of urban, and collective, living.

The state's continued support for and reliance on sociological studies throughout the 1960s contributed to functionalism's demise. This in turn fed the proliferation of different forms of housing, making the question of the ideal home, even in the populist guise of the Referendum Apartment or the *chalandonnette,* if not a nonsensical one, at least one able to be answered only by an inhabitant. It bears mentioning that the focus on appropriation and flexibility actually had its roots in the conception of individual happiness promoted in the 1950s-era domestic ideal. Homes didn't just have to be heated, bright, and easy to maintain, but they also had to satisfy inhabitants and contribute to their *épanouissement*. The domestic ideal nourished the conception of individual happiness, while the rhetoric and discourse of individual freedom also served the cause of single-family homes. Yet the contradictions remained between the privileging of individual agency while retaining state control of planning and construction to best serve the economy and government policies of *aménagement du territoire*.

Confusion reigned, too, about the desirability of collective housing. If during the 1940s and 50s, state planners' emphasis was on the modern, democratic interior, in the 1960s, they, like architects, turned their attention to the neighborhood and the city. Gaullist state planners sought to reconcile popular preferences while avoiding the politically fatal phenomenon of social segregation; instead of unifying the nation by building the same home for everyone—engineer, shopgirl, factory foreman, or artist—they now thought that mixed-density developments and intermediate habitats might model instead integration of different parts—of different *individuals*—into a unified whole. Since the beginning of the twentieth century, housing's "social question" had twice shifted: first from the promotion of good hygiene and moral behavior among workers and their families to the provision of modern comfort for all, and thence to the relationship of the individual to the city. While their experiments failed to bring about the desired results, the state continued, until the very end of the Thirty Glorious Years, to try to use home design to shape social life in urban France.

Notes

1. Georges Candilis, "Le mythe de l'habitat individuel," *L'Architecture d'aujourd'hui* 136 (February–March 1968), 14.
2. Julian Jackson, *De Gaulle* (London: Haus, 2003), 65.
3. Harloe, *The People's Home?*, 322.
4. See, for example, Voldman, *La reconstruction des villes françaises*, 387–88.
5. Wakeman, *Modernizing the Provincial City*, 127.
6. Flamand, *Loger le peuple*, 282; Roncayolo, *La Ville aujourd'hui*, 646.
7. Wakeman, *Modernizing the Provincial City*, 127.
8. Institut National de la Statistique et des Études Économiques, *Données sociales: Édition 1973* (Paris: INSEE, 1973), 118.
9. Rouaud, *60 ans d'arts ménagers*, vol. 2, 51.

10. Roncayolo, *La Ville aujourd'hui*, 647.
11. Anthony Sutcliffe, *Paris, An Architectural History* (New Haven, CT, and London: Yale University Press, 1993), 164.
12. Four other new towns were built outside of Lille (Villeneuve d'Ascq), Rouen (Val de Reuil), Lyon (Isle d'Abeau), and Marseille (les Rives de l'Étang de Berre).
13. Secrétariat d'État au Logement, Relations Extérieures, "Inauguration de Villagexpo," 23 September 1966, AN, CAC 19771153/3.
14. "Résultats du concours du Villagexpo," 13 April 1967, AN, CAC 19771142/19.
15. "Premiers résultats d'une enquête auprès des visiteurs de Villagexpo," in Ministère de l'équipement et du logement, *Statistiques de la construction* 11 (November 1967), bulletin found in AN, CAC 19771153/5, 51, 52, 54.
16. Yves Aubert, "Note pour M. Grange," 5 March 1968, AN, CAC 19771153/6.
17. Isabelle Gournay, "Levitt France et la banlieue à l'américaine: premier bilan," *Histoire urbaine* 5 (2002): 167–88.
18. Norma Evenson, *Paris: A Century of Change* (New Haven, CT: Yale University Press, 1974), 252.
19. On single-family housing construction, see Andrew Lorant (president of Levitt France), "In France, Too, Levitt Was Housing Pioneer" (letter to the editor), *New York Times*, 10 February 1994, and Kenny Cupers, "In Search of the User: The Experiment of Modern Urbanism in Postwar France, 1955-1975" (Ph.D. diss., Harvard University, 2010), 374.
20. Lorant, "In France, Too, Levitt Was Housing Pioneer."
21. Gournay, "Levitt France," 176.
22. Gournay, "Levitt France," 175 n.27; income statistics for 1965 taken from Baudelot and Lebeaupin, "Les salaires de 1950 à 1975," 16.
23. See John L. Hess, "French Home Buyers Pleased By a 'Levittown' Outside Paris," *New York Times*, 29 January 1967, 278; Hess, "In France, a Bit of Levittown, L.I., Not Far from Versailles," *New York Times*, 18 June 1972, 81.
24. Johann Dautant, "Entretiens avec Roland Prédiéri," 9 March 2009, for the Comité de Sauvegarde de Maurepas Village, http://www.maurepas-histoire.net/download/Entretien%20Predieri.pdf, 9.
25. Jacques Riboud, cited in Cupers, "In Search of the User," 374.
26. Cited in Tellier, *Le Temps des HLM*, 165.
27. Ibid., 166.
28. Ibid., 139.
29. Manuel Castells, *The City and the Grassroots: A Cross-Cultural Theory of Urban Social Movements* (Berkeley, CA: University of California Press, 1997), 82.
30. See Kenny Cupers, "The Expertise of Participation: Mass Housing and Urban Planning in Post-war France," *Planning Perspectives* 26, 1 (January 2011): 29–53.
31. Alain Touraine, *The Post-Industrial Society: Tomorrow's Social History–Classes, Conflicts and Culture in the Programmed Society*, trans. Leonard F.X. Mayhew (London: Wildwood House, 1974), 9.
32. Rod Kedward, *France and the French: A Modern History* (Woodstock, NY, and New York: The Overlook Press, 2007 [2005]), 402–5.
33. The Ministère de l'Équipement had become the Ministère de l'Équipement et Logement in April 1967.
34. Michael Joseph Mulvey, "Sheltering French Families: Parisian Suburbia and the Politics of Housing, 1939-1975" (Ph.D. diss., University of North Carolina at Chapel Hill, 2011), 201.
35. See section on "La maison individuelle" in Commissariat général du plan, *Le logement* (Paris: A. Colin, 1970).

36. So remarked a television journalist in 1964 in "Les Grands Ensembles de Créteil," *Journal de Paris*, RTF (Paris: Radiodiffusion Télévision Française, 11 April 1964). Video is available at http://www.ina.fr/video/CAF89027084/les-grands-ensembles-de-creteil-video.html. Revealing standard media prejudices of the time, the journalist prefaces his interviews of Créteil inhabitants by asking, "They have comfort, yes, but are they happy? What is life like for these uprooted inhabitants of a brand-new town?"
37. Flamand, *Loger le peuple*, 288.
38. Magri, *Logement et reproduction de l'exploitation*, 210.
39. P.T., "'Urbanisme de révolution' et 'urbanisme de réaction'," *Le Monde*, 19 January 1970, 12; Michel Vianey, "Vive la villa," *Nouvel Observateur*, 28 February 1972, 40.
40. Rémy Belhomme, "M. Nungesser a remis hier les clés aux premiers acquéreurs de Villagexpo," *Combat*, 17 November 1966, 1.
41. Vianey, "Vive la villa," 40; P.T., "'Urbanisme de révolution'," 12.
42. Henri Lefebvre, "Les nouveaux ensembles urbains. Un cas concret: Lacq-Mourenx et les problèmes urbains de la nouvelle classe ouvrière," *Revue française de sociologie* 1, 1 (1960): 186–201.
43. Susanna Magri, "Le pavillon stigmatisé: Grands ensembles et maisons individuelles dans la sociologie des années 1950 à 1970," *L'Année sociologique* 58, 1 (2008): 171–202, esp. 177.
44. Pierre Parat and Charles-Henry Arguillère, "'L'individuel': rêve, cauchemar, tendances," *L'Architecture d'aujourd'hui* 136 (February–March 1968), 7.
45. Ibid., 8.
46. Maurice Besset, *Nouvelle architecture française/New French Architecture* (New York: F. A. Praeger, 1967), 37.
47. Interview with Georges Candilis, published in *L'avenir des métiers de l'ameublement et de la décoration. L'ameublement et la décoration dans la vie moderne* (Paris: IPF, 1967), 15. Emphasis added.
48. Ibid., 15, and Besset, *Nouvelle architecture française*, 37.
49. Paul Clerc, *Grands ensembles, banlieues nouvelles: enquête démographique et psycho-sociologique*, Centre de recherche d'urbanisme, Institut national d'études démographiques, Travaux et documents 49 (Paris: PUF, 1967).
50. Ibid., 188, 189, 279, 387–89.
51. Mulvey, "Sheltering French Families," 201–2.
52. Nicole Haumont, *Les pavillonnaires: Étude psycho-sociologique d'un mode d'habitat* (Paris: Presse du Centre de recherche d'urbanisme, 1966).
53. Nicole Haumont, "Habitat et modèles culturels," *Revue française de sociologie* 9 (1968), 190.
54. See *Esprit* 37 (October 1969).
55. Georges Candilis, "Le fond du problème," *L'Architecture d'aujourd'hui* 130 (February–March 1967), 1, and, in the same issue, Pierre Parat and Charles-Henry Arguillère, "Habitat social: tendances, verrous, propositions," 3.
56. Parat and Arguillère, "Habitat social," 10.
57. André Hermant, "Pour une prise de conscience publique," *Esprit* 37 (October 1969): 540.
58. See Florent Champy, *Les Architectes et la commande publique* (Paris: PUF, 1998), 20.
59. See Moulin, "Avons-nous encore besoin des architectes?" *Esprit* 37 (October 1969): 396 n.17; Jacques Lucan, *France, Architecture 1965-1988* (Paris: Electa-Moniteur, 1989), 27.
60. "Les événements," *Techniques et Architecture* 3 (May–June 1968), 65.
61. Commissariat général du plan, *Le logement*, 126.
62. Robert Venturi, *Complexity and Contradiction in Architecture* (New York: Museum of Modern Art, 1966), 102.

63. See the March 1968 issue of *Architectural Forum*. This article was incorporated a few years later into their book with Steven Izenour, *Learning from Las Vegas* (Cambridge, MA, and London: MIT Press, 1972).
64. See Wakeman, *Modernizing the Provincial City*, 129–33.
65. CREPAH-GERASE, *Conditions et évolution de la production architecturale dans l'habitat social*, 16.
66. PAN still exists but now includes all of Europe and is known as EUROPAN.
67. J. Abram and D. Gross, interview with Robert Lion, cited in Gérard Monnier, *L'architecture moderne en France*, vol. 3, *De la croissance à la compétition 1967-1999* (Paris: Picard, 2000), 23.
68. See map in Secrétariat permanent du Plan-construction, *Plan Construction: Trois ans d'activité, mai 1971-décembre 1974* (Paris: Ministère de l'Équipement, 1974), 20.
69. Abram and Gross, interview with Lion, 23.
70. Mission de Contrôle des Prêts à la Construction, "Rapport sur l'Opération Villagexpo de St Michel-sur-Orge," February 1971, AN, CAC 19771153/6.
71. Monnier, *L'Architecture moderne en France*, vol. 3, 13.
72. Jacques Bardet, "La révolution de l'urbanisme reste à faire," *Esprit* 37 (October 1969): 550–51.
73. Jacques Bardet, "Assemblages volumétriques et tissu urbain," *L'Architecture d'aujourd'hui* 136 (February–March 1968), 28.
74. Haumont, *Les pavillonnaires*, 180–81.
75. Publicity material for Évry 1 housing development, in CAC 19780139/001 (n.d. [1973]).
76. Parat and Arguillère, "L'individuel," 10.
77. Débats parlementaires, Assemblée Nationale, compte rendu intégral des séances, 1st Séance of 17 May 1973, *Journal Officiel de la République Française*, 18 May 1973, 1329.
78. See, for example, Andrée Mazzolini, "M. Olivier Guichard décide d'interdire la construction des grands ensembles," *Le Figaro*, 22 March 1973; Étienne Mallet, "M. Guichard cherche à freiner la 'ségrégation par l'habitat," *Le Monde*, 23 March 1973; and R.P., "Moins d'HLM dans les communes ouvrières et 'guerre aux grands ensembles,'" *L'Humanité*, 23 March 1973. These articles are discussed in Mulvey, "Sheltering French Families," 216–17.
79. Castells, *The City and the Grassroots*, 76–77.
80. "Le Logement populaire en 1973: 'Des appartements encore plus chers et toujours plus petits,'" *Libération*, 30 October 1973, referenced in Mulvey, "Sheltering French Families," 217.
81. Haumont, "Habitat et modèles culturels," 181.
82. Henri Raymond, "Habitat, modèles culturels et architecture," *L'Architecture d'aujourd'hui* 174 (July–August 1974), 52.
83. COFREMCA, *Histoires de cellules: étude d'anthropologie sociale sur le vécu de certains logements Région parisienne* (Paris: Service Régional de l'Équipement de la Région Parisienne, 1975), 5. The architectural review *Techniques et architecture* disseminated this study, reprinting large excerpts from it in their December 1976 issue.
84. COFREMCA, *Histoires de cellules*, 53.
85. Ibid., 48.
86. Ibid., 45.
87. See Haumont, "Habitat et modèles culturels," 189–90.
88. See "Nouvelle pièce à vivre: la cuisine," *La Maison Marie-Claire* 1 (15 February 1967), 32; *La maison française* 281 (October 1974), 215.
89. Peggy A. Phillips, *Modern France: Theories and Realities of Urban Planning* (Lanham, MD, and London: University Press of America, 1987), 141.

90. Clanché and Fribourg, "Grandes évolutions du parc et des ménages depuis 1950," 85.
91. Godelinais and Lang, *L'Équipement des ménages en biens durables*, 20–22.
92. Duchen, *Women's Rights and Women's Lives*, 119; Prost, "L'évolution de la politique familiale de 1938 à 1981," 15.
93. Duchen, *Women's Rights and Women's Lives*, 92.
94. To see a number of plans similar to this one, consult Edith Girard's critique (influenced by Henri Lefebvre) of the doctrine of "flexibility": "Enfin libre et soumis," *L'Architecture d'aujourd'hui* 174 (July–August 1974): 10–17.
95. Jean Renaudie, "Faire parler ce qui jusque-là s'est tu," *Techniques et architecture* 312 (December 1976), 78.
96. *Évry 1, Concours conception-réalisation* (Paris: IAURP, 1971), D5, D10.
97. Excerpt from Françoise Lugassy's study for the Plan Construction of the inhabitants of the "immeuble Danièle-Casanova," published in *Techniques et architecture* 312 (December 1976), 80.
98. Cupers, "In Search of the User," 393–94.
99. Cited in Pulju, *Women and Mass Consumer Society*, 133.
100. Rapport final, groupe du long terme, Commission de l'Habitation, CGP, 1970, AN, CAC 19771142/036.

Conclusion

We make our environment; it makes us also.
—André Maurois, writer and member of the Académie française, 1952[1]

Published in 1950, *Le Blanchissage domestique,* Paulette Bernège's guide to laundering at home, not only detailed innovations in washing machine technology, but also took aim at the rat problem. Doing the laundry was still such an onerous task—involving at least fifteen different steps—that, unsurprisingly, larger items such as tablecloths and sheets or seasonal items might not get washed right away. For women who had access to large storage spaces, such as rural women, Bernège recommended hanging dirty laundry on a clothesline until the housewife could get to it. The problem with this was that rats might chew holes in the linens. So Bernège offered an "amusing" solution: that two glass bottles be threaded onto each end of the clothesline, and when the rats attempted to advance, they would step onto the bottle, which would spin and jettison the rat back to the floor.[2]

This anecdote crystallizes the status of French domestic space in the late 1940s and early 1950s: like state-of-the-art washers and dryers, the mechanized, consumption-based household was visible elsewhere (in the United States and in Sweden, for example), but French families knew that equipped, modern homes still lay only on their horizon. In the short term, they made do with cramped quarters, cold-water flats, and improvised "comfort." Bernège's book also reminds us of one of the many ways in which dwelling changed in France during the 1950s and 60s. When answering the question of where women should do the laundry, for instance, Bernège acknowledged that many women laundered in the kitchen because the French tradition of boiling clothes required very hot water, but, given that soiled clothes needed to soak for anywhere from 15 minutes to overnight, then hang to dry once they had been washed, laundry interfered with the kitchen's other primary function as the site of meal preparation. Soon, Bernège noted, more homes than ever would have bathrooms, which could accommodate laundering, since this space wasn't used after the completion of the morning toilette.[3] Before household appliances such as washing machines even entered the home, space *itself* was a luxury to urban working and lower middle classes. Ways of inhabiting the home changed during the Thirty Glorious Years, and this book has demonstrated how domestic space was a key component of the nation-building and social engineering projects of postwar French elites. State planners, tastemakers, and architects' modernizing projects for the home, were, in turn, a catalyst for transformations in dwelling practices and in mentalities. In this, André Maurois was right: the French made their modern homes, but the modern homes made them, too.

French modernizers of the home were both winners and losers; proud of their success in solving the housing crisis, they were not always aware of the ironies and contradictions inherent in their intentions, nor did many foresee the longer-term implications of their projects. The built environment materialized not only housing professionals' democratizing aspirations, but also their anxieties about the erosion of class boundaries, women's emancipation, and France's transition into mass consumer society. Elites did not acknowledge, for instance, the tension between their desire to contribute to a classless society and the classed dwelling practices that they normalized in social housing, nor did they recognize the contradiction between asserting that the modern home would increase leisure for everyone and then ascribing the new duties of scientific *and* artful homemaking to French women. Indeed, gender roles continued to evolve in ways that advocates of modernization had not anticipated. State housing professionals, architects, and the organizers of the Salon des Arts Ménagers forecast a modern home run by a stay-at-home mother, but by the end of the 1960s, a record number of over 57 percent of women between the ages of 25 and 39 were participants in the labor force, with a growing number of married women and mothers entering the labor market.[4] Nevertheless, as studies of time expenditure continue to demonstrate, French women, like women worldwide, have retained primary responsibility for homemaking.[5] Moreover, the pronatalist goals of Fourth Republic planners were met. Construction of new homes did allow for the creation of new households, and "young marrieds," while having smaller families, quickly produced more than De Gaulle's hoped-for 12 million beautiful babies in the first fifteen years after the new constitution.

Modernizers of the home believed they could contribute to a classless society because their functional apartment would eliminate variations in dwelling practices. Inhabitants of social housing, however, persevered in many of their habits and rebelled against the normative aspects of the *cellule d'habitation,* ultimately reshaping the modern home to conform to a variety of dwelling preferences. The resident feedback examined in chapter 5 revealed that many families demanded eat-in kitchens instead of lab kitchens, preferred long distributive hallways to communicating rooms or open plans, and favored standard-sized windows over outsize picture windows. On the other hand, new practices did emerge. Instead of spending several months of the year together around the kitchen stove for warmth, for instance, working-class families began to spend time in different rooms, inhabiting bedrooms for longer parts of the day. Instead of entertaining in parlors or dining rooms, middle-class families socialized in the *séjour*. (One striking aspect of mid-50s and -60s model apartments and magazine features is that one does not yet see many sofas; armchairs clustered around a radio or record player feature more prominently before the advent of televisions in each home. These upright chairs signal, in retrospect, a transitional period of comfort before the advent of reclining on a sofa.) Central heat led to people using their new shower stalls for bathing instead of for storing coal. Furthermore, as we saw in chapters 5 and 6, the home gained in priority as an object of household investment, and families began to use new credit mechanisms to furnish and complete their new homes, even as they grew accustomed to devoting larger proportions of their household income to rent. In this fashion, the French did indeed respond to elites' hopes that families would allocate more resources to and understand the importance of a comfortable home. The right to comfort produced by the provision of new homes effected a shift in mindset, and, for the first time families long used to rent control agreed to invest in and develop these "sites of happiness."

Finally, while the French failed, by and large, to "give the example" of their Modern art of living to the rest of the world—insofar as CIAM-inspired Modernism became known as International Style, and the specific designs of Le Corbusier, Charlotte Perriand, and Jean Prouvé remained cult favorites of a small group of aesthetes—those involved in housing design and construction had indeed raised the nation's standard of living and had improved housing conditions to the extent that there was no longer a sense of shame or decline in comparison to other European nations. Recall, in this context, Stanislas Fontaine (chapter 4), who described Sarcelles as a departure from 150 years' worth of "sad piles of houses," or Jacques and Jean-Claude at the Dijonnaise HLM apartment complex called Billardon (chapter 5), who saw modern homes as "great progress."

As part of France's regeneration, modernizing French elites like Jean Monnet had wished to inspire in their peers and in the average French person new ways of thinking, producing, consuming, working, and, as this book has shown, dwelling. Historian Richard Kuisel, writing about modernizers' proselytism, invoked the Monnet Plan's administrator, Étienne Hirsch: "A farmer on a tractor will no longer think like a farmer behind a horse."[6] Similarly, these elites assumed, families in modern housing would no longer think like those in *pavillons* or *hôtels garnis*. These aims were achieved, insofar as new ways of thinking, working, and dwelling rapidly became status quo, and families began to invest in home improvement. Where Jacques's wife interpreted her new home at Billardon as sheer "luxury," the transformation in expectations was such that by the end of the 1960s, flush toilets, gas stoves, hot water on demand, bathrooms, and washing machines no longer seemed like wild extravagances, but the basic requirements for an average home.

This does not mean, of course, that the French universally and equally gained access to the modern home during the Thirty Glorious Years. Indeed, though some Liberation-era housing professionals had regarded the modern home as a harbinger of the classless society, protesters during the May 1968 events vividly pointed out that the discrepancies between rich and poor, between privileged and marginalized, were alive and well in a prosperous, industrialized—and modern—France. The social housing built as HLMs in *grands ensembles* has fared especially poorly over time, becoming a signifier of the poverty and social exclusion it is often deemed to have caused. As recently as 2011, Marie-Christine Vatov, a journalist specializing in urban issues, observed that the razing of postwar towers like those at the legendary Parisian *grand ensemble* La Courneuve symbolizes the French state's commitment to repairing tears in the social fabric. She argued—correctly—that, unfortunately, the problems that the government is attempting to resolve reach far beyond the spaces themselves. Demolitions of towers and the erection of new, lower-rise apartment clusters will not lead to jobs for un- or underemployed youth or eliminate the drug trade from "sensitive neighborhoods."[7] Yet the fact that government money is available for new construction while there are fewer budgetary resources for education, job training, or additional police speaks to the continuity of the French state's faith in the determinism of space and its strategic role in social engineering.

Reexamining the Whos and Hows of the French Modernizing Project

Perhaps because HLMs and *grands ensembles* became so strongly associated with social malaise, mass housing is largely absent from accounts of postwar social transformation. In their book *Social Change in Modern*

France, Henri Mendras and Alistair Cole described the Thirty Glorious Years in the following terms:

> After a century of demographic stagnation (1840-1940), France's population rose dramatically after the war, from 42,000,000 to 56,000,000 within one generation. Simultaneously, economic production forged ahead and the structure of the French economy was radically altered. The nation's wealth increased in a totally unprecedented manner and economic production multiplied five-fold within several decades.
>
> The two dominant social classes produced by the Revolution, the peasantry and the bourgeoisie, have disappeared. The expansion of tertiary sector employment and the birth of the cadres have produced a complete overhaul in the nation's social class structure.[8]

This is a fairly standard way of looking at the rapid alterations of the postwar social world. But the emphasis on quantitative evaluation obscures agents of these changes. To put the focus on domestic space, as we have done here, is not to say that it was the only avenue for change. But equipped, modern homes were as much a catalyst for change as the appearance of the *cadre* in the social space. This becomes apparent if we consider what Mendras has called the *moyennisation* of French society. By this term Mendras means to describe both growth in the portion of the population who might be considered middle class, as well as a concomitant increase in the middle class's cultural influence. Mendras, like Jean Fourastié, uses the word "revolution" to describe social transformation, but Mendras sees the key developments as emerging after 1965. All the same, his three factors facilitating *moyennisation*—(1) the growth of mass production, which made consumer goods more affordable and available to larger swaths of the population; (2) the provision of welfare-state protections that reduced inequalities; and (3) the democratization of education—are all phenomena that took place over the course of the years 1945 to 1975.[9] Just as unemployment insurance, universal health care, and family allocations reduced income inequities, so too, I have argued, did the provision of a modern mass home. It is clear that model plans, mixed-class "one-size-fits-all" housing, and SCIC financing contributed socioculturally to *moyennisation,* since, as this book has shown, they played a role in the leveling out of income-based dwelling conditions and the spread of middle-class expectations regarding comfort and happiness during the 1950s, 1960s, and 1970s.

Incorporating the history of the modern home into the larger history of postwar France deepens our understanding of the complex reality of the period. More than a footnote to history, the postwar mass home materialized efforts by various groups to contend with other, more studied aspects of the period: the upheavals of war, decolonization, mass consumer culture, and Cold War ideological battles. Further, using the lens of domestic space allows us to see phenomena obscured when one only views these decades through an economic or a political lens. Our history of the ostensibly private sphere during the Trente Glorieuses underscores, for example, the unprecedented ways in which the modernizing state zoomed in on women in their role as workers, albeit domestic ones. If the Vichy Regime instantiated women's role as mother, and if postwar mass media representations of women were often focused on young women,[10] modernizers and postwar planners saw women through the lens of housewife. Rebecca Pulju has shown how women were targeted for their role as citizen-consumers, but she also indicates an intense focus on what she calls "the productivity drive in the home."[11] Taking their lead from prewar American and other European studies, postwar French technocrats measured, timed, and surveyed women qua homemakers, whether the woman in question worked outside the home for wages or not.

I would argue that the housewife was understood to be as much a worker as a consumer. The extraordinary attempts of home professionals to increase housewives' productivity (even if they were at times misguided about the nature of homemakers' tasks) emerge when we look, as we did in chapter 3, at the detailed and scientific literature on homemaking that appeared during this heyday of the home. Remember, too, that a number of housing complexes, as we saw in chapter 4, had home economics advisors' offices on site to assist or train women in the creation of a modern home. In the twenty-first century, few—except marketers and, in the United States, Martha Stewart—really care how housework is done or if space can be better organized to ease women's burdens; schools have largely abandoned home economics. Historians have made much of the sexism manifest in representations of women in the mass press of the postwar period, with these reducing women to teeny-boppers, sex kittens, or "mere" housewives. Our history of housing suggests, however, a concomitant effort by other actors in French society to take housework seriously. If literally building a kitchen around the body of the "average" French woman, as recommended by Jean Magendie in 1946, reified housework as women's work, it is no less true that bureaucrats, designers, architects, social workers, home economists, and tastemakers like Paul Breton were collectively toiling to ease the burden on women through what they understood to be good design. Writing women—and the contemporary understandings of their work within the home—"back in" to modernization narratives allows us to see how crucial women were understood to be to the national modernizing project.

Recalibrating the Balance Sheet of the Postwar Republics

Taking household labor seriously also inclines us toward a deeper appreciation of the contributions of the housing officials who steadfastly insisted upon outfitting homes with central heat and hot running water and of the home professionals who worked to educate women about using refrigerators and laundry rooms. To date, scholars have resisted such an assessment, often dismissing the significance of modern homes and their electric appliances by observing that a rise in housekeeping standards offset the advantages of electric appliances.[12] Yet there is a real difference between standards of housewifery—which women have agency to accept or resist—and the physical demands of outmoded or dilapidated housing. Integrating the latter into our analysis obliges us to credit the improvement in everyday life delivered by the modern mass home to someone like Paulette, whom we met in chapter 5. Paulette recounted that when she had her first child in 1948, the family lived in a one-room apartment, with only a sink and a wood- and-coal-burning stove. While her husband was at work, Paulette was in charge of procuring the coal and wood for cooking and heating. Moving into Billardon in 1955, Paulette and her friends were overjoyed at the prospect of no longer having to acquire fuel on a regular basis.

It would be a mistake, of course, to think that these women's joy was ubiquitous or permanent. The domestic ideal's emphasis on individual happiness, combined with the right to comfort that the modern home explicitly guaranteed, particularly as these were articulated and publicized at places like the Salon des Arts Ménagers, produced a level of popular expectation with regard to housing that the functionalist "cells" and the rapidly erected *grands ensembles* were, in fact, ill-equipped to sustain. Two decades after his Société centrale immobilière de la caisse spent millions of francs building thousands of units of HLMs to resolve the housing crisis, François Bloch-Lainé complained of their reception: "It was necessary to build quickly and cheaply. The Caisse did it. The beneficiaries of this effort, imploring during the wait, overflowed with gratitude at the moment of attribution. And, then, once moved in, they began to complain about details, to express shock that all the facilities weren't instantly available on work sites that were still in progress, to find excessive rents that were cheaper than in the surrounding areas. ..."[13] Bloch-Lainé's bitterness suggests that he never became fully cognizant of the pitfalls of planning that relied solely on experts and discounted user feedback, nor of the inherent limits to social engineering efforts and modernizing projects. Nor did he acknowledge that these same residents may have found their disappointment exacerbated by the promise—repeated in the numerous films and exhibitions of the housing ministry, offered by tastemakers like the Salon des Arts Ménagers, and celebrated in the glowing reviews in the feminine press—that these modern homes would bring happiness.

Yet there is also some truth to be found in Bloch-Lainé's claim that the "Caisse did it." A fair assessment of the Fourth and Fifth Republics' efforts in this arena requires understanding the problems that planners were trying to fix. Their solutions may have been partial and their victories short-lived, but there is still a strong case for considering housing to be one of the great postwar achievements. The present work thus contributes to the ongoing reassessment of the Fourth Republic, which has long had "an unhappy reputation,"[14] to use Philip Nord's expression, of parliamentary impotence and the disappointment of Liberation dreams. The example of housing helps us to see that in spite of the many debits it accumulated, a number of initiatives merit inscription on the credit side of the Fourth Republic's ledger. Modernization of the housing stock should be mentioned in the same breath as the economic miracle of the Thirty Glorious Years and the *État-providence*.

True, the welfare state, even as it confronts challenges, has aged better than many of the gargantuan *grands ensembles*. Should we lay this failure at the feet of Fourth Republic planners? Twenty-first-century social problems at *grands ensembles* might possibly have been avoided by using American-style developments of cheap detached homes to ease the housing crisis, but lack of private initiative, a population that preferred renting to buying, a lack of skilled manpower and materials, and the desire to reconstruct France by recourse to urban planning made a free-market Levittown appear quite out of the realm of possibility in the late 1940s and early 1950s. In subsequent years, the French looked at American suburbanization and were not tempted by the specters of white flight, ghettoization, and urban decay then making headlines. On the other hand, the *grands ensembles* could have been more sustainable and desirable places to live if more resources had been committed to soundproofing, to community organization and activities, and to collective amenities. In the pronatalist context of the postwar period, planners and housing professionals were so fixated on the dyad of home and family that they failed to think early or deeply enough the relationship of the individual and the family to the larger community. Architects and officials assumed that the collective form of the *grand ensemble*—loudly and fervently proclaimed to be a more humanist alternative to American-style anomic Levittowns—would organically foster and fulfill the community "function."

It wasn't until the urban sociologists of chapters 5 and 6 began articulating a critique of suburban exclusion and marginalization that serious efforts to ensure a connection of the individual to his or her community began to penetrate state policymaking, but by 1976, the oil crisis and corresponding economic crisis had truncated the state's involvement in housing design and construction. The Seventh Plan (1976) announced that priority would be given to "qualitative amelioration of habitat," and in 1977, the government voted a law ending direct state sponsorship of construction and overhauling financing in order to subsidize private investment in housing. The change was characterized as a shift from *aide à la pierre* ("stone" aid) to *aide à la personne* (individual aid). It is difficult to know how Fifth Republic ministers might have followed up on late 1960s housing initiatives had they been given budget credits, but certainly the efforts by Pierre Sudreau to increase resident participation and Robert Lion's attempts to support innovative design point to a certain awareness of problems and a willingness to engage with them. In this light, historian Brian Newsome locates the roots of Mitterrand's decentralized democracy in the Gaullist housing ministry;[15] this is debatable, but it is true that adding the qualitative experience of modern homes to the narrative of the postwar modernizing project demands that we recalibrate our judgments of both the Fourth and Fifth Republics.

Historicizing Modernism

A third implication of this examination of the modern French home is to qualify architectural historians' assertion of French Modernism's radical and collectivist values. To take just one example, architectural theorist and historian Mark Jarzombek has argued, "Overseas [in Europe], modernism was only marginally linked with domesticity. The French journal, *Construction moderne,* for example, did not discuss a single-family residence during the 1950s and 1960s. Modernity was equated with communal needs and aspirations, not with the individualistic needs of the family."[16] Nothing could be further from the truth. It is certainly true that French Modernists persuasively advocated for collective forms of housing as superior, for example, to tract developments composed of detached individual homes. Nevertheless, as demonstrated in chapters 2 and 4, within the four walls of domestic space, Modernist architects privileged the needs of the individual, followed by those of the family; the needs of the community placed a distant third. When architects zoned the living room for individual activities, discouraged the sharing of children's bedrooms, campaigned for the installation of equipped kitchens within each apartment, or, especially, broadcast the ability of the modern home to lead to an inhabitant's personal *épanouissement,* they gave their Modernist doctrine a humanist aspect. Indeed, by linking personal happiness exclusively to the new, architects and other Modernist tastemakers gave credence to the rights of the individual in modern France.

Along with architects and other promulgators of the domestic ideal, housing officials developed and literally built into the nation the notion that each person had an unalienable right to a basic level of comfort and leisure, as well as to the happiness believed to derive from these. Again, this right remained (and remains) unsatisfied for some segments of the population. That such a transformation in *mentalités* took place, however, can be seen in the change of the ideology behind slum clearance. In the second half of the nineteenth century, philanthropists and reformers advocated for improving the housing conditions of poor families for hygienic reasons. The repeated outbreaks of cholera over the course of the nineteenth century spawned an upper-class fear of contamination from the dirty and slovenly "dangerous classes." Eighty years later, while political motivations often played a role in decisions to renovate slum areas, activists and reformers invoked a moral argument of individual human rights, not hygiene, in order to persuade public powers to take action. This study thus challenges the history of French Modernism as it has often been understood, as prioritizing the collective and the monumental over a humanist and quotidian individualism.

In the twenty-first century, Modernist high-rise apartment buildings can still be found worldwide, housing the very rich and the very poor—though, of course, rarely at the same time. As we have just observed, careful historicization is needed to understand the functions of and the meanings ascribed to Modern architecture in varying sites and times over the course of the last century. It is also needed in order to avoid fetishizing Modernism's original anti-bourgeois stance, its purist aesthetic, and its economical approach to dwelling, all of which are still celebrated by architects and tastemakers. Jayne Merkel, a contributing editor for *Architectural Design/ AD* and *Architectural Record*, wrote an opinion piece for the *New York Times* in 2010, arguing against the false promises of McMansions that offered only redundant space and often a threat of foreclosure. Invoking a taste for restraint learned during the Depression, Merkel celebrated the "common sense" of 1950s-era dwellers for whom small, efficient homes were "positively stylish" and proposed that, in an age of recession, Americans could stand to learn much from the architect-designed minimalist ethos of postwar modern homes.[17] Yet our history of the domestic architecture of the Trente Glorieuses suggests that the acceptance of the right to comfort and the privileging of domestic space as a site for self-actualization led to increased expectations for home life. These in turn led to a proliferation of new practices and purchases within and for the home. The "taste for restraint" that Merkel admired was a product of hardship and the lower expectations of comfort that accompanied sustained deprivation.

This book shows that the French accepted half of the modern home's bargain: rejecting its rationalizing tendencies, they embraced its comfort. If some refused an art of living that demanded they dine in the living room, by the end of the 1960s they had accepted the premise that they were entitled to equipped housing in much the same way that they deserved health insurance and retirement benefits. As Paulette, the first-generation resident of Billardon, near Dijon, observed when discussing the one-room home she'd left with her family for the new *grand ensemble*: "If we had to relive what we experienced then.... Young people, they wouldn't do it these days."[18] One generation's luxury is another's necessity, and while many twenty-first-century middle-class Europeans and Americans have been learning to make do with less, mass acceptance of rationalized *existenzminimum* homes—even Modernist-designed ones—is wishful thinking.

The need to historicize domestic space is becoming more apparent in the twenty-first century, since ways of dwelling common to industrialized Western nations are again changing. Technologies like iPads and Blackberries, laptops, and wireless communication allow people to work and shop from home; Skype permits electronic socializing; adolescents within the home can remain in near constant contact with peers via Twitter or Facebook; children exercise indoors thanks to products like Wii and do their homework online. Family members now even interact with one another within the home via these technologies, with some parents waking their children for school by text message. This book has sought to explain how in one place, in one era, relationships of class, gender, and family formed and were formed by domestic space; how the home promoted a change in popular expectations of comfort and satisfaction; how work and leisure within the home were reimagined; and how modernizing projects and technocratic policymaking both took shape and met with various constraints. The lessons of the French postwar home may thus provide insights, inspirations, and caveats to the next generations of architects, policymakers, and urban planners.

Notes

1. André Maurois, "Maison et bonheur," *Maison et jardin* 2, 8 (April–May 1952), 45.
2. Paulette Bernège, *Le Blanchissage domestique* (Paris: Éditions du Salon des Arts Ménagers, 1950), 70–71.

3. French homes generally have a separate, usually quite tiny, room dedicated exclusively to the toilet—a true "water closet."
4. Olivier Marchand and Claude Thélot, *Le Travail en France (1800-2000)* (Paris: Nathan, 1997), 58. See also Duchen, *Women's Lives and Women's Rights*, esp. 146–49.
5. Arnaud Régnier-Loilier and Céline Hiron note that, despite recent redefinitions of a gendered division of household labor, laundry still falls 90 percent of the time to French women, as does ironing and cleaning the bathrooms; overall, twenty-first-century French women have responsibility for 80 percent of what Régnier-Loilier and Hiron call the "hard core" of housework. See their "Évolution de la repartition des tâches domestiques après l'arrivée d'un enfant," *Politiques sociales et familiales* 99 (March 2010): 5–25. A comparative study shows this is true in 33 nations, ranging from wealthy and poorer nations. See Jan Paul Heisig, "Who Does More Housework: Rich or Poor? A Comparison of 33 Countries," *American Sociological Review* 76, 1 (2011): 74–99.
6. Étienne Hirsch cited in Kuisel, *Capitalism and the State in Modern France*, 226.
7. Scott Sayare, "Razing a Neighborhood and a Social Engineering Idea," *New York Times*, 7 September 2011, A8.
8. Henri Mendras and Alistair Cole, *Social Change in Modern France: Towards a Cultural Anthropology of the Fifth Republic* (Cambridge and New York: Cambridge University Press, and Paris: Éditions de la Maison des sciences de l'homme, 1991), 1.
9. See Henri Mendras, *La Seconde Revolution Française 1965-1984* (Paris: Gallimard, 1988).
10. See, respectively, Francine Muel-Dreyfus, *Vichy et l'éternel féminin* (Paris: Seuil, 1996) and Susan Weiner, *Enfants Terribles: Youth and Femininity in the Mass Media in France, 1945-1968* (Baltimore, MD: The Johns Hopkins University Press, 2001).
11. See Pulju, *Women and Mass Consumer Society*, esp. chap. 3.
12. Following Ruth Schwartz Cowan (*More Work for Mother: The Ironies of Household Technology from the Open Hearth to the Microwave*) and Adrian Forty (*Objects of Desire: Design and Society Since 1750*) among others, Kristin Ross has articulated this line of thought for the case of postwar France: "Labor-saving appliances save no labor, if only because their introduction into the household is accompanied by a rise in the standards and norms of cleanliness" (*Fast Cars, Clean Bodies*, 104).
13. Bloch-Lainé, *Profession fonctionnaire*, 136.
14. Nord, *France's New Deal*, 1.
15. Newsome, *French Urban Planning*, 185.
16. Mark Jarzombek, "Good-Life Modernism and Beyond: The American House in the 1950s and 1960s: A Commentary," *Cornell Journal of Architecture* 4 (1990): 81. See also René Fraisse's comparison of individualist liberalism and functionalist collectivism in France, discussed in Phillips, *Modern France*, 157–59.
17. Jayne Merkel, "When Less Was More," *New York Times*, 1 July 2010, http://opinionator.blogs.nytimes.com/2010/07/01/when-less-was-more/.
18. Taboury and Gougerot, *Billardon*, 135.

Selected Bibliography

This selected bibliography lists the sources that would be most useful to a scholar researching the history of postwar domestic space. Specific bibliographic information about mass and trade press articles and archival sources can be found in each chapter's endnotes.

Primary Sources

Archives Nationales, Centre des Archives Contemporaines
19770660/7
19770775/4
19771096/1
19771142/19
19771153/3
19771153/5
19771153/6
19780319/001
19790660/11
19790660/2
19850023/4
19850023/19
19850023/118
19850023/120
19850023/121

Newspapers and Periodicals
L'Architecture d'aujourd'hui
L'Architecture française
Arts ménagers
Cahiers du CSTB
Cahiers du Ministère de la Reconstruction et du Logement

Combat
Le Décor d'aujourd'hui
Elle
L'Esprit
L'Express
Le Figaro
France Observateur / Le Nouvel Observateur
France-Soir
Informations sociales
Journal Officiel
Libération
Maison et jardin
La Maison française
La Maison Marie-Claire
Marie-Claire
Le Monde
L'Officiel hebdomadaire de l'équipement ménager
New York Times
Paris-Match
Revue de l'ameublement et des industries du bois
Science et vie
Techniques et Architecture

Audiovisual Material

"Les Grands Ensembles de Créteil." *Journal de Paris*, RTF. Paris: Radiodiffusion Télévision Française, 11 April 1964.

Marker, Chris. *Le joli mai*. Film. Paris: Sofracima, 1963.

Published Material

Aubert, Jeanne. *JOC, qu'as-tu fait de nos vies?* Paris: Éd. Ouvrières, 1990.

L'avenir des métiers de l'ameublement et de la décoration. L'ameublement et la décoration dans la vie moderne. Paris: IPF, 1967.

Balladur, Jean, Bernard Zehrfuss, and Bruno Vayssière. *Jean Balladur, Bernard Zehrfuss: le 7 février 1991.* Paris: Éditions du Pavillon de l'Arsenal, 1998.

Bernège, Paulette. *De la méthode ménagère,* edited by M.-L. Lemonnier. Paris: Jacques Lanore, 1969 [1st ed., 1928].

———. *Si les femmes faisaient les maisons.* Paris: Mon chez moi, 1928.

———. *Le Blanchissage domestique.* Paris: Éditions du Salon des Arts Ménagers, 1950.

Bertheim, C. Sidney. "Housing in France." *Land Economics* 24, 1 (Feb. 1948): 49–62.

Besset, Maurice. *Nouvelle architecture française / New French Architecture*. New York: F. A. Praeger, 1967.

Blachère, Gérard. *Savoir Bâtir: Habitabilité, durabilité, économie des bâtiments*. Paris: Éditions Eyrolles, 1971 [1st ed., 1966].

Bloch-Lainé, François. *Profession: Fonctionnaire. Entretiens avec Françoise Carrière*. Paris: Seuil, 1976.

Bloch-Lainé, François, and Jean Bouvier. *La France restaurée 1944-1954. Dialogues sur les choix d'une modernisation*. Paris: Fayard, 1986.

Boudon, Philippe. *Pessac de Le Corbusier*. Paris: Dunod, 1969.

Boulanger, Gisèle. *L'Art de s'installer*. Paris: Hachette, 1958.

Breton, Paul, ed. *La Civilisation quotidienne*. Vol. 14 of *L'Encyclopédie française*, edited by Gaston Berger. Paris: Société de gestion de l'Encyclopédie française, 1955.

Breton, Paul, and André Breton, eds. *L'art ménager français*. Paris: Flammarion, 1952.

Chancrin, R.-E.-Jeanne. *Nouvelle Larousse ménager 1955*. Paris: Librairie Larousse, 1955.

Chombart de Lauwe, Paul-Henry. *Paris et l'agglomération parisienne*. Paris: PUF, 1952.

———. *La vie quotidienne des familles ouvrières*. Paris: CNRS, 1956.

———. "Le logement et le comportement des ménages dans trois cités nouvelles de l'agglomération parisienne." *Cahiers du Centre Scientifique et Technique du Bâtiment* 30, cahier 257 (October 1957): 13–52.

———. "Ménages et catégories sociales dans les habitations nouvelles." *Informations sociales* 5 (May 1958): 2–12.

———. "Logement et comportement des ménages dans trois cités nouvelles de l'agglomération bordelaise." *Cahiers du Centre Scientifique et Technique du Bâtiment* 34, cahier 282 (November 1958): 9–27.

———. *Famille et habitation*. 2 vols. Paris: CNRS, 1959/1960.

———. *Un anthropologue dans le siècle: entretiens avec Thierry Pacquot*. Paris: Descartes & Cie., 1996.

Clerc, Paul. *Grands ensembles, banlieues nouvelles: enquête démographique et psycho-sociologique*. Centre de recherche d'urbanisme. Institut national d'études démographiques. Travaux et documents 49. Paris: PUF, 1967.

COFREMCA. *Histoires de cellules: étude d'anthropologie sociale sur le vécu de certains logements Région parisienne*. Paris: Service Régional de l'Équipement de la Région Parisienne, 1975.

Coing, Henri. *Rénovation urbaine et changement social. L'îlot no. 4 (Paris-13e)*. Paris: Éditions ouvrières, 1966.

Commissariat général du plan. *Le logement*. Paris: A. Colin, 1970.

Dautant, Johann. "Entretiens avec Roland Prédiéri," 9 March 2009, for the Comité de Sauvegarde de Maurepas-Village, http://www.maurepas-histoire.net/download/Entretien percent20Predieri.pdf.

Evry 1, Concours conception-réalisation. Paris: IAURP, 1971.

Fourastié, Jean, and Françoise Fourastié. *Les Arts ménagers*. Paris: PUF, 1950.

Gascoin, Marcel. "Le mobilier." In *L'Art Ménager français*, edited by Paul and André Breton, 45–180. Paris: Flammarion, 1952.

Habitations collectives à loyer modéré à usage locatif: Normalisation des caractéristiques. Paris: Journal Officiel de la République Française, December 1955.

Haumont, Nicole. *Les pavillonnaires: Étude psycho-sociologique d'un mode d'habitat.* Paris: Presse du Centre de recherche d'urbanisme, 1966.

———. "Habitat et modèles culturels." *Revue française de sociologie* 9 (1968): 180–90.

Hermant, André. "Les conditions générales d'un logement." Part 3 of chap. 2 of *La Civilisation quotidienne,* edited by Paul Breton. Vol. 14 of *L'Encylopédie française,* edited by Gaston Berger. Paris: Société de gestion de l'Encyclopédie française, 1955.

Institut National d'Études Démographiques. *Désirs des Français en matière d'habitation urbaine.* Paris: PUF, 1947.

Institut National de la Statistique et des Études Économiques. "Équipement ménager 1957," *Bulletin hebdomadaire de statistique* 557 (17 January 1957): n.p.

———. "Une enquête par sondage sur le logement (octobre 1955)." *Études Statistiques* (April–June 1957): 35–48.

———. *Données sociales: Édition 1973.* Paris: INSEE, 1973.

Journal Officiel. *Habitations collectives à loyer modéré à usage locatif: Normalisation des caractéristiques.* Paris: Impr. des Journaux officiels, 1955.

Le Corbusier. *Vers une architecture.* Paris: G. Crès, n.d. [ca. 1925].

———. *Almanach d'architecture moderne.* Paris: G. Crès, n.d. [ca. 1926].

———. *La Charte d'Athènes.* Paris: Éditions de Minuit, 1957.

———. *Le Corbusier: My Work.* Translated by James Palmes. London: Architectural Press, 1960.

Lefebvre, Henri. "Les nouveaux ensembles urbains. Un cas concret: Lacq-Mourenx et les problèmes urbains de la nouvelle classe ouvrière." *Revue française de sociologie* 1, 1 (1960): 186–201.

Lods, Marcel. *Le Métier d'architecte. Entretiens avec Hervé Le Boterf.* Paris: Éditions France-Empire, 1976.

Le Marché du réfrigérateur ménager. Paris: Comité d'action pour le développement de l'intéressement du personnel à la productivité des entreprises, 1955.

Mendès-France, Pierre. *Gouverner, c'est choisir.* Paris: Julliard, 1953.

Ministère de la reconstruction et de l'urbanisme [Yves Salaün]. *Se loger.* Paris: MRU, 1949.

———. Centre d'études de la Direction générale de l'urbanisme et de l'habitation. *Logements économiques et familiaux. Plans types: logements collectifs.* Paris: MRU, 1953.

———. *Logements économiques et familiaux. Plans types: logements individuels.* Paris: MRU, 1953.

Mongé, René. *Rendez-vous chez Chrysale.* Paris: UNCAF, 1956.

L'Office public d'habitations de la Ville de Paris. *L'Office public d'habitations de la Ville de Paris.* Paris: L'Office public d'habitations de la Ville de Paris, 1937.

Parker, Daniel. *La Famille en face du problème du logement.* Paris: Éditions Sociales Françaises, 1945.

Perriand, Charlotte. *Une vie de création.* Paris: Odile Jacob, 1998.

Petit Guide du Logement. Paris: Éditions sociales françaises, 1950.

Petit Guide du Logement. Paris: Éditions sociales françaises, 1957.

Renous, Pascal. *Portraits de décorateurs.* Paris: Éd. H. Vial, 1969.

Rochefort, Christiane. *Les Petits Enfants du siècle.* Paris: Éditions Bernard Grasset, 1961.

Roux-Spitz, Michel. *Réalisations.* Vol. 3. Paris: Éd. Vincent, Fréal & Cie, 1959.

Secrétariat permanent du Plan-construction. *Plan Construction: Trois ans d'activité, mai 1971-décembre 1974.* Paris: Ministère de l'Équipement, 1974.

Sonrel, Pierre. "L'habitation." In *L'Art Ménager français,* edited by Paul and André Breton, 15–42. Paris: Flammarion, 1952.

———. "Les nouvelles habitudes domestiques." Part 1 of chap. 2 in *La Civilisation quotidienne,* edited by Paul Breton. Vol. 14 of *L'Encylopédie française,* edited by Gaston Berger. Paris: Société de gestion de l'Encyclopédie française, 1955.

Sudreau, Pierre. *Au-délà de toutes les frontières.* Paris: Odile Jacob, 1991.

Touraine, Alain. *The Post-Industrial Society: Tomorrow's Social History—Classes, Conflicts and Culture in the Programmed Society.* Translated by Leonard F.X. Mayhew. London: Wildwood House, 1974.

U.S. Bureau of the Census. *Census of Housing: 1950,* Vol. I, *General Characteristics,* Part 1, "United States Summary." Prepared by the Population and Housing Division, Bureau of the Census, Washington, DC, 1953.

Venturi, Robert. *Complexity and Contradiction in Architecture.* New York: Museum of Modern Art, 1966.

Venturi, Robert, and Denise Scott Brown. "A Significance for A&P Parking Lots, or, Learning from Las Vegas." *Architectural Forum* (March 1968): 37–43.

Watson, Cicely. "Housing Policy and Population Problems in France." *Population Studies* 7, 1 (July 1953): 14–45.

Secondary Sources

Abbott, Andrew. *The System of Professions.* Chicago and London: University of Chicago Press, 1988.

Abram, Joseph. *L'architecture moderne en France.* Vol 2. *Du chaos à la croissance: 1940-1966.* Paris: Picard, 1999.

Anderson, Alex T. *The Problem of the House: French Domestic Life and the Rise of Modern Architecture.* Seattle, WA, and London: University of Washington Press, 2006.

Attar, Michèle, Vincent Lourier, and Jean-Michel Vercollier. *La Place de la forme coöpérative dans le secteur de l'habitat en France.* Paris: Éditions du PUCA, 1998.

Avril, Michel. *Raoul Dautry, 1880-1951: la passion de servir.* Paris: Éd. France-Empire, 1993.

Barjot, Dominique, Rémi Baudouï, and Danièle Voldman, eds. *Les Reconstructions en Europe, 1945-1949.* Paris: Éditions Complex, 1997.

Barre-Despond, Arlette. *L'UAM, Unions des Artistes Modernes.* Paris: Éditions du Regard, 1986.

Bastide, Henri, and Alain Girard. "Attitudes et opinions des Français à l'égard de la fécondité et de la famille." *Population* 4–5 (July–October 1975): 693–749.

Baudelot, Christian, and Anne Lebeaupin. "Les salaires de 1950 à 1975." *Économie et statistique* 113 (July–August 1979): 15–22.

Baudouï, Rémi. *Raoul Dautry (1880-1951), le technocrate de la République.* Paris: Éditions Balland, 1992.

———. "De Gaulle et la reconstruction." *Espoir* 103 (July 1995): 66–70.

Benevolo, Leonardo. *The History of Modern Architecture*. 2 vols. Cambridge, MA: MIT Press, 1971.

Bergren, Ann. "Female Fetish Urban Form." In *The Sex of Architecture*, edited by Diana Agrest, Patricia Conway, Leslie Kanes Weisman, 77–96. New York: Henry N. Abrams, Inc., 1996.

Bervoets, Liesbeth. "Defeating Public Enemy Number One: Mediating Housing in the Netherlands." *Home Cultures* 7, 2 (July 2010): 179–95.

Les bons génies de la vie domestique. Catalogue of the exhibition of the same name shown at the Centre Pompidou, 11 October 2000–22 January 2001. Paris: Éditions du Centre Pompidou, 2000.

Boucher, Frédérique. "Abriter vaille que vaille, se loger coûte que coûte." In "Images, discours et enjeux de la reconstruction des villes françaises après 1945," edited by Danièle Voldman, a special issue of *Cahiers de l'Institut d'histoire du temps présent* 5 (June 1987): 119–41.

Bourdieu, Pierre. *Distinction: A Social Critique of the Judgement of Taste*. Cambridge, MA: Harvard University Press, 1984.

Butler, Rémy and Patrice Noisette. *Le logement social en France, 1815-1981. De la cité ouvrière au grand ensemble*. Paris: La Découverte / Maspero, 1982.

Castells, Manuel. *The City and the Grassroots: A Cross-Cultural Theory of Urban Social Movements*. Berkeley, CA: University of California Press, 1997.

Castillo, Greg. *Cold War on the Home Front: The Soft Power of Midcentury Modern Design*. Minneapolis, MN: University of Minnesota Press, 2010.

Champy, Florent. *Les Architectes et la commande publique*. Paris: PUF, 1998.

Chapman, Herrick. "France's Liberation Era, 1944-47: A Social and Economic Settlement?" In *The Uncertain Foundation: France at the Liberation, 1944-47*, edited by Andrew Knapp, 103–20. New York: Palgrave MacMillan, 2007.

Clanché, François, and Anne-Marie Fribourg. "Grandes évolutions du parc et des ménages depuis 1950." In *Logement et habitat: l'état de savoirs*, edited by Marion Ségaud, Catherine Bonvalet, and Jacques Brun, 77–85. Paris: La Découverte, 1998.

Clarke, Jackie. "L'organisation ménagère comme pédagogie: Paulette Bernège et la formation d'une nouvelle classe moyenne dans les années 1930 et 1940." *Travail, genre et sociétés* 13 (April 2005): 139–57.

Clayssen, Dominique. *Jean Prouvé: l'idée constructive*. Paris: Dunod, 1983.

Cohen, Jean-Louis. *André Lurçat, 1894-1970: autocritique d'un moderne*. Liège: Mardaga, 1995.

———. *Scenes of the World to Come: European Architecture and the American Challenge, 1893-1960*. Montreal: Canadian Centre for Architecture, 1995.

Coley, Catherine. *Jean Prouvé*. Paris: Centre Georges Pompidou, 1993.

CREPAH-GERASE. *Conditions et évolution de la production architecturale dans l'habitat social*. Paris: Secrétariat de la recherche architecturale, 1982.

Croizé, Jean-Claude. "Normes et maîtrise du coût de la construction (1945-1980)." Vol. 4 of "Politique et configuration du logement en France (1900-1980)." Ph.D. diss., University of Paris X-Nanterre, 2006.

Cupers, Kenny. "In Search of the User: The Experiment of Modern Urbanism in Postwar France, 1955-1975." Ph.D. diss., Harvard University, 2010.

———. "The Expertise of Participation: Mass Housing and Urban Planning in Post-war France." *Planning Perspectives* 26, 1 (January 2011): 29–53.

Curtis, William J.R. *Le Corbusier: Ideas and Forms*. London: Phaidon Press, 1994.

———. *Modern Architecture Since 1900*. 3rd ed. London: Phaidon Press, 1996.

Duchen, Claire. *Women's Rights and Women's Lives in France 1944-1968*. London and New York: Routledge, 1994.

Dufaux, Frédéric, and Annie Fourcaut, eds. *Le Monde des grands ensembles*. Paris: Créaphis, 2004.

Dumont, Marie-Jeanne. *Le logement social à Paris, 1850-1930: les habitations à bon marché*. Liège: Mardaga, 1991.

Dunleavy, Patrick. *The Politics of Mass Housing in Britain, 1945-1975*. Oxford: Clarendon Press, 1981.

Dreyfus, Jacques. *La Société du confort*. Paris: L'Harmattan, 1990.

Éleb, Monique, and Anne Debarre. *L'Invention de l'habitation moderne. Paris 1880-1914. Architectures de la vie privée*. Paris: A.A.M./Hazan, 1995.

Éleb-Vidal, Monique, and Anne Debarre-Blanchard. *Architectures de la vie privée: maisons et mentalités, XVIIe-XIXe siècles*. Bruxelles: Archives de l'Architecture Moderne, 1989.

Evenson, Norma. *Paris: A Century of Change*. New Haven, CT: Yale University Press, 1974.

Flamand, Jean-Paul. *Loger le peuple. Essai sur l'histoire du logement social*. Paris: La Découverte, 1989.

Fourastié, Jean. *Les Trente Glorieuses, ou la révolution invisible de 1946 à 1975*. Paris: Fayard, 1979.

Fourcaut, Annie. "Banlieue rouge, au-delà du mythe politique." In *Banlieue rouge 1920-1960. Années Thorez, années Gabin: archétype du populaire, banc d'essai des modernités*, edited by Annie Fourcaut, 12–37. Paris: Éditions Autrement, 1992.

———. "Les premiers grands ensembles en région parisienne: ne pas refaire la banlieue?" *French Historical Studies* 27, 1 (January 2004): 195–218.

Fourcaut, Annie, Frédéric Dufaux, and Rémi Skoutelsky. *Faire l'histoire des grands ensembles. Bibliographie 1950-1980*. Lyon: ENS Éditions, 2003.

Frampton, Kenneth. *Modern Architecture: A Critical History*. London: Thames and Hudson, 1980.

Fribourg, Anne-Marie. "Évolution des politiques du logement depuis 1950." In *Logement et habitat. L'état des savoirs*, edited by Marion Segaud, Catherine Bonvalet, and Jacques Brun, 223–30. Paris: La Découverte, 1998.

Frost, Robert L. "Machine Liberation: Inventing Housewives and Home Appliances in Interwar France." *French Historical Studies* 18, 1 (Spring 1993): 109–30.

Furlough, Ellen. "Selling the American Way in Interwar France: *Prix Uniques* and the Salons des Arts Ménagers." *Journal of Social History* 26, 3 (Spring 1993): 491–520.

Giedion, Sigfried. *Space, Time and Architecture: The Growth of a New Tradition*. 5th ed., revised. Cambridge, MA: Harvard University Press, 2009.

de la Godelinais, Marie-Claude, and Gérard Lang. *L'Équipement des ménages en biens durables au début de 1976*. #213 of the Collections de l'INSEE, série M, #55, November 1976. Paris: INSEE, 1976.

Gournay, Isabelle. "Levitt France et la banlieue à l'américaine: premier bilan." *Histoire urbaine* 5 (2002): 167–88.

Grele, Ronald J. "Oral History as Evidence." In *Handbook of Oral History*, edited by Thomas L. Charlton, Lois E. Myers, and Rebecca Sharpless, 43–104. Lanham, MD: AltaMira Press, 2006.

Grelon, André. "In Mémoriam. Paul-Henry Chombart de Lauwe, 1913-1998." *L'année sociologique* 49/1999 (1): 7–18.

Guerrand, Roger-Henri. *Propriétaires et locataires: les origines du logement social en France, 1850-1914*. Paris: Quinette, 1987.

———. "Private Spaces," in *A History of Private Life*. Vol. 4. *From the Fires of Revolution to the Great War*, edited by Michelle Perrot, 359–449. Translated by Arthur Goldhammer. Cambridge, MA, and London: Harvard University Press, 1990.

Guerrand, Roger-Henri, and Roger Quilliot. *Une Europe en Construction. Deux siècles d'habitat social en Europe*. Paris: La Découverte, 1992.

Hård, Mikael. "*The Good Apartment:* The Social (Democratic) Construction of Swedish Homes." *Home Cultures* 7, 2 (July 2010): 117–33.

Harloe, Michael. *The People's Home? Social Rented Housing in Europe and America*. Oxford and Cambridge, MA: Blackwell, 1995.

Harris, Steven E. "Moving to the Separate Apartment: Building, Distributing, Furnishing, and Living in Urban Housing in Soviet Russia, 1950s-1960s." Ph.D. diss., University of Chicago, 2003.

Hecht, Gabrielle. *The Radiance of France: Nuclear Power and National Identity After World War II*. Cambridge, MA: MIT Press, 1998.

Heisig, Jan Paul. "Who Does More Housework: Rich or Poor? A Comparison of 33 Countries." *American Sociological Review* 76, 1 (2011): 74–99.

Henderson, Susan R. "A Revolution in the Woman's Sphere: Grete Lihotzky and the Frankfurt Kitchen." In *Architecture and Feminism*, edited by Debra Coleman, Elizabeth Danze, and Carol Henderson, 221–48. Princeton, NJ: Princeton Architectural Press, 1996.

Hoffman, Alice M., and Howard S. Hoffman. "Reliability and Validity in Oral History: The Case for Memory." In *Memory and History: Essays on Recalling and Interpreting Experience*, edited by Jaclyn Jeffrey and Glenace Edwall, 107–35. Lanham, MD: University Press of America, 1994.

Jackson, Julian. *De Gaulle*. London: Haus, 2003.

Jarzombek, Mark. "Good-Life Modernism and Beyond: The American House in the 1950s and 1960s: A Commentary." *Cornell Journal of Architecture* 4 (1990): 76–93.

Jencks, Charles. *Modern Movements in Architecture*. 2nd ed. New York: Penguin Books, 1985.

Jobs, Richard Ivan. *Riding the New Wave: Youth and the Rejuvenation of France After the Second World War*. Stanford, CA: Stanford University Press, 2007.

Joly, Pierre, and Robert Joly. *L'architecte André Lurçat*. Paris: Picard, 1995.

Judt, Tony. *Postwar: A History of Europe Since 1945*. New York: Penguin Press, 2005.

Kedward, Rod. *France and the French: A Modern History*. Woodstock, NY, and New York: The Overlook Press, 2007 [1st ed., 2005].

Khan, Hasan-Uddin. *International Style: Modernist Architecture from 1925 to 1965*. Köln: Benedikt Taschen Verlag, 1998.

Kopp, Anatole. *Quand le moderne n'était pas un style, mais une cause.* Paris: ENSBA, 1988.

Kopp, Anatole, Frédérique Boucher, and Danièle Pauly. *L'Architecture de la reconstruction en France, 1945-1953.* Paris: Éditions du Moniteur, 1982.

Kuisel, Richard. *Capitalism and the State in Modern France.* Cambridge: Cambridge University Press, 1981.

Kynaston, David. *Austerity Britain.* London: Bloomsbury, 2008 [1st ed., 2007].

Landauer, Paul. "La SCIC, premier promoteur français des grands ensembles (1953-1958)." *Histoire urbaine* 23 (December 2008): 71–80.

Langhamer, Claire. "The Meanings of Home in Postwar Britain." *Journal of Contemporary History* 40, 2 (April 2005): 341–62.

Léger, Jean-Michel. *Derniers domiciles connus: Enquête sur les nouveaux logements 1970-1990.* Paris: Créaphis, 1990.

Le Goff, Olivier. *L'Invention du confort: naissance d'une forme sociale.* Lyon: Presses universitaires de Lyon, 1994.

Lengereau, Éric. *L'État et l'architecture 1958-1981. Une politique publique?* Paris: Picard, 2001.

Lenoir, Rémi. "Family Policy in France Since 1938." In *The French Welfare State: Surviving Social and Ideological Change,* edited by John S. Ambler, 144–86. New York: NYU Press, 1991.

Leymonerie, Claire. "Le Salon des arts ménagers dans les années 1950: Théâtre d'une conversion à la consommation de masse." *Vingtième Siècle* 91, 3 (2006): 43–56.

Loehlin, Jennifer A. *From Rugs to Riches: Housework, Consumption and Modernity in Germany.* Oxford and New York: Berg, 1999.

Lucan, Jacques. *France, Architecture 1965-1988.* Paris: Electa-Moniteur, 1989.

Lyons, Amelia. "Invisible Immigrants: Algerian Families and the French Welfare State, 1947-1974." Ph.D. diss., University of California, Irvine, 2004.

Magri, Susanna. *Logement et reproduction de l'exploitation. Les politiques étatiques du logement en France (1947-1972).* Paris: Centre de sociologie urbaine, 1977.

———. "Le pavillon stigmatisé: Grands ensembles et maisons individuelles dans la sociologie des années 1950 à 1970." *L'Année sociologique* 58, 1 (2008): 171–202.

Marchand, Olivier, and Claude Thélot. *Le Travail en France (1800-2000).* Paris: Nathan, 1997.

May, Elaine Tyler. *Homeward Bound: American Families in the Cold War Era.* New York: Basic Books, 1999.

McLeod, Mary. *Charlotte Perriand: An Art of Living.* New York: Harry N. Abrams, 2003.

Mendras, Henri. *La Seconde Revolution Française 1965-1984.* Paris: Gallimard, 1988.

Mendras, Henri, and Alistair Cole. *Social Change in Modern France: Towards a Cultural Anthropology of the Fifth Republic.* Cambridge and New York: Cambridge University Press and Paris: Éditions de la Maison des sciences de l'homme, 1991.

Mengin, Christine. "La solution des grands ensembles." *Vingtième siècle* 64 (October–December 1999), 105–11.

Michel, Geneviève, and Pierre-Jacques Derainne. *Aux Courtillières: Histoires singulières et exemplaires.* Paris: Créaphis, 2005.

Mission Mémoires et identités en Val de France. *Les Carreaux 1955-1963: Naissance d'un grand ensemble en banlieue parisienne.* Villiers-le-Bel: Communauté d'agglomération Val de France, Mission Mémoires et identités en Val de France, 2006.

———. *Textes et images du Grand ensemble de Sarcelles, 1954-1976*. Villiers-le-Bel: Communauté d'agglomération Val de France, Mission Mémoires et identités en Val de France, 2007.

Mitterrand, Frédéric. "Mettre en valeur l'architecture du XXe siècle." In *1945-1975, une histoire de l'habitat: 40 ensembles de logements, patrimoine du XXe siècle*, edited by Île-de-France. Direction régionale des affaires culturelles. Paris: "Beaux-arts" editions/TTM editions, 2010.

Moissinac, Christine, and Yves Roussel. *Jules-Louis Breton, 1872-1940: un savant parlementaire*. Rennes: Presses universitaires de Rennes, 2010.

Moley, Christian. "La genèse du jour/nuit: scission de l'espace du logement en deux parties." *In Extenso*, 9 (1986): 259–81.

Monnier, Gérard. *L'architecture moderne en France*. Vol. 3. *De la croissance à la compétition, 1967-1999*. Paris: Picard, 2000.

Muel-Dreyfus, Francine. *Vichy et l'éternel féminin*. Paris: Seuil, 1996.

Mulvey, Michael Joseph. "Sheltering French Families: Parisian Suburbia and the Politics of Housing, 1939-1975." Ph.D. diss., University of North Carolina at Chapel Hill, 2011.

Newsome, W. Brian. "The Struggle for a Voice in the City: The Development of Participatory Architectural and Urban Planning in France, 1940-1968." Ph.D. diss., University of South Carolina, 2002.

———. "The 'Apartment Referendum' of 1959: Toward Participatory Architecture and Urban Planning in Postwar France." *French Historical Studies* 28, 2 (2005): 329–58.

———. *French Urban Planning 1940-1968*. New York: Peter Lang, 2009.

———. "French Catholics, Women and the Home: The Founding Generation of the Jeunesse ouvrière chrétienne feminine." *Historical Reflections* 37, 1 (Spring 2011): 18–44.

Nord, Philip. *France's New Deal: From the Thirties to the Postwar Era*. Princeton, NJ: Princeton University Press, 2010.

Pacquot, Thierry. "François Bloch-Lainé." *Urbanisme* 284 (September–October 1995): 5–10.

Parr, Joy. *Domestic Goods: The Material, the Moral, and the Economic in the Postwar Years*. Toronto: University of Toronto Press, 1999.

Phillips, Peggy A. *Modern France: Theories and Realities of Urban Planning*. Lanham, MD, and London: University Press of America, 1987.

Portelli, Alessandro. "The Peculiarities of Oral History." *History Workshop Journal* 12, 1 (1981): 96–107.

Pouvreau, Benoît. *Un politique en architecture: Eugène Claudius-Petit (1907-1989)*. Paris: Le Moniteur, 2004.

Power, Anne. *Hovels to High Rise: State Housing in Europe Since 1850*. New York: Routledge, 1993.

Prost, Antoine. "L'évolution de la politique familiale de 1938 à 1981." *Le Mouvement social* 129 (1984): 7–28.

Pulju, Rebecca J. *Women and Mass Consumer Society in Postwar France*. Cambridge: Cambridge University Press, 2011.

Raynaud, Michel, Didier Laroque, and Sylvie Rémy. *Michel Roux-Spitz, architecte 1888-1957*. Brussels and Liège: P. Mardaga, 1983.

Régnier-Loilier, Arnaud, and Céline Hiron. "Évolution de la repartition des tâches domestiques après l'arrivée d'un enfant." *Politiques sociales et familiales* 99 (March 2010): 5–25.

Reid, Susan E. "The Meaning of Home: 'The Only Bit of Life You Can Have to Yourself'." In *Borders of Socialism: Private Spheres of Soviet Russia*, edited by Lewis H. Siegelbaum, 145–70. New York and Basingstoke: Palgrave, 2006.

Rioux, Jean-Pierre. *The Fourth Republic 1944-1958*. Cambridge: Cambridge University Press, 1989.

Rimbaud, Christiane. *Pierre Sudreau: Un homme libre*. Paris: Le Cherche Midi, 2004.

Roberts, Mary Louise. *Civilization Without Sexes: Reconstructing Gender in Postwar France, 1917-1927*. Chicago: University of Chicago Press, 1994.

Roncayolo, Marcel, ed. *La Ville d'aujourd'hui*. Vol. 5 of *Histoire de la France urbaine*, edited by Georges Duby. Paris: Seuil, 1985.

Rosanvallon, Pierre. *The New Social Question: Rethinking the Welfare State*. Translated by Barbara Harshav. Princeton, NJ: Princeton University Press, 2000.

Ross, Kristin. *Fast Cars, Clean Bodies: Decolonization and the Reordering of French Culture*. Cambridge, MA: MIT Press, 1995.

Rouaud, Jacques. *60 ans d'arts ménagers*. 2 vols. Paris: Éditions Syros Alternatives, 1989/1993.

———. "L'esprit Arts ménagers." In *Les bons génies de la vie domestique*, exhibition catalogue, 51–58. Paris: Éditions du Centre Pompidou, 2000.

Rudolph, Nicole. "La cuisine, cellule de base de la modernisation française. L'architecture, la modernisation et le genre dans la France des Trente Glorieuses." Mémoire principal de Master 2, École Normale Supérieure / École des Hautes Études en Sciences sociales, 1999.

———. "Domestic Politics: The Cité Expérimentale at Noisy-le-Sec in Greater Paris." *Modern and Contemporary France* 12, 4 (November 2004): 483–95.

———. "'Who Should Be the Author of a Dwelling?': Architects versus Housewives in 1950s France." *Gender and History* 21, 3 (November 2009): 541–59.

———. "Model Homes: Negotiating Interiors in Postwar France." *Interiors: Design, Architecture, Culture* 5, 2 (2014): 239–56.

Sanyas, Hélène. "La politique architecturale et urbaine de la reconstruction. France: 1945-1955." Thèse de 3e cycle, Université de Paris VIII, 1982.

Schor, Ralph. *Histoire de l'immigration en France de la fin du XIXe siècle à nos jours*. Paris: Armand Colin/Masson, 1996.

Segalen, Martine. "The Salon des Arts Ménagers, 1923-1983: A French Effort to Instil the Virtues of Home and the Norms of Good Taste." *Journal of Design History* 7, 4 (1994): 267–75.

Ségaud, Marion, Catherine Bonvalet, and Jacques Brun, eds. *Logement et habitat: l'état de savoirs*. Paris: La Découverte, 1998.

Shennan, Andrew. *Rethinking France: Plans for Renewal, 1940-1946*. Oxford: Oxford University Press, 1989.

Sutcliffe, Anthony. *Paris, An Architectural History*. New Haven, CT, and London: Yale University Press, 1993.

Taboury, Sylvain, and Karine Gougerot. *Billardon, histoire d'un grand ensemble*. Paris: Créaphis, 2004.

Tafuri, Manfredo, and Francesco Dal Co. *Modern Architecture*. New York: Electa/Rizzoli, 1986.

Tellier, Thibault. *Le temps des HLM, 1945-1975: La saga urbaine des Trente Glorieuses*. Paris: Autrement, 2007.

Thébaud, Françoise, ed. *Histoire des femmes: Le XXe siècle*. Vol. 5 of *Histoire des femmes en Occident*, edited by Georges Duby and Michelle Perrot. Paris: Plon, 1992.

Thompson, Paul. *The Voice of the Past: Oral History*. Oxford: Oxford University Press, 2000 [1st ed., 1978].

Tilly, Louise, and Joan Scott. *Women, Work and Family*. New York: Holt, Rinehart and Winston, 1978.

Tipps, Dean. "Modernization and the Comparative Study of Societies." *Comparative Studies in Society and History* 15 (1973): 199–226.

Tise, Suzanne. "Between Art and Industry: Design Reform in France, 1851-1939." Ph.D. diss., University of Pittsburgh, 1991.

Topalov, Christian. *Le Logement en France: Histoire d'un marchandise impossible*. Paris: Presses de la Fondation Nationale des Sciences Politiques, 1987.

Urbanisme 322 (January–February 2002), special issue on the *grands ensembles*.

Vayssière, Bruno. *Reconstruction-déconstruction: le hard French ou l'architecture française des trente glorieuses*. Paris: Picard, 1988.

———."Des premiers objets de l'après-guerre aux années molles…." In *Les bons génies de la vie domestique*, exhibition catalogue, 132–36. Paris: Éditions du Centre Pompidou, 2000.

Vayssière, Bruno, Manuel Candré, and Danièle Voldman, eds. *Ministère de la Reconstruction et de l'Urbanisme, 1944-1954: une politique du logement*. Paris: IFA-PCA, 1994.

Viet, Vincent. "La politique du logement des immigrés (1945-1990)." *Vingtième siècle* 64 (October–December 1999): 91–103.

Voldman, Danièle. "À la recherche de modèles, les missions du MRU à l'étranger." In "Images, discours et enjeux de la reconstruction des villes françaises après 1945," edited by Danièle Voldman, a special issue of *Cahiers de l'Institut d'histoire du temps présent* 5 (June 1987): 103–18.

———. *La reconstruction des villes françaises de 1940 à 1954: Histoire d'une politique*. Paris: L'Harmattan, 1997.

Wakeman, Rosemary. *Modernizing the Provincial City: Toulouse 1945–1975*. Cambridge, MA: Harvard University Press, 1997.

———. "Reconstruction and the Self-Help Housing Movement: The French Experience." *Housing Studies* 14, 3 (1999): 355–66.

Weddle, Robert Brian. "Urbanism, Housing, and Technology in Inter-War France: The Case of the Cité de la Muette." Ph.D. diss., Cornell University, 1998.

Weiner, Susan. *Enfants Terribles: Youth and Femininity in the Mass Media in France, 1945-1968*. Baltimore, MD: The Johns Hopkins University Press, 2001.

Wright, Gwendolyn. *Moralism and the Model Home: Domestic Architecture and Cultural Conflict in Chicago 1873–1913*. Chicago and London: University of Chicago Press, 1980.

———. *The Politics of Design in French Colonial Urbanism*. Chicago: University of Chicago Press, 1991.

———."Prescribing the Model Home." In *Home: A Place in the World*, edited by Arien Mack, 213–25. New York: New York University Press, 1993.

Zipp, Samuel. *Manhattan Projects: The Rise and Fall of Urban Renewal in Cold War New York*. Oxford and New York: Oxford University Press, 2010.

Index

Abbé Pierre, 122–23, 130
Aillaud, Émile, 127, *133*, 172
Algeria and Algerian immigrants, 2, 27, 142, 173–74, 187, 198
aménagement du territoire, 36, 191, 218
amenities (heating, indoor plumbing, and utilities): central heating, 6, 8, 12, 19, 34, 38, 42, 46, 94, 102, 107, 124, *135*, 150, 165, 168, 214, 229; comfort, association with, 8, 34, 43, 51n45, 107, 166, 175; electricity and electrical outlets, 140, 155, 176; in *grands ensembles*, 175; hot water, 19, 45, 62, 63, 124, 125, 139, 146n26, 168, 174–75, 223, 226, 229; housing without, 6, 17–18, 120; individual acquisition of appliances, 138–42, 147–48n75; labor-saving devices offset by rising standards of cleanliness, 229, 234n12; LENs housing and, 124, 125, 146–47n26; MRU and, 22, 34; nationalization of utilities, 47; "new social contract," as part of, 12; in renewal paradigm, 42–43, 48, 214; at SAM, 92, 104, 107, 210; temperature requirements, 166. *See also* technological innovations
Andrault, Michel, 171, 192, 208, 209, 212
Appartement idéal (Ideal Apartment), 74, 74–75, 96–97, 107
Appartement référendum (Referendum Apartment), 150, 151–58, *154*, 159, 164, 166–67, 169, 176, 179, 189, 193, 213, 217
appliances. *See* amenities; technological innovations; *specific appliances*
architects, 8, 53–83; Appartement référendum rejected by, 155–58; art of living, concept of, 54, 76, 79–81, 161–62, 215; criticism of, 204, 211–12; in *Famille et habitation*, 161–62; Haumont on, 203–4; HBMs influencing, 54, 59–64, *60–63*, 75; housing crisis, *cellule d'habitation*, and restraints on, 129–33, 135–36; interest in domestic design issues, 6–7; May 1968, 204–5; middle-class concerns dominating designs of, 8, 54, 74, 75–79, 82; modernism influencing, 54, 59, 64–69, *68*, 82; needs-based architecture and development of 4P, 69–75, *73*, *74*; prefabrication, standardization, and mass production, 53, 55–56, 65, 214; Prix de Rome, 67, 204–5; profession of architecture in immediate postwar period, 54–59; responses to postwar housing, reactions to, 155–58, 161–62, 167–71, 180; social change, responding to, 213–16; state as client, repercussions of, 53, 58–59; on urban fabric, suburban life, and detached homes, 188, 200–201, 204–6; urban sociologists critiquing, 204, 211–13; of ZUPs, 190
armoires, 23, 78, 80, 98, 137, 138, 144, 154, 155, 169, 213
art of living, concept of, 4–5; architects and modernism on, 54, 76, 79–81, 161–62, 215; furnishings and, 80, 168–69; gap between architects and residents regarding, 168–69, 225; SAM and, 87, 102, 103, 107–8; in smaller homes, 136–39
Arts ménagers, 93, 97, 100, 108, 120, 137, 141, 155, 166

Balladur, Jean, 156, 171
Bardet, Jacques, 171, 208, 211
bathing facilities and bathrooms: appliances and laundry facilities in,

248 *Index*

139, 176, 224; as basic requirement, 226; cleaning of, 234n5; housing crisis and, 120, 124, 129, 131, 132, 134, 139; housing without, 18, 120; kitchens used for, 23, 28, 74, 76; in modernist architecture, 54, 62, 63, 66, 70, 71, 72, 74; MRU and, 18, 23, 28, 30, 34, 35, 38, 42, 45; as private spaces, 5; proximity to bedrooms, 30, 71, 74; responses of residents regarding, 155, 176; showers, 18, 34, 35, 38, 64, 94, 120, 124, 155, 214, 225; toilets inside versus outside, 23, 30, 34, 129, 130, 195, 234n3; in urban fabric and suburban living, 211, 212. *See also* toilets and toilet rooms

Beaudouin, Eugène, 28, 38–39, *39*, 67, 68, 69, 85n38, 126, 127

bedrooms: alcove, 159, 175; for children, 35, 74, 106, 120, 122, 130, 154, 159, 166, 168, 231; furnishings, 33–34, 138, 169; housing crisis and, 120, 122, 123, 129, 130, 134, 137, 138; modernist architecture and, 54, 61, 62, 63, 71, 72, 73–74, 78–79, 231; MRU contests and experiments, 23, 30, 33, 34, 35, 39; for parents, 23, 34, 35, 39, 72, 74, 79, 104, 106, 120, 130, 153, 154, 155, 166, 168–69, 203; as private spaces, 5, 63, 137, 169, 225; responses of residents regarding, 152, 154, 155, 159, 164, 165, 166, 169, 170, 175; SAM and, 106; segregation of children's bedrooms by sex, 106, 159, 166; *séjour* serving as, 104, *105*; separation of functions and, 23; size of, 23, 71, 137, 170; in urban fabric and suburban life, 203, 210, 211; young children sleeping with parents, 23, 34, 106, 120

Bernège, Paulette, 29, 50n31, 89–90, 92, 223–24

Billardon, Dijon, *grand ensemble* at, 172–78, 225, 226, 229, 233

Billoux, François, 20–21

Blachère, Gérard, 150, 172, 184n59

Bloch-Lainé, François, 123, 126, 132, 135, 182n21

Bonnevay law (1912), 59

Breton, André, 87, 92, 99

Breton, Jules-Louis, 89–91, 94

Breton, Paul, 87, 91–92, 94–97, 99, 100, 102, 103, 105, 107, 110n6, 138, 228

cadres, 185n97, 187, 195, 199, 202, 227

Candilis, Georges, *133,* 171, 186, 189, 200, 201, 204, 206, 210

Cassan, Urbain, 26, 57

Castors, and Baticoop, 37, 122, 194

Catholic activism, 11, 36, 37, 152, 158, 182n21, 200

CCAFRP (Caisse centrale d'allocations familiales de la région parisienne), 104–5, *105,* 107

cellule d'habitation: changing concepts of, 189, 201, 210, 216; Dreyfus and Tribel on, 167–71; failure to fulfill residents' needs, 150–51; in *Famille et habitation,* 161; *Histoires de cellules* (1962-1973 study), 211–12; housing crisis and development of, 8–9, 118, 128–36, *131, 133, 135,* 143–44; *Les Pavillonnaires* study and, 203; reconsidered in *Techniques et architecture,* 155; responses of residents living in, 150–51, 166–67, 171

central heating, 6, 8, 12, 19, 34, 38, 42, 46, 94, 102, 107, 124, *135,* 150, 165, 168, 214, 229

central service core, 130–32, *131,* 156, 170

Chalandon, Albin, and *chalandonnettes,* 198–200, 206, 207, 209, 217

Charter of Athens, 171, 200, 205

Chemetov, Paul, 171, *212*

children: adult versus child activities, 168, 169–70, 212; bedrooms for, 35, 74, 106, 120, 122, 130, 154, 159, 166, 168, 231; day care for, 30, 43–44, 143, 202; family size, 27, 30, 58, 134, 147–48n75, 163, 202; in *grands ensembles,* 176–77; parents, young children sleeping with, 23, 34, 106, 120; pronatalism and demographic renewal, 34, 43–44, 89, 91, 134, 146n50, 170, 214, 224; segregation of bedrooms by sex, 106, 159, 166

Chombart de Lauwe, Paul-Henry: Besset rejecting findings of, 201; on collective services for *grands ensembles,* 189; *Famille et habitation,* 150, 158–64, 180, 183n34, 200, 213; on functionalism, 149, 160, 161, 180, 210–11; on furniture, 159, 182n23; Haumont and, 203, 211; oral histories of first-generation *grands ensembles* dwellers and, 172; *Paris et l'agglomération parisienne* (1952), 158, 159; personal life and career,

158–60, 182n21, 183n46; reactions of state planners, engineers, and architects to, 164–68, 170; Tribel and, 184n48; on value of *grands ensembles*, 200; *La Vie quotidienne des familles ouvrières* (1956), 159
CIAM (Congrès international d'architecture moderne), 7, 64–65, 66, 68, 72, 171, 179, 225
Cité expérimentale de Merlan, Noisy-le-Sec, 25–32, 35, 37, 38, 39, 43, 45, 130
Cité Rotterdam, Strasbourg, 38–40, *39*, 126, 127, 149
Cités Radieuses, 126, 183, 195
class. *See* social class and housing
Claudius-Petit, Eugène, 17, 36–37, 40, 41, 44–46, 48, 48n1, 55, 92, 117, 121, 126, 132, 159, 167, 173, 191, 193
CNRS (Centre national des recherches scientifiques), 89, 112n31, 158
color, SAM's promotion of, 98–99
comfort: amenities and technological innovations associated with, 8, 34, 43, 51n45, 107, 166, 175; appliances, individual ownership of, 139–40; *chez soi*, detached homes and concept of, 203, 208; in Constitution of Fourth Republic, 17; establishment of right to, 11–12, 14n21, 232–33; evolving notions of what constitutes, 166; minimum standards of, 167; MRU's commitment to, 18, 34–35, 38, 43, 45; productivity related to, 42–43; rent and food costs versus, 41–42; social change and, 225
Communism, 20, 32, 36, 38, 44, 56, 72, 140, 186, 200, 209–10
Cornudet law (1919), 57
Courant, Pierre, and Courant plan, 121, 128, 130, 207, 210
CPTFM (Cahier des prescriptions techniques et fonctionnelles minima), 130, 155, 183n40
CPTFMU (Cahier des prescriptions techniques et fonctionnelles minimales unifiées), 165, 170, 183n40
CRI (Commissariat à la reconstruction immobilière), 21, 49n6, 57
CSTB (Centre Scientifique et Technique du Bâtiment), 32–33, 81, 91, 96, 125, 131, 139, 150, 159, 167, 170, 189, 207
Cupers, Kenny, 197, 216

DATAR (Délégation à l'aménagement du territoire et à l'action régionale), 190, 194
Dautry, Raoul, 19–22, 25–26, 36, 45, 72, 117, 188, 195, 198
day-night principle, 35, 38, 39, 49n17, 71–75, 134, 211
de Gaulle, Charles, and Gaullists, 6, 18, 19, 20, 36, 43, 47, 142, 151, 186–87, 190–91, 197, 209–10, 218, 224, 231
Delouvrier, Paul, 191, 207
Deroche, Jean, 171, *212*
detached houses. *See* urban fabric, suburban life, and detached homes
DGEN (Direction générale à l'équipement national), 21, 22
DGRST (Délégation générale à la Recherche Scientifique et Technique), 207, 208
DGUHC (Direction générale de l'urbanisme, de l'habitation, et de la construction), 21, 25, 42
dining arrangements: in Appartement référendum, 152, 153, 154, 155; combined living-dining rooms, 6, 24, 30–31, 39, 49n19, 61–62, 67, 71–76, 78, 129, 134, 137, 152, 165, 168, 169, 170, 211; eat-in kitchens, 5, 24, 24–25, 30, 38, 39, 49n19, 71, 153, 155, 159, 161, 164, 165, 167, 169, 170, 180, 212, 213, 225; housing crisis and, 129, 134, 137; in modernist architecture, 54, 61–62, 67, 71–78, 79, 82; MRU and, 23–25, 24, 28, 33, 35, 38, 39; proximity of kitchen to, 28, 35, 38, 39, 71, 73, 77, 211; SAM and, 104, 107, 120; separate dining rooms, 5, 23, 24, 24–25, 30, 40, 49n19, 170, 175; in traditional French homes, 5
Dreyfus, Jacques, 51n45, 125, 167–71, 180, 201, 212

eat-in kitchens, 5, 24, 24–25, 30, 38, 39, 49n19, 71, 153, 155, 159, 161, 164, 165, 167, 169, 170, 180, 212, 213, 225
economic recovery and national renewal, 3; amenities and, 42–43, 48, 214; gender and financial control, 97, 112n32; MRU, renewal paradigm followed by, 40–48; privacy and private space, 1, 2, 4; pronatalism and demographic renewal, 34, 43–44, 89, 91, 134, 146n50, 170, 214, 224; rise in real wages, 213–14; SAM and, 88, 94–95, 101–2, 109; social class

and, 45, 48; technological innovation and, 3, 40, 45
electricity and electrical outlets, 140, 155, 176
engineers, 57–58, 167–71, 184n59
ENSBA (École Nationale Supérieure des Beaux-Arts), 67, 72, 158, 204–5, 206
épanouissement, 46, 75, 81, 109, 112n35, 126, 128, 137, 143, 186, 218, 231
Essai d'habitation évolutive (Experiment in Adaptive Housing), 156–58, 157, 169, 171, 180, 214
ethnicity and immigration: Algeria and Algerian immigrants, 2, 27, 142, 173–74, 187, 198; *grands ensembles,* class and ethnic mix in, 172–74, 177–78; new wave of immigrants after 1962, 187
evolutionary housing, need for, 156, 167–71, 184n59
existenzminimum apartments, Frankfurt, 66–67, 71, 72, 75, 76, 84–85n45
Exposition des techniques américaines d'habitation et d'urbanisme (1946), 26, 55, 91

Famille et habitation study, 150, 158–64, 180, 183n34, 200, 213
family size, 27, 30, 58, 134, 147–48n75, 163, 202
Faucheux, Pierre, 74, 74–75, 107
Fée du Logis (Ideal Homemaker) competition, 7, 92, 100, 109, 112n37
Fifth Republic, 12, 151, 170, 189, 199, 213, 230–31
FNA (Front National des Architectes), 53, 56, 58, 72
FNAH (Fonds National de l'Amélioration de l'Habitat), 94, 120, 127
Fourastié, Françoise, 101, 107, 136, 138
Fourastié, Jean, 1, 45–46, 101, 107, 136, 138, 227
Fourcaut, Annie, 40
4P: Appartement référendum as, 153; art of living/dwelling, concept of, 79–81; as *cellule d'habitation,* 133, 133–36; challenges to, 9, 150–51, 201, 210, 211, 216; children of different sexes and, 166; defined, 6, 54; detached home compared, 203; evolution of, 69–75, 73, 74; middle-class concerns and design of, 74, 75–79, 82, 173; responses to living in, 150–51, 160, 166, 167, 180; SAM's awareness of need to sell, 103; size of, 135, 153, 165
Fourth Republic, 11, 17, 19, 21, 32, 43, 45, 47, 48, 135, 142, 224, 230, 231
France, postwar housing in. *See* housing in postwar France
Frost, Robert, 86n55, 88, 90
functionalism: challenges to, 9, 149, 160, 161, 168–69, 180, 210–11; failure to meet residents' needs, 150–51; gap between architects and residents regarding, 168–69; needs-based architecture and development of 4P, 69–75, 73, 74; SAM's articulation of domestic ideal and, 88, 92, 102–3; size of homes and, 136; UAM, as creed of, 68–69
Furlough, Ellen, 90, 91
furniture: armoires, 23, 78, 80, 98, 137, 138, 144, 154, 155, 169, 213; for bedrooms, 33–34, 138, 169; butterfly chairs, 80, 103; Chombart de Lauwe on, 159, 182n23; modernist art of living and, 80, 168–69; in MRU architectural competitions, 33–34; multi-use pieces for small homes, 137–38; at Noisy-le-Sec, 26–27; responses of residents and, 154, 167; SAM and, 95–96, 103, 137–38

Gascoin, Marcel, 66, 69, 78, 84n33, 106, 153
gender and domestic space, 8, 224; Appartement référendum, 150, 151–58, 154, 159, 213; architects' skepticism regarding women's views, 156–58, 161; division of labor, gendered, 102, 234n5; feminism, 90, 99, 109; financial control and, 97, 112n32; labor-saving appliances, effects of, 141–42; Lurçat on lack of women in Cité Rotterdam jury, 38; modernism evacuating considerations of, 70; modernization and, 5; needs-based architectural design and, 71; at Noisy-le-Sec, 28, 31; normative beliefs embedded in housing construction, 3–4; pronatalism and, 43–44; rationalist home design and, 28–29, 98, 99; responses of women to new homes, 9; SAM on, 88–89, 90–91, 97–102, 103, 108–10, 112n32, 224; stay-at-home motherhood, assumptions of, 29, 43–44, 89, 90–91, 99, 101, 109, 143, 214, 215, 224, 228; workers, women conceptualized

as, 228–30; working women, post-1960 increase in, 187, 198, 214, 215, 224
General Planning Commission, 10, 45, 47, 198, 205, 217
Germany: *existenzminimum* apartments, Frankfurt, 66–67, 71, 72, 75, 76, 84–85n45; postwar housing statistics in, 41, 60, 119, 194; Taylorism in, 29
government. *See* state; *specific ministries and other state bodies*
grands ensembles, 229, 233; associations with urban problems, 4, 11, 13n14, 184n50, 226, 230; collective facilities and services of, 163, 177–78, 183n35, 189; as communist/socialist hotbeds, 209–10; defined, 4; experimental nature of, 149–50; "failure of modernism" arguments and, 11; in *Famille et habitation,* 161; housing crisis and, 118, 125–28, 142–44; modernist architects and, 126–27; responses to living in, 9, 151, 160, 163–64, 167, 171–80, 181n2; social class/ethnic mix in, 172–74, 177–78; in urban fabric and suburban life, 187–91, 193, 194, 196–202, 205–11. *See also cellule d'habitation*
Gravier, Jean-François, *Paris et le désert français* (1947), 36, 190
Guichard, Olivier, and Guichard Circular, 209–10

Haumont, Nicole, 202–4, 208, 211, 213
Hautecoeur law (1940), 56
HBMAs *(habitations à bon marché amelioré),* 59, *62, 135*
HBMs *(habitations à bon marché):* Castors and, 37; Cité de la Muette, Drancy, 28, 39, 67; Cité des Oiseaux, Bagneux, 38; defined, 6; ILMs, 59–60, 62–63, *63,* 75, 76, 199, 208; influence on postwar architects, 54, 59–64, *60–63,* 75; Loucheur law (1928) financing, 19–20; model plans, *60–63,* 60–64; modernism and, 65, 67, 68, 75, 85n51; MRU taking over, 33
Héaume, Arthur, 35–36, 37, 39, 129
"Henri Becque" HBM model plan, *60,* 60–61, 84n24, 125
Hermant, André, 69, 80–81, 126–27, 128, 134, 137, 148n80, 161, 171, 176, 204
HLMs *(habitations à loyer modéré):* associations with urban problems, 10, 226; As and Bs, 130, 135; central heating and temperature requirements, 165–66; defined, 4; establishment of, 33; failure to meet residents' needs, 150–51; housing crisis and, 123, 124–25, 127, 130, 134, *135, 139;* kitchens and kitchen appliances, 139; LOPOFAs, 124, 130, *135,* 170; residents' responses to, 7, 150–51, 152, 155, 163–66, 170, 172, 173, 176, 180; size of, 134–39, *135,* 164–65, *165;* sociological studies of, 159–60; storage space in, 165; in urban fabric and suburban life, 190, 199, 203, 211, 212
hot water, 19, 45, 62, 63, 124, 125, 139, 146n26, 168, 174–75, 223, 226, 229
housing crisis (1945-1958), 8–9, 117–44; architects and, 129–33, 135–36; *cellule d'habitation,* 8–9, 118, 128–36, *131, 133, 135,* 143–44; domestic ideals promoted amidst, 142–44; furnishings and appliances, 136–42; *grands ensembles* arising from, 118, 125–28, 142–44; modernism and, 126–27, 128–29, 132–33; MRU/MRL and, 119, 121, 124, 125, 129–32, 137, 138, 139; origins and development of, 2, 118–26; size of homes and, 134–39, *135;* state efforts to resolve, 4; winter of 1953-1954, 122–23
housing in postwar France, 1–12; architects of, 8, 53–83 *(see also* architects); compared to UK and Germany, 41, 60, 119; in context of worldwide trends, 2–3; housing crisis (1953-1958), 8–9, 117–44 *(see also* housing crisis); interiors, focus on, 4–5; as modernizing project, 4–5, 9–10, 223–33 *(see also* modernizing project, French postwar housing as); MRU and (1945-1952), 8, 17–48 *(see also* MRU); "new social contract," establishment of, 11–12, 14n21; normative beliefs embedded in, 3–8, 31–32; one-size-fits-all/most approach, 3, 8, 12, 32, 53, 69, 88, 144, 164, 167, 179, 216, 227; renewal paradigm for, 3; responses to (1959-1961), 9, 149–80 *(See also* responses to postwar housing); SAM and, 8, 87–110 *(see also* SAM); state-driven nature of, 2–3, 6, 9, 10; urban fabric, suburban life, and detached homes (1966-1973), 9, 186–218 *(see also* urban fabric, suburban life, and detached

homes); WWII, destruction of housing in, 1–2, 17–18
hygienist agenda, 28, 61, 98–99

ILMs *(immeubles à loyer moyen)*, 59–60, 62–63, *63*, 75, 76
ILNs *(immeubles à loyer normal)*, 199, 208, 211
immigration. *See* ethnicity and immigration
individual appropriation of housing, 210–17
individual happiness, family life, and housing design, 8, 11, 17, 46, 55, 65–66, 70, 71, 75, 79, 86n63, 97, 106, 109, 126–27, 128–29, 134, 137, 176–78, 218, 231–32
individual homes. *See* urban fabric, suburban life, and detached homes
Indochina, French war in, 6, 117, 119, 123
INED (Institut national d'études démographiques), 5, 22–25, 35, 39, 42, 47, 49n14, 49n17, 69, 70, 82, 126
intermediary habitat, 207–9
International Style, 2–3, 64, 225
ISAIs *(Immeubles Sans Affectation Individuelle)*, 21–22, 37, 47, 54, 68, 71–75, *74, 75*, 103

Jourdain, Francis, 58–59, 68, 76, 79
Judt, Tony, *Postwar* (2005), 17, 42

Kérisel, Jean, 21, 26, 38, 46
kitchens: Appartement référendum, 153–54, *154*, 167; appliances in social housing, 139; Cité Rotterdam contest winner, *39*, 39–40; cooking odors from, 28, 50n30; dining arrangements, proximity of kitchen to, 28, 35, 38, 39, 71, 73, 77, 211; eat-in, 5, 24, 24–25, 30, 38, 39, 49n19, 71, 153, 155, 159, 161, 164, 165, 167, 169, 170, 180, 212, 213, 225; Frankfurt, *existenzminimum* apartments, 66–67; "Kitchen Debate," US versus USSR, 2; lab kitchens, 6, 71, 72, 73, 74, 76–77, 107, 134, 154, 156, 162, 176, 212, 213, 225; laundering in, 223–24; layout of, 5, 23–25, *24*, 35, 49n19; Maison des jours meilleurs (Better Days House), *131*, 131–32; modernism and, 231; needs-based architecture and development of 4P, 71, 72, 73, 74; at Noisy-le-Sec, 27–29, 30–31, 35; placement and orientation of, 35, 206; reactions to public responses to, 165; refrigerators, 34, 35, 38, 111n23, 139,
141; separation of functions and, 23; in social housing, 61, 62; in urban fabric and suburban life, 206, 211–13, 215

lab kitchens, 6, 71, 72, 73, 74, 76–77, 107, 134, 154, 156, 162, 176, 212, 213, 225
Labourdette, Jacques-Henry, 127, 170–71
laundry and laundry facilities, 29, 31, 96, 139–42, 168, 223–24, 229, 234n5. *See also* washing machines
Le Corbusier: CIAM and, 64; *Les 5 Points d'une architecture nouvelle* (1926), 67–68; in Cité Rotterdam contest, 38; Cités Radieuses, 126, 183, 195; Claudius-Petit and, 36; cult status of, 225; in *Famille et habitation*, 161; on functions of domestic life, 66, 84n32; on houses as machines for living, 46; Maison Loucheur (1928), *68*; open plan architecture of, 28, *68*; Pessac, workers' homes at, 67, 181–82n11; on rational home design, 65; relationships with other architects, 72, 73, 77, 137, 151, 156; *Towards a New Architecture* (1922), 7; transportation forms influencing, 66, 79; UAM and, 69; Unité d'habitation, Marseille, 21, 68, 71–72, 73, 138, 163, 170; *Vers une Architecture* (1923), 69
LENs (logements économiques de première nécessité/logements économiques normalisés), 124–25, 141, 145–46n26
Les Courtillières, Pantin, 127, 172–78, 185n97
Levitt, William J., Levitttowns, and Levitt France, 192, 194–96, 198, 230
Lihotsky, Grete Schütte-, 66–67, 76, 84–85n35
linoleum, 101, 107, 210
Lion, Robert, 207, 231
living room. *See séjour*
Lods, Marcel, 1–2, 28, 38, 39, 67, 68, 69, 71, 72, 80, 85n38, 127, 134, 161, 171, 196
Logeco housing: appliances in, 139; *cellule d'habitation* and, 128, 130, 134; failure to meet residents' needs, 150; furnishings for, 137, 138; Marly-le-Roi project, 127; model plan system, 121–22, 126, 147n55; Prefab Apartment, 166; size of, 134, *135*, 164, *165*; in social housing hierarchy, 124, 125; ZUPs compared, 190
Logis 48 and Logis 49, 104–7, *105, 106*

LOPOFAs (logements populaires et familiaux), 124, 130, *135*, 170
lotissements, 40, 44, 188, 191
Loucheur law (1928), 19, 59–60, 67
Loucheur, Louis, 67, 85n36, 89
Lurçat, André, 38, 56, 64, 69, 71, 72–73, *73*, 152, 171

Magendie, Jean, 29, 31, 43–44, 228
Maison des jours meilleurs (Better Days House), 130–32, *131*, 170
Marini, André, 32–33, 38
mass housing. *See* housing in postwar France
mass production, standardization, and prefabrication, 53, 55–56, 65, 103, 192, 214
master bedrooms, 23, 34, 35, 39, 72, 74, 79, 104, 106, 120, 130, 153, 154, 155, 166, 168–69, 203
Maubeuge ISAIs, 72–73, *73*
Maurois, André, 223, 224
May 1968, 199, 204–5, 216, 226
May, Ernst, 64, 66–67, 72, 75
Maziol, Jacques, 165, 191–92, 199, 209
MC (Ministère de la Construction), 151, 153, 155, 164, 166–67, 183n46, 187–88, 189, 191
ME (Ministère de l'Équipement)/MEL (Ministère de l'Équipement et du Logement), 188–89, 196, 197, 202, 206–7, 209
Mendès-France, Pierre (PMF), 123–24
Mendras, Henri, 227
middle class. *See* social class and housing
Modèles Innovations, 207, 208
modernism: Appartement référendum and, 153, 156–58; art of living, concept of, 4–5, 54, 76, 79–81, 161–62; beliefs and aesthetics of, 64–66; challenges to functionalism of, 9; Claudius-Petit and, 36, 37, 126, 167, 193; cult status of, 225; declaration of death of (1959), 179; democratic principles of, 3, 65–66, 69–70; "failure of modernism" arguments, 10–11; in *Famille et habitation*, 161–62; HBMs and, 65, 67, 68, 75, 85n51; historicizing, 231–33; housing crisis, *grands ensembles*, and *cellules d'habitation*, 126–27, 128–29, 132–33; influence on postwar architects, 54, 59, 64–69, *68*, 82; International Style, 2–3, 64, 225; middle-class concerns dominating designs of, 8, 54, 74, 75–79, 82; MRU and, 7, 36, 37, 53; needs-based architecture and development of 4P, 69–75, *73*, *74*; prefabrication, standardization, and mass production, interest in, 53, 55–56, 65; responses to postwar housing and, 10–11, 167–71, 179; SAM and, 108; transportation forms influencing, 66, 79, 84n34. *See also* functionalism
modernization theory, 9
modernizing project, French postwar housing as, 4–5, 9–10, 223–33; de Gaulle's concerns about, 186–87; defined, 1, 9; gender and, 224, 228–30; historicizing modernism, 231–33; responses of residents shaping process of, 224–25; social change and, 213–14, 226–28; social class and, 226, 234; state's role in, 2–3, 6, 9, 10, 229–31; traditional French dwelling design and, 5–6; wins and losses in, 223–26
Monnet, Jean, and Monnet Plan, 5, 10, 18, 32, 45, 119, 121, 225–26
MRL (Ministère de la Reconstruction et du Logement), 121, 122, 124, 129–32, 138, 150, 190
MRU (Ministère de la Reconstruction et de l'Urbanisme), 8, 17–48; administrative changes at, 32–33, 36, 121, 151; architects ranked by, 56–57; architectural competitions held by, 32–40, *39*; Castors and, 37; Claudius-Petit at, 17, 36–37, 40, 41, 44–46, 48, 117, 121, 159; comfort, commitment to, 18, 34–35, 38, 43, 45; creation of, 6, 18; Dautry at, 19–22, 25–26, 36, 45, 117, 188, 198; early research and survey work, 19–25, *24*; engineers at, 58; housing crisis and, 119; modernism, interest in, 7, 36, 37, 53; Noisy-le-Sec, 25–32, 35, 37, 38, 39, 43, 45; postwar challenges faced by, 17–18; reconstruction versus new construction, 20–21, 32, 36, 117, 119; renewal paradigm followed by, 40–48; SAM and, 88, 92, 94, 96, 108, 111n14; separation of functions, devotion to, 27–28, 30–32, 38, 48; urban planners and, 57

needs-based architecture, 69–75, *73*, *74*, 167–71

Nelson, Paul, 55, 58, 86n63, 91
"new social contract," 11–12, 14n21, 17
Newsome, Brian, 231
Noisy-le-Sec, 25–32, 35, 37, 38, 39, 43, 45, 130
Nord, Philip, 12, 230
Noviant, Louis-Georges, 69, 77
Nungesser, Roland, 192–94, 199, 208, 209

one-size-fits-all/most approach to housing, 3, 8, 12, 32, 53, 69, 88, 144, 164, 167, 179, 210–11, 216, 227
open plan architecture, 28, 30, 39, 68, 71
Opération Million, 124, 130, 133
OPHVP (Office public d'habitations de la Ville de Paris), 59–61, 67, 84n24
Ordre des architectes, 56–57, 205

PADOG (Plan d'Aménagement et d'organisation générale), 191, 194
PAN (Programme Architecture Nouvelle), 207
Parat, Pierre, 171, 192, 200–201, 204, 208, 209, 212
Parent, Claude, 137
parents: adult versus child activities, 168, 169–70; bedrooms for, 23, 34, 35, 39, 72, 74, 79, 104, 106, 120, 130, 153, 154, 155, 166, 168–69, 203; privacy, need for, 169–70; three-generation families, 120, 122
partitions and screens, 30, 31, 72, 75, 85n38, 104, 156, 175, 180
Les Pavillonnaires study, 187, 202–4, 211
pavillons. See urban fabric, suburban life, and detached homes
Perret, Auguste, 21, 35, 38, 196
Perriand, Charlotte, 68, 77, 80, 96, 107, 161, 225
Persitz, Alexandre, 35–36, 37, 39, 53, 55–56, 58, 69, 70, 81, 129
Picard, Jeanne, 152–57, 159, 165, 166, 169, 182n21
picture windows, 80, 136, 152, 174, 181–82n11, 225
Pingusson, Georges-Henri, 69, 161, 162, 171, 211–12
Plan Construction, 207, 215
postwar housing in France. *See* housing in postwar France
prefabrication, standardization, and mass production, 53, 55–56, 65, 103, 192, 214

privacy and private space: in bedrooms, 5, 63, 137, 169, 225; foyer, importance of, 30, 38; in HBM housing, 62–64; housing crisis and, 136, 137; Logis 49 recognizing need for, 106; modernism and, 68; needs-based architecture and development of 4P, 71–74, 82; parental need for, 169–70; picture windows, 80, 136, 152, 174, 181–82n11, 225; public-private division, 62, 72, 73, 203; renewal of nation through, 1, 2, 4; responses of residents regarding, 152, 153, 166, 168, 169, 170, 180; social class and, 5–6, 11; urban fabric, suburbs, and detached housing, 193, 203, 208, 212
pronatalism and demographic renewal, 34, 43–44, 89, 91, 134, 146n50, 170, 214, 224
Prothin, André, 10, 21, 34, 38, 135, 139
Prouvé, Jean, 28, 30, 38, 77, 81, 130–32, *131*, 161, 170, 225
PSRs *(programmes sociaux de relogement), 165,* 183n39, 184n41, 199
public housing. *See* social housing
public responses. *See* responses to postwar housing
public-private division of space, 62, 72, 73, 203. *See also* privacy and private space
Pulju, Rebecca, 228

rationalization, 28–29, 65–66, 78–79, 98–99, 118, 213, 217, 233
Réalisations Expérimentales, 207
reconstruction versus new construction, 20–21, 32, 36, 117, 119
refrigerators, 34, 35, 38, 111n23, 139, 141
regionalism, in France, 55, 193
Règlement de la construction (National Construction Regulations), 130, 131, 206
Renaudie, Jean, 171, 208, 209, 215, *216*
renewal paradigm. *See* economic recovery and renewal
rents and rent controls, 4, 5, 20, 33, 41–42, 48, 67, 119, 124, 166, 185n97, 225
Résidences du Chateau, Le Mesnil-Saint-Denis, 194–96
responses to postwar housing, 9, 149–80; Appartement référendum, 150, 151–58, *154,* 159, 164, 166–67, 169, 176, 179, 189, 193, 213, 217; architects' reactions to, 155–58, 161–62, 167–71, 180; engineers' reactions to, 167–71, 184n59; Essai

d'habitation évolutive, 156–58, *157*, 169, 171, 180, 214; *Famille et habitation* and, 150, 158–64, 180, 183n34, 200, 213; of *grands ensembles* dwellers, 9, 151, 160, 163–64, 167, 171–80, 181n2; media attention to, 179–80, 184n50; modernism and, 10–11, 167–71, 179; modernizing project shaped by, 224–25; on size of homes, 153, 160; state planners' reactions to, 164–70
Revue de l'ameublement et des industries du bois, 157
Riboud, Jacques, 195–96, 198
Rochefort, Christiane, 147–48n75, 179–80
Rome, Treaty of (1957), 111n23, 140, 142
Ross, Kristin, 109, 234n12
Roux, Marcel, 74, 74–75, 85n49, 97, 107, 153–54, *154*, 156
Roux-Spitz, Michel, 56, 71–73, 134

salle à manger. See dining arrangements
salle commune. See séjour
SAM (Salon des Arts Ménagers), 8, 87–110; Appartement référendum at, 150, 153, 154, 155, 166; color promoted by, 98–99; dilapidated housing, plans to eliminate, 190; economic renewal and consumer society promoted by, 88, 94–95, 101–2, 109; Essai d'habitation évolutive, 156; expectations of *grands ensembles* and, 176; *Fée du Logis* (Ideal Homemaker) competition, 7, 92, 100, 109, 112n37; functionalism and, 88, 92, 102–3; on furnishings, 95–96, 103, 137–38; gendered message of, 88–89, 90–91, 97–102, 103, 108–10, 224; homemaking and homemakers, concept of, 90–91; housing crisis and, 125; ideal/dream homes exhibited by, 74, 74–75, 96–97, 104–7, *105*, *106*, 130, *131*, 210; internationalization of, 111n23; lectures and panels, 92, 111n17, 141; MRU and, 88, 92, 94, 96, 108, 111n14; origins and interwar mission of, 89–91; postwar structure, activities, and attendance, 91–96; on rationalization, 98–99; social class and, 90, 91, 92, 103, 107; on taste and aesthetics, 102–8, *105*, *106*; technological innovations promoted by, 88–91, 99, 102, 108, 214; as vector for diffusion of ideas about modern living, 7, 87–89, 108–10

Sarcelles, HLMs at, 127, 142–43, 170, 178, 181n2, 209, 225
SAS (Syndicat des Architectes de la Seine), 156, 169, 170, 171, 180, 201
Schein, Ionel, 155, 158, 161
SCIC (Société Centrale Immobilière de la Caisse), 123, 127, 130, 132–33, 138, 143, 151, 167, 197, 208, 227
SEC (Service des Études de la Construction), 25–30, 33, 38
Second Plan, 121, 126, 144
Segalen, Martine, 88, 90, 93, 101, 109
séjour (living room), 6, 231, 233; as bedroom, 104, *105*; combined living-dining rooms, 6, *24*, 30–31, 39, 49n19, 61–62, 67, 71–76, 78, 129, 134, 137, 152, 165, 168, 169, 170, 211; housing crisis and, 120, 129, 130, 134, 137; in modernist architecture, 54, 67, 71, 72, 73, 74, 75, 76, 78, 79, 169; MRU experiments, surveys, and competitions, 23, 24, 28, 30, 31, 35, 39, 49n19; names given to, 76, 129; responses of residents and, 152, 153, 154, 155, 159, 164, 165, 166, 168, 169, 170, 175, 177; SAM and, 101, 104, *105*, *106*, 106–7; separation of functions and, 23; size of, 23; social change and use of, 225; in urban fabric and suburban life, 203, 208, 211, 212, 213
Sellier, Henri, 67, 89
separation of functions (room specialization): adult versus child activities, 168, 169–70, 212; day-night principle, 35, 38, 39, 49n17, 71–75, 134, 211; MRU's devotion to, 27–28, 30–32, 38, 48; at Noisy-le-Sec, 27–28, 30–32; order-disorder norms, 203; public-private division of space, 62, 72, 73, 203; social class and, 5–6; in social housing, 63; surveys on, 23–24, *24*; traditional housing's lack of, 6
"servant crisis," 76–78, 86n55, 99
sex, segregation of children's bedrooms by, 106, 159, 166
sexism. *See* gender and domestic space
showers, 18, 34, 35, 38, 64, 94, 120, 124, 155, 214, 225
size of family, 27, 30, 58, 134, 147–48n75, 163, 202
size of homes and rooms, 33, 134–39, *135*, 153, 160, 164–65, *165*, 174

social Catholicism, 11, 36, 37, 152, 158, 182n21, 200
social class and housing, 8; architects, criticism of, 212; *cadres,* 185n97, 187, 195, 199, 202, 227; categories of social housing based on class, 59, 62–64; comfort as aspect of working-class reform, 45; democratic principles of modernism, 3, 65–66, 69–70; *Famille et habitation* on, 162–64; *grands ensembles,* class and ethnic mix in, 172–74, 177–78; HLM, switch from HBM to, 33; modernist postwar housing design, middle-class concerns dominating, 8, 54, 74, 75–79, 82; modernization and, 226, 234; *moyennisation* of French society, 227; needs-based architecture and development of 4P, 69–75, *73, 74;* at Noisy-le-Sec, 27, 31; private space and separation of function associated with, 5–6, 11; renewal paradigm and, 45, 48; SAM and, 90, 91, 92, 103, 107; "servant crisis," 76–78, 86n55, 99; in surveys, 22–25; urban fabric, suburban life, and detached homes, 193, 199
social housing: appliances in, 139; ILMs, 59–60, 62–63, *63,* 75, 76, 199, 208; ILNs, 199, 208, 211; ISAIs, 21–22, 37, 47, 54, 68, 71–75, *74, 75,* 103; LENs, 124–25, 141, 145–46n26; LOPOFAs, 124, 130, *135,* 170; popular desire for, 210; PSRs, *165,* 183n39, 184n41, 199; size of, 134–39, *135,* 153, 160, 164–65, *165;* urban problems and, 4, 11, 13n14, 184n50, 226, 230. *See also* HBMs; HLMs; Logeco housing
Société française des habitations à bon marché, 44, 59
Solotareff, Marc and Léo, 37–38, 39
SONACOTRAL (Société nationale de construction de logements pour les travailleurs algériens), 173–74
Sonrel, Pierre, 70, 103, 117, 135–36, 143–44
Sotteville-lès-Rouen ISAIs, 71, 72, 134
specialized rooms. *See* separation of functions (room specialization)
Spinetta, Adrien, 38, 129, 132, 139, 145–46n26
standardization, prefabrication, and mass production, 53, 55–56, 65, 103, 192, 214

state: as architectural client, 53, 58–59; French postwar housing driven by, 2–3, 6, 9, 10, 229–31; reaction to public responses to postwar housing, 164–70. *See also specific ministries and other state bodies*
suburban living. *See* urban fabric, suburban life, and detached homes
Sudreau, Pierre, 149, 151–52, 156, 164–65, 167, 180, 189, 191, 193, 198, 231

Taylorism, 29, 64, 66, 90
Techniques et Architecture, 80–81, 155, 170
technological innovations: architects and, 54, 63–64; comfort, association with, 8, 34, 43, 51n45, 107, 175; gender and, 4; housing crisis and, 118, 141; individual acquisition of appliances, 138–42; labor-saving devices offset by rising standards of cleanliness, 229, 234n12; MRU and, 32, 35; at Noisy-le-Sec, 30; renewal paradigm for housing and, 3, 40, 45; SAM supporting, 88–91, 99, 102, 108, 214; in social housing, 63–64; traditional homes lacking, 6; urban fabric, suburbs, and detached housing, 205, 206–7, 210. *See also* amenities
Third Republic, 10, 40, 43, 45
toilets and toilet rooms, 18, 23, 30, 34, 38, 48, 103, 120, 124, 129, 130, 131, 175, 195, 211, 214, 226, 234n3
transportation forms, modernism influenced by, 66, 79, 84n34
Tribel, Jean, 167–71, 180, 184n48, 201, 212

UAM (Union des Artistes Modernes), 68–69, 74, 77, 78, 81, 91, 92, 96, 106, 138
UNCAF (Union nationale des caisses d'allocations familiales), 30, 92, 100, 104, 111n16, 139
Unité d'habitation, Marseille, 21, 68, 71–72, 73, 138, 163, 170
United Kingdom: access to amenities in, 120; Festival of Britain (1951), 2; French veto of membership in Common Market, 186; Ideal Home Exhibition, 7; International Style, postwar use of, 2; new towns in, 120; Noisy-le-Sec, British houses at, 26; postwar housing statistics in, 41, 60, 119, 194; "servant crisis" in, 86n55

Index   257

United Nations Economic Commission for Europe, Housing Committee, 176
United States: access to amenities in, 120; class-based housing construction in, 3; consumption-based households in, 223; de Gaulle's "third way" and, 186; George Washington Houses, East Harlem, New York City, 13n11; Hurricane Katrina, housing crisis compared to, 122–23; "Kitchen Debate," 2; Mitchell-Lama housing, New York, 176; Noisy-le-Sec, American houses at, 26, 30; Stuyvesant Town, New York, 13n11; suburban development in, 188, 192, 194, 201, 230; Taylorism in, 29
urban fabric, suburban life, and detached homes, 9, 186–218; architects on, 188, 200–201, 204–6; costs of individual homes, 195, 199, 225; *grands ensembles* and, 187–91, 193, 194, 196–202, 205–11; individualization, need for, 210–17; intermediary habitat projects, 207–9; media critique and, 199–200, 204, 209–10, 220n36; ME/MEL, 188–89, 196, 197, 202, 206–7, 209; negative choice, *pavillons* as, 201–2; new focus on detached homes, 187–88, 191–96, 198, 199; Paris, restructuring of, 190–91; *Les Pavillonnaires* study, 187, 202–4, 211; political agenda in France and, 186–87; row houses and duplexes, French dislike of, 193, 200; social class and, 193, 199; urban sociology and, 187, 200, 201–4, 211–13; Villagexpo, 187, 191–95, 199, 207, 208, 217; *villes nouvelles* and suburban developments, 191, 194–96, 198; ZUPs, 189–91, 192–94, 199, 206, 209, 211
urban planning, as profession, 57–58
urban problems and public housing, 4, 11, 13n14, 184n50, 226, 230
urban sociology: architects criticized by, 204, 211–13; Chombart de Lauwe and, 158–64; on detached housing versus *grands ensembles*, 200; Dreyfus and Tribel using, 168; emergence of, 9, 150, 158–59, 180; Noisy-le-Sec, social workers at, 29–30; *Les Pavillonnaires* study, 187, 202–4, 211; on *pavillons* as negative choice, 201–2
utilities. *See* amenities

Vayssière, Bruno, 14n21, 118, 181n2
Villagexpo, 187, 191–95, 199, 207, 208, 217
villes nouvelles, 191, 194–96, 198
Voldman, Danièle, 49n6, 57, 58, 145n2

Wakeman, Rosemary, 37, 206
washing machines, 102, 138–42, 147–48n75, 176, 178, 214, 223, 224, 226. *See also* laundry and laundry facilities
women. *See* gender and domestic space
World War II: destruction of housing in, 1–2, 17–18; French experience of, 3; Resistance during, 20, 36, 38, 48n1, 109, 122, 151, 156, 158; Vichy regime during, 3, 11, 20, 21, 43, 45, 49n6, 55, 56, 57, 193, 228

Zehrfuss, Bernard, 127, 129, 132, 161, 205
ZUPs *(zones à urbaniser par priorité)*, 189–91, 192–94, 199, 206, 209, 211

www.ingramcontent.com/pod-product-compliance
Lightning Source LLC
Chambersburg PA
CBHW072148100526
44589CB00015B/2138